4.63 - B+T - 7/66 (Sweeney)

OUR TIMES

The Best from
THE REPORTER

Edited by
MAX ASCOLI

FARRAR, STRAUS AND CUDAHY, INC.

NEW YORK

Library of Congress catalog card number 59-15071
First Printing, 1960

Published simultaneously in Canada by Ambassador Books, Ltd., Toronto. Manufactured in the U.S.A. by American Book-Stratford Press

16281

Contents

PART FOUR: PORTRAIT GALLERY

PART FIVE: GRAND TOUR

PART SIX: VIEWS AND REVIEWS

April 21, 1955

Foreword:

This Liberal Magazine

By Max Ascoli

In the last few years there has been a distinct tendency in our country to use the word liberalism with qualifying adjectives or to quarantine it within quotation marks. Meanwhile, the idea of liberty is paid constant tribute by American politicians of both parties as a disembodied principle so secure in the high heaven of abstraction as to require no effort to be made operational. Yet what is a liberal, if not a man who gives all he has to make liberty operational, and develops the highest possible degree of skill this vocation demands?

The Reporter's liberalism is based on the belief that liberty, far from being an ethereal thing, is always identified with and related to specific and present situations. In our day and country, for instance, freedom of the press or of information needs defense not against the enemy of past times—censorship—but against the peril of the present that is the oversupply of news. The point has been reached where freedom of the news, to be effectively operative, requires to be counterbalanced by a certain degree of freedom from the news. This is the specific situation in the publishing field to which *The Reporter,* this liberal publication, has applied itself. It manages to be quite selective in its handling of the news. It does not believe that all news items are born free and equal with a built-in or innate right to get into print. Other publications feel differently, but *The Reporter* sticks to its rule: It endeavors, as best it can, to sort out the meaningful and relevant from the trivial and gossipy; the natural-born, honest-to-God news from the synthetic facsimiles concocted in public-relations mills.

The oversupply of news is by no means the least cause making for the ever-spreading apathy and indifference that plague the public mind. In a remote way, everybody worries somewhat about the A- or H- or U- or C-bomb; no one relishes the idea of being vaporized. But who can do much about it all; who can prevent war from coming? *The Reporter* believes that there are quite a number of things that can be done, and that there are a definite number of men who can do these things, men with well-known responsibilities, addresses, and telephone numbers. These men must not be allowed to get away with high-sounding slogans, like instant retaliation—whether "massive" or "measured." The issues the men in power must cope with are well within the grasp of the American public, if the effort is made to give us not soporific slogans or slanted news but the truth. It is never easy to get at the truth, but according to the liberal belief there is such a thing, and—at great cost—men can reach it and be saved by it.

Liberalism is an exacting creed, and no wonder so many people are satisfied with paying lip service to the blessings of liberty and to the inevitable victory of the free world over the slave one. Of all political isms, liberalism is the only one that does not pre-scribe any ultimate goal to be pursued as an end in itself. Neither can such a goal be found in the particular exigency with which freedom happens to be identified. We cannot pursue anti-Com-munism as an end in itself, and yet there is no greater threat to the human race than the consolidation and spread of Commu-nism. We should know by now what a price we paid and are still paying for having pursued victory over Nazism as an end in itself.

Freedom is never unalloyed, and were some metaphysical laboratory ever to produce "pure freedom" it would not be worth having. Its unique, unsurpassable worth depends entirely on the way in which it is alloyed with specific interests and exigencies. The way to make freedom prevail over Communism is to prove that industrial production under democracy, with competing political parties and predominantly private enterprise, can ultimately give material comfort and spiritual well-being to an ever-increasing number of men. But the places where this ought to be proved are to be found in some of the spots near the Communist orbit where economic misery and political disorder increase the Communist temptation. Men are so made as to prefer sometimes a purposeful slavery to an aimless freedom. . . .

Liberalism is definitely intolerant of anything considered as an end in itself—including liberty. What can be said of life can be said of liberty: We cannot live life, but we can live, as fully as we are able to, that fragment of life which is ours. A liberal, a man who cultivates the skills that make freedom operational, is always a man on special assignment.

Because of its devotion to freedom, this magazine is always on special assignment.

This is a fortnightly of facts and ideas, or perhaps it would be better to say—gratefully borrowing from Whitehead—of ideas about facts. Being a liberal publication, it endeavors to harmonize the two, avoiding the promiscuous collection of news on the one hand and the reiteration of predictable, opinionated opinion on the other. News and opinion is the journalistic currency—frequently manipulated—by which facts and ideas are given circulation. Liberalism means an unending search for the right operational balance and, in the case of this publication, this means the right operational balance between facts and ideas. The two must check and control each other so that the facts are scrutinized and the ideas tested.

This liberal publication, of necessity, must be always objective and never impartial. Objectivity means a rounded, conscientious study of facts, so as to determine their causes and their weight. But this scrupulous care implies no detached reconciliation with their existence. Moreover many alleged facts, under close scrutiny, turn out to be phony.

Because of its liberalism, *The Reporter* is truly independent—independent, that is, of both political parties. One of the blessings of the way the two-party system is organized in our country lies perhaps in the fact that American liberalism has never been seriously tempted to become a party. On the other hand, it must be admitted that like our two parties American liberalism has been singularly leery of defining its own theoretical principles, the set of ideas by which its operations are guided. This has greatly contributed to the lack of commonly accepted standards even in the most articulate liberals.

Liberalism in our country has developed into an instinct, to be sure, exemplified by some of the noblest characters in public life. But this particular condition has been a very heavy handicap on liberalism lately, when it has had to withstand two different yet equally demanding tests. The first was the assault of ruthless, seditious demagoguery. The second was the task of presenting the American case to the outside world. Useful as they are, our political parties cannot do this job. It can be done only by liberals, assigned to this particular task. So far, unfortunately, the language of American liberalism has proved to be strictly for internal consumption.

Yet the need for ideas is urgent—and not only for communication with the outside world. For this reason, this magazine has had to indulge in more "think pieces" than it would have liked. The need being great, it has had sometimes to be satisfied in a hurry, without any chance of protracted reflection in an ivory tower—*Satisfaction While U Wait.*

PART ONE

Reporting

the Unreported

April 15, 1952

The China Lobby

INTRODUCTION BY MAX ASCOLI

The fall of Czechoslovakia in 1948, more than any other single event, rallied the western nations to that defensive partnership against Communism—the Mutual Security Pact. The fall of China in 1949 invigorated an entirely different kind of partnership—a partnership between Chinese and American factions eagerly involved in the internal politics of each other's country. The Chinese partners are the agents of a government that can rule China again only if the United States destroys Mao's forces in an all-out war. The American partners are an ill-assorted lot— honest men deeply concerned with the plight of the Chinese people and of Chiang Kai-shek; fanatics possessed by the nightmare of a Communist conspiracy centering on some of America's highest leaders; and politicians who will stop at nothing in their hunt for power.

This partnership of Chinese-American fear, ambition, and greed is the China Lobby—a nondescript tentacular affair that manages to use the craft of professional operators and the good will of well-intentioned amateurs.

During the war, Franklin Roosevelt decided that China was to be considered a great power. It was said then that if China did not exist, it would have to be invented, for it was the only great Asian power on which we could count after the war was won. Of all the Asian peoples, the Chinese are certainly the most numerous, and their numbers plus the vastness of their territory were taken as the sure evidence of greatness.

Winston Churchill, an expert on power, could hardly conceal his astonishment when Roosevelt insisted that China had to be one of the wartime Big Four. At the Cairo Conference, where Roosevelt took him to meet Generalissimo and Madame Chiang, Churchill thought the best thing all four could do was to go and take a look at the Pyramids.

For all his knowledge of our country, the half-American Churchill failed to realize two things. The first is the newly developed American habit of adopting favorite or pet countries—Spain (Republican or Franco), or China, or, for that matter, Britain. The second is the particularly warm spot China held in American hearts. The Chinese were different from us and did not care; their civilization was self-contained and yet friendly; they did not try to imitate our ways of living, as the Japanese did so pedantically. Indeed, the Chinese were the pet foreigners of most anti-foreign or isolationist Americans who by patronizing China could pay a safe tribute to the brotherhood of man. China was a sort of Shangri-La, exotic and in its essence unchangeable, yet touristically as well as emotionally accessible. Everything was different in China—even the Communists.

The passion for China seems to have acted like a curse on many outstanding people who were initially prompted by a sincere wish to stem the enemy advance on that forlorn front. The Lobby's full-time professionals have been quite clever in using the names and the reputations of all those who have had anything to do with China and want that country free. It would be a great injustice to confuse the many honest men who still have Chiang's cause at heart with the unscrupulous Lobby operators.

The Reporter has tried to give the historical background and a description of what the lobby actually is and does. We had to go into history, for one of the main efforts of the Lobby is to rewrite recent American history. As for the exposure of Lobby operations, we know that we have done little more than scratch the surface. A publication does not have the power of subpoena. But we thought that the job had to be done and that somebody had to make a start.

The China Lobby—Part One

By The Reporter Staff

The so-called China Lobby—which is much more than a lobby, since it exerts a relentless pressure on U.S. foreign and domestic policies—was born in 1940, when China stood alone and gallant against Japan. In June of that year, T. V. Soong, a clever and charming member of China's most powerful family, arrived in Washington, with no title, to get more help for the government of his brother-in-law, Chiang Kai-shek. His companion in this venture was a clever and charming Pole named Ludwig Rajchman, who had been a League of Nations health expert and was well acquainted in diplomatic circles. Now, twelve years later, the thoroughly Americanized Soong has withdrawn to a sort of exile in Riverdale, on the Hudson just above Manhattan. Rajchman too is in a sort of exile; far from Poland, he lives in Paris and runs errands for the Communist government of his country.

For several years prior to 1940, the United States had been helping China on a basis that was considered businesslike. Two stabilization credits of $50 million each were granted by the Treasury in 1937 and 1941, and in the interim the Export-Import Bank advanced $120 million against the sale of Chinese products to the United States. But to T. V. Soong, this was a few drops in the bucket of China's needs.

Soong, tall and, for a Chinese, burly, carries himself like a man of consequence. He was educated at Harvard and Columbia and clerked awhile in a National City Bank subsidiary before going back to China to make money. His father, a Shanghai printer named Charlie Jones Soong, had somehow saved enough to send his six children to America for their education and thereby had founded a dynasty. His second daughter married Sun Yat-sen, the founder of the Chinese Republic. His eldest daughter married a seventy-fifth descendant of Confucius (Kung Futse), H. H. Kung, a banker's chubby son known as "Daddy," or to his family as "Chauncey." The youngest daughter married Chiang Kai-shek in 1927, and T. V. Soong, who, one of his sisters said, "knows something about money," was named Minister of Finance in 1928.

In 1933, Chiang, whose relations with T. V. are often rancorous, relieved him of his Ministry and of the Acting Presidency of the Executive Yuan, and for the next seven years Soong devoted himself to the acquisition of a fortune he once estimated at $9 million. (A former friend put Soong's holdings in the United States alone at $47 million by 1944.) Soong's successor as Finance Minister was his brother-in-law, H. H. Kung, who also knew something about money. The bitter rivalry between Kung and Soong, in which Chiang usually took Kung's side, has been attributed in part to the fact that Mme. Kung had grown up to think of herself as the leader of the six children and did not easily yield to her impatient, often scornful younger brother. Mme. Chiang inclined to side with her sister rather than with her brother. The result of this family quarrel was that Chiang hated Soong and was contemptuous of Kung, Soong despised both the others, and Kung put up with Chiang's insults when he had to. But Kung and Soong have had one idea in common: to get all they could get from the United States for China, which in their minds meant China's ruling family. There is a story that when a legalistic American official once questioned Soong's authority to sign a document for his country, since he had no title, Soong replied: "I *am* China."

Americans have been impressed by Soong's flair for exotic, expensive gestures. In the spring of 1946 his wife, to whom he is deeply devoted, fell ill. Soong chartered a private plane in Nanking to go to Connecticut to pick up a cargo of dogwood, of which Mme. Soong is particularly fond. The bouquet must have cost between twenty and thirty thousand dollars.

T. V. Soong and Ludwig Rajchman sized up Washington rapidly when they arrived in 1940. Each of them had a highly developed genius for understanding how the disparate parts of a complicated structure like a government bureaucracy fit together. They soon saw that official Washington was a jungle of departments, often with overlapping functions and the usual hostility toward one another. The best way to get something done was to collect influential friends who could circumvent or overwhelm opposition.

Rajchman's Coterie

Rajchman was a past master at collecting influential friends. His sophistication, his charm, and his tough-minded sense of history made him particularly popular among the young New Deal reformers who had suddenly found themselves, somewhat uneasily, reforming not only a nation but a world. A talk with Rajchman was the intellectual equivalent of a trip around the globe. He led the young men from fascinating assumptions, like the one that China was a great power, to breath-taking vistas of things to come on a somewhat leftist wave of the future.

The best place for Soong and Rajchman to have friends was, of course, in the White House, whose master also favored the hypothesis that China was, or would soon turn into, a great world power. In December, 1940, President Roosevelt made his remarks to the press about what to do with your garden hose if your neighbor's house catches fire, and in March, 1941, Congress passed the first Lend-Lease Act. Advised by Rajchman, Soong set up China Defense Supplies, Inc., patterned loosely on the British Purchasing Commission. It was the obvious agency to represent China on Lend-Lease matters. At the President's own suggestion, Soong retained as head of this agency William S. Youngman, Jr., who had been a general counsel for the Federal Power Commission and had Roosevelt's confidence. Soong and Youngman staffed China Defense Supplies with influential Americans and a few persuasive Chinese. The Chinese were the "technical experts," the Americans the "advisers."

Youngman took with him a young lawyer named Whiting Willauer, who had worked with him in the government. The counsel for China Defense Supplies was Thomas G. Corcoran, to whom the White House door was always open. Corcoran's brother David also got a job, as did Harry Price, whose brother Frank was an important missionary in China. These men made good salaries and better contacts. Beyond the official personnel of China Defense Supplies, "Lulu" Rajchman drew to himself a sort of graduate seminar made up of bright young officials whom he introduced to some of the bright foreigners who were assembling in Washington. Soong himself made friends with such White House intimates as Henry Morgenthau, Harry Hopkins, Admiral Harry E. Yarnell, and Lauchlin Currie, and improved his acquaintance with such journalists as Henry Luce, Roy Howard, and Joseph Alsop. Soong once boasted to a State Department official: "There is practically nothing that goes on in your government of which I do not learn within three days." Rajchman went him one better. He claimed results in fifteen minutes.

With the way made smooth from top to bottom, Chinese requests for Lend-Lease items would be endorsed by Currie or Hopkins, "expedited" by China Defense men, and supported in Lend-Lease, where, as in other departments and agencies, disciples of Rajchman's or friends of Corcoran's were to be found. The zealots cut across lines of authority for what they considered a noble purpose. The Secretary of State, Cordell Hull, was by-passed and scorned in much the same way that Dean Acheson is now by-passed and scorned by the present friends of Nationalist China. Once the principle that the end justifies the means is firmly established, the means have a way of perpetuating themselves even after the end has been changed. The principle is one that the China Lobby, through all its metamorphoses, has faithfully observed.

Soon after Pearl Harbor, Chiang Kai-shek, with a keen sense of the new value of his resistance to the Japanese, let it be known that a loan of one billion dollars, half from Britain and half from the United States, would be greatly appreciated. The American ambassador in Chungking, Clarence E. Gauss, wrote home that the figure was much too high and would "invite attempts at misuse by banking and government elements," and thereby earned the hostility not only of the banking and government elements in China but also of their friends in the United States.

At about this time, Leland Stowe wrote a series of outraged dispatches for the Chicago *Daily News* Syndicate, only two of which ever saw publication—in the first week of January, 1942. In them he documented the charge that "Because the Burma Road has for years been dominated by racketeers and war profiteers, ten thousand Chinese soldiers have gone without rifles, hand grenades, or munitions." It happened that the owner of the Chicago *Daily News,* Frank Knox, who was also Secretary of the Navy, had been emphasizing in his speeches that Germany took precedence over Japan as an enemy. The Stowe dispatches put T. V. Soong in a fury. Soong, who had become Foreign Minister in December, 1941, protested vehemently to the White House. For a time, the talk in Washington was that China might quit the war. From a high authority came the order to kill the rest of Stowe's dispatches.

A few weeks later, on February 7, 1942, a bill granting China the half billion dollars Chiang had requested went through Congress in record time. The State Department's chief adviser on Far Eastern affairs, Stanley Hornbeck, did his best to get a clause into the agreement providing for consultation about how the credit was to be used, but Soong and his friends were able to override him, and the money was China's to use as its government chose.

The 'Good' Lobby

To the extent that Soong's wartime pressure group was a lobby, it was, in the eyes of nine out of ten of the Americans who helped it, a "good" lobby. The Chinese who pocketed some of the money and the Americans who profited later may have been in it with a degree of cynicism, but to the rest it was a patriotic effort to help a victim of aggression and, after Pearl Harbor, an ally.

Most of the fervor of the early New Deal had been transferred to getting the war won, but it was not uncommon in Washington to hear talk of the postwar New Deal in Britain, in Latin America, in China—even in Russia. Rajchman helped to focus the hopes of those who wanted a New Deal for China on T. V. Soong, although Rajchman must have known that Soong was usually on the outs with the rest of his family, that he had little popular following in China, and that the measure of Chiang's desperation was that he had turned to the brother-in-law he loathed. But Soong was the right man for Washington, and not much news got through from China in those days.

Since the late 1930's China had attracted many of the ardent anti-fascists who had devoted themselves to the cause of Republican Spain. Journalists, students, and the rootless converged on China from Europe and America; once there, they found themselves of use and importance. Some saw in the Chinese Communists a band more dedicated, more social-minded, and seemingly more patriotic than the Nationalists, and Americans began to read about the Long March and the land reforms. Some went to work for the Nationalist government, at better salaries than they could have commanded at home, and served it as propagandists, although they would not have used that term. Most of them endeavored to be objective reporters, but they were hampered by their admiration for China and by the conditions under which they themselves lived.

It is hard to be objective under bombing, and Chungking was incessantly bombed. It is hard to be objective when censored, and the censorship was strict. It is hard to be objective when the belly is stuffed, and the correspondents were lavishly wined and dined. To the accounts that they were sending home of China's glorious fight were added the reports, going straight to the grass roots, from the missionaries who had been flatteringly entertained by the Christian Generalissimo and his lady.

The activities of T. V. Soong and his group, therefore, were carried on under the happiest of circumstances. In the White House was a President determined to make China a great power; Soong had nursed his friendships there, particularly with Lauchlin Currie, one of his closest collaborators. The press treated China as a staunch ally. Private relief agencies, such as United China Relief, collected thousands of dollars for China, and the churches where the missionaries spoke collected thousands of pennies. And yet even in those days of idealism and hope, aid to China was being used as a lever to pry loose more aid.

The men in Washington were largely ignorant of the temptations and pitfalls of international power politics. They were impatient, determined to bring about the ends they sought before a change of the political wind could blow them out of power. And so they developed ruthless techniques that later were to be turned against them and against men who had little or nothing to do with the original controversy. A Tydings who couldn't be purged as a reactionary in 1938 was to be purged as a friend of liberals twelve years later.

There is a man who must smile at all this now. Ludwig Rajchman had a hand in making China a great power, but Mao Tsetung, not Chiang Kai-shek, is master of the Chinese mainland. Not even Ludwig Rajchman could foresee this outcome during his Washington days, but undoubtedly he did his bit to expedite the process of Chinese history. A free-wheeling Marxist all his life, he sees the work he has done in Washington largely vindicated by the unexpected results. In Washington, however, the wave of the future is not going toward the Left. In fact, the organization that was established there back in 1940, thanks largely to a marginal leftist, has been seized by the marginal Right.

The Pattern of Enrichment

"You must know the truth if China is to be saved," wrote the Australian newspaperman W. H. Donald to his friend Mme. Chiang Kai-shek in 1934, "and the truth is rotten officialdom—squeeze, corruption, militarism, overtaxation. . . . Unless you or someone initiates a move to install honesty quickly, China will die. It is dying now."

That same year Demaree Bess, now of the *Saturday Evening Post,* reported in the *Christian Science Monitor* that the Kuomintang was discredited and that either the Japanese or the Chinese Communists probably would win control of China. Three years later Japan struck, at the Marco Polo Bridge.

In the four years that China alone was at war with Japan, warnings like these were overlooked in this country. After Pearl Harbor, President Roosevelt's policy was that China was a great power or had to be propped up to look like one—as a counterweight to Japan and, if need be, the Soviet Union. This, of course, meant keeping China in the war as an active, if not very effective, belligerent. Since Chiang Kai-shek could say Yes or No to this, the fundamental weakness and disorganization of his government were ignored or played down.

For a time, little criticism of China's military effort was heard in the United States. But as the war went on, U.S. military leaders grew more critical. General Marshall picked General Joseph W. Stilwell to go to China and put more life into Chiang's resistance. Stilwell was carefully investigated by Secretary of War Stimson, who then arranged with T. V. Soong for Stilwell to be made Chief of Staff to Chiang Kai-shek, with virtual control over the Chinese Army. But Soong was afraid to make this clear to Chiang, which was the main reason for the bitter antagonism between Chiang and Stilwell for the next two and a half years, ending in Stilwell's dismissal.

The feud between Stilwell and General Claire Chennault—whose grandiose plan for developing China as an air theater appealed to the President—was corollary to the Chiang-Stilwell enmity. These quarrels soon involved diplomats, journalists, and the traveling representatives of everybody from the President to the aid societies. It was discovered—and vehemently denied—that Nationalist China was still as inefficient and corrupt as Donald and Bess had reported in 1934.

The conflict in China was reflected in Washington, and Soong's smooth-running machine began to break down. Lauchlin Currie made a trip to China in the summer of 1942, his second; he came back less enthusiastic than he had started out. Soong began to by-pass Currie and deal directly with Harry Hopkins or the President. Yet for a time Currie remained sufficiently deferential to Soong to support the appointment of Whiting Willauer—direct from Soong's own employ—to a Foreign Economic Administration post that gave him supervision over both Lend-Lease to China and purchases from China.

Joseph Alsop, another intimate of both T. V. Soong and Rajchman, went to China on a Lend-Lease mission, with a pipe-line to the White House. He stayed to join Chennault and be-come a bitter critic of Stilwell and of the State Department men who believed in military collaboration with the Communists. Yet these men have had no more gallant defender than Joseph Alsop against the charges that *they* were Communists.

By 1944, T. V. Soong had returned to China, gone through one of the Generalissimo's celebrated teacup-smashing tantrums, devoted himself for a time to the Chinese classics, and had once again been restored to power as Premier. With Soong up, Kung went down, and out as Minister of Finance.

Soong must have been well aware of some of the uses to which American aid was put in China. Under the eleven-year Ministry of Dr. Kung, those on good terms with the Minister of Finance had taken their cut of this aid—nothing unusual in a country where government-by-family had become a habit. The $500-million stabilization fund of 1942, on which the U.S. Treasury had pinned so much hope, was used to the hilt; Mme. Kung, for one, would buy Chinese dollars on the Shanghai exchange just before new credits to the fund were publicly announced, then sell when the announcement sent the currency up temporarily—thereby, of course, helping to send it back down.

The twenty-to-one fixed rate of exchange between the Chinese and the U.S. dollar that the Treasury had pressed for, before Pearl Harbor, enabled the Chinese government to sell currency to the U.S. Army at many times its open-market value, and to help its friends by buying their Chinese currency with U.S. dol-lars at the fixed rate. About $220 million of the $500 million that Soong got in Washington in 1942 was used to buy gold from the United States, ostensibly to stabilize the currency. Much of it was put on sale in China under circumstances that allowed insiders to make big killings in a single evening. One of the largest purchasers was Jeannette Kung, the Minister's second daughter.

Two hundred million of the $500-million loan was put aside to be used for eventual redemption of U.S.-dollar bonds and savings certificates issued by the Chinese government. The bonds were never redeemed, but the well-informed were able to unload before the redemption clause was publicly revoked. The savings certificates were quickly taken up by those who knew—as the general public did not know—that they, unlike the bonds, would in fact be redeemed. T. V. Soong, it has been reported, invested five million U.S. dollars in these securities as a patriotic duty. The Kung family, by the same report, was fourteen times as patriotic; its members invested $70 million. "It is most unfortunate," Henry Morgenthau wrote to T. V. Soong in 1945, "that the impression has arisen in the United States that the $200 million of U.S. dollar certificates and bonds and the gold sold in China have gone into relatively few hands with resultant large individual profits, and have failed to be of real assistance to the Chinese economy."

One day in 1945, after Dr. Kung had left the Ministry, his luggage was opened during a flight over the Hump into China and was found to contain a million dollars in cash. He said at the time that $9 million more was in New York awaiting shipment to him, and that the million he was carrying was insured in the United States for safe transit. In short, Dr. Kung really didn't much care. The air-force officials, who were forbidden to carry such cargo, made a hasty compromise. Chauncey and his baggage stayed on the plane, but the other nine millions stayed in New York.

As Premier, T. V. Soong got rid of Kung, but not of the government's old financial habits. T.V.'s brother T.L. ran the export-import office. Another brother, T.A., ran the salt-tax bureau. When UNRRA aid began flowing into China in 1945, T. V. Soong tried to bring its distribution under his control. This gave rise to bitterness, confusion, and inefficiency, as a result of which UNRRA fired its chief of mission and director of operations—the latter over the strong protest of Premier Soong. Chinese attacks on UNRRA began.

The reorganized staff stood by its guns and soon discovered that relief supplies were being mishandled. There were reports, for instance, that blood plasma was being sold on the black market. Congestion in the port of Shanghai and delays in landing essential supplies in favor of black-marketable material got so bad that UNRRA's Director General, Fiorello La Guardia, imposed a temporary embargo on most shipments.

A minor foreign-exchange scandal and a major quarrel with Chiang over control of China's economy (by this time heavily dominated by the military) forced T. V. Soong to resign as Premier in 1947. With Soong down, Kung went up, or at least regained control of the Bank of China. Shortly after that, Kung moved to the United States, transferring his office to the New York agency of the bank. Soong, after a sojourn in Europe, also came to this country, and the government was left in the hands of Chiang Kai-shek and the "CC Clique" of the brothers Chen.

How much of the American money sent to China has returned to this country for one purpose or another—pump priming for further assistance or just for personal enrichment—will probably never be known; government agencies cannot even agree on how much money has gone *to* China. Estimates of the latter, confused by different methods of computing material aid, vary from $5 billion down to $3.5 billion. Overseas holdings of private Chinese have been estimated at as much as $3 billion, and seldom at less than one. Some of this money has been used for speculation. Some has been used to persuade the United States to be even more open-handed.

Early in 1950, Alfred Kohlberg, a once obscure textile importer who by this time had come to have a profound interest in the fortunes of Nationalist China, wrote a joint letter to Drs. Kung and Soong, which was inserted with their replies in the Congressional Record by Senator William Knowland. Mr. Kohlberg quoted an item in *Newsweek's* "Periscope," which had said: "The Administration has an ace up its sleeve in case criticism of its Formosa and China policy becomes too hot. It is ready to disclose how Chinese Nationalist officials sold out their country by transferring personal funds and assets to the United States. The Treasury has the names and figures at its fingertips." Mr. Kohlberg suggested that Drs. Kung and Soong authorize the Treasury to publish the figures after their names, "as statements such as the above are a gross exaggeration."

Dr. Soong replied that he "did not choose to dignify the un-truthful attacks by pro-Communists in the American press by any notice"—thereby becoming the first person to call *Newsweek* pro-Communist—but later he authorized publication of the figures. Dr. Kung, who knew better than *Newsweek* how little the Treasury knew, wrote under the letterhead of the New York Agency of the Bank of China that he was "perfectly agreeable" to the publication of his "personal" accounts, and added: "Ow-ing to the Communist troubles, I have lost all my businesses and properties in China. What I was able to salvage was barely enough for the maintenance of myself and family for the time being."

Years of Disaster

In March, 1947, the Chinese Nationalists captured the Com-munist capital, Yenan, and Chiang Kai-shek told the American Ambassador, J. Leighton Stuart, that he would have the civil war won by the end of the summer. Instead, within a few months Chiang had lost his chance of mounting an all-out offensive that could destroy the Communist armies. Something had gone wrong.

By V.-J. Day, Chiang Kai-shek commanded the finest Chinese army in modern times. With American military advice and American Lend-Lease totaling more than $600 million in the ten months after the Japanese surrender, the Nationalists could con-front Mao with six first-class (by any standard) divisions, thirty-three divisions which had some U.S. training and equipment and were excellent by Asian standards, and two hundred or so more of inferior equipment and quality. In the fall of 1945, U.S. LSTs and planes ferried Chiang's troops into previously Jap-anese-held cities in north China and Manchuria to give them strong footholds in areas where in many cases the countryside had been long dominated by the Communists. Fifty thousand American Marines arrived to garrison Peiping, Tientsin, and Tsingtao. The United States was doing a great deal for Chiang —as much as or more than the "Get 'the boys' home" temper of Congress and the people would permit.

Then came the truce negotiations, which stretched out wearily and inconclusively for a year. At the full-scale resumption of the civil war early in 1947, Nationalist forces outnumbered the Communists by 2,600,000 to 1,100,000, and seemed to have the initiative in most of China. From the United States it looked, as it did to Chiang, as if victory was in sight.

The trouble was that the Nationalists were more interested in real estate, in announcing the capture of towns and cities, than in seeking out and defeating the Communist armies in the field. The Communist strategy was precisely the reverse. The loss of Yenan, for instance, meant little to Mao militarily; his government had abandoned it a few weeks before, leaving only a small force, which withdrew without a fight. While the Nationalists spread out thinner and thinner over north China and Manchuria, the Communists struck first in one area and then in another, whittling away Chiang's scattered forces with small loss to themselves.

To sum up, there is no evidence that Chiang ever tried to bring the Communist armies to battle; it is certain that he never succeeded in doing so.

Then there was the problem of graft and corruption in the Nationalist Army and government—the underfeeding of soldiers, the thievery by officers, the abandonment and even selling of U.S.-made arms to the enemy. Evidence of this comes from men who otherwise have had the highest opinion of Chiang.

Two important visitors to China in the summer of 1947, the season of Chiang's predicted victory, saw that the situation was nowhere near so rosy. They were William C. Bullitt and General Albert C. Wedemeyer. Bullitt, who traveled for *Life,* came back with a $1.3-billion plan for saving China in three years, claiming that Russia had been arming the Chinese Reds while the United States had been disgracefully withholding weapons, ammunition, and funds from Chiang. The Generalissimo himself was quoted in the New York *Times* of September 11, 1947, as telling a Kuomintang conference that he still had enough supplies for two more years of civil war. Chiang added that Nationalist losses had been "entirely due to the negligence of high commanding officers and to miscalculations of their own."

For all Bullitt's shifting of the blame to the late President Roosevelt, his own eighteen-point program of military and government reform included such measures as retiring half the Nationalist generals, jailing rich men who would not turn over funds in foreign currencies to the government, and cutting the army in half "by removing non-existent troops from the rolls" and "disbanding units of the lowest quality."

In a report not released until August 5, 1949, General Wedemeyer, who traveled for the President, urged a five-year program of aid to the Nationalists, a five-power guardianship for Manchuria with Russia as one guardian, or a U.N. trusteeship, and immediate "drastic, far-reaching political and economic reforms" by the Nationalist government. "Promises will no longer suffice," said the General. "Performance is absolutely necessary. It should be accepted that military force in itself will not eliminate Communism."

The real issue on which the Administration and the gathering forces of the China Lobby split was whether Chiang could or would carry out the reforms that everybody considered indispensable. Bullitt, who wrote: "In the pages of history Chiang bulks larger than any living American," said he could. The Administration, for a while, appeared to risk insisting on reform as the price for continued aid.

As it happened, the situation in China was so serious and the pressure from Congress so severe by the end of 1947 that the Administration proposed more aid than Bullitt had asked—$570 million for fifteen months (his program for that period came to $562.5 million)—and far more than the modest $250 million a year Governor Dewey was urging. What the Administration tried to avoid was all-out entanglement in a civil war which could imperil our program of resisting Communism in Europe.

In January, 1948, when the bill was about to be submitted, the Chinese Premier, General Chang Chun, announced his intention to reform the government. Before the hearings began, a "technical mission" of Chinese arrived in Washington, headed by Pei Tsu-yi, general manager of the Bank of China, and during the hearings its members were frequently seen around the rooms of Senator Styles Bridges's Appropriations Committee. The presence of this mission, its connections with some of the Americans who testified at the hearings, and certain other coincidences suggested that the Chinese government began at this time to try exerting extremely direct influence on pending U.S. legislation.

Both Wedemeyer and Bullitt testified in favor of the China-aid bill, as did General Chennault.

Another witness was Norwood F. Allman, who described himself as a representative of "many of the American firms doing business in China as well as a number of Chinese industrial and business firms," but whose expenses were paid by the Bank of China. From Washington, Mr. Allman, who is known to his friends as "Judge" because of his service with the Shanghai International Mixed Court, wrote to the governor of the bank substantially as follows: That he had been working hard on the Senators to counteract Marshall's opposition to any large aid program; that he had taken the line that Marshall, while in China on his Presidential mission, had tried to order Chiang Kai-shek around like one of his second lieutenants, and when Chiang refused to accept such treatment Marshall was piqued; and all this was having a good effect. Judge Allman was the first China Lobbyist to admit trying to discredit General Marshall.

In March, while the hearings were still going on, an old Christian Fronter named William J. Goodwin, who in 1941 had threatened that there would be civil war if America aided Britain, was hired by the National Resources Commission of China as an "advisor on public relations," or paid lobbyist. Mr. Goodwin's fee was $30,000 a year, of which he later said he had paid out $22,857 in expenses, largely for entertainment at such establishments as the Metropolitan Club in Washington and the Wee Tappee Tavern in New York. The following year he switched to the Chinese News Service, at a reduction in fee to $25,000 and in expenses to $9,783. Mr. Goodwin says he volunteered his services as a part of his "lifelong fight against Communism." When Goodwin was hired, he lunched with Ambassador Koo and was interviewed by a genial Chinese named Chen Chih-mai. Chen Chih-mai first came to the United States in 1944 to take charge of propaganda and is now Minister Counselor of the Embassy.

Goodwin began giving dinners at the Mayflower for Congressmen at which they could hear the opinions of Ambassador Koo and Counselor Chen. In an interview with Edward R. Harris of the St. Louis *Post-Dispatch* some two years later, Goodwin estimated that he had entertained about a hundred Congressmen a year, had converted at least fifty of them to support of more aid for Nationalist China, and had "helped materially" to lay the groundwork for Senator McCarthy's attacks on the State Department. Among the guests at his dinners were Senators Bridges, Knowland, Wherry, and McCarran.

Early in April, 1948, President Truman signed the foreign-aid bill, providing $463 million for China (about the twelve-month equivalent of the $570 million originally proposed for fifteen months), but Congress—this was the Republican Eightieth Congress—did not pass the actual appropriation until June, and it cut the figure for China to $400 million. On April 22, the Nationalists in Yenan surrendered almost without a fight.

In the June issue of the *China Monthly,* Alfred Kohlberg, after a trip to the Far East, quoted a man he identified only as "the greatest living American" as having said that America's troubles came from "stupidity at the top—treason just below." This was the first time Kohlberg had been able to quote anybody of the stature of General MacArthur on "treason" in the government.

In August, 1948, the Nationalist government at last announced a program of what sounded like drastic economic reforms. It was too late. In November, Chiang's demoralized Mukden garrison surrendered the well-fortified city to the Communist armies. This was the beginning of the end—the end that was to come so swiftly.

In November, too, the Chinese Nationalists suffered another major reverse—thousands of miles away; Thomas E. Dewey was defeated for the Presidency of the United States.

The days after President Truman's victory were dark and dramatic for the Chinese in America. In December, Madame Chiang made her desperate trip to Washington, had tea at the White

House, and found the President unwilling to commit himself to the all-out effort that would be needed to save her husband.

The Ubiquitous Major

Early in the evening of October 8, 1950, the telephone rang in the Manhattan apartment of a public-relations man named Leo Casey. Mr. Casey had done some publicity for the Republican Party in the late 1930's and had been an adviser in Wendell Willkie's Presidential campaign. More recently he had been hired by David B. Charnay, founder and head of a public-relations firm called Allied Syndicates, Inc. When the phone rang, Mr. Casey was having a quiet dinner with his wife.

Mr. Charnay, his boss, was on the wire in Beverly Hills, California. He ordered Mr. Casey to take a plane for Los Angeles to work on the Senatorial campaign of Representative Richard M. Nixon against Representative Helen Gahagan Douglas. Mr. Casey says he picked up $400 in expense money from an associate, Arthur Happenie, and caught a midnight plane.

In Los Angeles, according to Mr. Casey, his boss explained that the Nixon campaign would help to "open some doors" for Allied Syndicates, which was setting up a West Coast office. Mr. Casey and Mr. Charnay had a meeting with Mr. Nixon at the Hotel Ambassador. In the lobby of the hotel, Mr. Casey noticed with Laurence Witten, secretary of the firm, a Chinese gentleman whom he had frequently seen going in and out of Mr. Charnay's New York office, and who was referred to by others in the office as "the Major" or "the little fellow."

Mr. Casey organized an "Independent Voters Committee for Nixon." He worked hard, he says, to attract the Negro vote, on which Mrs. Douglas, a liberal, was counting heavily. Since Mrs. Douglas had been a sharp critic of the House Un-American Activities Committee, he also played up Mr. Nixon's part in the investigation leading to the conviction of Alger Hiss. His job well done and Mr. Nixon elected, Mr. Casey went back to New York.

He was warmly congratulated by Mr. Charnay and Mr. Happenie, who, according to Mr. Casey, was Mr. Charnay's right hand man at that time. Then, as Mr. Casey recalls it, Mr. Happenie suggested that he go to Washington and "deliver Nixon to the Major." Mr. Casey says he was puzzled by this, and Mr. Happenie explained: "You're not so naïve as to suppose you were out in California opening doors. You were working for the China account."

Mr. Casey knew, of course, that the firm was retained by the Bank of China, but he says he was shocked by Mr. Happenie's remark and told Mr. Charnay that he wouldn't think of "delivering" a Senator to a foreign agent. Soon afterward Mr. Casey left the firm, went to Washington, and told his story to Senator Nixon, who thanked him for the information.

David Charnay is a stocky, energetic ex-reporter for the tabloids, with a breezy, agreeable manner and iron-gray hair that stands up in Teddy-bear fashion. He founded his firm in 1947 and soon managed to "pitch," as he would put it, some valuable accounts, including Ballantine's Beer, Eversharp, and the United Mine Workers. Thus Mr. Charnay became good friends with John L. Lewis, whose autographed photograph ("with appreciation and good wishes") hangs on his office wall, and later with Mr. Lewis's friend and former $35,000-a-year co-trustee of the UMW's welfare fund, Senator Styles Bridges of New Hampshire.

In the summer of 1949—shortly after the Chinese had made their fateful decision to go after political power in the United States, and coincident with the publication of the State Department's "White Paper" on China—Mr. Charnay's firm was retained by the Bank of China at a fee of $60,000 a year, plus $17,-500 for Mr. Sullivan's law partnership, Sullivan, Bernard, and Shea. When he was asked recently how he happened to get the account, Mr. Charnay replied: "We pitched it." His job, as he explained it, was to prevent the recognition of the Chinese Communist government and the consequent freezing, for that government's benefit, of the Bank of China's assets in this country. Mr. Charnay states that he was never told how much those assets amounted to, but he has heard them estimated at "between one and three hundred million."

Mr. Charnay says that he did a "straight publicity job," getting editors and reporters interested in the mistreatment of

Americans by the Chinese Communists, particularly in the cases of captured Marines and Consul Angus Ward. Mr. Charnay set up the broadcast of Mme. Chiang Kai-shek's dramatic farewell to America in 1950 and was one of those who recommended Chiang's offer of Nationalist troops for Korea. Mr. Charnay also had a part in the production of a documentary propaganda film, "Death of a Dream," which before its general release was shown to gatherings of Nationalist China enthusiasts, Congressional and otherwise. He says that, though the picture had nothing to do with his work for the Bank of China, he acted as "a sort of catalyst" in getting it financed and made, and he denies, "as far as I know," the printed report that $20,000 of Chinese funds went into it. "They were private funds," says Mr. Charnay. He will concede, of course, that "private funds" from Americans might have been originally furnished by Chinese.

Mr. Charnay's account of the Nixon campaign, and particularly of the part played by Mr. Happenie, differs from that of Mr. Casey and of other former associates; the difference suggests a way in which the Chinese may work through an American firm but keep the boss free of responsibility for, or even knowledge of, its doings. Mr. Charnay says he went to see Hedda Hopper on another matter and she asked him to take over the direction of a committee she had organized for Mr. Nixon. He told her he could not do it personally, but got Mr. Casey for the job, and after seeing the campaign off to a start went back to New York. As for the Chinese major, "he may have been on the West Coast." As for his payment, "it all came from the committee." As for Mr. Happenie's being his "right-hand man," says Mr. Charnay: "He wasn't even in the firm."

Mr. Charnay says he has never met H. H. Kung. He does concede that "the Major," or "the little fellow," is Louis Kung, who was a major in the Chinese Nationalist Army (he is now a colonel) and is the second son of H. H. Kung. Mr. Charnay also concedes that Louis Kung is still a "very good friend." His former associates recall that Major Kung was in and out of the Charnay office a great deal during the 1950 campaign and predicted that the Republicans would pick up six seats in the Senate (they picked up five).

Louis Kung and his older brother David are favorites of their aunt, the childless Mme. Chiang Kai-shek. Their father, it will be remembered, was China's Minister of Finance while their mother and sisters were speculators in American aid—which could be why Dr. Kung has no objection to letting the Treasury reveal his own "personal" accounts. The parents now live quietly near Riverdale, New York City, and David has become the financier of the family. His father had him made joint managing director of the Central Trust Company in China ten years ago when he was only twenty-two. Among his present commercial activities, he is the largest stockholder of the Yangtze Trading Corporation, which was barred last June from licensing for foreign trade after it had illegally shipped tin to Communist China.

Louis Kung is twenty-nine. He attended Sandhurst, the British West Point, where his English acquired a clipped soldierly accent. He is nominally attached to the Chinese Military Staff Committee at the United Nations and is "technical adviser" to the Chinese Air Force in Washington, although he has never set foot in the office. He keeps houses in both New York and Washington. His Washington house is on Reservoir Road, and in it are several unlisted telephones. The Major is fond of calling up his friends and associates and identifying himself as "Lee" or "Smith." His friends include Senator Styles Bridges, who, according to Mr. Charnay's former employees, occasionally ran into "the Major" at the Allied office during the 1950 election campaign. Once when the Senator went off to rest up in a Western hideaway, Louis Kung was one of the people to whom he confided his phone number.

Louis Kung, the ubiquitous major, is far from the key figure in the Chinese division of the China Lobby; although important enough to be kept with diplomatic immunity while doing no diplomatic work, he is not much more than a courier or paymaster. And Allied Syndicates, Incorporated, is only one of the American firms or organizations that have been used by the Nationalist Chinese.

The China Lobby—Part Two

In the spring and summer of 1949, with the Chinese Communists swarming over the mainland, some of the most eminent of the dispossessed Nationalists set off for the United States. Here, too, they had recently suffered a major setback—in the Presidential election of 1948. But America was now the only place where they could find fresh hope for their nearly lost cause; as their army was driven to the China Sea and thence to Formosa, the only battlefield where they stood a chance of operating effectively was U.S. politics. They still had powerful friends in both parties, though they felt closer to the G.O.P. To spearhead the new campaign, the Nationalists counted on a few high Chinese officials who had spent the war years in Washington and knew the ropes.

Yet the prospect was dismal. One by one, the big cities and ports—Nanking, Hankow, Shanghai, Tsingtao—were falling to the enemy. The State Department, which had appointed a special committee to review U.S. policy in China, was about to publish its White Paper, and it was an open secret that the White Paper would slam the door on further aid to the Nationalists. For Chiang's agents in the United States, the darkest event of all had come at the beginning of that inauspicious year. On January 21, Chiang had stepped down from the Presidency of China and retired to Fenghwa, where he said he would devote his time to "sweeping the tombs of my ancestors."

Madame Chiang, who had arrived in Washington on December 1, 1948, took on the assignment of reorganizing Chiang's forces in this country. Until she left, on January 8, 1950, to rejoin her husband on Formosa, her task was to marshal the most skillful Chinese in the United States and to consolidate all the American support she could.

Much of Madame Chiang's work was done in the New York home of her brother-in-law, H. H. Kung. There she held weekly strategy meetings with various groups of Chinese who, by virtue of their past or present official positions or their private wealth, could accomplish most in the bumpy arena of American politics. The men who attended these sessions fell into two main groups. One, to which H. H. Kung and her brother, T. V. Soong, belonged, operated in and from New York and included men of means rather than government officials; the other, which worked in Washington, was composed of Chiang's most trusted chiefs of mission.

This was no ordinary group of political refugees. The Formosa régime was something more than a standard twentieth-century government-in-exile and something a good deal less than a real national government. It had found shelter on the island of Formosa, but it didn't want and couldn't hope to stay there forever. It had to go back to China or out of existence. The Kuomintang was eager to resume the fight, and its only hope was U.S. assistance on a gigantic scale.

Slowly, out of the Riverdale meetings emerged the line of action that the rebuilt China Lobby would follow. According to former Nationalist officials, it has never been a hard-and-fast program. But, by and large, it has kept the same general direction through the years since the fateful summer of 1949.

One top-priority objective was the removal of Dean Acheson as Secretary of State. Chiang's agents could not tell their master that they had been mistaken when they had advised him not to worry because unlimited military aid was coming. Somebody had to be the scapegoat. So they agreed on Acheson, who, they said, was besieged by Communists and fellow travelers in and out of the State Department and who was under the spell of Chiang's "arch-enemy," General George Marshall.

Probably none of these Chinese could have dreamed how wildly successful their piece of self-justification, expressly tailored for Chiang, would later on be with the American public. But at every opportunity, talking among themselves and with American friends, they hopefully spread word that the Administration was to blame for the Communist conquest of China.

Peace, for them, was unendurable and unthinkable; at all costs, America too had to be made to see that a third world war was inevitable.

The Washington group of Chinese who attended Madame Chiang's briefings usually included K. H. Yu, delegate to the International Bank; W. K. Li, representative to the Far Eastern Commission; General Peter T. K. Pee, military attaché of the Embassy; General P. T. Mow, head of the procurement office of the Chinese Air Force, who has since gotten into difficulties with the Formosa government; and Chen Chih-mai, Minister Counselor of the Embassy.

The New York group, by all odds the more colorful, had on its roster several of the most experienced and most mutually distrustful specialists in the lobbying business. This time they were to operate less flamboyantly than they had before. First and foremost came those ancient antagonists T. V. Soong, who returned to the United States in June, 1949, and H. H. Kung. Then there were Chen Li-fu, leader of the CC Clique (which had organized "thought control," the secret police, and a network of banks and industries), who had returned to this country by 1950, and Dr. T. F. Tsiang, the U.N. delegate.

Of the New York group, according to an ex-Nationalist official, only Dr. Tsiang received and spent Nationalist government funds. The others had to draw upon their own vast resources as circumstances and opportunity required. Chen Li-fu, for instance, reportedly pledged two million dollars from the funds of the CC Clique, some of which, incidentally, went and still goes to subsidize most of the Nationalist Chinese newspapers in the United States. His pet project has always been to blacken the character and motives of General Marshall, who back in 1946 had lashed out at the CC Clique.

H. H. Kung kept in touch with a wide range of Chiang enthusiasts, from Henry Luce to Senator Styles Bridges of New

Hampshire and Alfred Kohlberg, the New York importer. His son Louis, the "ubiquitous Major" of the preceding installment, was recruited by Madame Chiang as a courier, paymaster, and trouble shooter—a man-about-America.

As for T. V. Soong, his return to the United States was like a homecoming. He quickly set about making new friends and re-visiting old ones—among them his wartime associates Tommy Corcoran, General Claire Chennault, and Whiting Willauer, Chennault's partner in the profitable China Air Transport.

One sign of the changing times was Soong's approach to Alfred Kohlberg. It was something of a comedown for the man who had once asserted "I am China" to seek out the vociferous importer of Chinese embroidery. This was no Ludwig Rajchman, the political expediter and philosopher-at-large who had helped Soong set up the wartime China Lobby. But 1949 was a far cry from 1940, and Mr. Kohlberg looked promising. Through his China Policy Association and his magazine *Plain Talk* (later the *Freeman*), through his friends and fellow enthusiasts in Congress, Alfred Kohlberg was rapidly becoming a principal peddler of pro-Nationalist propaganda. Above all, he was spreading, even though to a limited audience, his uninhibited version of the State Department "conspiracy." And so in the winter of 1949-1950, not long before Senator McCarthy's first barrage, T. V. Soong sought out Mr. Kohlberg.

Ever since 1949, the official financing of the Lobby has centered largely in Washington, where Ambassador Wellington Koo presides uncomfortably and with little real power over the same group of men who used to attend Madame Chiang's weekly meetings in Riverdale.

The first lump sum in support of the Lobby's work, according to former Nationalist officials then in a position to know, did not follow the customary route. In the summer of that year $800,000 was transferred from Wang Shih-chieh, Chiang's chief secretary on Formosa, to Dr. Tsiang openly via the Bank of China in New York. This came to the attention of various Nationalist government employees, who at first believed it was intended to cover their salary payments, which as usual were two or three months in arrears. That, as it happens, was not what the money was intended for.

Before Madame Chiang left the United States early in 1950, she arranged for a fund of more than a million dollars, then under control of the Chinese National Resources Commission, to be put at the disposal of Counselor of Embassy Chen Chih-mai. General Pee, the military attaché, who reports directly to Chiang Kai-shek, also draws on large funds independently of the Embassy.

The ways of Lobby finance, like the finances of the régime itself, would drive any American C.P.A. to distraction. No one, including the Nationalist government, knows precisely what its assets amount to at home or abroad. In the incessant movement of Nationalist money, official and private accounts have become intertwined. In part, the reason is perfectly understandable. In 1949 a good deal of Nationalist money was put in private and numbered accounts for fear that the United States would recognize Mao Tse-tung's Communist government and freeze Nationalist assets over here. But this was not the only explanation. Of the enormous sums of government money that Chiang has parceled out to relatives and friends in this country and in Europe and South America since 1949, a substantial amount is known to have been allocated to the molding of American opinion.

The Smiling Counselor

Probably not even the U.S. government could trace the expenditure of the Lobby's money in the United States. But this magazine has been able to get the details of certain operations and frustrated operations in which the Chinese have been ready to put up anything from the price of a few cocktails to five million dollars. A case study of how Chinese money and persuasion are used is provided by the Washington career of Chen Chih-mai, the smiling Counselor.

Chen Chih-mai, who has been with the Chinese Embassy since 1944, knows a good many people in Washington. He had taken a Ph.D. at Columbia and taught at the National Tsing Hua Uni-

versity from 1933 to 1937. In 1938 he became Counselor to the
Executive Yuan, a position he held for six years before coming
to Washington. His connections with the Nationalist government, and particularly with the CC Clique, give him power and
responsibility considerably beyond his rank. It may be recalled
that when William J. Goodwin and Ambassador Koo first discussed Mr. Goodwin's lobbying job, the ambassador had Mr.
Chen interview Mr. Goodwin. Mr. Goodwin's fee for the first
year—$30,000—was paid by the Chinese National Resources Com-
mission.

In a cable of June 22, 1949, Chen Chih-mai reported to
Chiang:

> "Goodwin has commenced with his work already, which he pushes
> ahead feverishly. The leaders of both parties . . . are all supporting
> him . . ."

On August 1, 1949, Chen cabled again:

> "Goodwin . . . [is] working in an effort to disillusion the leaders
> of the Democratic Party about the Chinese Communists. We are be-
> ing very careful to avoid a partisan conflict and emotional attacks."

At one of Mr. Goodwin's dinners for Congressmen, a high
Embassy official briefed a group of Senators on the reasons why
W. Walton Butterworth, former U.S. Counselor of Embassy in
Nanking, should not be confirmed as Assistant Secretary of State.
Mr. Goodwin (who is now acting as one of Senator Taft's campaign strategists in New York) gave another of his dinners at
the Mayflower just after the White Paper was published, in August, 1949, at which Chen Chih-mai offered a vehement and detailed criticism of the White Paper. His talk provided ammunition for a three-day barrage by Senators Bridges, Knowland,
Wherry, and McCarran.

Chen Chih-mai was greatly helped in his work by the frequent
receipt of "information" on Americans from the Chinese secret
police. Senator McCarthy has admitted using information from
secret police, though he hasn't specified of what nationality, and
Mr. Goodwin has stated that he "helped materially" to lay the
groundwork for McCarthy's charges. Later the Senator was
briefed by Alfred Kohlberg, who also had access to Chinese files.

Mr. Chen also bought derogatory information on Americans from American sources; once, for example, he paid $300 for a report on Michael Lee, a Far Eastern expert in the Department of Commerce who was forced to resign in the fall of 1950 largely as a result of unproven charges that he had withheld aviation gas from Chiang.

Chen Chih-mai oversees the operations of the Chinese News Service headquarters in New York, to whose payroll Mr. Goodwin was switched in July, 1949. In the same month, the Chinese News Service employed a man named Norman Paige as a "press and radio consultant" at a reported salary of $30,000 a year. Mr. Paige, who changed his name from James Black de Puy for writing purposes, is a tall, heavy-set man of forty-five, with a thick black mustache. He had been a radio correspondent in the Far East, and after the war had become one-fifth owner of the Philippines Broadcasting Corporation until 1949, when he sold out and went to work for the Chinese. His regular duties have been to call on and win over publishers, editors, and radio broadcasters. He also gives cocktail parties and makes speeches.

The following excerpts from his confidential report to the Chinese News Service of January 29, 1952, show how Mr. Paige operates:

"American public opinion, so long swayed by the successful red smear campaign, is today far over to the realization that Generalissimo Chiang was sold down the river. People are beginning to realize that the position of the Nationalist government is today stronger than at any time since Marshall went to China and it is increasing daily. My campaign of realistic and honest approach, particularly with the press, is finding its right reward. . . .

"My recent contacts include:

"_____, owner of the _____, . . . is a Republican leader throughout the West. He can be considered an addition to our pipe-line. He will not only influence his own newspapers, but also others.

"_____, owner and publisher of the _____ _____. He too is a welcome addition to the main pipe-line. . . .

"_____ _____, feature writer—an old Asia hand and one who goes to any lengths to write or plant stories desirable." (*The names above are left blank because we have only this statement that the journalists referred to are parts of a pipeline.*)

All in all, Chen Chih-mai had a busy summer in 1949, what with riding herd on Messrs. Goodwin and Paige and entertaining Congressmen and other influential Americans. A complication arose from Chiang's resignation. Although General Li Tsung-jen had become Acting President in January, 1949, Chen Chih-mai and his colleagues continued to report to the Generalissimo—who was busy sweeping the tombs of his ancestors—as if he had never "retired."

Life at the Embassy became more devious than ever. Since Ambassador Koo was considered unreliable, all cables dealing with Lobby activities were dispatched to Chiang not through the Embassy but through channels controlled by Chiang's trusted agents. As the cables indicate, Chen Chih-mai, aided by General Pee, started intriguing against Acting President Li. On November 28, 1949, Pee cabled to Chiang as follows:

> "Congressman Judd gave us information by saying that the State Department may give Kan Chieh-hou [President Li's personal representative in the U.S.] the following promise. If Li were capable of getting rid of the old feudal system of evil forces and could succeed in obtaining military and political power, then aid from the American government will be forwarded immediately. The intention of the U.S. government is to deal a blow at you."

One of the most ambitious schemes of the Lobby appears in Chen's cable of September 15:

> "Yesterday, my humble self, Chen Chih-mai, met General Albert Wedemeyer. General told me that an aluminum magnate [J. Louis Reynolds of the Reynolds Metals Co.] relayed a message to him that the Chinese government intended to hire him at five million dollars if he would give up his military career in the United States government to go to China to assist us in the anti-Communist activities.
>
> "General Wedemeyer said he always has great sympathy toward our anti-Communist policy, and especially holds you in great esteem as a leader. He is willing to try his best, if he finds himself in a position to be of service to you as an individual.
>
> "However, his opposition to the present United States foreign

policy is a well-known fact. Therefore, if he comes to China as a private citizen in a private capacity, it will be certain that he would not be supported by the United States government. So nothing can be accomplished. He also said he could get by financially. If we have such a large sum of money, private or public, it should be used for the welfare of the people in order to enhance the force against the Communists."

According to Drew Pearson, General Wedemeyer has confirmed both the offer and his rejection of it.

According to former Nationalist officials, the idea of hiring General Wedemeyer originated with T. V. Soong, who, together with Ambassador Koo, was desperately seeking a means of reversing the policy advanced by the White Paper and paving the way for further U.S. aid. The scheme was that if a U.S. general like Wedemeyer were once established on Formosa, his unofficial mission could easily turn into an official one for the United States.

Thus Chen Chih-mai's private diplomacy was to bring to Formosa, pending the time the U.S. Army itself would arrive, a small private army of American officers. U.S. generals and admirals, retired or not, were encouraged to make private alliances, which Chen Chih-mai hoped and prayed the U.S. government would later on ratify.

China Rediscovered

The smiling Counselor was lobbying with a vengeance all through 1949. Perhaps he overstepped the boundaries of conventional diplomacy, but his government was in a very unconventional, indeed tragic, spot. Chen Chih-mai served his leader, for all we know, faithfully and well.

During the same year there were quite a few American citizens who, on their own initiative and with their own means, were moving in the same direction as the lobbyists controlled by Chen Chih-mai. The Counselor and his inner group saw to it that the volunteers were well stocked with information and sometimes with directives—but delicately. Each group and each leader needed special treatment. Volunteers are harder to keep in line than paid workers. Yet no foreign lobby in our country will ever succeed unless it can organize the spontaneous co-operation of well-meaning Americans.

Among China's most energetic volunteers in 1949, a notable one was Frederick C. McKee, a Pittsburgh industrialist, who has for years contributed zeal, time, and funds to causes he has believed in.

Since the fall of 1939, there have been in our country a number of organizations dedicated to a single foreign-policy issue. They cross political, economic, and religious lines, and, when their goal is reached, they are disbanded. In the most liberal of these organizations Frederick McKee was always to be found—an internationally minded fervent political do-gooder. In 1949, he appeared again and founded, with the aid of a few old friends, veterans of the William Allen White Committee, the Committee to Defend America by Aiding Anti-Communist China.

Strange Bedfellows

According to persons who know him, Mr. McKee is not overfond of Alfred Kohlberg. But they have a cause in common. Last June, ten of the fifty-one directors of Mr. McKee's committee were also directors of the American China Policy Association, which Mr. Kohlberg says he did not organize but "took . . . in hand" early in its career. The Association is a small group—it was deliberately kept so in the early stages, Mr. Kohlberg says, "because we didn't want anyone . . . who didn't agree with us" —but it includes citizens of fairly diverse views and reputation. Until summer, 1951, its president was Clare Boothe Luce. She was succeeded by William Loeb, the publisher of the Manchester, New Hampshire, *Union Leader,* a Republican who loves G.O.P. Senator Styles Bridges but loathes G.O.P. Senator Charles W. Tobey, whom he once called "dangerous to the future safety of the United States." Republican Senators George Aiken and Ralph Flanders he has described as "those two disgraces to the State of Vermont."

One of the directors of the China Policy Association is the Reverend Dr. James W. Fifield, a Congregationalist minister and head of Spiritual Mobilization, who has been widely criticized in

Los Angeles for the anti-Semitic overtones of his radio speeches. In a talk in 1948, Dr. Fifield singled out Mr. Kohlberg as "one of the five most vigorous, helpful and constructive individuals in the anti-Communist forces [who] happen to be Jews." Recently, when asked whether there was a China Lobby in the United States, Dr. Fifield said: "Yes, there is. Its head is Alfred Kohlberg, one of my dearest friends."

Early in 1949, when Madame Chiang was briefing the Chinese inner circle at the home of Mr. Kohlberg's friend H. H. Kung, Mr. Kohlberg suddenly renewed his attacks on the Institute of Pacific Relations after two years of comparative silence on the subject. In June he took off on a visit to Formosa. On his return he called on his friend Senator Bridges, wrote a report on China, and before long had his first meeting with T. V. Soong.

At about the same time, he was seeking what he called "the inside dope" on Ambassador-at-large Philip C. Jessup, under whose direction the White Paper had been prepared. Mr. Kohlberg wanted to find out, as he himself put it in an open letter to the columnist Robert S. Allen published in the *China Monthly,* whether Jessup "is just a confused liberal who has been used by more sinister subversives like Henry Wallace."

Around the time Mr. Kohlberg wrote his letter to Robert S. Allen, the first trial of Alger Hiss came to an end with a hung jury. The 8-4 verdict on Hiss's guilt just about represented the tormented indecisiveness of an extremely large number of people who for months had been debating among themselves, and many within themselves, whether Alger Hiss was guilty and whether, if he was, his lapse represented an accident in the life of one brilliant young man or a pattern of treason within the Administration.

This national ordeal of mutual suspicion and mulling over things past had started just after the war and reached a climax in the summer of 1948 with the outburst of confessions and accusations from Elizabeth Bentley, Whittaker Chambers, and Louis Budenz. These people, who became suddenly famous by reconstructing their pasts in public, released a wave of fear in a deeply disturbed nation: the fear above all that the new enemy the

United States was facing—far more dangerous than the ones that had just been defeated—could have received and might still be receiving assistance from men in high places.

On January 21, 1950, after his second trial, Alger Hiss was convicted on two counts of perjury and Dean Acheson said he would not turn his back on him. Three weeks later a man came up with "guts enough and dumb enough," as Mr. Kohlberg was later to phrase it, to accuse the makers of foreign policy of being traitors.

The man, of course, was Joseph McCarthy. On February 9, the junior Senator from Wisconsin made his now-famous speech in Wheeling, West Virginia, announcing that he held in his hands the names of 205 Communists in the State Department. He had based his charges on a jumble of material, some of which was derived from a two-year-old Congressional investigation, some from Mr. Kohlberg's own letters and articles, some from William Goodwin. What is surprising is that in this first broadside he made only a few passing references to China.

In February, soon after McCarthy's first outburst, Mr. Kohlberg met the Senator for the first time. They needed each other. McCarthy had the headlines and wanted ammunition; Mr. Kohlberg had never made the headlines but had a whole arsenal. Over dinner Mr. Kohlberg expounded his thesis that the I.P.R. was the instrument of Communist infiltration into the State Department. The Senator soon was furnished a collection of Mr. Kohlberg's favorite articles and releases.

At his first appearances before the Tydings Committee in mid-March, McCarthy quoted at length from both the Larsen article and an article by a Father Kearney, who later admitted that all his material had come from Mr. Kohlberg. Three days later McCarthy sent for Emmanuel Larsen and introduced him to his assistant, Don Surine. According to Larsen's later testimony, Surine explained that the Senator wanted Larsen's help. "If you string along with us," he added, "then it will go much easier with you." When Larsen insisted he had no evidence of espionage or pro-Communists in the State Department, Surine dismissed him.

To right-wingers of all shades all over the country, China suddenly became, under Senator McCarthy's impetus, the magic issue that might finally provide the road to power. Many of the fringe groups had until then never shown any particular interest in China. Take Dr. Edward Rumely's Committee for Constitutional Government, which ever since 1937 had been reviling the Administration on domestic issues. Its favorite author, John T. Flynn, had published in October, 1949, *The Road Ahead,* which the committee campaigned to put in every fifth American home. This book never mentions China.

But in November, 1951, Flynn published another book, *While You Slept,* entirely devoted to "our tragedy in Asia." Not the slightest responsibility for this tragedy is ascribed to Chiang. As Flynn has it, "the plan was laid in Russia" and "carried out in the United States by Americans, and by only a handful of Americans." The chief villains of the piece are Marshall, Acheson, and, of course, Roosevelt, who in Flynn's account once tried to induce Stalin to join a world government that would have made Roosevelt "President of the World."

Throughout 1950 and 1951 the chorus from the Right and even from some sections of the Center and Left grew shriller and shriller. Kohlberg could well be pleased with his part in preparing the score. "I am proud," he declared, "to have given Senator McCarthy a small part of the information he gathered for his fight . . ." A year later he had only one reservation about the Senator. "He doesn't go far enough," Kohlberg remarked. "He's too cautious about using his information."

People from the most disparate groups, Catholics and Klansmen, Jews and anti-Semites, labor men and "economic royalists," all were united in interlocking committees or interlocking ideas, all backing Chiang. This was not only the Lobby's doing, of course, but the Lobby gave the inspiration. In the clamor, more and more scruples came to be dropped. A man in whom rugged integrity and loyalty to Chiang had been struggling for years, Congressman Walter Judd, is reported to have begged McCarthy early in the game not to "call [them] Communists." But as the tide rose, Judd too was swept along.

Korea and Beyond

At the Chinese Embassy in Washington all the tumult and the shouting brought on by the Tydings hearings were looked on as a great triumph. William Goodwin, Chen Chih-mai's No. 1 lobbyist, said in an interview with Ed Harris of the St. Louis *Post-Dispatch:* "We'll have a new China policy as a result of all this by the end of summer. . . . And as for Secretary Dean Acheson, I can tell you that he's already fired by President Truman. It just hasn't been announced. He has to get rid of him because of all the pressure."

The Tydings hearings presented Counselor Chen and his colleagues with problems as well as opportunities. One particularly troublesome case was that of Owen Lattimore, who in 1941 and 1942 had been Chiang Kai-shek's chief American adviser and who now stood accused by Senator McCarthy of having been the Soviet architect of U.S. policy in China. On April 7, 1950, this cable was dispatched to Chiang:

> "Lattimore is being questioned at a Congressional hearing, and he produced two letters—one from you addressed to President Roosevelt, and one from Madame Chiang addressed to Lattimore, wherein you both commended him highly. As a matter of fact, Lattimore in recent years has attacked our government viciously, and has opposed any aid for us. He especially despises you very much. Now, he has used the above-mentioned two letters for his own defense. But we are in quite a bit of doubt about the existence of these two letters. Last night Congressman Judd intended to call Madame Chiang by long distance in order to debunk Lattimore. After a discussion, the Congressman preferred that the report be relayed to you by a cable from us instead."

On May 3, General Pee, the military attaché who had once described himself as having been "patient and tolerant to the extremity with General Marshall," sent the following message:

> "Last Sunday the New York *Times* editorialized about the China Lobbyists, and Ambassador Koo, Chen Chih-mai, H. H. Kung, and T. V. Soong were mentioned. The Lattimore case was created as a political weapon in a conflict between the two parties. But Lattimore and the Democratic Party intentionally pulled us into the case

and accused us of a sneak attack on the State Department and General Marshall. We are really in a very bad spot. For details, ask Chen Chih-mai in person."

Meanwhile, of course, the Lobby kept up the classic pressures of all lobbyists, as Counselor Chen had indicated in a cable to Chiang back in July 21, 1949:

"As far as our activities in the U.S. are concerned, it seems that we should cover the Administration, as well as the legislative branch, we should especially strive for a closer relationship with the latter. There is no danger at all if our procedure strictly follows the laws of the United States, but Dr. Hu Shih is opposed to getting in touch with the legislative branch. His opinion is off the beam."

By April 6, 1950, Chen Chih-mai was more than ever applying his tactics of working on the legislature. That day he cabled Chiang that he had had . . .

"a long talk with Knowland and Judd. They both said Mr. Acheson was strongly prejudiced against China to a most unreasonable degree, President Truman's ability is limited, and he is influenced by Acheson all of the time. Therefore, there is no chance for a change of China policy as long as Acheson is in power. However, Congressman Judd felt that our continuous air raids on the cities only killed many innocent people—he asked us to reconsider the military necessity of such action."

Two months later, on the eve of the war in Korea, Counselor Chen reported:

"Your subordinate Chen Chih-mai had a long talk with Congressman Judd, after he had shot a series of questions at Acheson today. After talking it over with others, the following conclusions were drawn: U.S. aid for China mainly depends on the outcome of General MacArthur's visit to Formosa. The most convenient formula for us to apply is to use the Japanese Peace Treaty, which is not signed as yet, as an excuse to work out with General MacArthur a so-called Formosa Defense Bill. Congress will support such a bill."

Three weeks later, war broke out in Korea, and Chen Chih-mai no longer had to press for a "Formosa Defense Bill." The

North Koreans took care of that—and more. President Truman sent the Seventh Fleet to neutralize and, if necessary, protect the island. Thanks to the Communists, Chiang was safe—at least for the duration.

To a diplomatic activist like Chen Chih-mai, the ally status that the U.S. government once more granted Chiang was a harbinger of better things. Gently and firmly, he set himself to speeding up the tempo of their coming. A key man to keep in touch with was, of course, Mr. Republican, who might head tomorrow's Administration. Chen managed to have a good talk with the Senator. A cable of July 28, 1950:

> "Senator Taft was immensely interested in the problems of Formosa. He at one time even advocated last January to send the U.S. fleet to defend Formosa. Your humble subordinate, Chen Chih-mai, gave Taft the following idea: We Chinese are willing to share the responsibilities along with General MacArthur in a fight against Russia and Communism; however, the economic strength in Formosa is weak and the source of manpower is limited—whereas, the mainland of China is teeming with guerrillas and a practically inexhaustible source of recruits. What they need is a proper leader and a proper organization. Your career in the racial revolutionary campaign, anti-aggression, anti-Japan, and anti-Communism, is brilliantly recorded in history, and you are the most natural leader of Asia and the best partner of the United States as well.
>
> "The above idea will be used by Taft in his speech which will in turn sell the same idea to the United States authorities."

A few weeks before his conversation with Taft, Chen Chih-mai had sought the counsel of a rebellious Democrat, former Ambassador to the U.S.S.R. William C. Bullitt, who, although fighting against the Administration, still knew who carried weight at the White House and the State Department.

Mr. Bullitt had, said a cable:

> "Recommended that we should get in touch—close and often—with Harriman and with the newly appointed Chief of the Far Eastern Division and Assistant Secretary of the State Department—Dean Rusk."

In the Embassy's opinion there was one great difficulty:

"Harriman is a rich man's son, and also he is very scrupulous."

Chen Chih-mai had another thing to hope for: Would Red China enter the Korean War? On September 13, 1950, he reported:

". . . What Americans fear the most is the forthcoming participation of the Chinese Communists in the Korean War. This development bears a very high possibility, of course, but at the present stage, our policy should be:

"a. Do not make any publicity about the northward moves of the Chinese Communist troops because such publicity will arouse the suspicions and fears of the Americans and would give the Americans an excuse that we are yearning for such a conflict.

"b. Instead, we should yell at the top of our lungs in an effort to persuade the Chinese people on the mainland not to be fooled by the Russians and Chinese Communists to participate in the Korean War. Then it would match perfectly with American psychology."

As far as the Formosa régime was concerned, events in Korea never lost their ambivalent quality, no matter how the war was going for the U.N. Chen Chih-mai saw the Inchon landing as an ominous portent of peace. On September 30, he cabled Chiang:

"The American people are quite excited over the recent victory in Korea. The American authorities will use this as political capital during the election year. The U.S. policy toward Formosa will have a tendency of a compromise. The attack from the Republicans will no longer be effective. American friends cautioned us that we were facing a most critical and dangerous situation. Our counter-measure is not to show our discouragement."

Chiang has been exposed to the danger of our making peace with Red China since the day when Red China entered the war, and the danger became particularly real when the war practically ended in a stalemate. As late as March 28, 1952, Chiang warned the U.N. against a truce.

Our Asian Policy: The Jammed Rudder

Our policy toward Chiang, since Franklin Roosevelt decided that we should have one, has been torn by the conflict between what our national interest requires of China and what the Kuomintang demands of us. The Kuomintang wants unconditional, unlimited assistance, both economic and military; the American national interest requires a strong, independent, and decently governed China. But no compromise has ever been possible between the American and the Kuomintang notions of strength, independence, and decency.

If Chiang Kai-shek were now the ruler of China, he would be cultivating good relations with Russia, just as, for all his internal anti-Communism, he always did as long as he held power on the mainland. Today the Formosa-bound Chinese ruler cannot play the balance-of-power game between the United States and Russia. He cannot threaten to turn against us. He has, however, through lobbyists and zealots in the United States, turned against our State Department, one agency of our government that has—or has had—the temerity to defend U.S. interests against the insatiable demands of the Kuomintang régime.

This operation against the American State Department, its policies, and its men may very well go down in history as a classic. By skill and by luck, the China Lobby has managed to jam the rudder of our Far Eastern foreign policy. Luck helped toward the end of 1949, when the Chinese Communists began ruthlessly mistreating American consular officials; on June 25, 1950, when North Korea started the war; and finally in November, 1950, when Red China went to the rescue of North Korea. Such domestic events as the trial of Alger Hiss also helped. The Lobby succeeded in exploiting all these advantages with such brashness and skill that even to admit having considered the recognition of Communist China has become anathema to the leaders of our foreign policy.

The Lobby's campaign has been just as successful against men as against policies. Most Americans were shocked when Senator McCarthy all but called General Marshall a traitor on the floor of the Senate. But General Marshall was probably not surprised at all. The first time he had been called a traitor was in a Kuomintang newspaper in 1948. Both in the United States and in China—particularly in China—he has had a unique opportunity to study the Lobby in action. His big obstacle as a mediator, apart from the bad faith of both sides, was the reassurance Chiang was getting from his friends in America. They told him that he didn't have to yield, so, of course, Chiang did his best to stall the negotiations that he had originally wanted. General Marshall had ample opportunity to learn that the Lobby's influence has been as nefarious in Chinese as in American politics.

Even before Red China showed its hostility toward us, the Lobby's campaign of intimidation produced results. In September, 1949, the No. 2 Communist leader Chou En-lai invited the U.S. ambassador to China, Leighton Stuart, to visit Yenching University in Peking, of which Dr. Stuart had been president. The State Department, still hoping to drive a wedge between Mao and Stalin, favored the visit, but President Truman, fearful that he might be accused of selling out Chiang at "another Yalta," vetoed the trip.

In January, 1950, when the question of expelling the Nationalist Chinese delegate came up in the Security Council, the American representative said that his government viewed the matter as a procedural one and would abide by the decision of a majority vote. In June, 1951, during the MacArthur hearings, Secretary Acheson said that it was not clear whether representation in the United Nations was a purely procedural matter. If it were a "matter of substance"—a point that only the World Court could decide—the United States could deliver a veto in the Security Council. And finally, when the Senate was considering the confirmation of American delegates to the latest General Assembly in Paris, one Senator asked all ten to declare their views on the recognition of Mao. Through this gradual stifling process the robotization of our China policy has been achieved. The State Department has had to accept it in order to keep some freedom of action in Europe and the Middle East.

One of the Lobby's favorite targets after General Marshall has been John Carter Vincent, Counselor of Embassy in China in 1942 and later chief of the Division of Chinese Affairs at the State Department. Mr. Vincent has now reached the point in his career when he might normally expect to become an ambassador, if only he could pass the test of Senate confirmation. Instead, the department assigned him to Switzerland as minister, and still later, under continuing pressure, to a less "sensitive" post at Tangier. Last spring Fulton Lewis, Jr., gave his public a glimpse of how the attacks on Mr. Vincent had originated. He announced that he had got hold of a report by Chiang's secret police, "one of several dozen" that were being circulated "in and around Washington." In his column he reported with relish how "Chiang's footpads" had "tailed" U.S. representatives all over China, rifled their files, and eavesdropped on their official and unofficial talks.

To judge from Mr. Lewis's examples, the secret-police reports were not very impressive. Mr. Lewis patched them together to make a picture of fellow-traveling career men conspiring to sell out Chiang to the Communists. He described Mr. Vincent, accurately enough, as "another of the State Department officials who went through the Nationalist Chinese intelligence wringer." According to Mr. Lewis, one of the secret-police reports "relates details on how Pat Hurley . . . had Vincent recalled to the United States from China." (Mr. Vincent left China more than a year before Mr. Hurley was appointed ambassador.)

The same document reported that John Stewart Service "rode in Army car No. 2070 . . . to the office of the Communist leader at No. 50 Tseng-Chia-Yen," and that he later "went in person to Yenan to see Communist Mao Tse-tung." Mr. Lewis did not explain that Mr. Service was the official liaison man between the U.S. Army Headquarters and the Communist 18th Army Group, or that his visit to Yenan lasted for almost a year, since he was a member of the official U.S. Army Observer Group that was dispatched to Yenan with the approval of Chiang Kai-shek. Or that Pat Hurley too "went in person to Yenan to see Communist Mao Tse-tung."

The attack on these individuals spread into an attack on the entire "China Service" which the State Department had created after the First World War. Because Chinese dialects, history, and customs are so difficult to master, the Department picked young men of particular aptitude and sent them to school in China for two years—and an optional third—of full-time study.

These men formed a sort of elite in the foreign service, but not on the basis of social snobbery. The "China Service" was a rugged, unglamorous, challenging assignment. Its men came mostly from families of modest means, frequently from missionary families, and many of them had spoken Chinese since child-hood. So much did they steep themselves in the language and in the thinking habits of the Chinese people that they became the most envied corps of diplomatic experts in the Orient. Neither the British nor the Russians had anything to compare with our China Service; not until 1942 did the Russians copy our methods to build a service that could match it.

Today this corps has been disbanded. Of the twenty-two officers who belonged to it before the Second World War and who are still with the Department, only two continue to work in the Division of Chinese Affairs. Both had the luck not to be in China during the war. The other twenty are scattered about the world. One, born of missionary parents and with twenty-five years' duty in China, is at Palermo. Another, with eighteen years, is in Ecuador. Twenty-nine years of experience in China of two men are now being utilized by the Department. The 285 years of the other twenty are being thrown away.

Officers who once wrote candid reports, expecting them to be read only by their superiors, have come to consider how each word they write would look when excerpted before some committee and then re-excerpted in the newspapers. A good foreign-service officer, like a good detective or reporter, used to get all the information he could and keep a close watch on trouble-makers. But now foreign-service officers have to restrict their acquaintanceship to people who will not seem objectionable. Our foreign service is becoming more and more like Soviet Russia's, which confines itself to telling its masters only what they want to hear.

Yet the need for correct decisions has never been greater. The July, 1951, issue of the *American Foreign Service Journal* put it this way: ". . . such has been the effect of happenings of the last years that, at the very moment in history when the Foreign Service should be at the peak of its capabilities, when it should be best prepared to meet the terrible responsibilities of a period of decision between war and peace, it should itself become besmirched before the eyes of the American people, its confidence, courage, and very belief in its own principles and precepts, seriously if not irreparably damaged."

The China Lobby: *In Conclusion* . . .

By Max Ascoli

It is strange, but it is a fact: In this day and age there still seems to be something indecent about the mere presence of foreign lobbies in our country. Our government has power of life and death over practically every country in the non-Communist world; not only cabinets but constitutions may survive or fall depending on the amount of economic and military aid that Washington grants. Any foreign government is derelict in its duty if it does not state its case as convincingly as it can to the people of the United States—particularly, in these times of Congressional supremacy, to the men who make the laws.

Just as every government that expects something from us has its lobby over here, we have a lobby in every country where our interests are at stake. The destinies of nations have become so intermeshed that the conduct of foreign affairs can no longer be monopolized, though it must be controlled, by Foreign Offices or Departments of State. This means lobbying, official and unofficial.

Congress, which should know everything there is to know about foreign lobbies, got around to recognizing their existence some years ago, when, following its fashion in dealing with unsavory things, it ordered all lobbyists to register. A few years later, it dealt with Communists the same way. Congress as a whole is still sour on all foreign lobbies, but quite a few Congressmen make generous exceptions in favor of some lobbyists.

With all the lobbying that is being done by foreigners here and ourselves abroad, there seems to be no reason why people should be squeamish about admitting that such a thing as a China Lobby exists—squeamish to the point that most publications still bracket the phrase chastely in quotation marks. If the Kuomintang didn't have a lobby here, there would be something radically wrong with it. As a matter of fact, there is something radically wrong with the Chinese Nationalist government—not that it carries on lobbying, but that it is little but a lobby.

Since the beginning of the war, the weakness of the Kuomintang on its home grounds has been offset only by the strength it has built up in Washington. It has always lived on credit with no collateral. Its leaders, lacking a real constituency among their own people, have been able to count mostly on their American constituency. This has put the China Lobby in a category all by itself, for it has always represented not a great nation but a régime playing at being a great power.

Since the China Lobby was reassembled here after Mao's victory, it has had to exert pressure on Congress, on the Executive, on public opinion, to get dollars and weapons in almost unlimited quantity. Yet not even billions or arsenals can satisfy it. Actually, nothing can, short of total war—a total war against international Communism that the United States has to start in the shortest possible time, for Chiang's position on Formosa is tragic, and his shrunken army has to reconquer a nation of nearly five hundred million people.

Never has there been a government that has asked so much of another. Yet the China Lobby has a formidable weapon in its hands: Since the alternative to Chiang is Mao, anybody in America—State Department official or private citizen—who is not for Chiang's restoration can be called a Red. Of course the China Lobby has money—a lot of it—and, particularly in the case of its Chinese agents, the resourcefulness that comes with despair. But what has helped most is the Red issue, which was first raised when the American people had grown aware of the Communist danger and were being overwhelmed with exposés on how the Communists had worked in America a few years before.

There are men possessed by a craving to detect conspiracies, hunt down suspects, and then wring confessions from those they have suspected. Almost invariably, these self-appointed vigilantes are those ex-Communists whose anti-Communism has become an obsession and a profession. Sometimes they find sponsors or employers whose anti-Communism comes from the urge to find a single cause for all the ills of the world. The professional ex-Communists serve their new masters as they did their old—with the same frenzied devotion, the scheming mental processes of the Communist mind. There is no other way they can think or, for that matter, live. They can't help suspecting everybody, planning purges, demanding confessions. *They* have confessed: Why doesn't everybody else?

These poor displaced people who, having gone through Communism, have lost their taste for a free society, cannot be at peace with themselves and cannot leave their fellow citizens in peace. Some of them have tried vainly to find a home and an occupation. The China Lobby offers them both.

The China Lobby asks every American to choose, and choose quickly, between Chiang and Mao and then to act accordingly, forgetting all else—what is happening in other parts of the world and what might happen to our own country should we plunge into all-out war against Red China. The Communists are masters of the black-and-white, either-or technique, and the professional former Communists have not lost that skill. Their fanaticism, which became aimless when they left the party, can, thanks to the China Lobby, help accelerate a train of events. Marxists always like to move in the van of history, like men who feverishly run up the steps of an escalator. Since the Chinese disaster, the invasion of North Korea, and the intervention of Red China, the train of events has seemed unmistakable. It leads to war; but to make the inevitable come sooner, the Lobby operators will stop at nothing.

There are men in America who know how to do the job—by no means all former Communists. But the refugees from Communism provide the techniques and the brains. Now, under the most respectable auspices, they can practice the subversion they could never successfully apply as Communists. They can work their way into some legal institutions—like Congressional committees—and pound at civil rights or stretch the statute of limitations with seeming respect for due process of law.

Actually, now for the first time America has been poisoned by Communism, and the men who unknowingly administer the poison are those very men who, under the glare of publicity, denounce it. They make the China Lobby—so different from all other foreign lobbies—the nearest thing to an effective Communist Party our country has ever had. There is no other outfit to which the China Lobby can be compared, with its hard core of fanatical, full-time operators, its underground, its legion of naïve, misled fellow travelers, its front organizations, and its foreign officials, in Washington with diplomatic immunity, who dutifully report to central headquarters. On a larger scale, the China Lobby is very much like the American Communist Party of the 1930's. Of course, people whose idealism or naïveté has been exploited by the Lobby or its fronts should not be blamed for the Lobby's misdeeds—unless one follows the prevailing theory of guilt-by-association.

During the last two years the life of the nation has been deeply disturbed by subversion and corruption. No cause of disturbance has been greater than the China Lobby. These have been weird years, years when things have happened that we must remember for a long time and never let happen again. There have been moments when this alliance of fanatic conservatives and incurable revolutionists, united under the auspices of Nationalist China, seemed rather close to remolding the politics of our country on a Chinese pattern—with war lords on parade and thought control on the rampage.

One of the most astonishing things about the China Lobby is that, as far as one can find out, it has no leaders, only mouthpieces. Yet they have been strong enough to cramp our national leadership.

December 23, 1952

The Wiretappers

By William S. Fairfield and Charles Clift

Wiretapping, a furtive practice that recognizes no legal bounds, has become the uninvited, unsuspected third party to the private telephone conversations carried on by American citizens of all persuasions and beliefs from all walks of life.

In 1934 Congress passed a law providing severe penalties for wiretapping, but only one person has ever been prosecuted and convicted under it, and that was in the early 1940's. Wiretapping today is actually the freest of free enterprises, highly expensive, but indulged in with virtual immunity from Federal prosecution by government agents, municipal police, political parties, business firms, witch hunters, divorce lawyers, private detectives, sharpers, freebooters, and blackmailers of all sorts—all of whom practice it in the serene conviction that there will never be any penalties.

This boldness stems from the knowledge that the Department of Justice is reluctant to press wiretapping cases to prosecution or even to gather evidence for them. Admittedly sensitive about the legality of tapping by its own agents, the Department of Justice hesitates to risk legal action that might focus attention on its own "extralegal" practices.

As a result of this lack of restriction, wiretapping is now a common practice in almost every troubled area of American life. A wiretapper eavesdrops indiscriminately. He catches in his net, together with the intended victim, all those who happen to use or to call a telephone being tapped, however irrelevant the call to the purpose of the tapper. And with police today monitoring many public pay-station phones in search of gamblers or prostitutes, the most innocent may find their private and sometimes very personal conversations recorded side by side with the business calls of a bookie or a procurer. If a line is considered worth tapping, and if someone has the money (or the staff) in addition to the inclination, he can have a tap installed on that line within twenty-four hours, no matter where in the United States it is located, no matter what the private or official capacities of its users. And once the tap is installed, the chances against accidentally discovering it would be at least ten thousand to one.

Neither Democrats nor Republicans have a monopoly on wiretapping. Past experience has shown that no matter which party is in power in Washington, Federal and Congressional leaders have a tendency to use their authority and the government's resources, including wiretapping, to pursue political feuds and personal advantage. Democrats have tapped Republicans and Republicans have tapped Democrats as if they were members of the underworld rather than leaders of a democracy.

Not all political wiretapping, of course, takes place in Washington or involves Federal officials. Wiretapping is practiced quite extensively in state politics. Governor Thomas E. Dewey of New York has not been averse to using tap-obtained information in attempting to get the goods on his Democratic foes in Albany. In 1940, a Congressional committee learned that a Democratic state legislator, Senator Ruth of Pennsylvania, had employed state policemen to tap the telephone lines of Mayor S. Davis Wilson of Philadelphia when the committee Ruth headed was investigating the city judiciary.

In the same year, Frank B. Bielaski's detective agency in New York, which had done much work for the Republican National Committee and for G.O.P. politicians in such states as Massachusetts and Pennsylvania, was exposed as having tapped the wires of public officials in Rhode Island. Although the two officials tapped belonged to opposing political parties, they had one thing in common: Each had earned the enmity of the Republican Governor, William H. Vanderbilt. When the taps were first discovered, J. Howard McGrath, then U.S. Attorney for Rhode Island, investigated. A few weeks later, McGrath reported that Governor Vanderbilt had privately hired Bielaski to do the tapping and had paid the detective some $11,000 for his efforts.

Political wiretapping is also practiced occasionally on the local level. In 1949, Clendenin Ryan, the wealthy self-appointed New York reformer, hired John ("Steve") Broady's detective agency to get what dirt it could on Mayor William O'Dwyer of New York. Broady, in turn, promptly hired the professional wiretappers Kenneth Ryan and Robert La Borde. Hidden microphones, or "bugs," were installed in the homes of Fire Commissioner James Moran and other city officials, and a mountain of information was collected. Then came retribution.

Police raided Kenneth Ryan's home, confiscated an estimated ten thousand dollars' worth of wiretap equipment, and found a list of dozens of city officials whose lines were to be tapped. Kenneth Ryan was taken to City Hall, where O'Dwyer personally questioned him. Ryan finally sneaked away from the interview while the Mayor's back was turned and climbed out a ladies'-room window.

In April, 1949, Kenneth Ryan and Broady were indicted for conspiracy to tap the wires of Manhattan Borough President Hugo Rogers, and Ryan was further indicted for escaping from custody. The next week, Ryan and Broady were also indicted for tapping the wires of a Brooklyn automobile company which was allegedly involved with politicians and racketeers.

About the same time, after Robert La Borde had blocked attempts to call him before a grand jury investigating the plot against O'Dwyer, he too was indicted for wiretapping—in a Brooklyn divorce case.

Kenneth Ryan insisted none of the officials on the list found in his possession had actually been tapped—because he had been arrested too soon. Police had to admit that neither Ryan, Broady, nor La Borde had ever been caught in the act of tapping city officials' wires. Eventually all went free. Soon afterward, O'Dwyer quit his post as mayor and left for Mexico, as U.S. ambassador.

Wiretapping, in any form, creates a basic American conflict. On one side are the ideals of freedom and individual privacy, on the other the arguments favoring the use of modern techniques to fight crime and to protect national security. Somewhere a line of demarcation must be drawn.

Some Law-Evading Enforcement Agencies

In 1916, the people of New York City were surprised to learn that their mayor, John Purroy Mitchel, had approved an investigation of local Catholic charities on the ground that these groups were out to destroy the public Charity Commission. Surprise turned to shock when New Yorkers read newspaper accounts of the investigative methods being used. With the co-operation of the New York Telephone Company, it was revealed, the Mayor had allowed the tapping of a Catholic priest's telephone.

The telephone company, in answering the charges leveled against it, pointed out that it had co-operated with city officials in this manner ever since 1895, when the police first conceived of the value of tapping telephone wires to obtain evidence.

The tapping of a priest's phone, however, was too much. Overnight, wiretapping became a subject of popular interest and indignation. A Congressman from New York, George Loft, called for a Congressional investigation of "this gigantic scandal," and a bill outlawing wiretapping was introduced in the New York State legislature. Positive action was delayed, however, by America's entry into the First World War, when the Federal government took over operation of the telephone companies. But in 1918 Congress put an absolute ban on wiretapping for the duration of the emergency.

After the war, with the telephone companies back in private hands and the Congressional ban lifted, wiretapping quickly came back into its own. The first great anti-Red drive was on, and Attorney General A. Mitchell Palmer ordered wiretaps regularly in preparation for his raids. In 1920, when the Eighteenth Amendment went into effect, Treasury Department prohibition agents also began employing wiretapping as a primary weapon.

Soon public reaction set in on a national scale. Citizens who had never considered wiretapping objectionable when used to catch criminals found it repulsive when applied to checking on fellow citizens who held unpopular beliefs. Other citizens objected violently to the use of tapping in prohibition enforcement—a few because they didn't want to see their private bootleggers jailed, many more because they feared that their own telephone orders for supplies might be recorded.

The protests reached Washington, and in 1924 Attorney General Harlan F. Stone, in a directive to the newly formed Federal Bureau of Investigation, proclaimed, under the heading "Unethical Tactics," that "Wiretapping . . . will not be tolerated . . ."

Unfortunately, Attorney General Stone's orders applied only to the FBI. Prohibition agents continued tapping without pause. In 1928, a repercussion from their efforts finally reached the Supreme Court. In the case of *Olmstead* v. *United States,* defense lawyers pleaded for a reversal of a client's conviction for bootlegging on the ground that the wiretapping used to gain evidence violated the Fourth Amendment restriction on search and seizure. In its 5-4 decision, however, the Court ruled that the Fourth Amendment applied only to "actual physical invasions" of privacy, and not to "projected voices." The four dissenters were Justices Brandeis, Holmes, Butler, and Stone.

The Olmstead decision only served to intensify public demand for legislation to outlaw wiretapping. In 1929, the first wave of a flood of anti-wiretapping bills engulfed Congress, despite J. Edgar Hoover's concurrent assurance to a House committee that "any employee engaging in wiretapping will be dismissed from the service of the bureau."

"While it may not be illegal," said the FBI Director, "I think it is unethical, and it is not permitted under the regulations of the Attorney General."

Two years later, in 1931, the Prohibition Bureau—still busily tapping away—was transferred from the Treasury to the Justice Department and Attorney General William D. Mitchell found himself forced to settle the internal conflict between FBI and Prohibition Bureau wiretapping policies. Disregarding J. Edgar Hoover's moral scruples, Mitchell decided in favor of wiretapping, subject to "authorization" of the Director of the Bureau.

Between the Olmstead decision in 1928 and the first session of the first Roosevelt Congress, numerous bills to outlaw wiretapping were introduced, and in 1933 Congress finally did force some control of tapping by banning its use in the enforcement of prohibition—which went off the books that year anyway.

During the depression years, as labor became more and more of a political force, its leaders complained with increasing anger about the use of wiretapping in anti-union espionage. With these voices added to those already demanding abolition of the practice, Congress was not long in acting.

In 1934 the Federal Communications Commission was established as an independent agency. Included in the enabling act, as Section 605, was a provision *intended* to outlaw wiretapping once and for all. It read in part: "No person not being authorized by the sender shall intercept any communication and divulge or publish the . . . contents . . . to any person . . . and no person having received such intercepted communication . . . shall . . . use the same or any information therein contained for his own benefit or for the benefit of another . . ." Violations were made subject to a $10,000 fine, two years in prison, or both.

While awaiting court interpretation of Section 605, Federal agencies, still operating under Attorney General Mitchell's 1931 approval of wiretapping, continued to tap telephone lines. Local enforcement officers and private detective agencies followed suit.

Three years later, in 1937, the Supreme Court reviewed its first case under Section 605, *Nardone* v. *United States*. Several defendants who had been found guilty of liquor smuggling now appealed their convictions on the ground that the evidence against them was the product of wiretapping by Federal agents and had thus been gathered in violation of Section 605. Government attorneys freely admitted the use of wiretapping, but argued that Section 605 did not apply to Federal agents.

The Court sided with the smugglers and reversed their convictions. Section 605, it ruled, was designed "to include within its sweep federal officers as well as others." Since Federal agents had violated Section 605 in intercepting telephone conversations and divulging their contents in court, the government's evidence was inadmissible.

The agents who tapped were therefore guilty of violating a Federal law. It was no surprise, however, that their superiors in the Department of Justice never bothered to prosecute. If the Department had done so, many lawyers feel, the courts would have upheld conviction of the offending agents.

Department of Justice v. the Law

Over the next three years, the Department of Justice continued to test in court various possible loopholes in Section 605. While it tested, it did nothing to halt continued wiretapping by Federal agents—not only (as was later admitted) in cases of national security, extortion, and kidnaping, but also in investigating such crimes as mail fraud, narcotics peddling, and bribery.

The next tests of Section 605 came in 1939 when the Supreme Court ruled out three more possible Justice Department loopholes in the wiretapping law. The first ruling involved the reconviction of Nardone and associates—this time based not on direct wiretap evidence but on evidence obtained from wiretap "leads." Justice Frankfurter, writing the majority opinion of the Court, termed this evidence "fruit of the poisonous tree." Such "fruit" was ruled as inadmissible in court as direct wiretap evidence, and the supposed smugglers were again freed.

In another 1939 case, *Weiss* v. *United States,* the Supreme Court closed two more potential loopholes. In one ruling, the Court stated that Section 605 must apply to *intra-* as well as *inter*state telephone conversations, since there was no way for a tapper on a line to determine beforehand whether a given call would cross state lines. In the other Weiss ruling, the Supreme Court refused to accept wiretap evidence when the authōrization of the "sender," as demanded in Section 605, was obtained *after* the tapping—in this case, by confronting him with the recorded conversations and by promising leniency.

In 1940, a circuit court of appeals further tightened up Section 605, in *Polakoff* v. *United States,* by stating that under the law, one party could not authorize interception of a conversation on his line unless the other party concurred. The Supreme Court refused to review the decision.

Thus, in their first interpretations of Section 605, the higher courts consistently ruled in favor of a strong wiretapping law. The court rulings were so explicit, in fact, that the Treasury Department began pressing Congress for specific authorization of wiretapping by Federal agents. In 1938, however, J. Edgar Hoover indefinitely postponed chances for such action by opposing a Treasury-drafted bill granting Federal agencies the right to tap. According to newspaper accounts, Hoover "said he had men who were expert in tapping wires, but if he let them practice it *to any extent* [italics ours] they would turn crooks in no time."

But, to some extent at least, the FBI and other Federal agencies were all tapping during this period. Meanwhile the Department of Justice continued searching for loopholes in Section 605.

On March 12, 1940, however, the Department's search was rudely interrupted by a Senate Interstate Commerce Committee report. The report, approving a proposed Senate investigation of wiretapping, was submitted by Democratic Senator Burton K. Wheeler of Montana. Wheeler stated: "Wiretapping [is] especially dangerous at the present time, because of the recent resurgence of a spy system conducted by Government police. Persons who have committed no crime, but whose economic and political views and activities may be obnoxious to the present incumbents of law-enforcement offices, are being investigated and catalogued."

Exactly five days after release of the Wheeler blast, the Department of Justice banned wiretapping. After nine years of almost unrestricted Federal use since Attorney General Mitchell's authorization in 1931, the practice was now totally prohibited. "In a limited class of cases . . . ," said Attorney General Robert H. Jackson, "wiretapping should be authorized under some appropriate safeguard. Under the existing state of the law and decisions, this cannot be done unless Congress sees fit to modify the existing statutes."

On April 9, Jackson repeated his assertion that the ban on wiretapping was not only ethically necessary but was made imperative by court interpretations of Section 605: ". . . the law on wiretapping is now clear and precise; and all future cases of wiretapping will be subject to prosecution in the Federal courts."

At the same time Jackson indicated why no one, even outside government, had been convicted of violation of Section 605 in the six years since its enactment: "I do not feel that the Department of Justice can in good conscience prosecute persons . . . for a practice . . . engaged in by the Department itself, and regarded as legal by the Department."

In the light of future events, the last statement was especially important. The following year, the Department embarked on its first and what turned out to be its only prosecution of a violation of Section 605—a violation in which an attorney named Jacob Gruber induced a switchboard girl in the Securities and Exchange Commission to cut him in on telephone conversations involving an investigation of one of his clients. Gruber was convicted, and the conviction stuck.

But only eight weeks after Jackson had declared wiretapping illegal, the Department of Justice quietly did a direct about-face and again authorized the practice. Federal agents have been wiretapping ever since.

The National Safety

Jackson's original statement of March 17, 1940, declaring the illegality of tapping, had come at an unfortunate time. Russia had recently defeated Finland. Germany was to overrun Denmark and invade Norway within a month. In the United States there was widespread talk of national defense and of possible sabotage.

During the Nazi invasion of the Lowlands, in May, President Roosevelt sent a mysterious memo to the Department of Justice— a memo that was never so much as mentioned until 1949 and which has still not been made public. According to a statement made in 1949 by Attorney General Tom Clark, the May, 1940, memo "approved . . . wiretapping when necessary in situations involving national defense." Why such a memo has never been publicly released is still a matter of conjecture. The best guess is that Roosevelt named specific suspected pro-Nazi Americans whose lines he wished tapped. In support of this theory, Senator Gerald Nye, a prominent supporter of the America First Committee, reportedly told a Washington columnist at the time that J. Edgar Hoover had privately informed him (Nye) that his wire was being tapped on orders from above.

Whatever the exact wording of the President's memo, however, the general content was enough to cause the Department of Justice to reverse its stand on Section 605. The law on wiretapping was just as "clear and precise" as Jackson had proclaimed it to be two months before, but FBI agents were again authorized to tap wires. Publicly, the Department said nothing; but behind the scenes it was again hunting a loophole in Section 605.

By the end of 1940, the Department had come up with another tenuous justification of its own activities. It had long been argued that, under the law, wiretapping was of itself no crime and that the only crime was to "intercept *and* divulge." The little word "and" made all the difference, since it meant that both acts had to be committed before anything illegal had taken place. In backing up this argument, the Department insisted that the entire Federal government was an entity, and thus an agent was not "divulging" to another when he passed wiretap information to his superior, and his superior was not guilty of "divulging" when he passed the information to another government agency or to Congress.

In March, 1941, Attorney General Jackson made this new construction of Section 605 public. "There is no Federal statute that prohibits or punishes wiretapping alone . . . ," Jackson said. "Any person, with no risk of penalty, may tap telephone wires and eavesdrop on his competitor, employer, workman, or others, and act upon what he hears or make any use of it that does not involve divulging or publication."

Jackson completely ignored, as the Department of Justice has ever since, the second part of Section 605: "and no person having received such intercepted communication . . . shall . . . use the same . . . for his own benefit or for the benefit of another. . . ." Obviously, without either divulging or using, tapping would be just an idle pastime.

After Jackson's statement, J. Edgar Hoover beat a prompt retreat from the ethical position he had publicly maintained against wiretapping since 1929. He still opposed unrestricted wiretapping, he said, but he thought it should be used in some cases, "such as espionage, sabotage, kidnaping, and extortion."

Hoover's list reflected the views expressed on then-pending wiretap legislation by President Roosevelt in a letter to Congressman Thomas Eliot in February, 1941—a letter in which the President, perhaps prophetically, warned of possible abuses.

The Court Retreats

In 1942, the Supreme Court, which had previously reaffirmed Section 605 at every opportunity, made its own retreat. In *Goldstein* v. *United States,* a mail-fraud case, Federal agents had persuaded two men, by showing them recordings of their telephone conversations, to testify in the prosecution of three others. The Supreme Court upheld the conviction of the three, saying that a person who is not a party to tapped conversations cannot object to their use.

The Court's specific decision, of course, applied only to a few cases. But it was the first interpretation of Section 605 that recognized the admissibility of wiretap-derived information in legal action. The Justice Department was now free to experiment with all sorts of wiretapping methods, evidence from which might or might not be admissible in court. Of one thing at least the Department could be certain: No agent would go to jail. To date, the Department seems quite satisfied with things as they are. In 1949, it did draft a bill to sanction Federal wiretapping. But two months later, when the anti-wiretapping forces began to organize, it promptly withdrew the bill. Meanwhile, despite Section 605, Federal wiretapping continues as a daily practice.

State laws are of little help in controlling wiretapping. Forty-two states restrict tapping in some manner, but only two—Delaware and New Jersey—outlaw divulgence in court, while at least seven others, including Massachusetts and New York, permit wiretapping by local law-enforcement officers.

Nor is the Federal Communications Commission any help. The Justice Department, not the FCC, is charged with enforcing Section 605, as the FCC has had to point out to many irate citizens, including a Detroit businessman who wrote recently to complain about a tap on the phone of a daughter who was suing her husband for divorce. The FCC could only refer him to the Justice Department and the Attorney General.

If the Attorney General answered the Detroiter at all, which is unlikely, he might have quoted his predecessor in office, Robert Jackson: "I do not feel that the Department of Justice can in good conscience prosecute persons . . . for a practice engaged in by the Department itself."

How to Tap a Telephone

Several years ago, a New York newspaper columnist informed local readers that now they too could discover if their telephone lines were being tapped. In New York, it was explained, anyone could check on a tap by dialing 711, waiting for the tone, then dialing 6 and hanging up. If the phone rang back, the line was free; if it didn't ring, a tap was in.

Actually, 711 . . . 6 was just a telephone-company test circuit. A ringback signified only that the line was in working order. The test could not possibly indicate wiretapping. The columnist's following was large, however, and after a deluge of dialing, the telephone company was forced to change the number of its test circuit.

The 711 . . . 6 detection method may well be the best-publicized wiretapping myth in the history of telephone, but it is not the most prevalent. That distinction belongs to the widely held theory that crackling noises on a line mean the wires are tapped. Telephone static is frequent and has various causes, including loose connections, moisture in the line, and dust between contact points. On the other hand, only the most amateurish "raw" tap could cause static. Usually the noise disappears on a second call. Seldom does it continue for more than two or three hours, and a wiretap is rarely installed for so short a period.

Ranking almost with the static test is the popular misconception that rapping on the mouthpiece of a telephone set with a pencil will make the conversation inaudible to the wiretapper. A hidden microphone, or "bug," *can* be neutralized by such rapping—as well as by clinking ice in a glass, jingling keys, or running water. But a wiretapper won't be bothered by noise in the mouthpiece any more than those who are holding the conversation. If they can hear, so can he.

Other myths hold that a bad tap will heat up the earpiece of the telephone set and that, if the conversation is being recorded, the scratching of the recording needle may be heard faintly. The first is electrically impossible, the second highly improbable.

As previously indicated, a sloppy job can result in continued static. It can also cause diminution of volume on the line, or even a complete shorting out. But few taps are installed by amateurs; the wiretapping business is dominated by former telephone-company employees and by agents trained in wiretapping at one or more law-enforcement schools.

Unfortunately, the telephone company, despite its frequently expressed concern, has not much more chance of discovering an unsuspected tap than the individual subscriber has. The company does test its lines continually, but the testing equipment is incapable of spotting an effective wiretap.

Occasionally, a telephone-company repairman on his normal rounds will stumble upon a tap and remove it. About as often, a private citizen will hire a wiretapper to check his lines for taps, the going rate ranging from twenty to fifty dollars. Some Federal agencies have regular tapcheckers on their staffs. None of this, of course, precludes a tap's being installed five minutes after a check is made. But physical inspection, at every possible point of installation from the phone itself right back to the "main frame" at the exchange, still remains the only positive means of detection.

Over the years, many machines advertised as capable of tap detection have been placed on the market, some for $200, some for much more. Congressmen and police officers have been among the purchasers. All have been bilked; no machine yet invented can positively identify a wiretap.

The simple fact is that a good tap upsets a telephone circuit much less than does normal line trouble, such as dust and moisture seepage, corrosion, and faulty contact points, all of which are far more prevalent. When the "detection" machine's red light glows or its bell rings, it is indicating more dramatically what the telephone company's test equipment also shows—imbalance in the circuit. Unless the machine is extremely sensitive, it will not register the slight imbalance resulting from a tap. And if it is sensitive enough to register a tap, it is also so sensitive that it will continually explode into false alarms.

Basically, the telephone circuit is not difficult to understand once one accepts the word "circuit" for what it means: a closed circle of wire in which current flows, that current in turn being able to carry voice vibrations.

At one end, the circle of wire enters the individual phone, passes through it, and emerges at the same spot. The entering wire and the emerging wire are then wrapped together as a "pair" for stringing back to the telephone exchange. At the exchange, the circle of those two wires is completed whenever the telephone is in use. In a normal local call, the pair of wires is joined at the exchange, through a relay, to the pair of wires leading to another telephone, and the conversation circuit is thus established.

Electric current must flow through the circuit, of course, in order to carry the voice vibrations. Every telephone exchange houses long banks of batteries to supply direct current, that current being thrown onto the line whenever the telephone is in use.

The wiretapper's fundamental equipment, based on this completed circuit, is quite simple. He needs earphones, and he needs a wire leading through those earphones, the ends of which can be easily attached to each member of the pair he wishes to tap, thus forming an additional path for current in the circuit.

The tapper also must interpose in his extension wires a condenser—an electrical device that blocks the passage of direct current while still allowing the detection of faint vibrations. Electricity always follows the line of least resistance. Without the condenser, part of the direct current from the exchange would flow through the tapper's earphones, by-passing the normal circuit. The voice volume on the tapped conversation circuit would diminish sharply, and the wiretapper would serve notice of his activities.

On the other hand, the tapper's condenser must be small in

its electrical capacity. If it is too large, it will also attract current from the normal circuit. A .01-microfarad condenser is fairly
standard in the wiretapping trade.

Along with the condenser, the wiretapper also hooks into his
line a large resistor—nothing more than a coil or a wire through
which current passes with difficulty. The resistor forces even
more of the direct current in the telephone circuit to follow its
normal established path, thus further cutting the drag from the
tap. The resistor does weaken the signal coming through the
tap extension, but the tapper can always compensate by adding
an amplifier to increase volume.

This, then, is the wiretapper's basic equipment: earphones,
wire, condenser, resistor, and, if necessary, amplifier. If possession
of these few electrical parts made a wiretapper, however, almost
everyone in the nation could be one. The parts are all contained
in the smallest home or car radio, the radio loudspeaker substituting for the earphones.

Actually, the expert wiretapper needs much more. He needs
to know how to trace an entire circuit from the individual phone
back to the exchange, and where to tap along that circuit without arousing suspicion. This requires a sound working knowledge
of the telephone company's entire physical plant, as well as
effective use of company lingo to obtain added information not
normally available to the outsider. The professional tapper also
needs additional equipment, including recording devices, adapt-
ors for these devices to permit telephone transcription, and machines to translate dial beats into actual telephone numbers.
He needs concealed space for himself and his equipment—a
"plant" where a line can be monitored for days and even weeks
without observation. And he needs assistants to help with the
twenty-four-hour-a-day job of monitoring. All these—equipment,
plant, and assistants—require sizable outlays of cash.

In choosing where to "go on" any specific telephone circuit, the
wiretapper is far more limited than might be expected. He can't
very well tap at the subscriber's end of the line without being
seen. Nor can he tap at the exchange. In times past, the telephone
company did permit certain official agencies to install "back-

taps" on the exchange main frame, but today, except in very special cases, it is reluctant to co-operate to that extent.

The tapper is limited in his hookups to that segment of the circuit removed from the immediate vicinity of both the subscriber and the exchange. Such a segment may stretch several miles. But again, the tapper is limited.

When the pair of wires leaves the subscriber's premises, it travels to a nearby terminal box, or "bridging point," where the two wires are connected to twin metal posts labeled with a pair number. The terminal box, however, also serves as a bridging point for the pairs of various other subscribers in the vicinity, all such pairs being similarly attached to numbered posts. Dozens and even hundreds of subscriber pairs may terminate in one box.

The pairs do not leave the terminal box separately. Instead, many are enclosed in a single cable for ease in transmission to the exchange—initially by poles in suburban areas, then by underground cable in the city. Inside the cable, all pairs look alike; singling out a desired pair for tapping is practically impossible.

In the cable, the pairs generally travel to a second bridging point, where they are again attached to posts bearing their pair number, where they are joined by additional pairs, and where the additional pairs are then encased with them for further transmission to the exchange. Before reaching the exchange office, a residential pair may pass through five or six bridging points, a business-district pair through three or four. The final cable leading into the exchange office often contains as many as 2,120 pairs.

The complete telephone exchange is thus much like a tree, with subscribers' phones as the outermost twigs. The twigs combine into branches, the branches into limbs, and the limbs into the trunk and roots, which are the exchange office.

To the wiretapper, it makes no difference whether a given cable contains twelve pairs or 2,120 pairs. Even if he opened the cable, he would be unable to identify the specific pair he wanted. His basic plan, therefore, is to learn the pair number, find the bridging points for that numbered pair, and then tap in at one of those points—the choice of which bridging point to tap being determined by the availability of space nearby to use for the "plant."

Because of the need for space in which to listen unobserved, a residential-telephone job is the wiretapper's toughest assignment. A hotel job, in which a room can be taken on short notice, is easiest, with apartment and office-building assignments running a close second.

The residential job is doubly difficult because the wiretapper can't afford to use the first bridging point—the terminal box on a nearby pole, from which the "drop" carries the subscriber's pair into his home. That terminal box is especially valuable to the tapper. It is not only the easiest bridging point to locate; it is also the only bridging point to which the subscriber's line can be directly traced and the pair number of that line thus individually identified. If the tapper were seen climbing that pole, however, his entire efforts might be nullified by the suspicions of his intended victim.

In such a situation, the professional wiretapper, unless he has access to inside information, relies on his knowledge of the telephone company, and on the fact that in a big city the company employees are so many that they can't all know each other by name. He starts only with his victim's number, obtained from the telephone book, and with the knowledge that the letters in that number indicate the exchange. He dials the same exchange letters, and follows with the series of digits he knows will connect him with the exchange repair clerk—in Washington, for example, 9960.

To the unsuspecting clerk the tapper gives a false name, says he's out checking trouble on a certain line, and repeats his victim's telephone number to identify that line. Then he asks for the pair and cable numbers—the latter mainly for effect. The clerk gives him both.

Having obtained the pair number, the wiretapper then calls cable records for the location of the bridging points of the desired pair. Again, he must have the telephone-company lingo down to perfection. In the Bronx and Manhattan exchanges, they are called "bridging heads." But in Washington, they are called "multiples," and elsewhere they are known as "appear-ances." The tapper must use the proper expression. If he is a professional, he will. If the cable-records clerk is no more than normally astute, the tapper will get the information he requests.

The wiretapper then knows the number of his victim's pair, and he knows that the pair runs from the original terminal box to a second bridging point on a telephone pole five blocks east, from there to a third bridging point on a pole five blocks south, and that from there it dives underground to a fourth bridging point in a cellar three more blocks south, where it finally enters an underground cable to the exchange. He can appear at any one of those bridging points without arousing the suspicions of his victim, and he can locate the line he wants by the pair number registered next to the terminal posts.

As to the "plant," the tapper may find a vacant house or apartment to rent near one of the bridging points. He then sim-ply attaches his clips to the twin terminal posts of the pair and strings his wire inside. If he can't find vacant space, perhaps he will find that one of the bridging points is in a secluded spot, where he can park without attracting attention. He then strings his wires down from the pole or up from the cellar and into car, where he sets up his battery-operated recording equipment.

If neither of these plans can be worked out to satisfaction at the bridging points in question, the wiretapper has one other alternative: In almost every terminal box, there are not only pairs in active use, but also "spare pairs." The spare pairs, like the multitude of bridging points, give the telephone system fluidity. If a new building goes up, the company doesn't need to string wires all the way back to the exchange. To service that building it can install telephones merely by bridging to nearby points and using spare pairs for transmission.

In the meantime, however, the wiretapper can use these spare pairs, easily identified because they are dead lines. He finds the spare pair at the same bridging point as the pair he wants to tap. He connects the spare-pair wires to the terminal posts of the vic-tim's pair. Then he calls the clerk at the trouble desk again, gets the bridging-point locations for the spare-pair number, and checks those locations for nearby vacant houses. Eventually, he is bound to find an ideal "plant."

Tapping hotel, apartment, or office-building telephones, as noted above, is far more simple. In a hotel, the pairs of all the phones on any floor generally lead to a terminal box or "house box" in the hallway on that floor. If the tapper gets a room on the same floor as his victim, he can just open the house box, where he will find each pair tagged by room number, and cross the pair of his own room phone over to the terminal posts of his victim's phone. The wires are thus pre-strung for the tapper; he just clamps his equipment to the bell box in his room and "opens the plant."

Apartment and office telephone tapping follows a like procedure as long as space can be rented in the same building—the only difference being that the terminal boxes in these buildings are generally located in the basement, where a janitor may have to be bluffed by telephone credentials or be bribed with money while the pair leading to the newly rented space is crossed to the terminal posts of the victim's pair.

Since wiretappers are not likely to be held to any expense allowance, money for bribes is readily available. And since most tappers are former telephone workers, the old pass can always be shown. "Some janitors are pretty smart, though," one professional tapper remarked. "They'll ask to see your tools, knowing they should be stamped 'Bell System.' When I went into the business, I bought a whole new set of tools, and gave them to a guy still working for Bell in return for his used tools. The only thing was, his old tools had the Bell stamp on them."

Hotel, apartment, and office telephone tapping may be complicated by inability to rent space in the same building. In such a case, the wiretapper must again go to the clerk on the trouble desk. But bridging points for such telephone circuits, while not so many in number as in a residential area, are generally located in the basements of other buildings. Some of these buildings are certain to have space available for a plant.

Before opening any plant, however, the professional wiretapper employs a technique that is little known even in telephone-company circles and that enables him to avoid tapping in while a conversation is in progress—an act which would immediately tip off the victim.

During a telephone conversation, direct current flows in the circuit. If the wiretapper snaps his clips to the terminal posts at the bridging point, some of that current will rush back to fill his condenser plate. And no matter how small that condenser, the listener will hear a "phhp" on the line as the tapper's condenser is charged.

To avoid this "phhp," the tapper attaches one clip to one terminal. Then, with the tap circuit still open, he places the other clip between his thumb and forefinger, licks his forefinger, and places the wet finger on the other terminal. The tap circuit is complete, but a wet finger is such a poor conductor that not enough current will flow through it to charge the tapper's condenser instantaneously. The "phhp" is avoided, but the tapper can still hear the conversation very faintly. Then, testing with the finger occasionally, he is able to delay installation of the tap until the line is free.

The expert wiretapper has several other ingenious little tricks that he uses on select occasions. One involves getting special numbers out of the telephone company. Actually, in many communities there are four classes of telephone numbers: listed (in the phone directory); unlisted (public but not yet listed); nonpublished (confidential); and special nonpublished (top secret). The first two anyone can discover. The third can be obtained by tracing the subscriber's wires from his phone to the terminal box, getting the pair number, and then bluffing the cable-records clerk into divulging the "drop number," or regular telephone number.

The records of special nonpublished numbers are even more difficult to obtain. There is one chance—by getting the pair number, tracing it through the bridging points to find the cable number, picking up a dozen other cable numbers in the process, and then calling the cable department and using the familiar language to request the "drop numbers" of all dozen cable pairs, including the desired one. In the cable department the number is not usually tagged as special nonpublished.

One last special trick is now outmoded. But in the first days of the dial telephone, the wiretapper was confronted with a serious problem. Since the tapped victim no longer spoke out the number he was calling, and since no one could count the clicks of the dial pulse accurately, the wiretapper found it impossible in many cases to report on whom the victim was calling. Soon a solution was discovered. The tapper learned that if he shorted a wire across the pair momentarily while the dialing was in progress, the victim would get a wrong number, or no number at all. After two or three misdials, the victim would dial the operator and give his number orally. The wiretapper could then jot down that number and let the next call go through unmolested.

To check the name of the subscriber at the number jotted down, the tapper could go to friends in the telephone company or could again bluff the "drop" name out of the clerk on the trouble desk. In some cities, however, the name of the subscriber, providing his number was published, could be obtained merely by dialing the same exchange letters as in the number, followed by a special set of digits. In Chicago, this applies today, the series of digits being 2080.

Since the days of shorting out to get a dial number, Kenneth Ryan, a former New York police detective who has been called the top wiretapping technician in the nation, has adapted a pulse-recording machine for intercepting purposes, a machine that punches out the pulses of the dial on tape, so that they can be counted and decoded into telephone numbers.

This machine, which has been sold by some for as high as $400, is only one of the devices an expert wiretapper uses today in addition to earphones, condensers, and resistors. Recording machines are also essential, and although Ryan says he can adapt the best machine in the country for tap work and sell it for $250, some wiretappers pay as high as $980 for a single machine, all possible attachments included.

Another machine used by some wiretappers is the voice-activated "start-stopper," one model of which retails for $90. The start-stopper is designed to start a tapped-in recording machine whenever voices come over the circuit, and to stop the recorder from three to fifteen seconds after the voices cease, depending on how the tapper sets it. Since the more expensive recording machines will transcribe for eight continuous hours, the stop-starter permits the wiretapper to dispense with paid assistants for monitoring work.

Kenneth Ryan, however, has no faith in the voice-activation principle. He claims that a stop-starter so activated will start at any noise at voice level on the line. But Ryan says he has just developed a current-activated start-stopper, based on the fact that direct current only flows through the line when the telephone circuit is completed. His machine, he claims, would make it possible for the first time to get efficient tap results from an unattended recorder.

In recent years, still another wiretapping device, the induction coil, has been publicized by national magazines ranging from *Popular Science* to *Business Week* and dramatically portrayed as the be-all and end-all of wiretapping—infallible, undetectable, and sinister. Actually, few self-respecting wiretappers would have an induction coil in their tool boxes.

The coil works on a simple principle: Electrical impulses flow through the pair in the completed conversation circuit. But these impulses also set into motion electrons in the air surrounding the pair, forming a field of radiation. An induction coil is so constructed that it can pick up this radiation in the air; and once picked up, quite normal tapping equipment can translate the radiation back into voices. Thus the induction coil removes the need for direct connection with the tapped pair.

Business Week's piece quoted William G. H. Finch, an outstanding electronics engineer, as saying that an induction coil selling at $4.85 could pick up telephone conversations through a wall and up to a distance of thirty feet. "A direct tap," said Finch, "belongs to the horse-and-buggy days."

Finch is a technical expert, and all but his last remark is probably true, under ideal conditions. But the fact is that an A.C. electric cord placed anywhere near the telephone pair in a room will cause enough radiation to drown out the radiation of the phone wires.

More important, an induction coil can be used only where the telephone pair to be tapped is not near any other pair. The coil will pick up all conversations from all pairs in a cable, for example. It is therefore of use only in a place where the desired pair exists alone and without interference.

In most telephone circuits, there is no such place. In a residential circuit, the "drop" from the terminal box to the home might be such a place, as might be the subscriber's premises. This, a professional wiretapper would be forced to point out, is a hell of a place to install a tap and open a plant. It would be simpler to marry the subscriber.

It seems obvious that the public remarks of men like Finch, who are genuine communications scientists but seem totally unaware of the pragmatic considerations involved in wiretapping, do nothing but propagate the myth of what might be called "Buck Rogers wiretapping," enormously widespread and impossible to control. Even limited wiretapping is not a pleasant thought to the free man. There is no point in exaggerating.

Listening In with Uncle Sam

Today the FBI is the only Federal agency that openly admits to any wiretapping, and it insists that the practice is limited to cases of kidnaping and of espionage, sabotage, and other "grave risks to internal security." But if it is a fact that FBI regulations do restrict tapping to certain "grave" cases, then it must also be a fact that the question of what is grave and what isn't is often left to the discretion of individual agents and officials, some of whom seem to cruise over a wide latitude of judgment.

There is further evidence that other Federal agencies, including the Central Intelligence Agency and various military intelligence units, have been avidly tapping away. J. Edgar Hoover, who should know, has said that his is not the only Federal agency employing wiretapping. While the others strongly deny the practice, some will frankly admit that they would deny it even if it were true; others admit that they would not hesitate to tap "in the interest of national defense."

Elsewhere in Washington, official denial of wiretapping is even more emphatic. The Treasury Department's Alcohol Tax Unit, Narcotics Bureau, and Bureau of Internal Revenue all claim they haven't tapped wires since 1939, although they do say that they gladly accept wiretap information contributed by the FBI or local police.

Sometimes private professional tappers are hired for specific assignments. Sometimes the FBI or local police are requested to do the tapping. But generally, Federal wiretapping is done by a regular member of the agency in question, a man whose skill is the result of former telephone-company employment or of training at the FBI Police Academy or at one of the Treasury Department schools that have taught wiretapping in Detroit and New Orleans.

The FBI, which probably does more wiretapping than any other Federal agency, is at constant pains to depreciate its use of the technique. J. Edgar Hoover's most recent public statement on the subject of tapping was made before a House appropriations subcommittee early in 1950, when the FBI director said his agents were tapping "less than" 170 telephones at the moment. Assuming five conversations over the average phone each day, 170 telephones would carry more than 300,000 tapped conversations a year. Such a figure is merely a guess, but it compares favorably with the concurrent testimony of Mrs. Sophie Saliba, head of the record-file room of the New York office of the FBI. Mrs. Saliba disclosed that more than thirty-five hundred disks of FBI-tapped conversations had been destroyed in 1949. Since a disk can easily hold five telephone conversations, probably these disks held at least 17,500 conversations—all obviously the work of the New York office alone.

Today, reports persist that the FBI maintains a constant tap on the telephones of all Iron Curtain embassies. Whether the telephone company, always uneasy about wiretapping, has actually co-operated to the extent of stringing these taps into a central switchboard makes little difference. It usually co-operates. Quite recently, when a company repairman found a tap installed at the basement terminal box in Washington's National Press Building, he reported his discovery to the company. "Forget it," he was told. "That's on the Russian news agency, Tass, upstairs." Earlier, another company employee had surprised two men at a terminal box in an apartment building where a foreign official was staying. When he asked for their company passes, they ran.

Later his boss called him in and introduced the two, both FBI men.

In the field of domestic crime, the FBI insists it taps wires only in kidnaping cases, although sometimes it expands this statement to include all cases "involving life and death." But here again, at least some agents of the FBI seem unable to stick to the Bureau's defined limits. In 1941, FBI men were found to be tapping the telephone of union leader Harry Bridges in the Edison Hotel, New York, in the course of deportation proceedings against him. In the same year, it was reported that the FBI had tapped telephones at Miami police headquarters during a corruption inquiry—and incidentally had had its own wires tapped in return.

In 1948, John L. Lewis, United Mine Workers president, accused Attorney General Tom Clark of using FBI men to tap UMW telephones. "Surely," said Lewis, "old Tom hasn't forgotten the day he sent one of his gumshoe men in to tap our telephones in our office and our boys threw him out on his ear. They caught him right at the control box in the basement, tapping her up, and they threw him out." Clark answered that no tap was necessary because Lewis roared so loud.

Outside the FBI, wiretapping on the Federal level is a somewhat disorganized business. No other government agency seems to have any set formula or any set method of operation. The Central Intelligence Agency, the Office of Naval Intelligence, and Army G-2 (Intelligence) all "do quite a bit of tapping," according to Kenneth Ryan, a professional tapper who practiced his trade with ONI's "ferret" squad during the war and who has also worked with other Federal agencies. "But mostly," Ryan says, "they tap on their own personnel or on each other."

Army G-2 is perhaps the most frank about its wiretapping practices. It admits it would tap "without hesitation in any case where the national security was involved." A spokesman points out that Secretary of the Army Frank Pace has publicly stated his opposition to wiretapping. "But," he adds, "Frank has never sent any directive on the subject to G-2, and I hope he never will." The spokesman further admits that G-2 has monitored all Pentagon lines from time to time, and will continue to do so. "The only way to prevent wiretapping leaks," he says, "is not to say anything over the telephone. These smart boys think they're talking in code, but a child could break it after three conversations."

From time to time, various Congressional committees, not to be left behind, also have found it expedient to listen in on telephone lines. The House District Committee once used Washington police to tap phones in the Hamilton Hotel during an investigation of milk bootlegging in the District of Columbia. The Kefauver Committee used wiretap information inadmissible in Federal court in its crime investigation. Most recently, the House's King subcommittee investigating tax scandals hired a wiretapper named William Mellin, who worked for the committee in December, 1951, as a "technical investigator." Mellin has never claimed any vocation but wiretapping.

Thus the pattern of Federal wiretapping emerges. As many of the details are missing as the agencies involved have been able to conceal. But enough has been uncovered to trace a general structure. It is a disjointed structure and not pleasant to look at —especially since it reveals men nervously defying a law they are supposed to be enforcing.

Cops and Robbers

When police arrested the young margarine heir Minot F. ("Mickey") Jelke and his associates in 1951 on charges of maintaining a vice ring, the New York Vice Squad could hardly credit its triumph to the kind of hard, plodding investigative work that is generally the mark of a good police force. After receiving a tip, police merely installed a tap on the playboy's apartment telephone, and in comparative ease recorded calls until they had enough evidence to move in and make arrests.

The approach was not new. In each recent year, New York police have used wiretapping in some three hundred criminal investigations. The tapping in all these cases was specifically authorized under a New York State statute which permits police wiretapping, subject only to the necessity of obtaining a court order. The technical legal question—whether state laws authorizing wiretapping are Constitutional—has just been settled by the Supreme Court: Wiretap evidence is admissible in state courts.

State law or no state law, local police in every major city in
the United States are today tapping telephone lines—from Boston
to Los Angeles, from Chicago to Miami. While Federal agents
professedly tap only in the most serious crimes, local enforcement agencies seem to do their tapping mainly in the fields of
gambling and prostitution, where incriminating evidence is recorded side by side with the conversations of many who may
hardly be considered as criminals, where publication of the recordings can thus subject the innocent to extreme embarrassment, and where secrecy can open the way for corrupt police to
blackmail the guilty.

State and local police can afford to wink at the Federal statute
against wiretapping, in view of the U.S. Department of Justice's
well-known reluctance to prosecute even private wiretappers. But
there is another reason why police have carried tapping so much
further than Federal agents.

Kenneth Ryan, a tapper with the New York police for twenty-
one years, has said of his trade: "It's just a timesaver; that's all
it is." In Detroit, Inspector Clayton Nowlin of the Vice Squad
agrees: "A lot of policemen are lazy," he says. "You can get the
information you need if you just go out and develop it. But some
of the boys would rather sit in an easy chair with the earphones
on."

Laziness must be the answer, for local police are well aware of
the extra-legal and unethical nature of wiretapping. When questioned, local enforcement officials will try, almost universally, to
deny the practice. A reporter who called the New York County
District Attorney's office recently was given a grudging admission
of wiretapping only after he mentioned the presence on the
D.A.'s staff of a well-known police tapper named O'Sullivan.
Some time later, the District Attorney's office introduced wiretap
evidence against Thomas (Three-Finger Brown) Luchese in a
New York State crime investigation. In Detroit, former Police
Commissioner Harry Toy told the same reporter that he had
used wiretapping to break up a hockey "fix" scandal several years
back and to crack a numbers ring. For details, Toy referred the
reporter to the present Deputy Police Superintendent, Lawrence

Kennedy. Kennedy promptly denied that Detroit police had ever tapped a telephone line.

Police forces conceal their wiretapping activities by various methods. Some use euphemisms for the practice, such as the official term "technical surveillance" in Chicago. Others give tappers assignments that hide their true duties.

In New York, for example, Kenneth Ryan was assigned to the Bomb Squad. In Washington, Vice Squad men do the wiretapping. The Washington police force also protects itself by refusing to buy any wiretapping equipment; it rents what it needs from private firms. The Los Angeles force has gone one step further; instead of having a tapper on the staff, it hires outside professionals whenever a job comes along.

The New York City police force has the most elaborate wiretapping organization in the nation. Perhaps fifty lines are tapped daily, sometimes under court orders, sometimes without such formalities. In addition to these full-time taps, spot checks are made regularly on the lines of hundreds of bookies.

The number of professional tappers on the New York City payroll has never gone higher than six, but these men—split between the city squad and the District Attorney's office—are sufficient. They install the taps and they remove them. Spare patrolmen and rookies, who know nothing about the techniques of wiretapping, do the monitoring.

Although most of the big names in the criminal world are tapped intermittently, ninety per cent of New York police wiretapping involves gambling and bookmaking. This in turn encompasses not only the phones of known bookies but also public pay stations at local baseball parks, race tracks, sports arenas, and even midtown restaurants, from all of which calls to bookies are often placed. At various times, the pay phones have been tapped at Ebbets Field, the Polo Grounds, Madison Square Garden, Pennsylvania Station, and—quite recently—at Toots Shor's and Dinty Moore's restaurants.

The tap on Toots Shor's pay phones paid off just last spring, when Phil Regan, the nightclub singer who entertained at the Democratic National Convention, called from Shor's to arrange an appointment between Mayor John V. Kenny of Jersey City and the high-ranking mobster Anthony Strollo, alias Tony Bender. Kenny considered Bender the only man capable of breaking up a current dock strike on the Jersey waterfront, and Regan set up a midnight meeting between the two men at the singer's apartment in the Warwick Hotel. According to the New York *Times,* detectives from the District Attorney's office were well staked out in the hotel lobby to observe the comings and goings of the principals. The news story did not indicate how the detectives had happened to be in the right place at the right time.

Any telephone tap involves recording the conversations of innocent people. One New York policeman has reported that while tapping a private line he recorded calls to the Juilliard School of Music, the Brooklyn Law School, the Mercantile Commercial Bank, a health club, a stationery store, a real-estate company, a garage, dentists, taverns, brokers, and a New York police station. The tapping of a public pay station obviously increases the problem many times, since both parties to a recorded conversation frequently have nothing to do with what the police are investigating. Over a tapped pay telephone, a man may hold legitimate but highly personal conversations with his wife, his lawyer, his doctor, his broker, or his business associates. On that tap sits an underpaid rookie. Suddenly he has information worth money—either to the man calling or to his personal or professional rivals. The temptation is obvious.

Wiretapping has brought many surprises to the tappers. Kenneth Ryan can recall the day in the mid-1930's when he placed a tap on the line of Vito Genovese, whose connection with Murder, Inc., was then under investigation by New York police. Genovese lived on Washington Square, in the building where Mrs. Franklin D. Roosevelt maintained an apartment. To tap Genovese's phone, Ryan got the pair number of the gunman's line, located his terminal box, found a "spare pair," or dead line, in the same box, cross-connected the spare pair to Genovese's pair, and then tapped in on the spare pair some blocks away.

Two days later, Ryan returned to the "plant" to see how the tap was going. "My God!" said the patrolman-monitor. "Do you know who we've got on here? F.D.R.!"

Ryan checked, and discovered that Mrs. Roosevelt had moved into her Washington Square apartment and had been given for her phone connection the same spare pair he was using. At the moment, she was talking about having a bath ready for the President, who was due in that night.

Ryan quickly returned to the Genovese terminal box, eager to remove his tap. But when he reached the box, he found it guarded by Secret Service men. "I wasn't happy about being on the Roosevelt line," Ryan says. "I wasn't even interested. But with the Secret Service on guard, all we could do was sweat it out."

In 1941, a case of police tapping police became a front-page story in Washington, D.C. During a House subcommittee investigation of the District police department, Captain George M. Little testified that nine men had been fired from his gambling squad and that wiretapping, at least in part, had led to the shake-up. Little cited the case of a night sergeant who was discharged after a telephone tap showed he was consorting with suspected criminals, one of whom had made an appointment to meet the sergeant at home. The captain attributed the tapping to a secret District police squad that employed two former telephone-company employees as "wire-work specialists," and added that the squad was undermining police morale. When other officers agreed, even to the extent of using the word "Gestapo," the secret squad was quickly disbanded.

Before its dissolution, the special District squad had done a wide variety of wiretapping and other investigative work, not only in local cases but also on request from the Bureau of Internal Revenue, the FBI, Army and Navy Intelligence, the House Un-American Activities Committee, and an assortment of other Congressional committees. Because of the District police department's dependence on Congress for operating funds, a limited number of wiretapping requests from Capitol Hill have continued to be honored by the department.

The Federal Communications Act of 1934, even if it has not been enforced, has at least made wiretapping more difficult. Before 1934, telephone-company officials rarely refused to help police tappers. The "back tap," installed as a company courtesy on the main frame at the exchange, made police telephone interception a relatively simple matter. But the Communications Act, along with several wiretapping scandals, forced company officials into retreat. Back taps are no longer available, and local police forces have learned to be satisfied if the telephone company just maintains a hands-off policy. "A company repairman will stumble on a police tap, then pretend to have something in his eye until the tappers can clear out," a member of the Chicago Crime Commission has said in explaining telephone-company policy in his area.

State police, of course, are just as thoroughly enmeshed in wiretapping as are city and county law-enforcement agencies. On the state level, however, the tapping generally has political overtones. Often it is a matter of the party in power's tapping to get information on rival machines.

Such was the case in New York State in 1943, when Thomas E. Dewey, the crusading district attorney who owed so much to wiretapping and who had done so much to promote the practice, moved into the Governor's Mansion at Albany. One of Dewey's first moves was an attempt to crack down on the O'Connell brothers, brewery owners and leaders of Albany's well-oiled Democratic machine, whose power was neatly summarized in the slogan of their beer: "Hedrick or Else!"

Dewey, as the story has it, called in some of his former New York City police assistants, and a wiretap was promptly installed on several O'Connell telephone lines, state police doing the monitoring.

One day not long afterward, the state trooper in charge of the wire work dropped in on Dewey's executive assistant, Paul Lockwood, and remarked that the telephone conversations of the brothers O'Connell were something to startle even a hardened eavesdropper. One afternoon when affairs of state were a bit dull, Lockwood repeated the trooper's remark to Dewey, and the two officials decided to hear for themselves.

Soon the able assistant and the distinguished young Governor were huddled together at the listening post, earsets adjusted.

Both started with anticipation as one of the O'Connell brothers put in a call to a New York State Supreme Court Justice.

The circuit was completed, and O'Connell began discussing a business deal—with such frankness that the judge warned O'Connell to be careful, since his wires might be tapped. At the listening post, pleasure, according to the legend, lighted the faces of Dewey and Lockwood. But the smiles vanished when O'Connell replied, "I don't give a damn what that [obscenity] little mustachioed [obscenity] Dewey hears me say, and that goes for his fat-pratted assistant Lockwood, too!"

Lone Wolves and Private Ears

Most free-lance wiretappers are satisfied to farm out their talents to a number of private detective agencies that hire on a job-to-job basis. No detective agency maintains a regular wiretapper on its staff, for tapping assignments are not that frequent. Even the most high-powered private agencies employ the practice in fewer than ten cases a year. The average client simply will not foot the costs, pyramided as they are by the skilled personnel, by the special equipment required, and by the risks involved.

One New York wiretapper asks fifty dollars a day for his services, plus such additional funds as may be needed for bribing janitors and renting space for a "plant." Another New York professional gets a five-hundred-dollar fee for installing the tap, plus twenty-five dollars a day for maintenance. To such costs must be added the detective agency's cut, and the client who ends up paying less than seven hundred dollars a week for a tapping job can consider himself fortunate.

While these prices hold private wiretapping to a minimum, the professional can make a good living as long as he gets his share of assignments and as long as he can supplement his income with jobs in related fields of electronic detection, such as installing secret microphones and checking lines of worried clients for the taps of others. The private wiretapper, in fact, makes dozens of line inspections for every tap he installs. Competent tapchecking is no simple matter, for each bridging point must be personally inspected to assure a tap-free line. But since checking involves no elaborate equipment, no bribery, and no law violation, its costs are quite reasonable. The professional generally charges between twenty-five and fifty dollars for a complete line inspection, although some big names in the underworld have volunteered to pay much more.

Actually, the telephone company itself will inspect a subscriber's line for taps if requested to do so. But the company often refuses to disclose results of its checks. If the tap is police-installed, it will not even be removed. The suspicious subscriber, hardly satisfied with such service, looks elsewhere.

Often he goes to a detective agency, but occasionally he may find a telephone-company lineman who will do the job on the side. In 1951 the Kefauver Committee heard testimony from exactly such a lineman, James F. McLaughlin of New York. While working for the telephone company, McLaughlin testified, he had met one Irving Sherman. Sherman introduced him to Frank Costello, who paid McLaughlin $50, $100, and even $150 to check Costello's wires at frequent intervals over a three-month period. McLaughlin was soon also checking the lines of such celebrities as Dandy Phil Kastel and Nat Herzfeld, as well as the wires of Mayor William O'Dwyer. Sherman made all the contacts.

Nat Herzfeld, McLaughlin said, had a switchboard on which every line proved to be tapped. McLaughlin recalled telling Herzfeld of the taps and added that Herzfeld replied: "As long as I know they are there, I don't care. Let them stay there."

Herzfeld's reaction is not unusual. John ("Steve") Broady, the studiously casual head of one of New York's more fabulous private detective agencies, claims he never removes a tap found on a client's telephone line. "We can use that tap to make the opposition eighty per cent ineffective," he says. "I've fed false information into a tapped phone and sent opposition agents all the way to California and even overseas chasing down phony leads. Work out the conversations with my clients just like a movie script."

Broady is a periodic employer of the two leading wiretappers in New York, Kenneth Ryan and Robert C. La Borde. Each of these men completed his apprenticeship with the New York Telephone Company many years ago. Both tapped wires for the

New York Police Department before entering the field of private tapping. Each has since been arrested for wiretapping more than once, but each has escaped conviction so far.

In temperament, however, the two men are far apart. Ryan is the scientist, quietly proud of his work and of his contributions to the mechanics of wiretapping. La Borde is the artist-showman of wiretapping, a man who brings a kind of rough glamour to his skill and his accomplishments. Ryan is a boyish-faced family man, living contentedly in a small home in Yonkers, puttering in his basement workshop, and commuting to the city only when necessary. La Borde, large of body and florid of face, prefers a Broadway office as the dramatic setting for his activities.

Many consider Ryan the top wiretapping technician in the country. But even though he developed the dial-pulse recorder and several other wiretapping refinements, he has never made much money. For some twenty-one years, until 1947 in fact, he was satisfied to work for a police salary—"with no extras"—and to turn his inventions over to friends without charge.

La Borde deserted the police force for more lucrative fields far earlier, and has lived well ever since. His only contribution to the science of wiretapping is a machine that he claims will register taps, but that unfortunately will also register any other trouble on a line. La Borde's shrewd promotion of the machine, however, has paid off handsomely.

"La Borde is a real publicity hound," a rival wiretapper has said. "Once he even asked the newspapers to come take pictures of him tapping wires. I called him up and said, 'For crissake, Bob, cut it out. You're putting everybody on guard against tapping.'"

Like other professional wiretappers, Ryan and La Borde have employed their talents in a wide variety of investigations. But usually divorce cases seem to lead the list. This is especially true in New York, where adultery is the sole ground for divorce and where secret trysts can often be discovered through wiretapping, but it also applies wherever a wealthy man wishes to shed an unfaithful mate without paying alimony. Wiretapping is also quite common in the world of business. Like divorce tapping, business tapping is sometimes lent an aura of legality by a company's giving authorization to tap its own lines.

Exactly this sort of legality was claimed by Steve Broady in 1949, when he, Kenneth Ryan, and two others were indicted in New York for tapping the wires of Kings County Buick, Inc., a large Brooklyn automobile agency. The charge against Ryan was eventually dropped, but Broady's case went to trial. Before a blue-ribbon jury, the suave investigator insisted he had tapped only at the request of fifty per cent of the company's stockholders, who had hired him in 1947 to investigate charges that mobsters were controlling the agency and were getting an abnormal share of the new cars then so difficult to obtain. After a seventeen-hour session, the jury acquitted Broady.

Robert La Borde has reported working on several similar cases. During the war, he was hired by E. R. Squibb & Sons to investigate missing consignments of drug concentrates. With the authorization of company executives, La Borde tapped various office telephones, and soon he had recorded proof of the guilt of a handful of underlings, who had simply driven the drugs off in trucks and had then sold the loot to cut-rate druggists. When the guilty employees promised to repay the loss, Squibb executives, wishing to avoid bad publicity, dropped prosecution.

"Most corporations I've worked for would rather settle things quietly," La Borde says. "A little later, I tapped the office phone of the treasurer of a large corporation and got a straight confession that he'd embezzled $185,000. When he promised restitution, the corporation decided not to prosecute, but he's never repaid a cent, to my knowledge."

Much business tapping, of course, is directed at discovering the plans of competitors. The utilities magnate Samuel Insull and David Lamar, the "Wolf of Wall Street," both are said to have employed wiretapping regularly to keep tabs on business rivals, and with very profitable results.

Over the years, labor unions have also been a major target of business wiretapping. Fifteen years ago, many union telephone lines were regularly tapped for leads on possible strike actions. And although the tapping diminished as unions grew strong and were able to fight back, the National Labor Relations Board is still presented with occasional cases of wiretapping in labor espionage. In 1950, the Seafarers International Union charged the Cities Service Oil Company with using wiretapping to prevent labor organization, and detectives later admitted they had been hired by Cities Service to spy on its employees.

The same year, it was later brought out at a hearing of the National Labor Relations Board, the telephone company itself was found to be tapping the home telephone of one of its switchboard operators at Weirton, West Virginia. The tap was on for eleven hours, and the girl, who was a member of the Communications Workers of America (CIO) and who at the time was trying to organize the Weirton exchange, was fired four days later. The company admitted the tap but contended that it was used to determine whether the employee, in violation of a company-union agreement, was using her telephone to solicit union memberships from other operators on duty at the switchboard. The NLRB, while observing that "certain circumstances disclosed by the record cast serious doubt" on the good faith of the company's contention, nevertheless concluded that there was not sufficient evidence to refute it and upheld the girl's dismissal.

In 1951 the telephone company was charged with tapping in Michigan during a nation-wide CWA strike. The strike was of the hit-and-run variety; each day the workers at a different exchange would walk out. The company could mobilize its supervisory employees to fill the gap, but first it had to know where the gap would be each day. CWA officials, using telephones they suspected were tapped, planted information that a certain exchange would be out the following day. Then, by word of mouth, they ordered a second exchange many miles away to go out instead. When the company's supervisory staff showed up at the first exchange, with nothing to do, union officials seemed well justified in claiming that their wires were tapped.

Because of its habit of using taps to check the efficiency of its own employees at work, the telephone company has been called "the biggest tapper in the business." Actually, within an exchange the work of each operator is regularly checked by a supervisor who taps in through a special switchboard. On a higher level within the company, some officials' telephones are fitted with special test distributor circuits so that they can dial any private number and be automatically tapped in. The result may be efficiency, but it can also be suspicion and uneasiness.

Private wiretapping also produces a vast potential for blackmail. But although many professionals will check the lines of men of notoriety for taps, few will tap for criminal purposes.

"I've recorded dirt on all sorts of important people," says Robert La Borde. "I've thrown away millions in blackmail by turning completed tapes over to my clients." Others might not be so scrupulous.

One man reportedly did make a fortune in blackmail by tapping at various expensive resort hotels, discovering who were paying the bills for attractive female guests.

"I used to know this cop on the force who later retired, bought a string of hotels, and moved into a big estate out on Long Island," La Borde says. "One day he came into my office flashing a big roll of bills, and I asked him how come he was doing so well.

"He just smiled and said, 'Recording. How else?' "

Electronic Eavesdropping

Among a people long fascinated by gadgetry—and now coming to accept systematic snooping by private and official agencies—men skilled in the advanced techniques of electronic surveillance have found a ready market for their services. Take the case of Bernard B. Spindel.

Shortly after the war, Spindel, a Signal Corps veteran engaged in the industrial-training-films business, was approached by a police captain in his New York neighborhood. The captain had heard that Spindel was tinkering with Army-surplus recording equipment on the side. He offered to pay $250 for a unit adapted to wiretapping. Spindel says he later learned the device was used by the captain to make sure he was getting the agreed-on percentage rake-offs from the bookies in his precinct. When this police official led to a second and third, and when Spindel found himself not only purchasing and adapting machines but also servicing them, he gave up his industrial-film activities and took out a license as a private detective.

The wiretap recorder is, of course, only one of many electronic machines that the confidential investigator, like his government counterpart, now finds extremely useful. The technological revolution may have come late to the private-detective industry, but it has arrived with a rush.

"Bugging," or the installation of concealed microphones, has undergone the same revolution. Twenty years ago the job could be accomplished only by obtaining space next door and drilling a hole through the wall to plant the microphone—an operation that is practical only in hotels and in a few half-filled apartment and office buildings. Today, however, any room to which entry can be briefly obtained can be "bugged" without difficulty.

The postwar development of "printed circuits," whereby complex wiring can be simply stamped with conductive paint on a wafer-thin plastic disk, and the invention of transistors, which perform the same functions as a radio vacuum tube but are often constructed in sizes smaller than a pencil eraser, have made possible minute radio transmitter sets that can be concealed almost anywhere. A battery-operated model the size of a safety matchbox, with a transmission life of at least two days, can be easily hidden in an armchair or lampstand. For more permanent installations, another model the size of a pack of cigarettes can be fitted behind an ordinary wall socket, operating off the building's electric power rather than a battery. In either case, the investigator is able to pick up conversations from as far as two blocks away.

If neither of these bugging methods is practical, a Washington specialist points out, the "carbon button" microphone in the mouthpiece of a telephone can be utilized, even while the phone remains on the hook. The simplest way of accomplishing this, he says, is to remove the two-wire cable leading from the individual telephone to the wall connection, substituting for it a four-wire cable of the same size and type. As soon as the two additional wires are attached to the telephone mike, the room is "bugged."

Transmitting conversations picked up on the extra two wires is no problem, the detective adds. "If you don't want to install a radio transmitter behind the telephone wall socket, you can always lead your wires out through the regular phone conduits."

In the old days, hoodlums, fearing such bugs, would hold their business conversations in bathrooms, opening all faucets wide on the then sound theory that the "whoosh" of water covered practically all audible frequencies and thus would drown out human voices. Now, however, the private investigator can record voices right through the noise of running water by filtering out most of the interfering frequencies so that the voices can be heard over the remaining frequencies.

In one of the most elaborate electronic detection assignments ever attempted, Bernard Spindel once employed a combination of bugs, wiretaps, and pocket-sized Minifone wire recorders on behalf of a Midwestern labor leader whose operations were currently under investigation by two separate official bodies.

Flying west, Spindel spent three days checking the union president's home and office for concealed listening devices. He found and removed no less than seven partially completed installations for microphones. In the next four weeks, working only at night, he ripped out all the cables at union headquarters, rewiring the entire telephone system (consisting of eighty-six lines and a total of six hundred connections) so that all lines led into one sealed terminal box, the only key to which was placed in the labor leader's hands.

Duly impressed, the union president next asked Spindel to install wiretaps and telephone bugs in the offices of a dozen union lieutenants of whose loyalty he had doubts. A week later this job was also completed, the monitoring wires all being strung to a listening post in the president's office.

The job might have ended there had not a local grand jury suddenly decided to question all the union officers. In this emergency, Spindel was asked to stay on and do what he could to prevent any backsliding. He solved the problem by providing eight Minifone units, complete with recorders in shoulder holsters and wrist-watch microphones. As each union lieutenant was called into the private chambers of the grand jury, the apparatus was strapped to his body and turned on. As soon as he emerged, the machine was removed and the record played. The labor leader was gratified to learn that all his aides were completely loyal.

Spindel's itemized bill included $762.50 for cables, $100 for telephone-company "tips," $638 for expenses, $3,000 for the eight Minifones with all attachments, $650 for the two special recorders, $750 for the three days of tap checking, and $2,500 for installation. The total payment for these and some other little items was $9,329.

Two years ago, Spindel installed another elaborate surveillance system for the manager of an eastern aircraft factory. The executive, whose plant buys more than $300 million in parts every year, originally became suspicious of some of his purchasing agents after receiving a call from one potential supplier who complained that he couldn't get a single order from the purchasing department even though he knew perfectly well he was offering parts at lower prices than the factory was then paying.

Operating as a telephone-company repairman, Spindel placed wiretaps on the lines of forty-odd purchasing agents and installed three strategically placed telephone bugs. The tap and bug cables were strung to a closet in the plant manager's office, where they were fed into a bank of ten recording machines. Separate control systems were built into a bookshelf cabinet and into a desk drawer. The manager, using an inconspicuous hearing aid and a rotary selector that picked out only the busy telephone lines, could then switch in on any of the forty-odd lines and automatically record all suspicious calls by means of a ten-button control panel.

The results were impressive. Nine purchasing agents were recorded while arranging kickbacks with various suppliers. Not only was the practice stopped but the manager was able to recover more than $200,000 from the guilty suppliers by threatening to cut off all future orders.

The manager was so well satisfied, in fact, that he asked Spindel to set up a permanent electronic surveillance system—one that is still in operation. To maintain a constant watch over the activities of plant employees, Spindel has installed no less than twelve bugs—four in the men's washroom, two in the women's washroom, and six in the company dining hall. Now that the purchasing department has been cleaned up, the wiretap leads have been switched to cover the phones of all foremen and department heads. Five additional telephone bugs have been installed on the lines of the plant manager's top assistants. "That's one factory where nobody pulls wool over the boss's eyes," Spindel boasts. "The manager has found the setup very useful. He knows just which employees are acting up on the outside. He knows which junior executives are loyal to him and which are his enemies, and that way he knows who to promote and who to fire."

Methods of preventing electronic snooping have lagged far behind the development of the devices themselves. One leading investigator, who cannot be identified because his tactics clearly involved the obstruction of justice, can recall only one occasion on which he was able to thwart successful electronic-detection techniques employed by others. "My client, an East Coast exporter, had orally contracted to buy a bunch of parts for shipment overseas," he explains. "But when the manufacturer didn't deliver on time to meet commitments and when my client found out that the guy was actually turning over most of his production to a rival shipper, he refused to pay."

The manufacturer took the exporter to court, claiming breach of contract. In hopes of getting an immediate settlement, he then let it be known that he had made secret recordings of the oral agreement.

That was his crucial mistake. It took the investigator just three hours to build a powerful battery-operated electromagnet and to fit it into an innocent-looking leather briefcase. On the day of the trial, the exporter's lawyer simply walked into court with the briefcase and set it down next to the recording machine the opposition had placed on ominous display.

"In a fraction of a second," the investigator recalls, "the tape was completely erased—on the same principle by which the little magnet in a regular recording machine is used to erase the tape. The manufacturer's lawyer turned the machine on, and nothing happened. He fiddled with it and fiddled with it, and still got just a blank hum. They even took a recess to get new recording equipment. Finally, the judge threw the case out of court for lack of evidence. The look on that lawyer's face was worth more than the fee."

August 11, 1955

The "Engineering of Consent"
—A Case Study

By Robert Bendiner

Back in the days of Ralph Waldo Emerson it was thought, at least by Dr. Emerson, that if a man built a better mousetrap than his neighbor, the world would beat a path to his door. Today, thanks to public relations, we understand that the builder must first arrange for "the engineering of public consent" to mouse-traps. Next he must acquire "earned recognition" for his particular model. And then, according to extreme practitioners, he must, if necessary, "create situations of reality" by setting up, for example, a National Citizens' Committee for the Urgent Capture of Mice.

As to the second of the three quoted phrases—all culled from the sober pronouncements of eminent publicists—there can hardly be any question of logic or propriety. To seek recognition for the merits of a product or an idea is clearly as inevitable as it is blameless, Dr. Emerson's theory to the contrary notwithstanding. But when it comes to "engineering" people's minds, the question naturally arises as to the moral mileage we have covered from The Public Be Damned to The Public Be Maneuvered.

Edward L. Bernays, father of the "engineering" line and one of the most vociferously idealistic men in the business, undoubtedly had in mind only proper objectives for his approach, presumptuous as its phrasing may sound, but the case study we are about to make shows what can happen when "opinion engineers" are given their head. It is a short step, it turns out, from wangling public consent to kidding the public into imagining its consent has already been given—a thought that Carl Byoir & Associates, Inc., it would seem, daringly worked up to a whole creative system for manufacturing "situations of reality."

(P.R.) Men at Work

It is this system, with its overtones of modified Barnum, that underlies, colors, and gives public meaning to the $250-million anti-trust suit formally titled *Noerr Motor Freight, Inc. et al. v. Eastern Railroad Presidents Conference et al.*, but better known in the trade as the railroad-trucker brawl. Should this case ever come to trial in the United States District Court in Philadelphia, where it has long been at rest, it would doubtless sustain *Tide's* prediction of the "most hard-fought and bloody of the century's legal battles." But even in the event of a settlement, now strongly indicated, enough has spilled out in pre-trial skirmishes to afford a remarkably complete and lively panorama of public-relations men at work—at least one variety of the species.

There is no intent here to judge the case or to pass on the relative merits of hauling freight by rail or truck. Neither is it suggested that the "engineering" that went on in this celebrated battle is synonymous with public relations in general, though in varying degree its aspects are to be encountered elsewhere in the craft. To find them all together it was clearly necessary to pick an extreme case rather than describe a typical one.

Nonetheless, what gives the affair its special claim to attention is that the rival concerns—Byoir for the railroads and David Charnay's Allied Public Relations Associates for the truckers—are whirring dynamos in the business, that their clients are economic powers of the first rank, and that in their raucous clash not merely a public-relations firm is on trial but some of the commonly practiced techniques of public relations as well.

On January 21, 1952, Pennsylvania's Governor John S. Fine faced a hard decision. Without his veto a measure called by its sponsors the "Fair Truck Bill" and by its opponents the "Big Truck Bill" would automatically become law. That outcome, the Governor knew, would not sit well with the railroads, traditionally a power in Pennsylvania politics roughly comparable to oil in Texas and sin in Nevada. On the other hand, both houses of the Legislature had passed the bill, which would have raised the weight limit for long-haul trucks allowed on the state's highways from forty-five thousand pounds to sixty thousand. Except for Kentucky, the Pennsylvania limit was the lowest in the country, far below that imposed by any of its neighboring states. The trucking business, smarting under the drastic curb, had itself become a force in the Pennsylvania capital, perhaps not as entrenched as exponents of the older form of transportation, but brasher, with considerable appeal to voters, and an ample supply of ready cash.

Caught in this crossfire of special interests, the Governor may well have acted on what he conceived to be the pure merits of the case when, six minutes before the deadline, he vetoed the weight-increase bill. If Governor Fine had been cross examined on the reasons for his action, he could certainly have made out an excellent case.

In the first place, the Maryland State Roads Commission was co-sponsoring a test of the relative damage done by various axle loads to concrete pavement, and with what appeared to be providential timing, an advance copy of an interim report had come to Governor Fine's attention. The tentative findings were hard on heavy trucks.

The Governor also understood that the Pennsylvania State Association of Township Supervisors, a quasi-official body, was all out against the "Big Truck" bill. Tens of thousands of post-cards were pouring out under its imprimatur addressed to the car owners of the state, and it had produced a television program on the Maryland road test.

The Pennsylvania State Grange appeared to be equally aroused against the bill. Material had streamed out of its headquarters during the legislative battle, and the Governor must have known that the Grange had worked on state Senators, especially those from politically doubtful districts, to vote against the measure.

So insistent, in fact, was the opposition—even after passage of the bill—that the Governor felt obliged to hold public hearings two days before the deadline for his decision—and at those hearings the anti-big-truck witnesses had made an extremely impressive case.

The result of all this civic activity was the veto. *Vox populi* had been heard and heeded. Or so it seemed, for few persons outside the offices of Carl Byoir & Associates knew until much later:

¶That the public relations man of the Maryland State Roads Commission, which had co-sponsored the road test, had been advising the Byoir office, on an expense account, and was later to go on the payroll of Byoir's client, the Eastern Railroad Presidents Conference (E.R.P.C.), at $1,000 a month.

¶That those tens of thousands of postcards mailed out to motorists in the name of the Pennsylvania State Association of Township Supervisors had been prepared and mailed by the Byoir organization and billed to the E.R.P.C.

¶That during the fight for the bill, a Byoir lieutenant, according to his own subsequent testimony, made his headquarters in the Pennsylvania State Grange, whose literature was similarly drawn up by Byoir men and billed to the railroads.

¶Or, finally, that the impressive showing at the hearings was not the spontaneous plea of affected Pennsylvanians, but the carefully coached performance of Byoir-organized witnesses.

Allowing for a certain freedom from shyness essential to the profession, let Reynolds Girdler, then a Byoir executive, tell the story of the "CB&A team" in his own words:

"When January, 1951, opened, there seemed every reason to believe that the truckers would get their bill through, increasing the allowable weight to 60,000 pounds. The 17 railroads of Pennsylvania then started fighting. . . . They fought the bill for four months and then threw up the sponge. They reported to their superiors that they were licked. Even so the lobbyists in control of the railroad activity continued to oppose allowing the CB&A people to operate in Pennsylvania. Their superiors then thrust us down their throats."

Recommending a special award for C. Colburn Hardy, who

commanded the Byoir forces in the Battle of Harrisburg, the interoffice memorandum continued:

"The team went to work in Pennsylvania beginning in June, 1951. Not only did they begin to generate publicity against the bill, but they were successful in getting a long list of organizations and individuals publicly to oppose the bill. Those organizations ranged from the CIO to the Pennsylvania State Grange. . . . Even after the bill was passed by both houses, clamor against the bill continued. . . . The CB&A team thereupon went out and organized twenty-one witnesses for twenty-one organizations against the bill. They prepared their statements and the publicity . . . Veto of this bill meant that some five million dollars worth of freight was retained on the Pennsylvania Railroad, because the trucking limit was not raised. This represented one of the most dramatic illustrations of the power of organized public opinion that anyone could hope to find. . . ."

The opinion may have been more organized than public (Mr. Hardy, the award-nominee, modestly dismissed this description of his efforts as "overenthusiastic"—"a sales pitch"), but the illustration was certainly dramatic enough. According to Edward Gogolin, general manager and first vice-president of the Pennsylvania Motor Truck Association, the veto "triggered the industry" into action.

While the truckers had never been a retiring sort, it was clear now that massive retaliation was in order. It was not surprising, then, that in May, 1952, they engaged the services of David Charnay and his Allied Public Relations Associates. As the Pennsylvania truckers' president, Floyd B. Noerr, put it, "We were trying to find out who was stabbing us in the back, and then if we did find out, to pull out the dagger and bring suit."

The identity of the assailant could hardly have been as much of a mystery as all that. Certainly, Gogolin, Noerr's lieutenant, had a good notion since, as he was later to testify, "Practically every morning, to get to my office, I had to stumble over C. Colburn Hardy, the Byoir man, who was using the Grange office on the first floor of our building as his headquarters." Nevertheless, it was plain that Charnay's services were not being engaged merely to "engineer public consent" for the hauling of freight by truck. He was hired as well to do a detective job on a fellow publicist.

Long before the Governor's veto or Charnay's entry into the picture, the American Trucking Association was aware of the Byoir tactics against the long-haul truckers.

The reason for this was dramatic and simple. One day in July, 1951, a young lady named Sonya Saroyan, originally Sonya Jigarjian, walked into the American Trucking Association's Washington office to tell Walter Belson, its public-relations director, all about Life with Byoir.

After two years as secretary to the Byoir executive in charge of the Eastern Railroad account, Miss Saroyan—twenty-nine and variously described as "an attractive brunette" and "a very strange dish of tea"—had resigned or been fired, a point not easily determined. With her went a large packet of memos, reports, directives, letters, and releases, mostly carbons or copies she herself had made and which she therefore somewhat naïvely regarded as her "own property." All of it was intended to show how the art of public relations was practiced by her erstwhile employer. Belson accepted her offerings, along with two days of tape-recorded "testimony" at $50 a day, plus expenses. For nearly a year that seemed to be the end of Miss Saroyan's brush with adventure.

What her motives were cannot be pinned down with certainty, but, as often happens, they seem to have been a blend. Richardson Dilworth, chief of the truckers' legal battery when he was not engaged as Philadelphia's district attorney, explained that she "had become thoroughly disgusted with the methods being used in the handling of this account" and had therefore gone to the other side as a matter of conscience. Sonya herself takes a somewhat less lofty view, explaining that she "very impulsively" walked out with the papers when she was bypassed for a promised promotion to the Tintair account.

At any rate, the truckers appear to have been extraordinarily slow to see the value of Sonya's contribution to their cause. At one point in the Battle of Harrisburg, Belson telephoned Gogolin to report that some pertinent material had been delivered to headquarters by an ex-employee of the enemy and to ask whether the trucking executive was aware of "certain things" going on in the state, more significant even than Gogolin's tripping over Hardy every morning on his way to work. Soon after, the Pennsylvania truckers dispatched an agent to examine the material in Washington and take notes. But it appears that if the Charnay organization had not taken over, the Saroyan dossier, in all its colorful detail, might have been left forever to gather dust.

It was in April, 1952, that three officials of the Pennsylvania Motor Truck Association called on David Charnay, an enterprising young man whose favorable impression on John L. Lewis had made him a major publicist, putting him in a position to ask the truckers, and to get, $36,000 a year, plus expenses, for his services. The sum was modest enough compared with the $150,000 a year the railroads were paying Byoir, plus expenses running up to $250,000, but still rather impressive for a man who only a few years earlier had been reporting nightclub doings for the New York *Daily News*. Besides the United Mine Workers of America account and a colorful and rewarding stint for the Nationalist Bank of China, Charnay had lined up such notable clients as Ballantine Beer and Eversharp. A man of versatile talents, he has managed to promote the fortunes of such diverse figures as Franklin D. Roosevelt, Jr., Richard Nixon, Robert F. Wagner, Vincent Impellitteri, and Louis E. Wolfson, the man who tried to take over Montgomery Ward.

In its preliminary phase the truckers' account was put in the hands of a former newspaper man named Henry Paynter, whose first order of business was to get a private detective on the track of Sonya Saroyan. She was located in New York, in May, and throughout the summer and fall, she says, Paynter and Charnay pressed her to release the material she had turned over to the American truckers office (which apparently would not yield it up to the Pennsylvania group otherwise), and to tell them more about the workings of the Byoir enterprise.

She was offered a job, according to her testimony, but turned it down. Eventually, as she tells the tale, she succumbed, on the understanding that the documents and her testimony—she had added an additional $1,050 worth—were to be turned over to a Congressional committee for investigation. Next thing she knew, she says, was the announcement in the papers of January 18, 1953, that the Pennsylvania Motor Truck Association and thirty-seven trucking companies were suing the Eastern Railroad Presidents Conference, thirty-one railroads, thirty-four individuals (mostly railroad presidents and ex-presidents) and the public-relations firm of Carl Byoir & Associates.

"I have every reason to believe," wrote Sonya Saroyan less than a month later, "that the suit is based, in great part, on my testimony." Dilworth seemed to agree. When a railroad attorney offered to produce without subpoena certain items of interest to the truckers in exchange for the Saroyan papers, Dilworth is reported to have answered, "This would be like swapping a ticket to South Pacific for a Minsky burlesque ticket."

The Dilworth evaluation was probably accurate, but the truckers had other sources of information as well. In the fall of 1952, the Charnay office enjoyed the services of John G. (Steve) Broady, a private investigator who has since then added to his fame and drawn an indictment as the alleged "master ear" of a Manhattan wiretap ring. Paynter says that Broady's contacts were solely with him, rather than with Charnay, and the fruits of his efforts, whatever they were, were turned over directly to Dilworth. Both sides have complained of rifled files, and Dilworth charged that the Byoir firm had destroyed some of its own records rather than have them subpoenaed—a charge vigorously denied by Byoir.

Allowing for the natural exuberance of lawyers, especially in pretrial procedures, it seems reasonably clear that in a public-relations war anything up to and including piracy may well be expected. In any event, what emerged from the Charnay firm's preliminary labors, as defined by the distinguished Philadelphia law firm of Dilworth, Paxson, Kalish & Green, amounted to the following charge:

That the defendant railroads had conspired, through vilification, slander, bribery, and assorted devices to drive the long-distance truckers out of business, with the objective of "carving out exclusive, monopolistic spheres of operation in the freight transportation business." To this end, the complaint ran, the

Byoir firm had been hired and it "immediately initiated a vicious, corrupt and fraudulent campaign" to "obstruct, hamper and impede interstate transportation by motor vehicle," all in willful violation of the Sherman Antitrust Act. In its reply, the Byoir firm flatly denied these allegations.

Boiling down the charges as they related to Byoir, Dilworth at the pre-trial hearings specified "misinformation . . . front organizations . . . distorted photographs . . . planting of stories . . . 'boilerplate' announcements . . . phony polls," and the like. To which Philip Price of the defense staff replied that much of the case seemed to be that the "defendants got together and called the plaintiff bad names."

Whether such activities as those alleged form a pattern that is vulnerable under the Sherman Antitrust Act may safely be left to the courts and the fullness of time, but the open discussion of these techniques, illegal or merely tricky, is of general interest to the public and of special interest throughout the whole hypersensitive realm of public relations.

If there is one obvious lesson to be derived from the railroad-trucker affair, it is that the fulsome interoffice memorandum is a luxury to be resisted. A specimen of the sort that prompted Dilworth to say he would guard with his life the collection of Byoir papers carted off by Miss Saroyan is this gem that Reynolds Girdler, the former Byoir executive, composed in 1949 to set the tactical line for promoting the firm's new railroad client:

"You can see from the foregoing that this account is utterly unlike the conventional one. *Here we do not have a client for attribution.* [Italics mine.] Of course we will release some stories under client attribution, but they will be of lesser propaganda importance than those we can generate from motorists, property owners, taxpayers, farmers or women's groups. In sum, we not only have to create publicity ideas; we also have to go out in the field and create the groups and occasions so that those publicity ideas will become realities."

One of the groups they created, in the New York sector of the battle line, was the Empire State Transport League. When Girdler first testified about this organization, he modestly credited its formation to a small group of upstate New York

businessmen. They were aided, he said, by Thomas Kiely, a
Byoir man, but "only in the nicest kind of way," and besides
the impetus was their own. Confronted, however, with a memorandum he had dashed off to his superior on the subject—another of the documents spirited out by the impulsive Miss
Saroyan—Girdler freely admitted authorship. It read in part:

"We formed the Empire State Transport League in New York
because we needed an organization that could legitimately mail
all types of propaganda on the general subject of trucks and
highways."

The League had an address, of course—11 North Pearl Street,
Albany, it said on the letterheads—but no office that a Dun &
Bradstreet investigator could locate. A public stenographer took
the mail and, presumably, relayed it on to the Byoir office. But
the organization did have a constitution and bylaws, and for
reproducing copies of these, along with membership-application
forms, the Byoir firm duly billed the Eastern Railroad Presidents
Conference on December 9 and 12, 1949.

The League was then all set to send out releases, reprints, and
other such material, none of which would have been quite so
persuasive if it had had to bear some such imprint as "Carl
Byoir & Associates, Public Relations Counsel to the Eastern
Railroad Presidents Conference" instead of "Empire State
Transport League."

David I. Mackie, chairman of the E.R.P.C., has insisted that
". . . the real issue is not between the heavy truck operators and
the railroads, but between an informed and militant public and
the highway freighters." The League, it seems, was just a slice
of that informed and militant public boiled down to a letterhead.

Another slice apparently was called the "New Jersey Citizens
Tax Study Foundation," which was launched just as the Byoir
office was warming up the campaign against the truckers. Among
its original incorporators was one C. Colburn Hardy, then com-
manding the Byoir railroad campaign on the Jersey front. As
Hardy later testified, "This was a personal matter that I did as
a citizen, similar to a great many other civic projects in which I
happened to be interested."

It was odd, though, that at the pretrial proceedings fifteen canceled checks amounting to $3,700.58 were produced from the Byoir files, made out to Fred W. Goodwin, executive director of the Foundation. The E.R.P.C. was also billed for the Foundation's envelopes, letterheads, and releases, as well as for "contributions" by the Byoir firm.

Still harder to square with Hardy's purely civic role in the Foundation was the directive he addressed to his staff with all the characteristic candor of Byoir executives:

"We are also assisting in the formation of a new group: New Jersey Citizens Tax Study Foundation . . . ALL LITERATURE, ETC. from this group must be on plain paper and mailed from New Jersey."

Yet the Foundation solemnly turned out studies on highway finance and even conducted a poll that showed the public fairly panting for a mileage tax on heavy trucks. "As a fact-finding group," said the covering release, "the Foundation takes no position, merely reports the results." With equal solemnity the Foundation later released to the press a letter to the New Jersey Motor Truckers Association denying that it was a "front" for the railroads.

The New Jersey Automobile Owners, Inc., was clearly not started by Byoir, having been incorporated back in 1938. But, testified Hardy, "I helped in reactivating" it. The pattern was similar to the relationship between Byoir and the civic-minded tax students. Again checks were produced from the Byoir files. Again the E.R.P.C. was billed for material put out in the name of the do-good organization. And again there was the unfailing memorandum. This one, also from Hardy, said:

"We are cooperating with an autoist group, New Jersey Automobile Owners, Inc. . . . This group sends out considerable literature. It MUST be mailed in New Jersey."

There was a further injunction: "Whenever any letter goes from the N.J.A.O., a copy MUST be mailed to Robert A. Fox, New Jersey Automobile Owners, Inc., 155 Evergreen Place, East Orange, N.J. . . ." A sensitive touch, perhaps, but it probably seemed only right and proper for Mr. Fox, as executive secretary, to be informed of what his organization was up to.

Practically every public-relations firm makes use of citizens' committees of one sort or another—and generally legitimate use. But as elsewhere in this business the area is cloudy, with only a shadowy line separating the relatively pure from the purely bogus. Thomas J. Deegan, chairman of the E.R.P.C.'s subcommittee on public relations, plays the ambiguity for all it is worth. Pressed by Dilworth, he expounded his views on fronts— "noble and ignoble":

" 'Front' can be the very evil one that we both talked about a moment ago, the Commy. 'Front' can be something as simple and genuine as Bing Crosby smoking a Chesterfield. 'Front' can be someone else with a co-interest saying the story that you are interested in, too, which, to my humble knowledge, is a perfectly genuine, proper thing to do. 'Front' has taken on even other connotations—Marilyn Monroe."

Gerry Swinehart, president of the Byoir firm and evidently far more active in the railroad account than Byoir himself, shrugged off the implications of the "front" technique altogether. "There may have been one or two instances where we organized groups," he said, "but those groups knew what they were doing." No one was fooled but the public.

While few public-relations men share Swinehart's openly indulgent attitude toward the synthetic front, practically all of them endorse a close working relationship with what the trade calls "co-interest groups." In truth there would seem to be no reason why they shouldn't hitch a client's public-relations activities to the parallel program of another organization—as long as the thing is done openly. The rub is that it is not always, or even generally, done openly. Certainly not in this case.

The Grange, a good example of a co-interest group, was certainly operating in Pennsylvania before Carl Byoir & Associates were, and it continued to function there long after Messrs. Girdler and Hardy pulled out their "team." It was real and legitimate, but how independent it was in this particular campaign against the truckers is something else again. We have already indicated that a good quantity of the Grange's propaganda in that fight was created by Byoir men, though the Grange was not their client, and that printing, mailing, and other publicity charges were regularly paid for by their office. Weekly work reports from Hardy and his team, later cited at the hearings, indicate that the Grange's lobbying was supervised by, and even its letters written by, Byoir lieutenants:

June 28, 1951: "With Grange, set up special program to contact Senators in doubtful counties. . . . Wrote material for Grange News Letter."

July 29, 1951: "Letters to editor from J. K. Mahood, Pennsylvania State Grange, to answer inaccurate charges of proponents of S 615 [the truck bill]."

May 9, 1952: "Hardy wrote letter from Master, Pennsylvania Grange, to accompany reprint of National Grange Monthly reprint."

June 27, 1952: "Mailing reprints over signature of Master of State Grange."

The Pennsylvania State Association of Township Supervisors similarly enjoyed the talents of the Byoir establishment, courtesy of the E.R.P.C., not to mention financial assistance. So, it appears, did the Citizens Tax League of Rochester, New York, and the Citizens Public Expenditure Survey of Albany.

It often happens that a potential co-interest group has to be subtly persuaded of its co-interest. In such cases, there is no substitute for the services of an eloquent member, and like all professional services these are not performed gratis. Such a "pro" par excellence is Mrs. Bessie Q. Mott, a veteran clubwoman, pamphleteer, and great-grandmother.

Questioning Swinehart at the pretrial hearings, Dilworth sardonically suggested that Mrs. Mott was "getting to be practically a regular" at profitable crusading. Yes, Swinehart agreed, "She works for a great many people. . . . She is a specialist in the field of reaching women's clubs, women's interests." Indeed she is, having given unstintingly not only to the railroads, but also to the Great Atlantic & Pacific Tea Company, when Byoir was fighting that chain's case in defense against the Justice Department, and, before that, to oleomargarine, which she served under the banner of Batten, Barton, Durstine & Osborne, Inc.

"But I don't take on a fight," says Mrs. Mott (Smith, '99),

"unless it's something I believe in." However, the lines between her personal crusades and the interests of her organizations tend to get blurred. She is said to have allowed Byoir to pay for letterheads of the American Home Department of the New York State Federation of Women's Clubs which showed Bessie Q. Mott as vice-chairman and were used to invite ladies to a forum likewise paid for by the Byoir office. A pamphlet under her signature, called "Are We Being Railroaded into Socialism?" is alleged to have been printed and mailed at Byoir's expense, though the author was carefully identified only with the Public Affairs Department of the Federation.

When the truckers formally complained in their suit that the lady was using her position as a platform for Byoir and the railroads, the president of the Federation could only concede to the press that as chairman of the public-affairs committee, Mrs. Mott had in fact issued antitruck propaganda and that the Federation had felt obliged to tell her to stop.

Mrs. Mott had been receiving $500 a month and expenses from Byoir. Canceled checks were produced to show that the civic-minded lady had drawn more than $7,500 for work on the railroad account. Evidently she was worth it, however, because when her name bobbed up again on the Byoir work reports, after a quiet spell, Swinehart inquired about her new activities. The answer, from staff-man Horace Lyon, was as follows:

"She is on retainer ($500 a month) for months of May and June ONLY—when the state and national Fed. of Women's Clubs and Bus. & Prof. Women's Clubs are holding their annual conventions, setting up next year's program plans, etc.—to do these things:

"1. Get our program guide on the need for a modernized national transportation policy published with the endorsement of the Nat. Fed. of Women's Clubs.

"2. Get transportation on the program agendas for next year. . . .

"We are getting results, and value, on both counts."

Byoir's own comment, as quoted by *Fortune,* was: "Sure we hired a clubwoman to get the women's clubs. What are we supposed to do? Hire a veteran to speak for women's clubs, and a woman to speak for veterans' organizations?"

Inevitably, the spectacle of a Bessie Q. Mott manipulating women's clubs to the greater glory of a group of railroads has in it something of high comedy. Unhappily this element is lacking in the alleged working arrangements between the Byoir establishment and Clinton H. Johnson, public-relations agent for the Maryland State Roads Commission. The truckers' complaint uses harsh words and charges that Governor Fine's last-minute veto of the truck bill had been influenced by Johnson, who was in a position to have advance knowledge of the road test and who, at the same time, it said, had been receiving payments from Carl Byoir & Associates.

Johnson denied these allegations, but he conceded certain points that at least raise the question of propriety. Johnson's basic case is a simple one: He was not an employee of the State of Maryland but an independent contractor engaged to handle the public relations of the Roads Commission. His contract did not prevent him from engaging in other public-relations work as long as he did not let it interfere with his labors for the commission. Yes, he did make twenty to thirty trips to the New York offices of Carl Byoir & Associates, but his motive was to get their help in doing his job for the Maryland highway program.

At the same time, he gave the Byoir organization factual information about highway construction costs, overweight violations, and the like. At no time was he paid for services. Certainly he never took bribes nor did he misrepresent data or have any idea how the Byoir office got hold of the report on the road tests so far in advance of the general release. And, finally, he intended to bring suit against the truckers for libel and slander.

From Girdler's deposition we get a somewhat different perspective. Johnson did "interpretative and research work" for the Byoir office, he recalled, and was paid largely on the basis of the number of hours he put in. Girdler couldn't recall exactly the rate, and the arrangement does seem to have been pretty hazy all around. He recalled that amounts were given Johnson for expenses—Johnson confirmed this—without written statements, without itemizing, and often in cash. Girdler thought the expenses ran to $50 or $75 for an afternoon, night, and following day.

Hotel bills—Johnson usually stayed at the Biltmore—were often sent direct to Byoir. One of these, introduced as plaintiff's Exhibit P-65, covered a Labor Day weekend for Johnson and his wife, and must have been something of a bonus. Including theater tickets and meals, it came to $190.38. Johnson said it was for writing a free article for the Byoir firm—an article that, as it happens, never quite got finished.

In spite of Johnson's failure to remember payment for "services," several memos from Hardy to the bookkeeping department and at least one check bear the words "for research" or "services rendered." The sums were not high, but on January 1, 1953, Johnson went on a part-time basis with the Roads Commission and signed up as a consultant to the Eastern Railroad Presidents Conference for $1,000 a month. When plaintiff's counsel asked him, rhetorically enough, whether he considered this a "pay-off," his lawyer advised him not to answer. But he admitted that the Maryland Attorney General's office was investigating his relationship with Byoir while he worked for the Roads Commission and that as far as his state job was concerned, he was then on leave without pay. In a report later issued by the Attorney General's office Johnson was given a clean bill of health, but considered to have shown "poor judgment."

In the first of its many memoranda, in which it agreed to take on the railroad account, Carl Byoir & Associates laid down a few operating principles, to wit: The basic appeal must be directed not only to friends of the railroads but to motorists, conscious of hazards on the highway, and to taxpayers. Motorists are "ripe for action of some sort; but as yet they have not found a way to make themselves vocal or to express their resentment in legislation. . . . It is our task to accelerate these spontaneously generated currents."

Accordingly, the magazine department was ordered to start work "on the long process of researching and writing major magazine pieces." The radio department was "alerted to write scripts and create events acceptable to networks and local stations." It is a subject, wrote Girdler, that should "give us plenty of scope for the ingenuity that distinguishes CB & A departments. . . ."

Excerpts from early work sheets show the turn that this ingenuity took almost from the start:

"Production Department: 10/4 . . . Selecting pictures . . . featuring worst truck tragedy within the past year. . . .

"10/14 . . . Making layouts, selecting pictures, writing captions for Central States News Views featuring spectacular wreck near Gary, Ind., of large van-type truck. . . .

"Radio Department: 10/21 . . . Securing radio script with mention of 'nasty truck driver.' . . ."

Not all the railroad people took kindly to this sort of thing. Walter J. Tuohy, president of the Chesapeake & Ohio, was sharply critical of an inter-office Byoir memorandum that read in part:

"At belated last, this is confirmation of my understanding of our conversations concerning the desire of the account . . . to portray truckers as evil, sinister wrongdoers. Actually, the proposed program fell into three categories. . . . 1. An effort by me to create and sell scripts to existing dramatic programs with the trucking theme as basic plot, picturing the trucker as a lawbreaker, etc. As we discussed, invariably to conform with network requirements the 'bad' truckers may have to be compensated for by 'good' truckers but the poison will still be there and the damage done. 2. We will make all possible efforts to enlist the aid of regular and free-lance writers to utilize the truckers as a 'heavy' . . ."

William White, then president of the New York Central, testified that he had criticized some of these Byoir effusions as being in "an eager-beaver jargon that I didn't like."

On the other hand, Thomas J. Deegan, who besides being chairman of the E.R.P.C.'s public-relations subcommittee was vice-president in charge of the Chesapeake & Ohio's public relations, thought the stress on horror pictures perfectly proper because of the danger to the public from trucks carrying explosives. "Seeing the explosives truck photographed riding along the highway with nothing happening is interesting, perhaps, but certainly not striking," he remarked, "but seeing it exploded and children and mothers lying on the ground torn to bits brings one up short."

Of course, life in the publicity departments was not all melodrama. There were serious articles to be worked out with reputable writers for reputable magazines. To judge from a memorandum written by Patricia Lochridge, head of Byoir's magazine department, the firm was sometimes able to go rather far in the molding of articles. Staking a claim to one of the monthly awards that provide incentive in the Byoir establishment, Miss Lochridge wrote to a superior:

"Still a third nomination from the magazine department for the article, "You CAN Have Better Roads," which appeared in the April issue of *Country Gentlemen*. This was a co-operative venture pulling together the work of the account and the department in a year-long endeavor. . . . This was a difficult job to put across, entailing two complete rewrites of the article to satisfy both a pixie author and a difficult editor. This was accomplished without too much pain and the underlying philosophy of the . . . account came through in the final draft. . . ."

At the pretrial proceedings Dilworth was unkind enough to confront Miss Lochridge not only with her memorandum but also with a note assuring the writer of the article that "tomorrow John Connor will send you some additional money as a working fund." It was "purely expense money," Miss Lochridge explained, to pay the author for research expenses prior to the article's acceptance. On rereading the piece, she felt "it was very much of Emily [the 'difficult pixie'] and very little of me." As for the memo itself, she dismissed it as "flowery," especially the part about the underlying philosophy. Then she added, by way of explanation, "Well, gee, I wanted to get the prize that month."

In many other ways the firm of Carl Byoir & Associates lived up to the dictum allegedly laid down early in the game by Hardy that "all publicity and activity should come through third parties," that the firm would "provide a vast amount of information but, for the most part, its source should remain anonymous." Polls and surveys appeared under high-sounding names, but the financing and, in some measure, the phrasing of the questions, originated in the Byoir office.

A Byoir work report for May 29, 1952, includes such items as: "Hardy revised material for speech by H. A. Thomson, Township Supervisors" and "Hardy wrote editorial for Pennsylvania Association Township Supervisors Magazine, endorsing weight-distance tax." Sonya Saroyan swore that press releases issued in the names of prominent persons were written and distributed from the Byoir office, including one from the insurance commissioner of Pennsylvania, in which big trucks were blamed for an expected boost in automobile-insurance rates. And even the New Jersey Rural Letter Carriers Association, which had also been enlisted in the cause, complained that the Byoir office had framed a resolution for the country mailmen and then reworded it in the press release they prepared.

They work hard at Byoir's.

Resort to Law

Confronted with this feverish activity and broad assortment of stratagems, the truckers, on Charnay's advice, fell back on the law. It is not for the observer to contend, as the defendants have repeatedly contended, that the suit was brought as a counterattack in a publicity war. Assuming the plaintiff's perfect good faith in going to court, however, we can still appreciate the considerable tactical advantages that have accrued to them as a result.

By the very nature of the action, the enemy was put on the defensive. The plaintiffs also had an opportunity to strike an injured but gallant air and, through a "situation of reality" of their own making, get some pretty colorful publicity.

Two months after the intermittent pretrial sessions got under way, Robert McCay Green, co-counsel for the truck operators, filed an affidavit richly summarizing the testimony given up to that time and replete with stories of false fronts, weighted polls, and the doing of such persons as the remarkable Mrs. Mott. Five thousand copies went out to members of the Pennsylvania Motor Truck Association, the press, and interested outsiders. "Absolutely inexcusable," protested Byoir attorney R. Sturgis

Ingersoll. But Dilworth blandly suggested that this was "obviously a protest inspired by your client, one of its happy ideas." Otherwise, he pointed out, the complaint would have been made to the court. Co-counsel Green added that by publicizing the document in this way, they had merely "kept the plaintiffs properly informed." And when Ingersoll sharply asked "Are the politicians in Ohio plaintiffs?" Dilworth settled for "This is too nice and too quiet a morning and we refuse to be needled."

It is true, of course that the doings of the truck operators and their publicists likewise became a matter of record, but because they had never put on anything like as intricate a campaign as their opponents and were not victimized by the disclosure of interoffice memoranda, there was much less for the railroad lawyers to work on. The latter were forced to make do with such scoops as the allegation that the truck operators had a war chest of $600,000, that they kept a hotel room in Harrisburg for "entertainment" (just as the other side did), and that even-handedly they doled out money to both parties shortly before elections.

Edward Gogolin, the Pennsylvania Motor Truck Association's general manager, didn't seem quite sure of the reason for this last custom. When Byoir's lawyer pressed the point that "nobody but a damned fool would bet a thousand dollars on each team" at a ball game, Gogolin agreed, but as to why the truckers did essentially the same thing, he could only explain, "Well, I've been told all big business did that." While the testimony may have rubbed some of the gloss from the truckers' shield, it was mild stuff when compared with the single admission from the other side that five members of the Pennsylvania Legislature at the time were on the payroll of the Pennsylvania Railroad, four of them on the Senate Highway Committee.

The suit had, from the truckers' viewpoint, the further merit of providing another public review of the career of Carl Byoir, surely one of the gaudier records of the era. The slight, conservatively dressed man of sixty-four scarcely looked the part of one of the great press agents of history, patent-medicine entrepreneur extraordinary, publicist for such diverse clients as Machado, Masaryk, and the German Tourist Information Office of the Nazi era, and finally head of the largest public-relations firm in the world.

In perhaps needless detail, Dilworth dwelt on Byoir's medicine-man period in the 1920's, when he collaborated with one X. La Motte Sage, A.M., Ph.D., LL.D., in the manufacture of Nuxated Iron. "The valuable blood, nerve force, and tissue-building properties of this preparation are due to organic iron . . . in combination with nux vomica," the label read. But the American Medical Association found less than four cents' worth of iron in a dollar bottle. Reminded of this finding by Dilworth, Byoir said, "That may be accurate," but it was still the best iron tonic on the market at the time. The trouble was with the distribution system, which he thought made such products too expensive. Another of his products was brought up—Seedol ("Natural Seed Bowel Tonic Works Wonders"). And furthermore, he had to defend his campaign in behalf of the A & P, which in 1946 cost him a conviction for conspiring to violate the Sherman Antitrust Act and a fine of $5,000.

Much of this line of questioning may have been irrelevant, as Byoir strenuously pointed out. "Ever since these depositions started to secure evidence," he complained, "that material has been used in many other ways by the Pennsylvania Truck Association to smear Carl Byoir." But the grilling did serve to put Byoir on the defensive, and that evidently was the purpose.

In the nature of things, the suit so far has aided the fortunes of Carl Byoir & Associates considerably less than those of David Charnay. But ironically, a settlement would prove still better for the latter than an eventual trial in open court, even one that resulted in a smashing victory for the truckers. Charnay is in this enviable heads-I-win-tails-you-lose position for the simple reason that in spite of the suit he has for some time been publicly and privately promoting the notion that the two branches of the transportation business "must decide to live together competitively and at peace."

Tide reported that in certain quarters "he is being touted as an 'industrial statesman'" for having brought railroad men and truckers together in a Council of Eastern Rail & Truck Common Carriers (C.E.R.T. for short) which seems to have found a potential meeting ground in the development of "piggyback"—the transport of truck trailers on railroad flatcars.

Charnay claims to have made "overtures" for a get-together of this sort even before the suit was filed, and he told this reporter of having offered Walter S. Franklin, President of the Pennsylvania Railroad, the friendly tip that "While you two roll around in the mud, that drone you hear overhead is air cargo." Perhaps more eloquent are two simple facts concerning C.E.R.T. David Charnay is a member of the Council; Carl Byoir is not.

Meanwhile, it is hardly possible to overlook the significance of what has been happening in Harrisburg. Once again, a bill to increase the weight limit for big trucks was put into the hopper. But instead of calling the Byoir men back into action again, the railroads almost immediately ran up the white flag. Associated Railroads of Pennsylvania, otherwise known as the railroad lobby, quickly announced that it would not oppose the measure. Its chairman, long one of the most trenchant foes of "big-truck" bills, did not exactly go all out for the measure, but it was plain that sweet reasonableness was the order of the day. "After a thorough study of the bill," he said, "we feel that it is reasonable in view of the laws of surrounding states." The bill was passed by the legislature and signed by Governor George M. Leader, Fine's successor.

Should a settlement sprout in this altered climate, what will have been the net effect? Two firms will have demonstrated the power of public relations as it has rarely been demonstrated before—one almost single-handedly defeated an important piece of legislation; the other stepped in and the bill was passed. The railroads and long-haul truck operators, neither of which has been made to look any better to the public as a result of their costly public-relations war, will have come to an understanding —after an enormous outlay of time, money, energy, and talent— that they almost inevitably would have reached anyway without benefit of public relations.

Whatever impact the railroad-trucker affair may have had on the principals or on the public, the publicity seems to have sent tremors through a calling already jittery with self-doubt. For in spite of a surface brashness, the public-relations industry in general is surprisingly marked by self-searching, ambiguity as to function, and an almost pathetic yearning for recognition by the American public.

Yet alongside this introspective anxiety—whether or not in a causal relationship had better be left to others—goes a bland assumption that public-relations men know best what is good for you; that their techniques can provide solutions to most problems, industrial, national, and international; and that they should, of necessity, be high in the councils of the Republic.

Actually, elaborate self-justification is a little bewildering to the layman, who does not doubt that public relations has a legitimate and constructive role to play, one required by modern society. At its best it is a compiler and disseminator of useful information. More than that, it is increasingly a molder of policy in business and industry.

The more complex the community and the more varied the interests of the individual citizen, the more essential public relations becomes. Not only must institutions convey their purposes and merits to particular sectors of the public, but they must in return have the needs and desires of those they seek to interest conveyed back to them. The public-relations man is the interpreter in this two-way traffic of ideas—not only for railroad presidents and processors of cheese, but for university chancellors and yo-yo manufacturers, for Federal agencies and private trade associations, for aspiring aldermen and the governments of foreign states.

Perhaps it is this impression of mounting importance that gives some of the best people in the business a feeling of uncertainty, a sense that considerably more responsibility is in order.

As *Tide* commented, "Understandably, the pre-trial deposition-taking in the truckers' suit . . . has quite a few PR men wondering about ethics and behavior of the business."

May 16, 1957

Clouds from Nevada: *A Special Report on the AEC's Weapons-Testing Program*

By Paul Jacobs

Within a few days the detonation of a nuclear weapon will begin Operation Plumbbob, the new series of tests that is being conducted this spring and summer by the Atomic Energy Commission at its Nevada test site.

When that first "device" is detonated from the control point, midway between Frenchman and Yucca Flats ninety miles northwest of Las Vegas, there will be a blinding flash of light, a great bang, and a shaking of the earth. In the days following there will be more detonations. The seven-hundred-foot tower on which one of the devices is mounted will disappear as a huge cloud rises and forms the now familiar mushroom shape.

These are no longer novel sounds and sights to the people living in Nevada and Utah near the test site. Those gathered around the crap tables of Las Vegas will hardly break off from their concentration on "making the hard four" to connect the sound or flash with its cause. But others, when they see or hear the explosion, will be filled with apprehension and dread; justifiably or not, they regard the Atomic Energy Commission as an army of occupation.

At the Fallini ranch, near Warm Springs, Nevada, about a hundred miles north of the test site, a somber group of children and adults will see the flash of light and bitterly recall that all

114

through the spring of 1955 little Martin Bardoli, then seven years old, had waited excitedly on test days—along with six other children, all going to school at the ranch, and about a dozen adults—for the mushroom clouds to appear. Martin, a tow-headed kid everybody called "Butch," died last year of leukemia in a Reno hospital.

His mother, Martha Bardoli, says, "I think my Butch died because of the tests." And after the boy's death, one of the doctors who attended him stated that it "may have resulted from the atomic explosions in southern Nevada." At that time and now, the Atomic Energy Commission emphatically ruled out that possibility. Although the AEC has stated that leukemia can be induced only by much larger doses of radiation than Martin could have received, the fact is that the AEC does not know exactly how much radiation exposure "Butch" Bardoli received as a result of radioactive fallout from its weapon-testing programs.

Nearly thirty miles east of the Fallini ranch, in the middle of a desolate valley close to the Grant mountain range, is Nyala, Nevada. Nyala is really only the Gerald Sharp ranch, but years ago it was a sub-station post office and it is still listed on the map.

Minnie Sharp, her husband, and their grown sons live at the ranch and raise cattle. During many of the tests, Mrs. Sharp worked bare-headed in her garden, occasionally looking up at the clouds drifting north from the test site and nestling low along the mountains near the house. These days Mrs. Sharp is never without a bandanna or a hat, for she has lost every hair on her head and body. She thinks that the loss of her hair may be due to radiation fallout from the tests. The AEC denies this possibility, although again it can only estimate on the basis of incomplete data just how much radiation exposure there has been at the Sharp ranch.

Loss of hair was one of the reasons why Dewey A. Hortt, Elma Mackelprang, and Aaron Leavitt sued the United States government after the 1953 test series. They claimed that they had been repeatedly exposed to low-level doses of radiation fallout, resulting in illness. The AEC denied the claim and eventually their suit was dropped.

Mr. and Mrs. Dan Sheahan, fairly recent residents of Las Vegas, are not as indifferent to the tests as most other people of that city. Mrs. Sheahan believes she contracted cancer when she and her husband were operating the Groom mine, just outside the area of the Nevada test site. Again the AEC denies the possibility, although it admits that there has been heavier radiation exposure at the mine than at almost any other area outside the testing grounds.

Two hundred miles northeast of the test site, in Cedar City, Utah, some sheep ranchers must be reading about this year's Operation Plumbbob with a singular personal concern. They believe that the death of thousands of sheep grazing near the test site during Operation Upshot-Knothole, the 1953 series, was the result of radioactive fallout. In 1956 the AEC won a lawsuit brought by these ranchers. The Federal judge presiding over the case did find, however, that "there were no advance warnings given or other precautions taken to safeguard the herders or their sheep."

The 1,268 residents of Hurricane, Utah, were among the 16,200 people in Nevada and Utah exposed to radiation in 1953 from a detonation that, according to the U.S. Public Health Service, "added measurably to the total external exposure for the test series." Twenty miles west of Hurricane, the signs of the same kind of "exposure" can still be detected in radioactive moss growing high on the red hills overlooking St. George, Utah, whose 4,545 residents were once kept indoors two and a half hours after a detonation. The residents of St. George are probably not aware that they "were continuously exposed for sixteen days to atmospheric contamination" which during one twenty-four-hour period was 1,260 times greater than the provisional permissible concentrations established for radiation workers by the National Committee on Radiation Protection of the National Bureau of Standards.

It is only about ninety-five miles from the proving grounds to the now deserted Riverside Cabins off U.S. Highway 91. About fifteen people were living at the seven-cabin motel on the bank of the Virgin River early in the morning of April 25, 1953, when a shot was detonated from a tower on Yucca Flat. A few hours later a radioactive cloud silently deposited on the motel the heaviest doses of fallout ever recorded in the United States on an inhabited place outside the immediate test site. The fifteen people presumably do not know that they were exposed. At the time of exposure, the AEC was as silent as the cloud. No public statement of the incident was made until three months later, when the AEC issued its fourteenth semi-annual report, and even then the motel was not identified by name. No record of the names of the fifteen was kept by the AEC, and nothing is known about their present physical condition.

Citizens' Safety, National Defense

Meanwhile, amid increasing anxiety both in this country and abroad concerning the biological and genetic effects of radiation and in the face of ever more critical appraisals of weapons testing, the AEC continues to put forth its soothing assurances that both the pathologic and genetic harm from radiation fallout have been exaggerated by irresponsible, overly emotional, or politically biased individuals.

Early in 1957, Dr. Warren Weaver of the Rockefeller Foundation, chairman of the National Academy of Science's Committee on Genetic Effects of Atomic Radiation, concluded a discussion of weapons testing before a Senate subcommittee by stating, "I do not think it is fair to the people of the United States or the people of the world to give them the impression that there is no danger involved in this, for there is." But a month later an AEC official said, "When some books and articles continue to be written with a view of scaring the public and selling the material, it seems to be the right time for us to repeat the known facts in a sober and scientific look at the problem."

For some years, it was extremely difficult to get the "known facts" about radiation fallout near the test site from the AEC. (Martha Bardoli, for example, doesn't know exactly how much radiation her son "Butch" was exposed to. Neither does the AEC.) Some of the information the AEC does have on the general subject is buried in documents that are classified. Exact fallout figures and figures on radiation exposures of the civilian population in all the tests prior to 1955, even when known—an important proviso—are contained in reports that are still classified and not available to the public. From these classified documents, which the AEC says contain military information, some reports on radiation exposures, based on incomplete information, have been issued to the public. Sometimes even when military security was not involved, material affecting health and safety has either been classified or released only in a way designed to avoid what one AEC official has called "very bad psychological effect."

The job of balancing the demands of public health and weapons development has been something of a dilemma for the AEC ever since it was created. Because of the exigencies of world politics, its most important function has been the development of nuclear weapons. Yet at the same time, it is responsible for protecting the public from the dangers of radiation.

To assist in its primary function, the AEC was provided with its own security system, giving it the right to classify "all data concerning (1) design, manufacture, or utilization of atomic weapons; (2) the production of special nuclear material; or (3) the use of special nuclear material in the production of energy . . ." Convinced of the superior importance of its primary mission, the AEC has frequently used its security system to protect activities that have little to do with military security. The practice has been habit-forming.

Even though no danger to public health from the AEC's continental testing program can be established with any certainty, it is clear that some of the AEC's established patterns of behavior raise grave questions of public policy.

When Congress gave the AEC the right to build an impenetrable wall around its own activities, effectively cutting off those inside from giving out information, it also prevented those outside from getting information except at the discretion of those within.

The Whims of Fallout

The problem of possible danger to public health from the fallout of radioactive particles after the explosion of a nuclear device has existed since the very first test of an atomic weapon at Trinity Site near Alamagordo, New Mexico, back in 1945. Indeed, a program of monitoring the area away from the test site for radioactivity was made part of the plans for that first detonation.

The explosion of a nuclear weapon produces four major effects —blast, heat, immediate nuclear radiation, and residual radioactivity. The first three of these effects are almost simultaneous with the detonation, while the fourth is held in the cloud produced by the explosion. The size and path of the radioactive cloud, its height, and the amount and character of radioactivity within it are chiefly dependent upon the energy yield released by the weapon, its height above the ground at the time of explosion, and the weather conditions prevailing at the time of detonation. Any nuclear detonation immediately forms about sixty different radioactive substances representing some thirty-five elements. Most of these substances begin a decay process that may eventually produce about 170 isotopes with radioactive lives ranging from a tiny fraction of a second to many, many years.

The fallout problem results from some radioactive isotopes dropping to earth together with others that have mixed with bits of matter and in turn made them radioactive. This other matter may be fine particles already in the air, much larger dust particles sucked up from the ground if the explosion took place close to the earth, the physical material enclosing the device, or even the tower on which it was mounted.

The devices exploded at the Nevada Test Site have been of much less energy yield than those detonated in the Pacific, although they are still capable of great destruction and are highly radioactive. Until now the Nevada tests have been restricted to simple nuclear-fission devices of the A-bomb variety, while in the Pacific tests such "small" devices have been used to trigger the release of still larger quantities of heat and radiation.

Because the small Pacific islands near the test area are practically uninhabited, close-in fallout, which occurs within the first ten or twenty hours following an explosion, is not as great a problem there as it is in Nevada. But as far as the rest of the world is concerned, the intermediate fallout (which takes place during the first weeks after the explosion) and the delayed fallout (the slow dropping of tiny radioactive particles from the air over a period of years) are much greater from the high-yield thermonuclear tests in the Pacific than from the low-yield devices exploded in Nevada. Most of the problems of genetic and pathologic damage to human beings concern the Pacific tests, but the Nevada tests have also contributed to the world's radioactive burden.

Some Contradictions

Publicly at least, the AEC has adopted the position that there is as little danger from close-in fallout to the population around the Nevada test site as there is to the world population from the intermediate and delayed fallout as a result of the Pacific tests. And yet while it has been issuing reassuring public statements during the past five years, the AEC has been trying to reduce the amount of fallout in the Nevada tests. This has been done by developing better methods of predicting weapon yield, by more accurate weather predictions, by building higher towers, by surfacing the ground around the explosion area, and, in the forthcoming tests, by using balloons tethered two thousand feet in the air as well as towers for detonation platforms. The monitoring system to check exposures off the test site itself has also been expanded and improved for the forthcoming series.

But despite such past public statements from the AEC as its 1953 report that "the precautions taken to prevent hazard to the public from the continental weapons tests have proved to be adequate," there are indications that some of the test personnel themselves believe the precautions taken were, in fact, somewhat less than adequate.

During the discussion that led up to the AEC's establishment of a site for testing smaller weapons within the continental limits of the United States, serious consideration was given to the fall-out problem. Two significant fallout phenomena had been observed in the 1945 Trinity explosion—one well known, the other discussed very little. It is fairly well known that a number of cattle, grazing twenty-five miles from ground zero, the detonation point, received burns on their hides. Not so well known, however, is the fact that a radioactive "hot spot" was formed at a point also about twenty-five miles from ground zero. This "hot spot" was an area of high ground-level radioactivity completely surrounded by areas of much lower activity.

Since the AEC's primary mission was the rapid development of nuclear weapons, almost all its decisions—including the one about the establishment of a domestic test site—have been heavily weighted by that responsibility. Although most of the staff were finally convinced of the desirability of a domestic test site, many in the AEC were also aware of a grave responsibility to the civilian population.

Nevada Is Chosen

During 1949 and 1950 the pace of weapons development had accelerated and it had "become clear that the program would require more frequent tests than could be conducted feasibly in the Pacific." In the judgment of the AEC, "The rate of development of new and improved nuclear weapons depended on whether or not a continental site could be utilized." There was also a fear—never, of course, mentioned in public—that because of the Korean War either the scientists or the devices might be captured by Soviet or Chinese Communist forces. The question was raised, as Dr. Graves, the director of the Nevada tests, has said, "whether or not it might not be dangerous to actually take these things away out in the Pacific and the scientists that were involved."

After a survey of available locations, the Nevada site was finally selected. For the AEC the site had the advantage of being fairly close to Los Alamos and Albuquerque, both key points in the weapons-development program. "In addition," states the AEC report of January, 1953, "the location and relative isolation of the Nevada site provided safety factors in relation to blast and fallout, particularly because the prevailing winds blow from the test site for many miles across a relatively unpopulated region."

The decision to establish the continental test site was made late in 1950. "Careful review of all available research and test data relating to fallout indicated," the AEC has declared, "that under the controls planned, there was adequate assurance of public safety." (The AEC Chairman at the time was Gordon E. Dean, recently appointed after the resignation of the first Chairman, David E. Lilienthal. Lewis L. Strauss took office in June, 1953.)

The 1951 Tests

The first tests in Nevada were held in January and February of 1951. Five devices were detonated. All of them, according to Richard G. Elliott, director of the AEC Office of Information at Albuquerque, were "relatively high air bursts" with "very little ground fallout anywhere in the [Nevada test site] region." Minor radioactivity was detected, however, thousands of miles away in the snow at Rochester, New York, by the Eastman Kodak Company and by the University of Rochester Atomic Energy Project.

The monitoring program, designed to check on local fallout and air contamination away from the test site, was under the direction of the Los Alamos Scientific Laboratory. Those who actually did the work included, besides employees of the laboratory, other AEC employees, AEC contractor employees, and Air Force personnel. Almost complete secrecy enveloped the entire operation; there were only terse public announcements of detonations that had already been made. On January 27, 1951, for example, the AEC released this statement:

"One of the periodic tests announced by the Commission on January 11, 1951, was held early this morning.

"Full security restrictions of the Atomic Energy Act apply to the work at the site and the AEC section of the reservation will be closed indefinitely to all persons except those directly connected with the experimental programs. No reports yet received have indicated a hazard."

That final sentence, stated in a variety of ways, has been the constant theme of the AEC press announcements.

The security provisions were so rigid that not even the people living around the test site were given advance information about the detonations. The records of Dan Sheahan, who was living with his family at the Groom mine just outside the test site, indicate that they "were not told what day any of these bombs would be set off and no AEC men were here during any of the tests in this series. By late morning or midafternoon a man usually called in to check for radiation. The tests set off before daylight on February 2 shook our house violently, breaking open our front door and cracking windows in several buildings."

In the meantime, plans had been made for another test series in Nevada. Operation Buster was to be held in the fall of 1951. In the early summer of 1951 a new series, Jangle, was added to Buster. Jangle included a surface and an underground burst, both of which were liable to cause heavy fallout. Following the addition of Jangle to Buster, according to a Public Health Service report, "A 'Feasibility Committee,' appointed by AEC, held several meetings at which the possible hazards from off-site fallout were discussed thoroughly. With meager data from previous tests, it was difficult to predict the probable extent of such fallout."

A mathematical method of predicting fallout was developed, based largely on data from the pre-Hiroshima Trinity test of 1945. "The Feasibility Committee," the Public Health Service report goes on, "drew up certain criteria to be met by the Jangle Test." The committee "tentatively" set external radiation tolerance levels and "permissible" air concentration for personnel off the site. Planning for "possible hazards from off-site fallout" during the series was based, according to the AEC, "on the fact that the first shot would be very low yield on a tower, and the next four would be air bursts—none of these resulting in significant fallout in the region—and a surface and an underground shot (in November) which although of limited yields would result in heavy fallout close to the Test Site."

As in 1945, safety precautions were the responsibility of the

Los Alamos Laboratory. Monitoring was done by personnel from Los Alamos, from the military services, Civil Defense, the Public Health Service, and the Atomic Energy Commission.

For the five tests of Operation Buster, a maximum of six mobile teams was used to monitor radio-active fallout. According to the Public Health Service, "Measurable air-borne activity and ground contamination were found on all Buster shots but one."

On November 19, 1951, following a surface detonation, a radioactive fallout cloud moved north toward the area where "Butch" Bardoli, then four years old, was playing outside his father's ranch house. Not far from the Bardoli ranch, Mrs. Minnie Sharp worked bareheaded in her garden, while about thirty miles west the Fallinis worked and played at their ranch. Once again, during Buster-Jangle, the AEC issued reassuring reports.

During this same series the Sheahans, then living at and working the Groom mine, just outside the test site, had some of their first contacts—friendly ones then—with the AEC. Bitter lawsuits, accusations, and denials about Mrs. Sheahan's cancer and the loss of their mine because of heavy radioactivity were to follow, but during those exciting early days the Sheahans gladly opened their home to the people on the test staff. "We don't know whether we have become honorary members of the Sheahan family or whether the Sheahans are honorary members of the AEC," one of the AEC staff wrote in Dan Sheahan's diary on a day when six members of the test group came to observe a blast from the mine site. Despite the fact that the mine was closed down a number of times at the AEC's suggestion because of radioactivity, the AEC denies that test shots have interfered with the peaceful use and equipment and operation of the premises.

The 1952 Tests

After Buster-Jangle, another series of tests, Tumbler-Snapper, took place in the spring of 1952, even "before all of the Buster-Jangle data could be analyzed" according to the Public Health Service.

The plans for Tumbler-Snapper included a number of tower shots that "created considerable concern about fallout" (a PHS report). It turned out that there was fallout—from four detonations this time—in the area of the Bardoli and Sharp ranches, and once again it was publicly reported only in minimal detail.

It is known that the Groom mine was again subjected to sufficiently heavy fallout to call for evacuation of the premises. On May 5, 1952, Mr. Sheahan found a note on his front door saying, "A dusty shot will be made early the morning of May 6. It is strongly urged that Groom be evacuated before 6:00 A.M., 5/6. Return to Groom will be possible by noon unless otherwise informed. There will be one man at the sampling station with radio." The exact fallout data for this series, as for the earlier ones, are contained in documents still classified.

During Tumbler-Snapper it was, however, observed, according to the Public Health Service, that "on at least three occasions significant activity, predominantly airborne in nature, could be found at points far removed from the fallout pattern. This occurred at a time when it was known that the main cloud had advanced well beyond the 200 mile line." Two of these three unforeseen instances took place in California, where "significant activity" was found in Downey, an industrial suburb of Los Angeles, and in a lettuce field near Fresno. The incidents were not made public by the AEC but were reported by a West Coast NBC news program, "Top Story."

In late May of 1952, the Sheahans report that fallout once again hit their camp, this time containing "a great many bead-like particles, some over a sixteenth inch in diameter," many of which were "iron metal and were assumed by several AEC men to be part of the tower upon which the bomb was placed."

Nation-wide fallout data "gave no indication," according to a PHS report, "that the 'tolerance levels' set previously by the Jangle Feasibility Committee were exceeded. However, in general, air and ground levels of radiation were higher than for previous tests. Some time after the operation, about 100 cattle were reported to show visible skin changes from beta radiation. These reports were confirmed on investigation."

The 1953 Tests

A year later, in the spring of 1953, there was significant activity in the Dixie Valley, 125 miles east of the test site. The valley got

its name when its Mormon settlers came to the southern Utah
desert country in the middle of the nineteenth century and started
to grow cotton. The cotton crop has long since been replaced by
pomegranates, figs, dates, almonds, walnuts, and grapes, but the
old name still remains. The Dixie country is a green and lush
oasis surrounded by the desert from which it was wrested by the
hard-working followers of Brigham Young.

The Dixie country lies due east of the Nevada Test Site and
was subjected to fallout during Operation Upshot-Knothole, the
series conducted in the spring of 1953. Eleven nuclear shots were
detonated during Upshot-Knothole, with seven being fired from
towers and one from a 280-mm. cannon. Following three of the
tower shots there was "measurable" fallout in the Dixie area,
and after the ninth detonation in the series the fallout was serious enough to cause the AEC to warn the residents of St. George
to remain indoors for two and a half hours. This was the same
shot that caused the 16-day air contamination mentioned earlier.

For some reason the AEC did not give similar warnings to the
residents of all the communities in the area, even though the
fallout in some of them was heavier than that in St. George.
Some but not all of the schools in the affected region were
warned to keep their pupils indoors during the fallout period
after this ninth detonation. There is little doubt that one reason
for the AEC's failure to warn all the people and schools in the
affected region was limited manpower. Communication facilities
for monitoring were still under the direction of the military
during Upshot, but some changes were made in the operations—
changes that reflected, according to the AEC, "growing awareness
of the desirability of maintaining closer contact with people in
all off-site communities. . . ." There was also a shift to the use
of more civilian monitors, "in particular contrast to Tumbler-
Snapper where the bulk of monitoring personnel were military."

It was during these 1953 tests that the Public Health Service,
for the first time, took part in the off-site safety operations. Since
then this organization has played an increasingly important role,
although it is still subordinate to the AEC staff. In 1953, PHS
personnel were little more than observers of the results, while in

1955 the entire matter of off-site safety was assigned to them. Indeed, the fact that the Public Health Service was given a greater part in the making of decisions during the 1955 tests may very well have been a consequence of the procedures followed in the 1953 tests. For there is little doubt that the 1953 series created more unsolved problems of public health than any tests before or since.

Seven stockmen who sued the government for more than $222,-000 damages said that radioactive fallout from Upshot-Knothole detonations in 1953 was responsible for the illness and death of a number of sheep. Immediately after the second shot of the series, Dr. Lyle B. Borst, a nuclear physicist then at the University of Utah in Salt Lake City, warned that Utahans might have received harmful doses of radiation from it. Dr. Borst, former chairman of the Department of Reactor Science and Engineering at Brookhaven National Laboratory, and presently chairman of the Department of Physics, New York University, attacked the AEC for covering up information. He said that when he was at Brookhaven, "any building as contaminated by radiation as Salt Lake City was after one explosion would have been evacuated immediately."

Fallout from Upshot-Knothole was the basis of the lawsuit filed by Dewey A. Hortt, Elma Mackelprang, and Aaron Leavitt, who claimed that their illnesses and loss of hair had been caused by radioactive fallout. It is an established fact that fallout from Upshot-Knothole resulted in burns to horses grazing outside the test site; the government accepted responsibility and paid indemnity, although it refused to admit responsibility for injuries to cattle. The residents of the Riverside Cabins got their radiation during Upshot-Knothole; St. George and Hurricane got their doses during Upshot-Knothole; and it was during this series of tests that many vehicles on the highway, including a Greyhound bus, had to be decontaminated.

Many aspects of the AEC's behavior, private and public, during and following the Upshot-Knothole series are certainly open to criticism. In the period after the series was completed, contamination of water holes around the test site was the subject of much concern to the stockmen in the area whose cattle and sheep grazed on the range. Yet in October, 1953, public relations was apparently at least as important as public health to the AEC official who queried the Commission's Division of Biology and Medicine concerning an AEC report on radioactivity levels in the water holes: "The livestock owners in this area have been told that the water in this area is safe for stock; however, in view of the results of these recent analyses, I would appreciate your opinion as to the significance of the indicated radioactivity and what is considered a permissible level in water for livestock. I would like to point out that if in your opinion the above indicated levels warrant closing the waterholes, the livestock picture would become rather complicated as

"(1) We have already indicated that radiation is not the cause of deaths, and if it were determined that these levels are hazardous to stock, it would probably be impossible to convince the owners that we are not at fault, and

"(2) To deny the owners the use of waterholes would bring about new problems to both the owners and the government."

The water holes were not closed. The manner in which the problem of the Papoose Lake water hole was handled within the AEC is illuminating. Early in June, 1953, two brothers, Dell and Cornell Stewart, friends and neighbors of the Sheahans, claimed that some horses and cattle that had ranged near the Papoose Lake water hole had been badly affected by radioactive fallout. Sixteen horses, said the Stewarts, had been burned and six cattle had dropped dead after leaving the water hole. The government indemnified the Stewarts for the horses but not for the cattle. Apparently the practice is to admit responsibility only for damage that can be seen—such as beta burns—and to deny everything else.

After the incident was reported to the AEC, a sample was taken from the water hole. The radioactive content was examined and a report made to the Las Vegas office of the AEC stating that the results were only for "the time of counting with no extrapolation attempted, since the exact shot from which the activity originated is not known, and, further, it may be a combination of shots making the extrapolation very complex, if not impossible." Fallout from the "combination of shots" might have resulted from any of five detonations, all of which were tower shots that brought fallout which "added measurably to the total external exposure for the area."

On June 11 the AEC official in Los Alamos who made the original report wrote to Las Vegas that the samples "do not indicate sufficient activity to be the cause of the effects noted in the afflicted animals." And although the first report said extrapolation was "very complex, if not impossible," the new report said that "Although data has not been obtained at this time to identify the origin of the material, it is highly improbable that by any reasonable extrapolation factor could this concentration have been serious." A day later, in spite of this letter from Los Alamos, the Las Vegas office reported that neither of the two Los Alamos officials "would state whether level is dangerous to cattle or horses as they cannot determine the length of contamination. Collison [one of the officials] stated it to be dangerous on permanent basis but not dangerous for short periods. The cows and horses could have licked metallic particles of mud off salt blocks."

It is clear from its own reports that the AEC did not know much at the time about the significance of the radioactive level of the water, and that there was at least some possibility that the cattle could have been adversely affected.

May Sheep Safely Graze?

The AEC's water-hole investigation was carried on simultaneously with its inquiry into the sheep losses, about which the Commission seems to have decided in advance what the results of its study would be. In the lawsuit that followed the investigation, a U.S. district judge decided that radiation was not responsible for the damage. What is still at issue is not the conflicting scientific evidence concerning sheep deaths but the conduct of the AEC.

Following a report of the death of a number of sheep, in June, 1953, the AEC had requested two veterinarians, Major Robert Veenstra of the San Francisco Naval Radiological Laboratory and Dr. R. E. Thompsett of Los Alamos, to join an investigating party of other veterinarians, Public Health Service officials, AEC staff members, and the spokesman for the sheep owners. Both

Thompsett and Veenstra had had some experience with the effects of radiation upon animals.

Veenstra's report to the AEC on his investigation stated that in his opinion "radiation was at least a contributing factor to the loss of these animals." Thompsett's original report was similar, with a strong statement that in his opinion the AEC had contributed to great losses. He said, "There is no doubt as to the origins of the lesions on the sheep . . . I believe that the sheep came in contact with radioactive dust from plants in the area."

The AEC was apparently convinced long before the investigation was completed that radiation was not responsible for the losses. A few weeks after the investigation was started, the AEC reported, in July, 1953, that "malnutrition was a major factor in the deaths" of the sheep.

For the remainder of the year, intensive studies of the sheep deaths were made by the AEC, the Public Health Service, the Utah State Health Department, and a number of other interested agencies. Experiments were conducted by the AEC on other sheep at Los Alamos, and discussions were carried on with the stockmen, who were convinced that the deaths were the direct result of radiation. Inside the AEC, opinion remained divided among the scientists and veterinarians. In October, 1953, Thompsett, back at Los Alamos, where sheep experiments were being conducted, informed the AEC in Las Vegas that "they had produced burns on test sheep comparable to those showing on Cedar City sheep in May and June, 1953." According to Thompsett, the AEC was "in trouble."

By January, 1954, the AEC's investigation was completed, to its own satisfaction at least, and apparently it was convinced that its statement of July, 1953, had been proved correct. This conviction was not shared by the Utah State Department of Health, which had a number of serious objections to the AEC procedures and report. One objection, for example, was that "there has not been sufficient supported evidence presented that these animals could not have been exposed to higher radiation as the monitoring teams certainly did not cover the complete fallout area. What coverage was done was along areas of easy access and not in the more rugged areas where the sheep were grazing and where there were not adequate roads and easy access was not available." Furthermore, the Utah Health Department was not convinced that the Los Alamos experiments on sheep conclusively proved that radiation had not been responsible for the deaths of the Cedar City sheep, as had been decided after an AEC meeting at which the Thompsett report was discussed. As a result, the Utah Health Department refused to accept responsibility for the report when it was released.

Self-Investigation

Two years later, Dan S. Bushnell, the attorney for the sheepmen who had sued the government, discussed with the court the integrity of the AEC scientists who had investigated the sheep deaths. He said, "Initially they placed great emphasis on the fact that there could not have been, in their calculation, any significant amount of radiation. So starting with that hypothesis, they jumped to the next point, that the sheep could not have been damaged by radioactivity, and they then proceeded to prove or substantiate that position.

"I think they were influenced to some extent by this: If they found to the contrary, they were, in essence, condemning themselves. This was an investigation by the department which did the act. It was not an impartial investigation. There's been, in my opinion, a lot of corroboration to the fact that it was not an objective and far-reaching investigation. My opinion is that a lot of these fellows jumped to their conclusions, and then proceeded to substantiate it. And they were the men in control."

Keep Smiling

During and following Upshot, it became clear that some very important safety procedures needed improvement, although there was little or no public discussion of these problems. Whatever private doubts there may have been inside the AEC concerning these safety techniques, only optimistic and reassuring reports were presented to the public.

In its report of January, 1953, entitled "Assuring Public Safety in Continental Weapons Tests," the AEC flatly stated that "cattlemen using adjoining ranges are notified a few hours before a test." Yet in March, 1956, Dr. Alvin Graves, AEC test director in Nevada, admitted that the test organization had not known "where any particular herd of sheep was on any given date when a test was being set up," had made no attempt to locate "every herd of sheep," did not know "how many herds of sheep would be involved in an area within 100 miles from the point of detonation," had not instructed the radiological safety officer "to determine the location of these sheep herds prior to the time that detonations were to be set off," did not know how much radiation the sheep were "subjected to in any particular test," did not know "the specific or precise location of sheepherders in that area," and therefore could not warn them.

But this lack of knowledge did not disturb the test organization very much since they also felt, according to Dr. Graves, that there were no sheep or men "in a region where they would get enough radiation to injure them." In response to a question on this last point Dr. Graves said, "We may have been wrong in that." But no indication of such doubt had come through in the AEC's report of July, 1953, that none of the "observed fallout levels" was "high enough to create a human health hazard."

The AEC now admits that between 1950 and 1955 "there were occasions when shots were fired under a swinging weather pattern." But in February, 1955, the AEC stated that "All tests are planned for times when forecast weather conditions minimize the possibility of fallout hazard." The Commission made no mention in its report of the fact that during Operation Upshot-Knothole in 1953, the heavy fallout on St. George, Utah, came after a final prediction was made "for no concentrated fallout on any community."

The weather pattern must have been "swinging" during and after that detonation because the AEC now reports that "instead of a broad pattern of light fallout, the concentrated winds following the shot resulted in a very long and narrow fallout pattern which extended just north of St. George, with higher fallout at much greater distances." The fact is that before 1955 the AEC's fallout predictions were "all dependent upon wind variations; upon assumptions that winds outside the test site are the same as those at the site and that there will be no change in the winds after the time of detonation." If the people in the Dixie Valley suffer any ill effects from radiation in the years to come, it will be largely because these assumptions went wrong.

The monitoring of off-site fallout was no less in need of improvement than the weather forecasting, if the 1953 procedures are any criteria. Even the routine monitoring runs to check fallout dosages on roads and populated places proved to be inadequate. Specific readings given for many places affected by fallout during the 1953 series were actually only estimates, since they were merely extrapolations of the readings obtained along the roads and in the fixed monitoring stations; some cross-checking was provided by data obtained in aircraft. According to the Public Health Service, "The terrain, limited manpower and limited facilities made more detailed investigations impractical."

Thus, even though it is known that there was some fallout north of the test site after at least two shots, the AEC does not know the exact dosages accumulated by "Butch" Bardoli, his sisters and parents, the people at the Fallini ranch, the Sharps, and others in that area. The monitoring maps for the series indicate that no runs were made by the mobile teams on the road near the ranches in that area.

The Ninth Shot

The AEC's basic dilemma was clearly illustrated during the fallout on St. George and other communities after the ninth shot of the 1953 series. The AEC had been repeating its assurances that every precaution against accidents had been taken at the Nevada test site when suddenly, on the morning of May 19, there was an unexpected change in weather conditions that caused the fallout cloud to move over well-traveled state highways and inhabited communities. With only a limited number of mobile monitoring teams available, it was necessary to set up roadblocks on the highways an hour and a quarter after the shot in order to examine all vehicles and wash them if it was required.

The cloud moved over the towns of Mesquite and Bunkerville, Utah, both of which had gotten a dose of radiation only three weeks earlier at the same time as the motel. Two and a half hours after the shot, the people in these two towns were told to stay indoors for the next forty-five minutes. The AEC does not state in its reports whether the people living on isolated ranches and farms in the path of the cloud were also warned. The school principals in the two towns were called and advised to keep the children indoors.

The cloud continued eastward to St. George. Fallout on the five thousand inhabitants there began at 8:45 A.M., and the monitors reported it to the control point of the test site. At 9:25 A.M. the control point instructed the monitors to advise the people to stay indoors. The sheriff, the Cedar City radio station, and the school principals joined the monitors in advising the public of the situation, and by 9:40 A.M. most of the people were indoors. At noon they were released, ten minutes after various officials from the test site had arrived to survey the situation.

But what of Hurricane, twenty miles east, with its thirteen hundred people? The school principal there recalls being phoned and told to keep the children indoors during recess. The AEC makes no mention of warning the residents of Hurricane, even though the fallout there was greater than it was in St. George.

And what of Gunlock, Utah, thirty-five miles north of St. George, where about one hundred people live in a hollow surrounded by lava hills? The schoolteacher there has no recollection of ever being told to keep indoors the dozen children who attend the one-room schoolhouse. Neither she nor the owner of the general store recalls ever seeing any monitors in or around Gunlock during the Upshot-Knothole tests of 1953.

"I've become a little nervous about the fallout because of all the talk," says the schoolteacher. Perhaps fear of making schoolteachers nervous was one of the reasons why the AEC's 11:30 A.M. press release on the day of the fallout did not point out that people in Mesquite and Bunkerville had been told to stay indoors. In that press release Hurricane didn't exist at all. The entire matter is disposed of in a few sentences in the AEC's semi-annual report of July, 1953: "Just after the 9th detonation, a shifting of winds indicated that the atomic cloud would pass over St. George, Utah. While no hazard to health was anticipated, the residents of St. George were requested to remain indoors from about 9:30 to 11:00 A.M. during the time of the actual fallout."

The fact that hundreds of motor vehicles were stopped at a number of places on the highways after shots 7 and 9 and the fact that it was found necessary to decontaminate more than a hundred of them are discussed in the same report in an equally brief and perfunctory manner: "Following two separate detonations, monitoring teams reported fallout material on some portions of U.S. highways 91 and 93, near Glendale, Nev. Vehicles traveling along these highways were monitored, and were washed at AEC expense if their interiors averaged 20 milliroentgens (0.02 roentgens) per hour or higher." Nothing is said in the report of the fact that in St. George the air contamination at one time was 1,260 times more than the provisional permissible concentration established for radiation workers and that high degrees of contamination continued for sixteen days after the shots.

The AEC seems to have been shifting from one foot to the other, torn between its belief that weapons testing is one aspect of the rich possibilities of the atomic age and its commitment to the protection of public health. Of course most of the AEC staff firmly believe that there is little danger from the kind of weapons testing carried out in Nevada. But a man's conviction that the tests are safe might help to rationalize his belief that they are valuable, or his conviction that they are valuable might help to rationalize his belief that they are safe.

A combination of these subtle forces was probably operating on the seven AEC scientists and administrators who attended a meeting at Los Alamos, New Mexico, in October, 1953, after Operation Upshot-Knothole, to discuss the problem of radioactive contamination in the Papoose Lake water hole near the test site. This is the water hole that was involved in the loss of livestock alleged by the Nevada ranchers. Liquid and dirt samples had been drawn from the water hole and tests run for radioactivity. The meeting discussed the fact that the tests showed radioactivity to be "two to three and one-half times the suggested permissible limit" established previously. It was pointed out to the group that "in view of the sensitive conditions which exist with respect to livestock and fallout in this area," the results of the tests could not be ignored "without providing convincing argument that the activity is not hazardous." The group then raised the question that there was "considerable doubt as to the significance of these results" and that "the permissible limit" cited was "only one of the several limits by various authorities." In other words, if there are doubts about the permissible limit, take the one that suits you. Since the water holes were not closed, it can be safely presumed that in effect that's what the AEC did.

Another matter discussed at the same meeting was a proposed bulletin of the Atomic Energy Commission's Advisory Committee to prescribe the radioactive level that would be safe for the general public. Would it be advisable to recommend that the full safety level be allowed for the people of Nevada while the rest of the nation would get only one-tenth of that amount? During the discussion at the meeting it was "recognized that this would have a very bad psychological effect on the people of Nevada."

One of those present therefore suggested "that, in view of the problems that such an issuance would create, especially among the people of Nevada, a better approach would be to state the permissible level and then state that only 1/10th of this value should be allowed in areas not subjected to controlled conditions and that the Nevada tests are conducted under controlled conditions."

Another AEC official told the meeting that "the lab would take exception to any [bulletin] that would create a bad psychological effect with respect to our Nevada operations."

The 1955 Tests

The problem of possible "bad psychological effect" also influenced the AEC's attitude in 1953 toward the use of film badges on the civilian population to measure radiation dosage. Such badges have been required for all AEC employees exposed to any amount of radiation for years, and a permanent record is kept of each employee's total exposure. Up to and including the 1953 tests the fallout monitors wore such badges. But when it was suggested that such badges be placed extensively on civilians and in public places exposed to fallout during the 1953 tests, the suggestion was vetoed within the AEC, partly because of administrative difficulties but partly also because of fear that the placing of such badges would create "psychological" problems among the population.

But during Operation Teapot, the 1955 test series, the Public Health Service, which by this time had much more responsibility in the test organization, placed thousands of such badges upon people and sites throughout the Nevada-Utah area. It was these badges that for the first time provided the AEC with fairly complete information on civilian dosage. The more extensive monitoring force used during Teapot was composed almost entirely of regular or reserve Public Health Service personnel given special training for their assignment. Final authority for making public-health decisions, however, was still in the hands of the AEC test organization. Under Public Health Service direction, plans were made during Teapot for regular and extensive milk and water sampling, which had hitherto been done only on a sporadic basis. Before the 1955 test series began, Public Health Service personnel visited communities throughout the area to explain the forthcoming tests, "to facilitate good public relations," and to lift some of the uneasy secrecy that had surrounded the earlier tests.

Just before the 1955 series many communities were visited by representatives of the test organization who explained the value of continental nuclear tests and outlined the precautions taken for public safety. This whole program, involving direct contact between the monitors and the communities to which they were assigned, was regarded as good practical public relations, according to the official report on the 1955 tests. This, incidentally, was the first unclassified description of off-site safety activities issued for a test series. After describing the program, the report concluded that "while it may not have altered completely basic public opinion regarding the tests, it at least made the explanations of zone personnel more acceptable."

'How Were We to Know'

There were exceptions, of course, to the cordial welcome accorded the AEC. "It must be recognized," states the report, "that although relations throughout the off-site area were generally good, there are some specific areas of difficulty. An example of this is the attitude of the newspaper edition in Tonopah [Nevada] who contrary to editorial opinion in general, has maintained a highly critical attitude towards test activities." The community referred to is northwest of the test site, and the nearest town of any size to the Bardoli, Fallini, and Sharp ranches. The editor is Robert A. Crandall, and his paper is the weekly *Times-Bonanza.*

One of the first occasions on which Crandall was "critical" of the AEC occurred in March, 1955, when he wrote an editorial about the AEC's alleged failure to keep Tonopah "posted on local conditions following atomic detonations." Crandall was specifically concerned about the fallout after Turk, the fourth shot of the 1955 series. The first three shots of the series had resulted in comparatively little fallout on inhabited places, most of it going east and southeast of the test site into isolated sections. The fallout clouds had followed fairly closely their predicted paths. But Turk, the fourth shot, was quite different. First, the test description states that a comparison of the prediction and the actual weather "indicates an extreme overprediction. This came about as a result of a frontal system change which occurred near shot time. This frontal change resulted in a drastic reduction in wind speeds and a rapid shifting of wind directions." The fallout prediction map shows the radioactive cloud moving south and west of the test site. Instead of going south, the clouds moved east, northeast, north, northwest, and west—in every direction except south!

Crandall wrote in his paper at the time that "As the cloud crept slowly northward, anxious AEC monitoring teams followed its progress. They now admit the cloud wasn't supposed to be there but a last-minute switch in wind direction sent it billowing and weaving across parts of Nye and Esmeralda counties."

After describing the movement of the cloud over the Tonopah

area and toward Warm Springs, Crandall detailed his unsuccess-
ful attempts to contact either AEC monitors or public-relations
men for information. "We did not believe the fallout was
hazardous but in the absence of any reliable reassurance how
were we or anyone else to know?"

In the same article Crandall told about a state game warden
who came to the newspaper office in Tonopah to report that
"the mud on his pickup ran the Geiger counter off Scale II—and
the region around Warm Springs, from which he had just come,
was so hot you could hardly use a Geiger." An AEC monitor
who happened to be passing through town assured the game
warden that the reading was not considered dangerous. Most
Geiger counters cannot be used to judge the amount of radiation to which a person is exposed.

But over at the Fallini ranch, nobody was getting any reassurance from the AEC. Seven children were attending the
ranch school that term. It was "Butch" Bardoli's first year there,
and he lived with his two sisters and his mother at the ranch
during the week. After school was over on Friday afternoons, the
four Bardolis drove thirty miles east and spent the weekend at
their own home with Mr. Bardoli.

Throughout the whole test series in 1955, all three of the
Bardoli kids, two Fallini children, and two children of the
Wheeler family, who came over every day from Warm Springs
eleven miles away to attend school, went outdoors during school
recess and watched the radioactive clouds. So, too, did their
teacher, Joanne Davis. Mrs. Fallini and Mrs. Bardoli were working outdoors in the yard much of the time, and Mr. Fallini was
usually off at the back of the ranch. Occasionally Mrs. Fallini
would take a color picture of a cloud as it drifted lazily overhead.

It was after the passage of one such cloud that all the adults at
the ranch recall a peculiar taste in their throats—"an acid-like
taste"—for which the AEC has no explanation and claims never
to have heard described before. It was also after the passage of
one cloud, perhaps the same one that worried Crandall and the
game warden, that Joe Fallini took his Geiger counter into the
schoolroom and checked the radioactivity there. Startled at the

ominously rapid clicking of the counter—the reading was so high that it registered more than the meter could count—Fallini drove to Tonopah the next day and discussed the incident with a number of people. As he described how he took the reading inside the schoolroom, an AEC monitor, who had just joined the group, stopped him with a rather surprising question: "What schoolroom are you talking about?" It turns out that the existence of the Twin Springs school had not been known to AEC officials at the test site.

The film-badge records for the school corroborate Fallini's story. While film badges were placed on every school in the area either before or just after the first shot in the test series, the school at the Fallini ranch did not get a badge until March 30, after nine shots had already been detonated. But the AEC maintains that there was a badge half a mile from the school, placed there four days after the test series began, that showed a low total dosage for the series. The AEC claims that the amount of radioactive contamination could have had no effect on the children.

Information Is Hard to Get

Like most editors, Robert Crandall gets most of his news about the AEC from that agency's Information Services Division. Crandall feels strongly that the AEC has tried to subject him to pressure.

"Every time we've had an adverse comment in the paper," he says, "or what might be interpreted as adverse by the AEC, I've had a couple of boys—or three or four—come in to see me. They come into the office and their tactic has always been along these lines—'Well, you don't believe that the AEC for a moment thinks that there is any possible harm in the tests or that any civilian could possibly be injured in any way?' Then they go on to talk about all the precautions they take. I recall one time when one of the AEC men said, 'Suppose there was some woman living around here who had a weak heart and you were to run a story to the effect that this radiation fallout was harmful. And suppose that she had a daughter or small child that was out there. Do you realize that this woman might suffer a heart attack because of the fact that you were spreading alarming stories?'

"At other times," says Crandall, "they say something like this, 'Well, of course the Communists would like us to stop the tests, too.' "

During October, 1956, Crandall ran an article quoting Dr. Linus Pauling, of the California Institute of Technology, on the aging effects of exposure to radiation. Under the headline LOCAL CITIZENS "GIVE UP" 1000 YEARS, the story quoted Dr. Pauling as saying that "the life expectancy of 'some Nevada residents' may have been shortened three months by radiation from atomic tests in this state." The article then went on to discuss the National Academy of Sciences report on the effects of radiation and quoted Dr. Pauling to the effect that radioactivity can "weaken the body so that it is susceptible to various diseases. It can actually cause such diseases as leukemia, which is directly traceable to radiation, either cosmic, background or fallout." The same issue of the paper carried a story on the death of Martin Bardoli from leukemia.

The AEC's reaction was immediate. Crandall received a long letter from Richard G. Elliott. "As you know," Elliott wrote, overlooking a good deal of past history, "we have tried consistently since January, 1951, to keep you and the people of the general Tonopah area advised of the facts concerning our operations at Nevada test site. This has been particularly true with regard to radiation fallout.

"Your article October 26, 'Local Citizens "Give Up" 1000 Years,' presented a statement as to radiation fallout experienced in Nye and Esmeralda counties which is inaccurate. We feel that it should be corrected and that you will want to correct it."

Crandall did not print all of the two-page statement that accompanied this letter but did quote from sections of it, writing that "statements attributed to Dr. Linus Pauling of the California Institute of Technology regarding possible harmful effects locally from radioactive fallouts have been challenged by an AEC spokesman." The AEC's statement disputing Pauling cites the report of the National Academy of Sciences to the effect that "doses [of radiation] up to about 100 roentgens, when spread

over years, have not been shown to shorten human life . . . if
very large numbers of people were exposed to a gradually accumulated dose of 100 roentgens or even less, their life expectancy might well be lowered by a minor, but statistically observ-
able, amount."

The three dots at the end of the first sentence indicated, of
course, that the AEC official had deleted something from the
original quotation. The deletion was of one sentence—"On the
other hand, we cannot yet say that there is a minimum amount
below which the effect does not take place."

Extrapolation and Hot Spots

Elliott's long letter to Crandall chided the editor for making
statements that "are entirely inaccurate and contrary to official
fallout reports." Some of these "official fallout reports" were
included in the letter, including one for Nyala, where the Sharp
ranch is located.

There is at least a possibility that this "official" report is as
"inaccurate" as the AEC claims Crandall's article to have been.
Until the 1955 tests the AEC had no accurate knowledge of fallout doses at the Sharp ranch because prior to 1955 it seems to
have been monitored only once, and, more likely, never at all.
Even in the 1955 tests, the film badge that was used to estimate
the dosage at Nyala was placed at the ranch weeks after the tests
had already begun and fallout clouds had passed over the area.
The "official fallout" report for Nyala is, in fact, no more than
an educated guess.

Until the spring of 1957 the public-information policy of the
AEC was to call such educated guesses "official fallout reports,"
without indicating that some of the dosages listed were based
only on "extrapolations." It was not until March, 1957, when a
booklet called "Atomic Tests in Nevada" was distributed to the
residents of the area, that the AEC finally admitted that some of
the doses it listed for the Nevada-Utah-Arizona communities
were "estimates of the effective biological doses which might have
been experienced."

The booklet lists cumulative fallout dosages for 118 communities, but no mention is made of the fact that at least twenty-

three of the 118 were either never monitored or were monitored only once through all the tests up to 1953. The pamphlet still does not mention unexpected "hot spots" and the possible danger from them.

'Response to Inquiries'

It is characteristic of the AEC's public-information policy to give out a good deal of important information only in response to inquiries. Following the publication of the AEC's fourteenth semi-annual report in July, 1953, an AEC public-information director informed the Las Vegas AEC office that "Under fallout section of 14th report reference is made to tourist camp near Bunkerville. Upon inquiry you may confirm that this is Riverside Cabins."

Over a period of years there has been some relaxation of the regulations on the dissemination of public information. Gradually, under pressures from the outside and from within, the terse public announcements of the first weapons tests have been replaced by more detailed stories in later series. The New York *Times* commented in 1955 on this change by saying that "this year, for the first time, the public is getting virtually the full publishable story from Atomic Energy Commission officials about the Nevada atomic tests." The *Times* also pointed out that four years ago "the Commission's policy was 'tell nothing.'"

But even with this gradual relaxation of public-information standards, the AEC has continued to retain control of much data that seems to be unrelated to the need for security. Take, for example, the reports made to the AEC in 1953 by the two veterinarians concerning the deaths of the sheep, allegedly brought about as a result of fallout. Early in the investigation, the Utah State Health Commissioner wrote the AEC for the reports of Drs. Veenstra and Thompsett. In reply, the Commissioner was informed by the AEC that the reports had not yet been "received or reviewed by our classification board. Consequently, we cannot tell you at this time when you may expect to receive the information or how it may be used."

Thus, even with the best will in the world, the AEC officials were not free to release, even to a state Commissioner of Health, reports dealing with possible fallout effects on sheep in Utah.

The classification status of Veenstra's report came into the picture again at a meeting the AEC held with the aggrieved stockmen on January 13, 1954, in Cedar City. Members of the AEC staff explained to the stockmen that their investigation had absolved the AEC from responsibility for the sheep deaths. During the meeting one of the stockmen, Douglas Clark, asked for copies of the dissenting reports made by Veenstra and others. He was told that these reports were classified "for military reasons."

When questioned about this matter recently, an AEC official in Washington stated that the Thompsett and Veenstra reports were not given out to the stockmen because they were "internal documents of the AEC," and because Thompsett's report had been lost in the files. In addition, he pointed out that the AEC knew in advance that the reports were incorrect and therefore there was no reason to release them.

It was not until 1955, when the stockmen sued the government, that they were finally able to obtain the Veenstra and Thompsett reports.

Because of the supreme military and strategic importance of all atomic matters, the Atomic Energy Act of 1946 provided that all information—all of it, every document, every letter, every report, and every scrap of paper dealing with atomic energy—was born "classified" and remained in that state of grace until it was declassified. There was thus created a huge government monopoly over atomic-energy information, based on the accumulation of vast amounts of "Restricted Data" which the AEC disseminated in accordance with strict security provisions.

Scientists and Politicians

When the AEC was created in 1946 and given complete authority to control the development of atomic weapons and energy behind a wall of secrecy, Congress established the Joint Committee on Atomic Energy to supervise the Commission's activities. The Committee, composed of eighteen members divided equally between the House and Senate, has described its function as that of a "watchdog" over the AEC, to exercise "the public scrutiny which ordinarily follows government operations."

But the Joint Committee itself has had to operate under the same conditions of secrecy as those it must try to penetrate. As overseer of the AEC, the Joint Committee has pointed out that its findings "have had to be accepted by the rest of the Congress and by the public because the Commission has of necessity had to operate behind very strict security regulations." Further, the Committee has said that it has "had to examine the operations of the Commission to see whether or not such operations came within the law since there is no way that the Commission's operations can be reviewed by a court."

Congress is often unable to "learn the merits" of a bill—either because it lacks the necessary scientific training or because of the secrecy imposed on AEC operations. Since Congressmen cannot become scientists, scientists can scarcely avoid assuming political responsibility. The result is that the AEC gains too much power in both science and politics.

As the employer of thousands of scientists, either directly or through contracts to universities and research institutions, the AEC must perhaps inevitably impose a certain amount of governmental conformity within the scientific community. If a scientist opposes an AEC policy, he runs a risk, as J. Robert Oppenheimer did, of having his motivations questioned: He must either rationalize his scientific activity in political terms or else suffer the penalty of becoming an outsider in his own community.

When Dr. Thompsett wrote his original report on the sheep deaths in Utah, he stated that radiation was undoubtedly one of the factors causing the death of the sheep, and added that he thought the "AEC had contributed to great losses." After a lawsuit was filed against the government by the sheepmen, he wrote a letter to the assistant general counsel for the AEC in which he changed his opinion. When asked if the man to whom he had written the letter was a personal friend, Thompsett replied, "I would say he is a very good friend, yes." He could not recall whether he had been "directed" by his "very good friend," the AEC counsel, to "address this communication to him."

It must often be a great strain on an AEC scientist to play simultaneously the two roles imposed upon him by the circumstances in which he must work—the role of the scientist concerned with the investigation and presentation of facts and the role of the public official who must provide scientific arguments to justify political decisions.

Take, for example, Dr. Willard F. Libby, an AEC Commissioner and a distinguished scientist. On April 11, 1957, Commissioner Libby made the flat statement that "There is a great deal we do not know about the precise effect of radiation on the human body, but we do know that the effect of radioactive fallout from nuclear tests is not, nor is it likely ever to be, the danger to the human race in this generation or in later generations which many people have been led to believe."

Not only does Dr. Libby's statement run counter to the considered opinion of a number of other distinguished scientists not employed by the AEC; it also appears to contradict the position now taken by Dr. Charles L. Dunham, director of the Division of Biology and Medicine of the AEC. Dr. Dunham has said, "Any cell which has been irradiated has suffered an insult of a greater or lesser degree depending upon the amount of radiation received. The induction of a favorable mutation is a very rare exception. It is, of course, this injurious effect of radiation which makes it essential that all unnecessary exposure to ionizing radiation be avoided. To put it another way, there should be *no exposure of persons to radiation without at the same time some useful purpose being served for the individual or for the group.* In fact, we should go one step further, as has recently been urged in the report of the National Academy of Sciences-National Research Council on the biological effects of atomic radiation. Even when a useful purpose is served, whether in industry, in national defense, or in the practice of medicine, all radiation exposures should be kept at a minimum, especially exposures to the germ cells."

Discussing the question of radioactive fallout, Commissioner Libby concluded his remarks with these words: "Are we willing to take this very small and rigidly controlled risk, or would we prefer to run the risk of annihilation which might result if we surrendered the weapons which are so essential to our freedom and our actual survival."

But is the risk "very small"? Some scientists disagree sharply about the nature of the risk.

And has the risk been "rigidly controlled"? Federal District Judge Christenson would not agree that it was, at least in the case of the sheep that died following the tests in Nevada. The Judge said in his decision: "It seems so manifest as hardly to be subject to suggestion to the contrary that those charged with security provisions in connection with the tests owed to those who might be substantially damaged by resulting radioactive fallout, the duty to use reasonable care to ascertain their whereabouts within areas to be affected and to at least give them timely warning so that they would be in a position to protect themselves and their property if necessary. There were no advance warnings given or other precautions to safeguard the herders or their sheep."

Nobody told the people of the Dixie Valley to be careful of future exposure to radiation because they had already been exposed to almost the "upper limit" advised by the National Academy of Sciences for the general public. Has the AEC followed up the recommendation made at the conclusion of the 1955 tests concerning reports of eye irritation "that this matter should be investigated in order to prove or refute the wide-spread belief that this is due to test activities"? And is it certain that St. George, Utah, will not again be exposed to air concentrations of radioactive beta and gamma emitters which, for five hours, exceeded by twenty-five per cent the emergency "tolerance" limits set by the Feasibility Committee for the Nevada tests?

The British Example

Obviously, the AEC's two responsibilities—that of investigating the hazards of radioactivity and that of developing weapons which produce radioactivity—have had many unfortunate consequences. It is conceivable that two of the AEC's chief goals—that of research "directed at improvement of current weapons models and development of new models to meet the requirements of the Armed Forces" and the "protection of atomic energy workers and the public against the harmful effects of radiation"—may prove to be so contradictory as to require a division of responsibilities, as, indeed, they have been divided in Great Britain.

Although the Atomic Energy Authority, Britain's counterpart of the AEC, is also responsible for protecting the public "against the harmful effects of radiation," it relies on a separate organization, the Medical Research Council, for technical data on maximum permissible levels of exposure to radiation.

The Council is composed of twelve members, who are appointed by the Privy Council Committee. Of the twelve, nine are appointed for their scientific qualifications, while the remaining three—at least one of whom must be a member of the House of Lords and another a member of the House of Commons—are appointed for general rather than scientific qualifications. The Council employs a staff of about one thousand and has full liberty to appoint its own research officers and to pursue its own scientific policy.

There is now no real counterpart in the United States of the British Medical Research Council. But something in the same pattern that would produce the same effect might be possible—an entirely independent scientific agency that would derive its authority from Congress. There might be some duplication between the new agency and the AEC, but the duplication would be well justified by the additional assurances of safety that would be provided.

Following the fundamental pattern of our government, the responsibility for weapons development should be separated from that of guarding public health. Probably the major trouble with the AEC lies in the fact that its enormous power is not subject to adequate checks and balances.

The history of the Nevada weapons tests shows how badly these checks are needed.

Insomnia

BY SEC

Count the small liberties as they leap over the stile and disappear, One by one—

One, To Differ (those who believe in other ways betray)

Two, To Listen (this lecture is canceled; the thoughts might lead astray)

Three, To See (this movie is banned because some call it obscene)

Four, To Enter (this man cannot immigrate, he erred at eighteen)

Five, To Read (those books are no longer permitted on the shelves)

Six, To Be Silent (those who refuse to speak convict themselves)

Seven, To Question (this judge who consulted his conscience must be impeached)

Eight, nine, ten, eleven, twelve (the limit is not yet reached)—

Count the small liberties as they leap over the stile and disappear, One by one.

A Grip of Fear

August 30, 1949

The Case of Alger Hiss

By ROBERT BINGHAM AND MAX ASCOLI

Two trials were conducted at the same time in the same court-room: one against Alger Hiss, indicted for perjury; the other against the ghost of liberalism in the 1930's. The first was a judicial trial, following the rules of law; in the second, emotions imposed *their* rules of evidence. Retroactive passions and present-day fears made the case of Alger Hiss a simultaneous, double-feature performance. Men and women stood in line for hours outside Judge Samuel Kaufman's courtroom, munching sand-wiches out of paper bags, waiting for the doors to open, while other men and women reached hungrily for the bold headlines, fretfully expecting some fantastic disclosure, as if at any moment new pumpkins stocked with new stores of secrets might be dis-covered somewhere.

A lawsuit is always a theatrical ceremony, a ritualistic public re-enactment of the felony to allow the sentinels of justice, who were caught off guard when the crime was committed, belatedly to demonstrate their power. A trial, like a good tragedy, purges the emotions, first by this re-enactment, then by the punishment of guilt. In this particular trial, emotions were not purged, but fanned.

In Judge Kaufman's court practically everybody—the de-fendant, the main witnesses, the lawyers—over-acted, each of them truer to type than life ever seems willing to permit. It was

153

as if all the leading characters had worked so hard at rehearsal that, at the moment of actual performance, their words sounded strained and improbable. As in a play conceived by a pedantic and slightly obsessed playwright, virtue could not be so virtuous, nor vice so vicious, nor forensic rhetoric so rhetorical.

The spectators' minds were alternately absorbed by the trial and wandering away from it, trying to figure out from what was said the things that were left unsaid. Some people—mostly inveterate haters of the New Deal—had long since conducted their own trial according to a fairly uniform pattern. They passionately took the prosecution's contention for indisputable fact: Not only was Alger Hiss guilty, but so was the whole group to which he belonged. According to these people, the case was clinched, because, in their opinion, there had always been connivance between what they considered the eternal enemy, Soviet Russia, and at least a large number of New Dealers. The trial was better than guilt by association: It was at the same time the forcible establishment of the association and the proclamation of its guilt.

In their over-rehearsed, over-played performance, the main actors were remarkable. Lloyd Paul Stryker was always at the center of the stage—the strutting, sneering, posturing defense attorney. His opponent, Assistant United States Attorney Thomas Murphy, provided the perfect contrast as the mighty-muscled, walrus-mustached vaudeville cop, persevering but not too bright. Alger Hiss was the ever-courteous and smiling Eagle Scout whose shining virtue had been called into question; Whittaker Chambers, the mysterious man-of-a-thousand-faces, appeared this time as the homespun dairy farmer. A comparable performance was given by nearly everybody who came to the bar—all the supporting actors, the bit players, and the Greek chorus of celebrities who chanted an affirmation of the integrity of their Orestes, who was still pursued by the Furies of the House Committee on Un-American Activities.

Mr. & Mrs. Chambers

The plot of the drama was obscure. Alger Hiss was not charged with espionage—the Statute of Limitations ruled that out; he was accused of lying when he said he was not a spy. Specifically, he was charged with having committed perjury on December 15, 1948, before a Grand Jury, when he denied having furnished restricted State Department documents to Whittaker Chambers —a denial that Hiss had made dozens of times previously and continues to make. For good measure, he was also indicted on a second perjury count for saying that he had not seen Whittaker Chambers after January 1, 1937; this was in effect a repetition of the first count, since the Bill of Particulars that went with it cited the specific times Hiss saw Chambers as the occasions when he allegedly delivered the papers during the first three months of 1938.

The evidence that the prosecution brought forward consisted mainly of the testimony of Whittaker Chambers. A plump, jowly man with graying hair, who wore a black suit and a black tie, Chambers was self-conscious but deadly earnest. His deep voice was cracked, tired, almost inaudible as he told his version of the facts.

Supporting Chambers's testimony were the films of State Department documents he had pulled out of a pumpkin on his farm last December, almost certainly typed on a Woodstock typewriter that once belonged to Hiss.

That was all of the directly relevant evidence introduced against Hiss at the court of justice. At the court of emotions, all those who had already found Alger Hiss guilty of treason looked for different evidence. Wasn't there a clear connection between giving state documents to a Russian colonel in a Brooklyn movie theater and, a few years later, accompanying President Roosevelt to Yalta?

The curse of overstating and overacting was shared by both sides. Mrs. Chambers, who had nothing to contribute directly about the issues in the case, was put on the stand to show that considerable intimacy had existed between the Hisses and the Chamberses. Mrs. Chambers, like Shakespeare's Mistress Quickly, had the gift of total recall. She was a stark little woman playing a parlor game, trying to recall the pattern on some wallpaper she had seen fourteen years earlier and proudly fetching up the fact that "Mrs. Hiss doesn't like ice cream." Unfortunately for her husband and Mr. Murphy, some of her recollections contra-

dicted certain other evidence and even her own previous testimony. About all she really proved was her unfaltering loyalty
to Mr. Chambers. Asked whether some of her husband's actions
were inconsistent with "decent citizenship," Mrs. Chambers, who
always wore a big black hat, stiffened angrily, pointed her finger
dramatically toward the heavens, and made the pronouncement:
"I resent that—my husband *is* a decent citizen—and a great man!"
At this point there was muffled, uneasy laughter from the
audience.

Mr. Murphy marched a platoon of FBI agents into the courtroom to support parts of the narrative. These men—to whom
Stryker referred contemptuously as "FBI's"—were notable for
their standardized physical appearance and their uniformly ex-
cessive politeness. Stryker lit into the "FBI's" as if they were
public enemies, trying to imply that they had threatened violence
and offered bribes to the witnesses. It was their exhaustive research, he insinuated, that had provided both Mr. and Mrs.
Chambers with the substance of their testimony about the Hiss
household. Murphy complained disconsolately, "It's open season
on the FBI."

The testimony of Henry Julian Wadleigh was singular. Cor-
roborating Chambers's testimony about him, Wadleigh very
blandly described, with impeccable diction, the part he had
played in the espionage work, confident that the Statute of Limitations protected him. Here was a tasty tidbit for the ghouls, full
substantiation of their claims about flirtations and even assigna-
tions between the bright young men of the New Deal and the
minions of international Communism. But Wadleigh, of course,
yielded himself too easily; the pack wanted a victim who, like
Hiss, would fight. Wadleigh slipped almost unnoticed into the
virtuous garment of an anti-Communist and went his way in
peace, deriving considerable self-esteem for having done his bit
to aid justice, as well as royalties for a serialized account of his
salvation in the New York *Post*.

No one could ever surpass Lloyd Paul Stryker in overacting.
The robust, rosy-cheeked barrister was after every last drop of
sympathy for the handsome defendant, who looks—or looked—
much younger than his forty-four years. Hiss wore glasses the

first day, but never after that; the strategists must have decided he looked more boyish without them.

With disgust dripping from his rich voice, Stryker tried to build up an emotional horror towards Chambers, the man he called a "moral leper." Stryker's insistence that Chambers had failed to follow the dictates of middle-class morality all his life got very tiresome as the days wore on. Among the prejudicial evidence brought in against Chambers were the facts that he flunked geometry in high school, that he did not return some books he had borrowed from the Columbia University Library, that he lived for a while with a woman to whom he was not married, and that his grandmother was a little addled.

Of course, the main thing against Chambers was his admitted former allegiance to the dark power of Communism. Stryker leaped on that: "If I knew he had engaged in a criminal conspiracy over a period of years—*to tear down that flag*—I wouldn't believe him no matter if the FBI erected a stack of Bibles as high as the building and he swore on it."

Chambers admitted that in his testimony on Hiss, before Congress and the Grand Jury, he had perjured himself nine times. But even some of the facts he insisted upon remained dubious. One such was the matter of a trip to Peterboro, New Hampshire. Chambers testified that Mr. and Mrs. Hiss drove him in their car to visit the late Harry Dexter White at Peterboro early in August, 1937. He remembered that they stayed at an inn called Bleak House, which belonged to Professor Samuel Morrison of Harvard, and that they had attended a summer stock production of "She Stoops to Conquer" the evening of August 10. All the details were clear in his mind.

The defense lit into this story. They presented Mrs. Lucy E. Davis, the operator of Bleak House, who said that no trio resembling the Hisses and Chambers had registered at Bleak House during the early part of August, 1937, and that she always insisted most particularly that every guest register. Mr. J. Kellogg-Smith, proprietor of a children's camp at Chestertown, Maryland, where Hiss's stepson, Timothy Hobson, used to spend the summer, testified that Hiss was at the camp every day of the first two weeks of August, 1937, taking care of his stepson, who had

broken his leg. The fact that Harry Dexter White is now dead
was made to seem suspiciously convenient for Chambers. Even
the FBI was unable to support Chambers's story. If Chambers
fabricated the Peterboro trip, might he not have fabricated the
whole accusation?

In Anglo-Saxon law, the defendant is not required to prove his
innocence. The prosecution must prove his guilt. But it certainly
helps if the defendant is able to offer a plausible explanation
of the situation. Hiss's staff had no plausible explanation of one
very important point: the travels of the Woodstock typewriter.
Raymond Sylvester Catlett, who worked for the Hisses as a yard
boy in the 1930's, testified that Mrs. Hiss had given him the
famous Woodstock some months before the papers could have
been typed by anyone, and that the machine thereafter stayed in
his house. No one suggested that Mr. Catlett had done the typing, and the prosecution tried instead to show that the defense
witness's memory may have been faulty, and that he might have
received the machine after the documents were typed. None of
this, of course, is proof that Hiss *did* have the typewriter, certainly not proof that he did the typing and gave the papers to
Chambers.

Hiss's defense decided to question Chambers's fitness to accuse,
rather than to insist coldly that under our law a defendant's
guilt must be proved. It would be an understatement to say that
by the time Stryker began to make his summation to the jury,
he had exhausted the usefulness of this technique. In identifying
Alger Hiss with Home, Mother, and the Flag, and gasping at
the depravity he claimed to see in Whittaker Chambers, Stryker
temporarily deafened the ears that might have detected insin-
cerity in Chambers's testimony. In his summation, Stryker ham-
mered the matter of "reasonable doubt" to a meaningless pulp,
and sidestepped the damaging circumstantial evidence against
Hiss. All he said was, "Whether these documents were on that
typewriter, I don't care," and, "Where, when, and how he
[Chambers] got them [the papers]—I don't know." His reluctance
to provide any remotely tenable hypothesis made one wonder if
such speculation had been forbidden by Alger Hiss, for one
reason or another. Eight of the jurors interpreted this reluctance

as a sign of the defendant's guilt, but the other four must have felt that even an innocent man might have his reasons for simply denying the charge and saying no more. Among these reasons there might have been the conviction that the law was on his side.

Murphy's summation was a masterpiece. He pretended to offer a rational alternative to Stryker's spellbinding, but what he really did was to gather up all the emotional forces that Stryker had set in motion and turn them against the defendant. This was a rare feat for Murphy, after his uninspired performance during the rest of the trial, but like his brother, "Fireman Johnny" Murphy, who used to be a relief pitcher for the Yankees, Thomas Murphy was capable of a good showing in the late innings. He summed up the evidence that supported Chambers's story: (1) Chambers had in his possession copies of State Department documents; (2) the dates of the documents all fall in the first three months of 1938; (3) all except one of the papers were copied on the Woodstock. How did Chambers get them, Murphy demanded, if Alger Hiss hadn't furnished, transmitted, and delivered them?

A Trial or a Case?

Judge Kaufman, a meticulously dressed man who displayed an increasingly grave look as the trial progressed, has been criticized for showing partiality to the defense. He did, it is true, sustain many of the defense's objections, but that might be explained by the fact that Stryker, who has been trying cases a few decades longer than Murphy, may know the law a little better, as well as by the fact that the defense is traditionally given the benefit of the doubt in criminal cases.

Judge Kaufman's principal mistake was his insistence on behaving as if he were presiding over a lawsuit in which only ascertainable facts, not opinions and passions, were to be considered. One of the things he said that his critics may or may not see fit to hold against him was: "Circumstantial evidence, to be sufficient in this case, must not be merely consistent with the guilt of the defendant; it must be inconsistent with any reasonable hypothesis of innocence." He also explained the perjury laws: To convict there must be two witnesses or one witness and independent corroboration.

Perhaps he thought there was only one trial at his bar, the trial of Alger Hiss for perjury, and that he was the presiding officer of that trial. He was the only one of the performers who did not overact. Even the jurors, as soon as they decided that they could reach no decision, felt that at last the time had come to have their say, and several of them did not hesitate to share with the press their opinions about how a judge should behave and about how a trial ought, ideally, to be conducted.

There is an intermission now, for the emotions need a rest in the torrid summer of 1949. But Attorney General Tom Clark has announced that the trial will be resumed in the fall, when the docket of the District Court is less crowded.

Will it be the second trial of Alger Hiss for perjury, or the next act of this great public drama—The Case of Alger Hiss? For the two things are far from identical: Indeed the relationship between them becomes more and more remote. This invariably happens whenever a case in a court of law becomes the object of public passion. The guilt or innocence of Captain Dreyfus or of Sacco and Vanzetti came to have little significance in *L'Affaire Dreyfus* or the Sacco-Vanzetti case.

Alger Hiss will have to go to court, and of course attend all of the sessions dedicated to him. But at the same time the case that bears his name is more and more removed from him. In the people's minds the image of Alger Hiss is already as depersonalized as a rogues' gallery picture. Little attention has been paid to the two contradictory positions this young man has held: General Counsel of the Nye Committee—the farthest point that isolationism has ever reached—and Secretary General of the San Francisco Conference—the summit of militant internationalism.

The Hiss case, started by the House Committee on Un-American Activities as part of a general attack on New Dealers, has now, because of its morbid features, caught the public imagination. It has been, one must admit, a striking success for the committee. The case does not need to be inflated now by new revelations from former Communist couriers. The excitement of the public is enough to keep it going. The case will carry itself along—with a live man attached.

Actually, neither Alger Hiss nor the New Deal is on trial, but justice. The ritual of justice cannot be exposed to tests like this one. The trial of law is designed to settle individual cases and is always centered on the individual who is to be proved innocent or guilty. It can never try a crowd or a mob. It cannot work when the aroused imagination or the passion of the crowd over-flows in the court. Justice, the blindfolded goddess, cannot be exposed to the bellowing of the mob. Perhaps the members of the hung jury felt something like this in their tired bones while lingering around the courtroom, like students still keyed up after an examination, on the night of Friday, July 8.

Will it then start over again? Are we going to see again the pictures of Mr. and Mrs. Whittaker Chambers, Mr. and Mrs. Alger Hiss? Perhaps Mrs. Whittaker Chambers, in the fall or winter, will not wear the same big black hat. Mrs. Alger Hiss may or may not wear the same white gloves. All of us will once again talk for hours and hours, passionately and inconclusively, about Hiss and Chambers and the Woodstock typewriter. The same nightmarish orgy of gossip will start over again, so that once more large masses of decent, normal men and women will talk and feel with the frenzy of a mob.

Or perhaps there is something we can do about it. Each one of us could refuse to be drawn into the mob. The newspapers and the radio would render a unique public service to the nation if they would give a minimum and inconspicuous coverage to the second Hiss trial. We don't need to hear again about Whittaker Chambers's teeth, or the wallpaper and decorations in the vari-ous Georgetown houses in which the Hisses lived at various times. We can look at something else, talk of someone other than the unfortunate, worn-out protagonists of this case, Mr. and Mrs. Whittaker Chambers, and Mr. and Mrs. Alger Hiss.

July 8, 1952

Lives and Deaths of
Whittaker Chambers

By Max Ascoli

In writing *Witness,* Whittaker Chambers has opened the second round of what he calls "the Case." This may turn out to be a service to the nation if—and it is a very large if, in no way dependent on Chambers—"the Case" is thoroughly and fearlessly debated, if his testimony is examined and cross-examined, as that of any witness must be. So far, there has not been much evidence of this.

Yet this time we are not taken by surprise, buffeted by headlines, stirred up by revelations or lurid gossip. This time we have a huge book in front of us to read and to ponder. The adventures of Alger Hiss, as told by Whittaker Chambers, are meant to corroborate the indictment to which Mr. Chambers, in his own terminology, bears witness. This indictment is against the prevailing values of our democracy and against the leaders who guided our nation through the New Deal and the war.

These men stand accused of having worked for the victory of our deadly enemy, Communism, although only a fraction of them did so knowingly. "Thus men who sincerely abhorred the word Communism, in the pursuit of common ends found that they were unable to distinguish Communists from themselves, except that it was just the Communists who were likely to be most forthright and most dedicated in the common cause. This political color-blindness was all the more dogged because it was completely honest. For men who could not see that what they firmly believed was liberalism added up to socialism could scarcely be expected to see what added up to Communism."

The author brings forth his indictment not in a bill of particulars but through a detailed description of what he himself has done and seen throughout the whole range of his life. What happened to him is made to carry a message of universal and of immediate importance. The basic themes of his message are reiterated rather than explained, for the author, like other religious writers, relies on the habit-forming persuasiveness of reiteration.

Mr. Chambers's book must stand or fall on the validity of his indictment. It is not up to him to decide whether the religious message of his book has canonical virtue or is apocryphal. *Witness* cannot just be considered as a piece of literature or a contribution to the history of our times. We cannot put the book on the shelf, after having given the author an "A" as a storyteller, a "C" as a philosopher of contemporary history, and a "D" as a theologian. To do this is to exhibit at its weakest that facile liberalism which Chambers scorns.

The book is all of one piece. With artful and deliberate lack of discretion, the dismal, at times nightmarish life of this human being is exhibited to millions of Americans by the man who has had the hard luck to live it. For all its emphasis on religion, *Witness* is a political book and a major event in present-day American politics.

Chambers's is no isolated voice. For years it has been first whispered, then said, then yelled into all the microphones of the nation that an unspecified number of our national leaders have knowingly or unknowingly connived with the enemy. In creating these fears and apprehensions, no influence was greater than that of "the Case"—first round. Now all those who are prone to believe in the undefined, unspecified guilt of an Administration or of a generation will be heartened, for "the Case"—second round —has found the Book.

Motives and Justifications

In giving us the tale of his life, the author has set himself a number of different goals. He wants to denounce the Communist danger at home, to confess what his own role has been in the Communist conspiracy, to explain the queer halting course of his denunciation of Alger Hiss. He manages to give a justification for every instance where his behavior has been odd, as on the various occasions when he perjured himself. He wants to make of his past testimony in courts and in Congressional committees the evidence of his right to be a witness for his God.

Above all, he wants to get even with his enemies, as many another author of a religiously inspired book has done before him—Dante first of all, who, even from the height of the *Paradiso,* never stopped lashing out at those who had wronged him.

Scarcely anything that has been said against Chambers is left unchallenged or unanswered in this book. To those who questioned his sanity and searched for the peculiarities of his family background, he offers a clinical, detailed, sometimes lurid description of the traits that he inherited and the environment that shaped his youth. He stretches himself on the couch, and tells the analysts—whom he hates en masse—all the things that they want to hear from him, and that fall into their set categories. Thus he reports how horrible he felt when, as a boy, he had to kill a chicken: "I tied the chicken's legs and hung it, head down, from a nail, and as quickly and as mercifully as I could, severed its head. The knife fell as if gravity had jerked it from my hand. Then I hid."

Then he proceeds: "All right. As a man, I will kill. But I will kill always under duress, by an act of will, in knowing violation of myself, and always in rebellion against that necessity which I do not understand or agree to. Let me never kill unless I suffer that agony, for if I do not suffer it, I will be merely a murderer." This passage is characteristic of the whole book; the author lifts himself to the pulpit by the bootstraps of his public self-analysis.

It was in his childhood, he says, that he developed "a deep distrust of the human race." "I never had any real friends." "By degrees I told myself: I am an outcast. My family is outcast. We have no friends, no social ties, no church, no organization that we claim and that claims us, no community. We could scarcely be more foreign in China than in our alienation from the life around us."

There is a ring of unquestionable truth in this description of his squalid childhood. For Chambers, schooling—the process of formal learning—never became an education. According to his own record, he never acquired that modesty, that patience in comparing his ideas and feelings with those of other men before him and around him, which is education. All his life he has remained somewhat unrelated and lonely. For him the only way of communicating and perhaps of grasping ideas is by inflating to enormous proportions the accidents of his life.

In his youth he was an omnivorous reader. But of all the books he read the only one that made a dent on him was *Les Misérables* by Victor Hugo, that writer who created gigantic figures—all reeking of ham.

There are pages of *Witness* that cannot be read without a sense of horror, pages describing things that happened to the author which the reader wishes he had never read, for such things should not happen to any human being. This is the case, for instance, in that scene where, in Chambers's house one night, his father beat and nearly killed his brother, until Chambers grappled with his father. Toward the end of the book, his description of his last attempt at suicide—when the Hiss case was reaching its climax—does not spare us any detail: Chambers lying in bed, breathing the poisonous fumes, the pictures of his children, one in each hand, and the letters on the table to be read after he is dead. But he has to tell the reader about the contents of these letters.

There seems to be no reason why millions of Americans should be made privy to such wretchedness—unless it be that although reading Chambers is no pleasure, being Chambers must be incomparably worse. The author knows this, and uses it to the hilt.

His Private World

In all his leaps from the episodic to the universal, from occurrences to ideas, Chambers seems to have a rather personal and peculiar notion of ideas that is unrelated to their socially established meaning.

Such is the case with his concept of history, which he obviously borrows from Marxism. The words "history" and "historical" appear with extraordinary frequency in the book, often several times on one page. Invariably "history" means necessity—a superhuman power that makes men act, and on which human will cannot exert much of an influence. To Chambers, history is not something that men make and for which they have a share of responsibility. The "logic of history" told Chambers that Communism was the only way out for the twentieth century. The man who leaves Communism finds "himself facing the crisis of history."

History, according to Chambers, moves in one direction: toward Communism. Communism "is the central experience of the first half of the 20th century." It gives men "a reason to live and a reason to die."

This insistence on men dying for their faith runs through the book. There seems to be no higher criterion for either a man or a faith. Twice he quotes his assertion, made on a broadcast, that he still shares with Alger Hiss "the conviction that life is not worth living for which a man is not prepared to dare all and die at any moment." According to Chambers, a well-spent life seems to be a form of staggered suicide.

This is a peculiar attitude, since there has seldom been an absurd cause for which men have not been ready to die. Among those who are at all times ready to die can be found many whose lives aren't worth living. For the hard business of living is ordinarily one of paying for what we do with a different coin from that of our life—coins called work or success. Chambers has remained a frustrated Kamikaze—first in the cause of Communism, then in that of anti-Communism.

Non-Omnipotent God

Even what Chambers calls Communism bears little resemblance to what is generally known by this name. Communism, he says repeatedly, is based on faith in Man. Communism as previously known is based on faith neither in Man nor in Men, but in a total subjection to a merciless, undeviating history. Indeed, it is the mystical, irrevocable character of this subjection that has made many people reject their Communist allegiance.

Actually, Chambers, who is obsessed with the idea of Communism, underestimates its danger, for he sees it acting primarily as an underground conspiracy. But the tragedy of our time is that there are millions of men who embrace Communism to free themselves from some of the ills that torture them—and thus are enslaved. Not the spy or the secret agent, but the professional agitator, skillful in finding his work wherever there is human suffering, and in creating human suffering, represents the major threat to our society.

Chambers talks of God. Indeed, he has dedicated his life to God. God has spoken to him at least once. It was one day when he was coming down the stairs in his Mount Royal Terrace house in Baltimore. "As I stepped down into the dark hall, I found myself stopped, not by a constraint, but by a hush of my whole being. In this organic hush, a voice said with perfect distinctness: 'If you will fight for freedom, all will be well with you.'"

This sounds like one of those compacts which the first Patriarchs entered. But it is difficult to see how Chambers's god can keep his part of the compact, for he is a horribly weakened god, abandoned by large masses of men who have gone to the other side—the side which Chambers maintains is winning. There is not much hope to be found in this book that the trend may be reversed and that the attempt to stop Communism can be anything but a suicidal foray on the advancing conquerors. Yet, through Chambers, this god asks for the tribute of men ready to die. This mortally wounded Moloch is not the God of the Judeo-Christian faith.

In the whole book, Christ is hardly if ever mentioned, although the verbiage of Christian ethics and Christian charity is largely used. But the person as well as the meaning of Christ are not to be found anywhere—the respect for the human person that the Christian faiths consider sacred because Christ accepted human shape.

For it is true that the struggle of our time is a religious one: a struggle where various Molochs (called Communism or nationalism) stand against men's will to rule themselves and to maintain their communion with God through many churches or through no church—as Christ told the Samaritan woman. This faith in the human person, always meshed into politics yet somehow independent of it, has become the faith of our civilization, East and West, and is shared by hundreds of millions of baptized and unbaptized people.

It is faith in freedom. This unfortunate man Chambers has extremely vague notions of freedom. He says, "freedom is a need of the soul, and nothing else." He does not know how freedom is organized and released, or what a system of law is, or how laws exert their checks on men's instincts. Indeed, not only the democracy of the New Deal but the idea of political freedom is alien to him.

One night, when he was about to leave the Communist Party, he says, ". . . I faced the fact that, if Communism were evil, I could no longer serve it, and that that was true regardless of the fact that there might be nothing else to serve, that the alternative was a void." It was not just on that one night that he faced the void which his education had not filled and which Communism could not cover up. What that void means is no values, no purpose, no design, no faith in life. The Russians have a word for it: nihilism.

There is so little hope left in Whittaker Chambers that whatever happens in his favor seems to him a freakish reprieve from doom. Chambers has no qualms about aligning himself with whatever institution or interests Communism fights. And why should he? Whatever Communism attacks is not destined to live long.

Nihilism, in his case and in that of some other former Communists, is what remains of the Marxist conception of history in the minds of men who still adhere to it but no longer want to be its agents. Since he refuses to be the tool of the inevitable, the nihilist enjoys a vacation from history. He can get a free ride on any forlorn counterattack against the inevitable.

Yet this unfortunate, lonely man is now offering millions of Americans the opportunity to relive, through his book, his own life. Thanks to his profession and his native gift, he has acquired a remarkable power of communication. But what he can communicate is, above all, his nihilism, the lonely experience of his own self, of a man never entirely identified with anything, either Communism or God, and forced to replace all these accepted standards of value with his own homemade substitutes. He communicates to his fellow citizens universal distrust of their leaders, not a promise of salvation. But he does impart to them that thorough despair for which only the iron discipline of Communism can be a cure.

Other former Communists had already advanced the Rasputin-like theory that to fight Communism, which is the evil of our times, one must have been a practitioner of evil. But no one had ever gone as far as Whittaker Chambers. He still boasts of his attachment to some of the most typical Communist values. He even makes a plea for his onetime profession, spying: "Like the soldier, the spy stakes his freedom or his life on the chances of action."

Constantly he exhibits, flagellates, ultimately extols himself. Constantly he makes it quite clear that whatever he has done to others, it is he who has suffered the most. His whole story is construed as a slow, tortured ascent, Chambers's immolation to what he is the witness for. This becomes particularly striking where he describes what he underwent while denouncing Hiss.

In answer to the question that a journalist put to him at the time, "What do you think you are doing?" he replies, "I am a man who, reluctantly, grudgingly, step by step, is destroying himself that this country and the faith by which it lives may continue to exist." When he decides not to destroy the microfilms, he says, "I knew, too, that whatever else I destroyed, I could do what I had to do only if I was first of all willing to destroy myself." Later, when he considers suicide, he says, "Whether I lived and bore a witness of justice, or killed myself and bore a witness of mercy, I would in either case destroy myself."

Once, in answering Mr. Nixon, who had asked him about his motives in accusing Alger Hiss of Communism, he said, "There are in general two kinds of men. One kind of man believes that God is a God of Justice. The other kind of man believes that

God is a God of Mercy. I am so constituted that in any question I will always range myself upon the side of mercy." He must have forgotten at that moment that there are also the Communists in this world, who do not believe in God—either of Justice or of Mercy.

His last attempt at suicide, at the time he was testifying before the New York Grand Jury, he describes as having been at least partly successful. "Still, no one who has been through such an experience can be expected to be quite the same man again. He is both freer and stronger, because he is, ever after, less implicated in the world. For he has been, in his own mind at least, almost to the end of everything, and knows its worth."

In a chapter entitled "Tomorrow and Tomorrow and Tomorrow," the author makes it clear that there is not much of a tomorrow left for him. After the trials, there is not much energy left, either—aside from whatever energy might have been required for the writing of these 799 pages. At the end, the book has the inexorable accent of the *Consummatum Est.*

Without Fear or Malice

Just because this book is no ordinary piece of literature, but a very important political fact, it is imperative that it be answered and not just reviewed. The episodes it reports may be all true. But the frame of reference and the perspective are, to say the least, arbitrary.

From the sense of doom, of inevitable Communist victory, only the enemy can benefit. Moreover, this pessimism is utterly unjustified, for in fact we are fighting against Communism and we certainly will win if we do not let nihilism becloud our vision and sap our strength.

It is not possible to derive from this book any other sentiment than a profound pity for Whittaker Chambers. But all the accidents, the quirks, the oddities of his life cannot be considered representative and exemplary, even if his desperate loneliness is endowed with the power of communication—amplified by the *Saturday Evening Post* and the Book-of-the-Month Club. We do need to revise our recent history, for we can no longer rely on the happy improvisations that allowed Roosevelt's America to emerge from the depression and from the war. But these blanket indictments of all who have led us during the last twenty years, and of the democratic tenets our nation lives by, cannot remain unchallenged. Only too frequently of late the sewers have been overflowing into Main Street. Behind Chambers, anguished in his search for God, come Lait and Mortimer—and the rest.

Perhaps we ought to have less shyness and self-consciousness in asserting our religious beliefs. Our times are so serious, the fight against Communism so demanding, that we must call on all the support we can get from the faith that has made our civilization. We all have our share of guilt for the life that is described in this book, and we can never pity its author enough.

But we will not trade Christ for Chambers.

August 17, 1954

"Big Brother" in Foggy Bottom

BY WILLIAM HARLAN HALE

All the eleven thousand people in the State Department and far more outside it have heard of him and what he does, but only a small fraction have actually seen him. His name often appears in the newspapers, yet he has taken to avoiding the press because of the "bad publicity" he says it gives him. He occupies a fourth-floor suite in the New State Building on a corridor peopled with senior policymakers and earnest young desk officers, yet the atmosphere that surrounds his own office is something apart. Burly, silent men enter and leave; doors are kept shut; his secretaries discourage callers; he himself is often incommunicado for days. It is as if in the midst of the decorous halls of the State Department's chaste new edifice in Foggy Bottom one had blundered into the headquarters of the chief of a municipal homicide squad. Rumors go around about the dossiers he is said to have on his superiors as well as on all those below, and about a special room in the Department's Annex "4" in which suspects are grilled with the help of a lie detector. "Lots of people," he admits gruffly, "think I'm an ogre."

When you reach his outer offices, you find his chief secretary, Gwen Lewis, a former lady athlete, seated under a motto of Elbert Hubbard on the wall: "An Ounce of Loyalty Is Worth More Than a Pound of Brains." Admitted to the inner chamber, you discover a man of forty, with a football player's build, horn-rimmed glasses, quick eyes, and a tendency to jowls, who gets up to greet you from under his array of several dozen signed photographs of leading Republicans (including one of Senator Mc-Carthy inscribed "To a great American") and breaks into an affable and disarming grin. "You know," he says, "Foreign Service people come into my office all upset and say, 'Where's Scott McLeod?' When I say, 'I'm McLeod,' they can't believe it. 'Why,' they say, 'you don't have horns' . . ."

Exalted Gendarme

You are in the presence of one of the most powerful and controversial officials of the United States government—a man who only a few years ago was an obscure FBI agent in Concord, New Hampshire.

McLeod is known to the world as the State Department's security chief—the first time a cop has risen to the rank of an Assistant Secretary of State. As McLeod himself protests, he is a good deal more than just a security man; he has a subordinate, Dennis A. Flinn (also an ex-FBI man), who is the *real* security man. Last spring, his superior, Thruston B. Morton, Acting Under Secretary for Administration, emphasized the same point when he was concerned about the bad press McLeod was getting: "We shouldn't have let Scotty be ticketed as the top security officer . . . We should have built up Flinn."

McLeod's position carries the longest ranking title in the Department—"Administrator of the Bureau of Security, Consular Affairs and Inspection," and it gives him a $15,000 salary along with Assistant Secretary's rank. Until last March he also controlled the Office of Personnel, which made him the equivalent of two Assistant Secretaries. His title conveys much about his job, but not all. That job, unprecedented in the Department, was set up by the McCarran Immigration Act of 1952, which established a Bureau of Security and Consular Affairs that was to contain a Passport Office, a Visa Office, "and such other offices as the Secretary of State may deem to be appropriate . . ." McLeod also wanted and got the Personnel Office, declaring that its function and that of Security were "inseparable." Actually, Security and Personnel had always been kept separate before, on the ground that policemen should not function as judges. But the newcomer's doctrine was accepted, and, as he told a House committee, "It was on this premise that I accepted the post . . ."

Later, as his bad press increased and such veteran counselors as Douglas MacArthur II and H. Freeman Matthews advised the front office that a mistake had been made, Personnel was publicly shifted away from him. Yet appearances were deceptive: In practice McLeod's police powers and alliances enabled him to continue to dominate the personnel decisions being made down the hall. His own boss, Morton, said as much when he told me in May that "no real change" had been brought about by the sundering. Meanwhile, Secretary Dulles recompensed McLeod by giving him full control over still another key function, Inspection.

Today, Administrator McLeod holds not one but several portfolios, all of them filled with dossiers. In the State Department of 1954 he plays the assorted roles of chief policeman, supervising psychiatrist, top consular and immigration-policy man, special contact man on security matters with the FBI, the CIA, and interested committees on Capitol Hill; and inspector general of the entire State Department and Foreign Service.

In his first role, as security chief, or rather super-chief, he has been directing the most intensive intramural investigation undertaken in the history of our government—a "full field" study, within the space of a year, of every single member of the Department's present eleven thousand-person complement, from ambassadors down to supply clerks, in Washington and scattered among 267 diplomatic and consular posts abroad. This has been done under the provisions of President Eisenhower's Order 10450 of April 27, 1953, which brought such factors as a jobholder's drinking habits, sexual interests, and possible "neurological disorders" under the purview of security officers rather than the usual personnel authorities—another "first."

In his next or consular role, he gives supervision to Mrs. Ruth Shipley's largely autonomous Passport Division, which determines what citizen may or may not travel abroad under U.S. protection, as well as to Edward Maney's Visa Division, which advises consular officials overseas as to which foreigners may or may not come in. (The McCarran Act of 1952 sets forth thirty-one separate grounds on which an alien may be refused admission.) Further, he watches over the Office of Special Consular Services, which aids Americans on business or in trouble abroad; a Munitions Control unit; and, more immediately, a special office set up to administer the Refugee Relief Act of 1953, under which more than 200,000 escapees from Communism, displaced orphans, and others specially exempted from immigration quotas are supposed to be admitted by the end of 1956. As head man for the relief of refugees, McLeod co-ordinates the efforts of six departments (State, Treasury, Army, Justice, Labor, and Welfare) and directs the screening of each applicant, including the orphans—a process he began by hiring a staff of special investigators, who in turn had to be investigated first.

All these functions take the Administrator far afield, but his most recently acquired one—inspection—brings him to bear again on the staff. The theory of the Foreign Service—all of whose career officers hold Presidential commissions as this nation's representatives abroad—has been that as a special corps it should manage and inspect itself, just as the Army, Navy, and McLeod's own former outfit, the FBI, do, and not be subject to outside policing. So it has regularly detailed senior officers of its own number to serve as traveling inspectors of our diplomatic missions abroad, where they arrive with a mandate to look into every human nook and organizational cranny of the operation, on the premise that all they learn will be held in strict confidence.

But on April 15, Secretary Dulles turned this delicate function —along with that of inspecting the Department's entire home establishment as well—over to McLeod, with an instruction to the staff that this made him the focal point for receiving "new ideas . . . criticisms," and for "personally" hearing "from any of our people" anything about "problems official and personal." This phrase, coming over the Dulles signature, seemed to give topside sanction to a practice which everyone below the Dulles level knew had come into existence under McLeod's administration, namely, that of informing on other officials whom you either suspected or just didn't like.

"Can't you see our decent people taking their personal problems to a cop?" snorted a top State Department official when I was alone with him. "And that kind of a cop?"

Security über Alles

On paper, the massing of all these powers into one hand would look like an administrative grab bag if it were not that one concern had evidently brought all of them together: the new overriding security interest. A singleness of purpose and outlook unites the chief officials around McLeod, all of whom, with the exception of the passport and consular chiefs, are new appointees to their jobs. At his right stands his gray-haired, heavy-eyed Deputy Administrator, Robert F. Cartwright, another former FBI agent, brought in from an investigative post in the General Accounting Office. Then come two special high-level consultants, James Egan, who for thirty years was also an FBI agent and in recent years assisted Congressman John Taber's House Appropriations Committee, and Frank Waldrop, the brawny former editor-in-chief of the Washington *Times-Herald* under Colonel McCormick's ownership. Of the duties of these two lieutenants, McLeod will say nothing except that Egan has been conducting a management survey and that Waldrop is engaged on "special research."

On the next level is McLeod's Assistant Deputy Administrator, Frances Knight, a brisk spinster nearing fifty, who formerly served as a management assistant in the State Department's Information Program, where she became known as a special confidante of the Taber and McCarthy Committees across town. Then comes the immediate boss of "SY" (Security), the affable Dennis Flinn, who after twelve years in the FBI switched into the career Foreign Service and who is pointed out, when people charge that McLeod's organization doesn't like the Foreign Service, with such words as, "What do you mean, we don't like the Service? Look at Denny Flinn right here!"

Ex-FBI man Flinn was installed by ex-FBI man McLeod to

replace the Department's previous SY director, John Ford, and promptly emulated his chief by bringing in his own new brooms as well. From the Atomic Energy Commission came William Uanna to run the much-needed job of tightening up "physical security," while a Civil Service Commission investigator, Otto Otepka, was imported to head the more subtle task of "evaluating" all reports turned in about the habits and behavior of our diplomats and desk officers.

If under Order 10450's injunction to SY to "develop information" concerning any behavior, activities or associations which tend to show that [an] individual is not reliable . . ." an investigator discovers that Counselor X stationed in country Y fathered a child out of wedlock fifteen years ago, it is up to Otepka and his staff to "evaluate" this, after which it goes to Flinn, who then notifies McLeod of the find, who then "recommends" to the Under Secretary what action should be taken. First, however, this is "co-ordinated" with Personnel, at which point another member of the McLeod circle, George F. Wilson, Deputy Assistant Secretary for Personnel, comes in.

Wilson, a dry, secretive Midwesterner, is another new face at the Department, brought in at McLeod's urging from a job as administrative aide to Senator William Knowland. The Congressional-relations value of giving so central a post to a protégé of the Republican Majority Leader was evident. A University of Arizona graduate whose last job in private industry was that of assistant credit manager of a milling concern in Los Angeles, Wilson is looked on by Foreign Service officers as a man of limited background, suspicious of graduates of Eastern colleges, of Harvard accents, of intellectuals generally, and of people who have spent much time in Europe in particular.

"We work very closely with Wilson," says Flinn. McLeod's team did not work so closely with Wilson's former boss, Assistant Secretary Edward T. Wailes, a strong-minded career officer who was a stranger in their midst, but Wailes resigned last spring.

These are the men who have come to power over the most crucial points of Secretary Dulles's foreign-affairs establishment. One thing they do not control is Communications. Early this year, a rumor flew about Department corridors that McLeod was maneuvering to snap up that division as well. It turned out to be false. "I don't need the cables," he told *The Reporter*. "I can see them easily enough." That he does see them—along with any other policy traffic that interests him—everyone in the service either knows or suspects.

What matters more than the fact of concentration of powers under McLeod is the concept with which he approaches them and the uses to which he and his staff of more than a thousand put them.

A policeman is paid to keep an eye on suspicious characters down the block and make sure all doors are locked. McLeod and his fellow agents are clearly well-trained house detectives, and there is general respect for their work at spotting outside eavesdroppers and careless officials and double-checking any leads to actual subversion. But a house dick's negative mentality has limitations when you give him something really big to accomplish. Thus, during the first ten months of McLeod's administration of the Refugee Relief Act, written to authorize over 200,000 emergency entries, double and triple security checks resulted in enabling only nine aliens to enter the country under its terms. "You can imagine what would happen," said McLeod's program chief, Robert C. Alexander, "if we made a single mistake."

But something more than just the FBI approach dictated McLeod's response to President Eisenhower's Order 10450, which called on Department chiefs to specify any "sensitive" position on their roster, the holders of which would then be subjected to a "full-field" investigation. Unlike the previous Truman order, which had required the government to produce evidence of disloyalty against a man before he could be fired under it, 10450 made people dismissable simply on "suitability" grounds. If a man happened to have a Communist landlord or an elderly maiden aunt still living in Warsaw (these are actual cases), it could be shown by an enterprising SY man that his continued employment was not "clearly consistent with the interests of the national security." In non-Federalese English, "When in doubt, throw him out."

Entering Dean Acheson's old preserves seventeen months ago, McLeod was frankly anxious to throw the maximum out, and he told his investigators to be "completely ruthless." A device lay at hand: It was to declare that in the State Department, not just key positions but *every* position was "sensitive" under the terms of 10450, and thereby to subject every employee right down to the last warehouse assistant to a search into all he had ever done, said, written, or read. "Usually, somewhere, you turn up *something*," a SY investigator remarked to me. McLeod himself, in an interview given last January to the friendly *U.S. News & World Report,* stated that in perhaps fifty per cent of his investigations, "you develop . . . so-called derogatory information"—which he then translated to mean, "you run into somebody who doesn't like the man." "You see," McLeod's alter ego, Dennis Flinn, explained to me, "we've done better than any other department."

Most officers whom I have queried do not agree that McLeod's group has done so well. The effects on morale of turning loose a task force to ferret out at high speed the life histories of eleven thousand employees have been widely and unfavorably reported. The effect on day-to-day operations, at a critical period in our foreign relations, has been equally crippling.

Not only new appointments but assignments, transfers, and promotions of officials already in the service have been held up for six and even nine months, since no personnel action can now be taken until SY has completed its full study of the "case." In mid-June, the pivotal Operations Coordinating Board was still awaiting clearance of Department officials requested for its staff in 1953, while at overseas missions some six hundred positions to which officials had been assigned similarly stayed unfilled. In the particularly urgent area of communications, some forty overseas code-clerk posts were empty, also awaiting McLeod's green light.

To help with his Herculean task, McLeod has had to hire a battalion of new investigators, building up to a force of 350, including 120 borrowed from the Civil Service Commission—a number greater than the size of the entire State Department on the eve of the First World War. Trained men, particularly "evaluators," he admits, are hard to find these days. Other government agencies and private industries are also busy taking on fresh squads of such talent. Dennis Flinn, who hires them, has observed that most of those he can get are very young men who have never had a job before; but, he adds confidently, "I insist on a college education." These young men are the ones visitors have noticed ambling in numbers up and down the State Department corridors during the past year, checking names on doors against those they carry in identical little black loose-leaf books, and then entering to interrogate veteran officers on how they have spent their careers. Here are some questions they have asked:

Of an officer accredited to the legitimate (Republican) government at Madrid during the Spanish Civil War: "Did you have any contact with the Rebels? The Communists, I mean."

Of a former consul-general: "At what age were you married? Did you have sexual intercourse before marriage?"

Of a diplomat who had served in Finland while it was in the war on the Axis side: "So you were working to get Finland and Russia to agree? Hm. Let's see, who was President then?"

"Yes, I've had trouble with some of our boys," Flinn admits. "They handled officers as if they were starters, too, and wanted to know their qualifications for the job." A policy official put it rather differently: "The trouble with these boys is that they don't know, period. By sending droves of them all over the lot, Mc-Leod has actually made it more difficult to take a searching, grown-up look at what's *really* sensitive. A security system shouldn't be cops-and-robbers stuff, but a means to an end."

But what actually is the purpose of the system, as McLeod and his clan see it? "In a sense, I am a politician," he stated in his first major speech, given before the American Legion convention at Topeka a year ago, "in that I was appointed by the present Administration to a political office"—which surprised those who thought he had been appointed to a security office. Then he went on to state his object clearly: The Department must be purged of traitors, homosexuals, and bad risks, certainly, but also of Democrats. "Sometimes," he lamented, "it is extremely difficult because of the Civil Service Act, the Veterans' Preference Act, and the Foreign Service Act to replace an individual whose viewpoint does not coincide with that of the Republican Party.

. . . Until such time as we can re-educate those employees or replace them with proper personnel the progress which we make is sometimes very slow." In another speech, before the Rock Creek Republican Women's Club in Washington, he stated that his object was not to establish "if a man is loyal or disloyal, but if he is a good security risk"—and what was a good risk? "Not *all* New Dealers are necessarily security risks," he added with a laugh.

A "holdover," though, could readily be made to seem like a risk. There was the case of Reed Harris, deputy chief of the Department's Information Program and a survivor of seventeen years in government, who was shown back in his college days to have written a heated attack on commercialized campus football, and whose resignation was brought about through prearranged signals between McLeod and the McCarthy Committee. Two of his key subordinates in Information—a happy hunting ground for "scalps"—were ousted on sexual grounds: They weren't charged with anything perverse, simply with some affairs with women that made them vulnerable to the new Puritans. In the case of the veteran career diplomat Charles E. Bohlen, McLeod interceded personally at the White House to fight his appointment as ambassador to Moscow on the ground that his participation at Yalta and other conferences under the Democratic régime made him a "public-relations risk."

Next came the case of Bohlen's brother-in-law, Charles W. Thayer, also a prominent career officer long experienced in Russian affairs, whom McLeod "got" (Under Secretary Donold B. Lourie concurring and Secretary Dulles looking the other way) when he could not get Bohlen. Thayer's dismissal was calculated to shock the entire Foreign Service into awareness as to where the new power lay.

Most recently, the top case on SY's list has been that of career officer John Paton Davies, Jr., the Old China Hand who, after having been cleared in eight investigations of the charges hurled at him by Senators McCarthy and Jenner, in June was haled into the dock for his ninth.

Although McLeod wanted Republicans to take over, he was particular about what kind. In his Wichita speech a year ago, he remarked, "The progress toward change has not been as rapid as many of us had hoped it would be," implying that the moderates around Dulles were holding him back. Last December, the warning from McLeod's camp became unmistakable: David Lawrence's *U.S. News & World Report* came out with an unsigned six-page blast that had evidently been fed it by interested sources inside the Department ("Turmoil Inside the State Department: Acheson Men Cling to Power, Republicans Struggle to Get In"), in which a dozen anonymous and unidentified officials were quoted as attacking top appointees such as Assistant Secretaries Walter S. Robertson and Samuel C. Waugh and also Under Secretary Walter Bedell Smith on grounds of harboring "holdovers" and the holdover mentality. The hero of the piece—which was reputed to have been "set up" by a particularly zealous employee of McLeod's, now safely tucked away in the Historical Section—was McLeod himself, whom Smith and the others were said to have "boxed in."

The *U.S. News* story made statements so wild that Under Secretary Smith "blew his top" and succeeded in getting editor Lawrence to print corrections next month. For instance:

Charge, December 18: "The new chief of the Policy Planning Staff, put in by the Republicans, actually served as a policy aide to Acheson. His deputy is a New Dealer who was trained by Felix Frankfurter."

Correction, January 15: "The new chief of the Policy Planning Staff is Robert R. Bowie. He never served as a policy aide to Acheson—he never even worked in the Department in Washington. . . . As for his deputy chief, he is Jacob Beam, a Foreign Service career officer who was not trained by Supreme Court Justice Frankfurter, and doesn't even know him."

To McLeod and his team, the idea of a professional nonpartisan service to conduct our foreign affairs is something alien, even un-American. Like his friend George Wilson at Personnel, McLeod mistrusts many of the ways of our diplomatic corps: "It should be remade into a mold more American and less European," he told a home state paper, the Des Moines *Register,* "U.S. diplomats imitate the dress, accents, mannerisms and even the thinking of foreigners." To *The Reporter,* he was more brusque: "They think they can make policy in a vacuum . . . They're happy when they get the next pay check." And to one of his own security lieutenants stationed in mid-Europe, who reported to him last year that Foreign Service officers were growing restive about their delayed promotions, he remarked bluntly, "Look, I'm sitting on those myself. If they don't like it, they can get the hell out."

The Foreign Service Institute, training ground of young officials, also saw a new point of view taking over when it fell into the lap of educators McLeod and Wilson last year. They doubted the value of such professional schooling—certainly as it had been given—and entirely suspended its intermediate course, letting its director out and installing a caretaker until they could decide what disposition to make of it. Of this stopgap appointee, Edward J. Bash, formerly with the Department of Agriculture, the Wriston Committee on Foreign Service Reorganization reported in June: "He does not pretend to have the accepted characteristic of 'an educational leader of distinction.' " The content of those courses that did survive was checked by SY investigators, who sat in on seminars taking notes. Special SY clearances were required for anyone invited to lecture at the school.

In order to free key foreign-affairs positions from professionalism and open them to deserving Republicans, McLeod last year asked the Civil Service Commission to turn back more than three hundred from the career service to the status of political appointees. This is also known as the spoils system. The Commission grudgingly released about a hundred. Then McLeod set about similarly getting his SY investigators "exempted," which caused an uproar in the ranks of veteran SY men when they saw their established rights of tenure threatened by political appointments dependent entirely on McLeod's whim. By February 1954, some twenty of his most experienced men had quit, and one of them, William D. Huskey, special agent in charge of guarding foreign visitors, walked out charging that McLeod had created "an atmosphere of fright and intimidation."

But the problem of getting higher jobs unstuck still bedevils McLeod, and sometimes drastic remedies have to be applied.

Some months ago, Assistant Secretary Samuel C. Waugh of Economic Affairs was confronted with information from Mc-Leod's office to the effect that a certain man on his staff was a "risk" and had to go. Waugh challenged his judgment. Then it emerged that McLeod's office had been particularly anxious to "open up" that spot because it had an office seeker all ready and waiting for it. "I don't mind taking in Republicans," another high official told me. "I'm a Republican myself. But I do object to taking in ward heelers."

The McLeod Dossier

Who is this man, and how did he get the job?

R. W. Scott McLeod was born forty years ago in Davenport, Iowa, and in his boyhood moved to "acreage" in Ottumwa and then to Cedar Rapids, where his father managed to give him $100 and one suit of clothes to attend Grinnell College. After trying to pay his way there by working a laundry and dry-cleaning route while also playing quarterback, he had to drop out after freshman year to earn money. ("Of course," he recalls, grinning, "the school didn't win a game after I left. They all came around to see if I was coming back.") After a year of odd jobs he *was* back, a sophomore whose deity was Harry Hopkins and whose roommate—so one Washington correspondent understood him to say—was a district organizer for the Communist Party. In response to my own inquiry, McLeod amended this to say that the young Communist simply roomed on "the same floor" with him, and that the chap was "theoretical, not practical." In any case, it is not known whether this derogatory information is contained in McLeod's own SY dossier. Meanwhile he had taken to trying his hand at journalism, writing a column for the campus paper and editing the college annual, *Zephyr.*

On being graduated, he called at the employment office of the Des Moines *Register,* where he got a job—not as a reporter, but only as an adtaker at $17 a week. "I was a terribly ambitious kid," he recalls, "and I took this disappointment very hard." Then he turned his back on Harry Hopkins, he says, and on the New Deal as a "philosophy of despair." By 1938 he had found himself a police reporter's job on the Cedar Rapids *Gazette,* whose editor was Verne Marshall, soon to become one of the most voluble leaders with Charles A. Lindbergh of the isolationist America First group. McLeod became Marshall's protégé on the paper.

By 1941, the zealous Verne Marshall had been fired from the paper as his cause declined, and McLeod was casting about for other employment. His work as a police reporter had brought him into contact with the regional FBI office, which after Pearl Harbor was having difficulties recruiting new men. McLeod was inducted as an FBI special agent and soon assigned to Concord, New Hampshire, where he remained until 1949.

In Concord, McLeod one day called on Senator Styles Bridges to express his appreciation of a bill for improved FBI pensions which Bridges had backed, and therewith a friendship began. In 1949, Bridges took him, as his administrative assistant, to Washington where McLeod worked hard for his chief and got to know such important men as Senators McCarthy and McCarran. (George Wilson was simultaneously doing similar work for Senator Knowland.) McLeod's skills in the political field first appeared in the spade work he did for Bridges's share in the dissenting Senate tract denouncing the dismissal of General MacArthur and the Administration's entire Far Eastern policy ("Individual Views of Certain Members of the Joint Committee on Armed Services and Foreign Relations"). Then, when 1953 came around, Donald B. Lourie, who had been tapped as Under Secretary for Administration and was looking for an assistant who stood in well with the McCarthy-McCarran-Bridges wing on the Hill, heard of McLeod. "Fine appointment," said Senator McCarthy, "excellent man . . ."

Secretary Dulles, for his part, was little interested in the matter of who was to be his new SY chief. As he told Secretary Acheson in their brief meeting just before the changeover, his intention was to rid himself of the administrative problems of the Secretaryship and devote his attention to high policy. In fact, it was not until a New York *Times* reporter confronted him that Dulles even became aware that McLeod had been given not only SY but Personnel as well. "Is that bad?" he asked innocently. When told that in any case it was unprecedented, he simply answered, "I leave these things to Smith."

While Dulles remained above the smoke, a contest for position had been going on between Walter Bedell Smith, an Eisenhower man, and the other Under Secretary, Lourie, and his men, all built up in the desire to appease non-Eisenhower Republicans on the Hill. Within a few months McLeod was able to say: "For the first time in twenty years . . . the House Un-American Activities Committee under Chairman Velde, the Senate Internal Security Subcommittee under Senator Jenner, and the Special Investigating Subcommittee under Senator McCarthy have received the complete and unequivocal support of the State Department." One of his first acts, as his Iowa newspaper friend Clark Mollenhoff reported it to the Des Moines *Register,* was to reach a "compromise" with Senator McCarthy whereby the Senator's long-standing demand for classified State Department personnel files would be met by giving him information from them "when deemed proper," although the files themselves would not be handed over. By April, a flow of such information was moving from McLeod's office to the committee, and Roy Cohn, for instance, showed himself to be in possession of the minutest details of a strictly confidential Department Loyalty Review Board "interrogatory" as sworn to by one official.

Another close contact for McLeod at the other end of town remained his former employer, Senator Bridges, to whom in March he leaked the advance information that Charles Bohlen was to be picked as Ambassador to Moscow. Bridges told McCarthy, who told Senator McCarran, who made a denunciatory speech that blew the story's lid. This tactic, especially when he followed it up by going around to see Major General Wilton Persons, the President's own liaison man with Congress, to ask support in blocking the Bohlen nomination, almost cost McLeod his job. Secretary Dulles stated somberly to the press that he himself must have "final responsibility" in the matter of clearing or not clearing Bohlen, and Under Secretary Smith was detailed to demand McLeod's resignation. But within a few days, the Department thought better of it.

The Price

Today, the total price of not having done something about McLeod—and of taking him and his team in the first place—can be reckoned. Figures do not tell the story, since SY distorts them; the price is written down in the breakdown of the integrity of the government's No. 1 civilian department. On actual casualties, McLeod testified in January before the House Appropriations Committee that last year 534 "risks" had been dropped, of whom eleven were ousted for "pro-Communist activities or associations." But it has since appeared that about half of those "dropped" were in fact just transferred to other U.S. agencies, and McLeod will give out no details as to how many—if any—have been fired on evidence of actual disloyalty. He admitted he couldn't find any trace of a list of fifty-seven alleged Communists in the Department that McCarthy claimed to have seen; he has yet to point to any one man or woman actually charged with subversion. He states that only eleven suspects so far have made use of the appeals machinery set up to rehear cases, from which he argues that the rest, by implication, have thereby admitted their "guilt." Of course this leaves out of account all those who have been too terrified to brave a second round with McLeod, with its possible legal cost and public pillorying, and who have preferred just to drop out of sight quietly.

McLeod and his team do not admit that letters have been opened, rooms have been wired, reading matter checked, or telephone conversations tapped. Yet a career minister attests that letters coming to him through the Foreign Service mail room have been steamed open "in a very amateurish way." Officials on the Policy Planning Staff have charged—as reported in the New York *Times* last March 7—that SY investigators have been put on their trail to discover which of them read officially circulating copies of certain magazines, including *The Reporter*. Although both McLeod and Flinn insist that offices have not been wired, most officials don't believe them and guard their talk closely, "just in case." When I discussed with McLeod's top adviser, former editor Frank Waldrop, allegations that diplomats abroad were now reluctant to present objective reports in their dispatches, for fear

that SY might subsequently hold something against them, he exclaimed, "Any man who doesn't report the truth ought to be
fired." Yet at the same time a young secretary formerly with the
FBI has been assigned to the "highly sensitive" Policy Planning
Staff, whose members have observed her reading and making
notes on old dispatches.

The new system, in short, has outgrown even its originator.
Sustained by his all-pervasive agents, it has become one of actual
or implied blackmail. Throughout the "10450" manhunt this
year, junior officers have been called on by SY agents to tell all
they know about their supervisors' habits. In turn, the secretary
of a junior on the West European desk, when reprimanded for
dawdling, threatened to go to McLeod and tell all she thought of
him. A security limbo exists into which officials pass when SY
finds something against them—not enough to cause suspension or
dismissal, but just enough to make SY veto their promotion or assignment to especially important jobs; and there are stories
around the corridors about how even an anonymous denunciation by a rival can land you in this particular degree of hell.

"Risks," furthermore, are earmarked for firing without notice
to their immediate superiors who are in the best position to know
their performance. If a superior wants to stick his neck out and
fight for retaining someone branded a "risk" by SY, he must do
so in a paper that then goes into his own dossier—with the result
that in case further derogatory material turns up (as an SY man
put it to me) "It's *his* neck."

In this condition, Dulles's Department has inevitably become
so fear-ridden and flat as to convey an absence of tone. A British
diplomat assigned to Washington remarked to me, "From one day
to the next, I can't find out any more what your people are thinking. They're either jumpy or silent. I can't learn what their long
view is—if they have a long view." Middle-rank advisers in particular, often the suppliers of new ideas or approaches, are now
little heard from; the key Policy Planning Staff, which used to
meet daily, now has so little to say that it gets together only every
second or third week.

While political officers sit waiting at their desks, FBI veteran
Flinn is today completing his investigations and busying himself,

as he told me, with "developing" information as to "public-relations factors" concerning them. Frank Waldrop, the intellectual of the McLeod camp, holds forth in his book-lined mansion against "liberal crap . . . student exchange and all that crap . . ." Mr. Morton, as Assistant Secretary for Congressional Relations, privately apologizes for some of McLeod's behavior, but says that since the State Department (unlike Agriculture or Labor) has no "constituents," it must go out of its way to making itself palatable up on Capitol Hill. "Scotty," he tells me, "is a damned fine kid."

When Dulles took in "Scotty," he evidently thought he was buying a man who could persuade the extreme right wing on the Hill to take its heat off the Department. Instead, he bought a system that has turned *up* the heat and means to keep it there. He did not stop to think that while a good policeman was needed, such a man's frame of reference was limited professionally to simple black-and-white judgments. To invite the cop upstairs to participate in complex matters of high policy and management was both to mistake the cop's qualifications and the scope of the needs. Dulles asserted he was interested only in the ends of policy, not the means. Since any means would do, McLeod's were the ones he got. And so he now must witness a law of governmental physics in operation that insists on filling that vacuum—not only with adventurers but this time with a Big Brother.

What Happens to a
Victim of Nameless Accusers

By Anthony Lewis

On July 29, 1953, Bernard Goldsmith was living what most Americans would regard as a life of exceptional economic and psychological security. He had been in the same government agency since 1931, working up from a clerk's job at $1,440 a year to the directorship of a staff of sixty-three people and a salary of $8,360. He made a little extra money practicing law in his spare time. He had twice been commended by his agency for exceptional service and had recently suggested and carried out an office reorganization expected to save the government many thousands of dollars.

He was buying a home in Parkview, a housing development that had been built by the government in a Maryland suburb and later sold to a residents' corporation that Goldsmith served as general counsel. He was, or had been, president of the Parkview Citizens' Association and Parent-Teacher Association, and a director of the Lions Club. His wife was chairman of the Parkview Community Chest drive and a leader in Jewish and nonsectarian charity organizations. His fourteen-year-old daughter had just won a county-wide contest for an essay on Independence Day. She was awarded a $25 defense bond and her picture was printed in a Washington paper.

Half an hour before quitting time on July 29, 1953, Goldsmith and his assistant, Sam Rosen, were asked to go to the personnel director's office. Goldsmith, who was called first, thought he knew what it was about. Rosen was moving to California. His resignation had already been accepted, but he had agreed to stay on a few weeks so Goldsmith could take a scheduled vacation. Presumably the personnel director wanted to talk about Rosen's replacement.

When Goldsmith walked in, his own immediate superior was sitting in the office with the personnel director. The latter handed some papers to him. They were three letters, all dated July 29. The first began:

"Subject: Removal from duty—proposed.

"This is notice of proposed adverse action against you. The action contemplated is removal from duty, based upon information available which reflects upon your suitability as an employe from the viewpoint of security. Accordingly, it is proposed to remove you . . . in the interests of National Security, based on the following charges. . . ."

There were eight numbered charges. The broadest, and gravest, accused Goldsmith of being part of a "radical" group at Parkview. The others accused him of attending a meeting, subscribing to a paper, and joining an organization more than ten years earlier, and of associating with persons suspected of Communist leanings, some of whom Goldsmith recognized as Parkview residents or law clients of his and others whose names he did not recognize at all.

The second letter said:

"In view of the action contemplated, your access to any classified materials is hereby terminated . . ."

The third letter referred to the other two:

"Reference (a) advised you of your proposed separation . . . Reference (b) deprived you of the right of access to any classified materials. . . . The purpose of this letter is to advise you that in the further interest of National Security . . . you are suspended from duty at 0815 on 30 July 1953. Before leaving the premises on 29 July 1953 you will deliver your identification badge and pass to the Badge Office, Room 105."

The Accused

Goldsmith is forty-three, a small man with a small brown mustache and gray-streaked hair. He looks tired. Goldsmith's wife Alice, forty-two, is slight and pert, with rosy cheeks, black hair pulled back. They have four children.

Like most of the families in Parkview, they have a two-story row apartment. The only books visible in their living room are *Alice in Wonderland* and twenty-four volumes of the Harvard Classics.

Goldsmith is a registered Democrat who often votes for Republicans—or, as he later told a reporter, "At least I used to. I voted for John Marshall Butler in 1950 against Tydings. We got a postcard that seemed to be handwritten by Butler. So I thought, if the guy is thoughtful enough to send me a card I'll vote for him."

Mrs. Goldsmith's reaction to the accusation against her husband was: "If someone had told him about it ten minutes before it happened, he'd have bet ten years' salary—that's how sure he was that such a thing couldn't happen in this country. Especially when you've lived the kind of life we have."

Goldsmith tried to recall July 29 in the personnel office. "When I finished reading the letters, I told them the charges were absolutely false and I could prove it readily. I remember I said: 'If it's taken this agency twenty-three years to decide I'm a security risk, God help it.'

"When I walked out of the office, I still didn't realize I was suspended right away. I used to be a member of our own loyalty board under the old system, and we never did anything like that." (Under policy followed in the Truman Administration, agencies could suspend an accused man or not, depending on the charges and the sensitivity of his job. Under the new security program anyone accused must be suspended immediately.)

"Back in my own office I sat down and read the letters again," Goldsmith said. "I realized I was suspended and had to turn in my badge. I walked over to the security office and turned it in. As I walked back, Rosen came out of the personnel director's office. He was crying. I didn't need to ask him what had happened.

"On the way home all I could think was: 'How am I going to tell my wife?' I was thankful the two older children weren't home

—they were up in Worcester with my sister-in-law. They're very impressionable . . .

"I had decided to eat dinner and wait. But as soon as Alice looked at me . . ."

Mrs. Goldsmith told the reporter: "I said, 'What happened? Is everyone all right?' "

And Goldsmith replied, "I've been suspended."

"I can't tell you exactly what happened for the next four days," Goldsmith continued. "We didn't eat. We stayed up all night talking. I think I lost nine or ten pounds."

"We drew the blinds and locked the doors," Mrs. Goldsmith said, "and it was a hot summer. When we finally went over to my sister's place and told her—it's funny looking back. You won't understand, but we closed the doors and took her in a small room."

Goldsmith's sixty-three staff members were told that he had been suspended and that security was involved—no more. A girl in Goldsmith's office telephoned him and told him there was a rumor that his brother was a top Communist. Goldsmith doesn't have a brother.

News of his suspension spread around Parkview. A woman who plays mah-jongg with Mrs. Goldsmith telephoned and said a man in Washington had told a friend of hers that Goldsmith and Rosen had been "picked up on espionage."

Someone tipped off the *Times-Herald,* Colonel Robert R. McCormick's Washington newspaper. A reporter called Goldsmith and said he might as well talk freely about the case because the story would be printed anyway. Goldsmith did not talk. No such story ever appeared in the *Times-Herald.*

A Few of the Boys

Parkview Housing, Inc., which had bought the development from the government, was on Goldsmith's mind. He was its lawyer, and Rosen had formerly served as president. Both had been leading supporters of the decision to set up the corporation and buy the houses, and it was a controversial decision.

The government had been trying to sell Parkview for years. Goldsmith and the majority of residents felt they would be better off buying the development themselves than letting it go to an outside real-estate firm. But a minority group of low-income families who had been given low rents had hoped no one would buy Parkview and the government would have to stay on as landlord.

At the end of 1952 the sale had been completed. Parkview Housing had given every resident a year to decide whether he wanted to buy his home. The end of that year was approaching and some of the minority were bitter because they were going to have to move out and also because Parkview Housing had had to raise rents.

Goldsmith felt vaguely that somehow the housing fight might have had something to do with the security charges against him and Rosen. He was also afraid that their suspension might get Parkview Housing in trouble.

"I felt in all fairness I should notify Bob Chase, the president," Goldsmith said. "I didn't want to see him alone because he works for the government and I thought he might be accused of something—it was crazy, I know. We asked him and his wife to come over, and again we locked the doors. I told him, 'If you think this will embarrass you in any way . . .'"

Chase and the board of Parkview Housing gave Goldsmith a formal vote of confidence. A few days later the corporation held a farewell party for Rosen, who had decided to make his planned move to California and attempt to clear his name from there.

"It was our first public appearance," Mrs. Goldsmith said. "There was a terrible storm, and we were late. Before we got to the hall a gang came up and called Rosen a dirty Jew and a Communist."

Goldsmith found out later what had happened.

"Sixteen of the minority who hadn't joined Parkview Housing were up in the American Legion hall drinking. It wasn't an official Legion meeting—I want to make that clear—they just sell beer there. The sixteen got pretty drunk, and they thought maybe if they attacked the party they could break up Parkview Housing and stay in their apartments.

"They called all the newspapers and the state and county police and said there was going to be a riot—they were going to break up a Communist meeting. They got into three cars, but because of the storm only one ever got to the hall. Luckily the Parkview police chief was there. He refused to arrest them. They wanted to be arrested so it would get in the papers."

During the black first days after he was suspended Goldsmith wanted religious help. His rabbi is a government chaplain, and Goldsmith was afraid of getting him in trouble, so he called the minister of Parkview's Protestant church.

"The minister came over here and talked with us one night until about three in the morning," Goldsmith said. "To show you how wonderful he was—he was leaving on a trip, and he gave me an itinerary so we could call him wherever he was and he would come back if we needed him. He gave us back our faith in people. He said it wasn't just our fight, it was everybody's fight."

People began calling and offering to help—friends, employees in Goldsmith's office, people they hardly knew. There were 250 telephone calls from Parkview residents alone.

"That's the one wonderful part of this," Goldsmith said. "You find out for the first time in your life what people think of you. You know, you could go through a lifetime and never know who your friends are. In that way we're fortunate.

"We were afraid people would think of themselves, but most of them didn't. I mean especially the ones in the government, people who knew if I were not cleared, their jobs would be in jeopardy.

"A delegation came over from the office with ice cream and cake and candy and wanted to know what they could do. When I warned them they might be jeopardizing their jobs, they said they had confidence in me."

Mrs. Goldsmith said men from the office kept dropping in.

"One man said to me: 'All that I am today I owe to Bernie Goldsmith.' Another wanted to know if his wife couldn't cook for us, and if they couldn't take the little children off our hands."

"Another friend got me aside and said: 'Bernie, I just got a $2,500 check. I want to turn it over to you. Don't worry about paying me back—just give me some when you can.' He pulled out the check, but I wouldn't take it. I guess if I had taken all the money I was offered, we could have gone down to Florida and retired."

Money was the first problem Goldsmith had to tackle once he had decided he would fight for his job and his name. He had sixty days' leave coming, so he thought he would be paid for that long anyway.

"I called one of the men at the office and said: 'I just wanted to check and be sure I'll be paid during my annual leave.' Immediately he started hemming and hawing, and I realized he was even afraid to talk with me because he thought I might be a spy or something. Then finally he said he'd check and I should call back. He didn't want anyone to say he'd called me. In the end I had to call the personnel man, and he said they could not give me the annual leave. I asked him what people do about eating while they're fighting these charges. He said something to the effect of 'That's not our problem, it's yours.' "

Mrs. Goldsmith's parents and two brothers offered to support the family so Goldsmith could press his appeal without looking for other work, and he accepted that offer.

The next problem was to find a lawyer.

"I didn't know what lawyer handled these cases," Goldsmith said, "but I called a friend and got some suggestions.

"The first man said I was a guinea pig for the new security program and it certainly looked like an interesting case. He said since I was a lawyer he'd give me a break on fees—five hundred down and forty dollars an hour. I told him it would take a while for me to find the down payment, and then he said he made it a policy never to get into a case at all until he gets the down payment.

"The second lawyer wanted five hundred down, half immediately, and twenty-five an hour if I did a lot of the work myself. He was willing to put a ceiling of two thousand on the fee. Something could have been worked out, but we still weren't sure he was the right guy. After all, it wasn't only the money, it was our life."

The third man Goldsmith saw was Joseph Fanelli, a nervous, forceful attorney who had handled some cases under the old loyalty system, and Goldsmith took only a few minutes to hire him. Fanelli's fee was thirty dollars an hour, with a maximum of one thousand dollars and no down payment.

Under the Eisenhower security regulations Goldsmith had thirty days to file a formal answer to the charges. His department could clear him on the basis of the answer alone, but Fanelli realized that was unlikely. (The department never mentioned this possibility, as it turned out.) Then Goldsmith had the right to appeal in person at a hearing before a board of three men drawn from other branches of his department. Finally, he was permitted to file friends' character affidavits with the hearing board.

Fanelli and Goldsmith finished the formal answer to charges August 20.

Bill of Particulars

These were the written charges against Bernard Goldsmith, and the answers:

¶"You have associated for a considerable time with persons who are known Communists. Among others, this association applies to Abner and Doris A_____, and Henry and Grace B_____."

Goldsmith answered: "I have never associated in any way with any known Communist . . . Communist sympathizer, radical, or any kind of pink.

"I do not know Henry and Grace B_____ at all. An old Parkview residential listing indicates that Henry B_____ lived in Parkview prior to 1949. I think that I have heard he is a chemist. Beyond that I know nothing of him or Grace B_____, who I assume is his wife.

"There is an Abner A_____ who lives in Parkview. He called at my home on just one occasion late in 1951. As a lawyer I had just filed a slander suit against Parkview Services, Inc., in behalf of a man formerly employed by this company. Mr. A_____ was a director of Parkview Services, and he came to ask me something about the suit.

"The foregoing is the full extent of my acquaintance with Abner A_____. I do not know any Doris A_____. I assume she is Abner A_____'s wife."

¶"You have been an associate of one David C_____, who has been described as having Communistic tendencies, and it is of

record that his wife signed Communist nominating petitions during 1939. Mr. C_____ was formerly employed in your department and resigned while under investigation relative to his status as a security risk."

Goldsmith's written answer said that C_____ was a director of Parkview Housing, that he had seen C_____ at meetings but had never been to his home, that he had been C_____'s lawyer in the attempted purchase of a delicatessen, and that he had nothing to do with C_____'s working for his department and had in fact denied C_____ a job in his own office because he was unqualified.

¶"There is a record of your attending a meeting at which donations were required for the United American Spanish Aid Committee, which is on the Attorney General's list of subversive organizations. You solicited and requested other individuals to attend the meeting."

Goldsmith answered: "Prior to receipt of the charges I had never heard of this committee. My counsel informs me that the organization had something to do with the Spanish Loyalists.

"I have never attended a meeting at which donations were required. I have never solicited or requested anyone to attend a meeting concerned with aid to Loyalist Spain.

"Sometime after we moved to Parkview in 1939 my wife and I were invited to a party. As new residents we were glad to go. Many Parkview residents were there, including the Mayor. The party was social. However, games (in the nature of quizzes) were played. They cost twenty-five cents or maybe fifty cents, with a small prize for the winner. My recollection is that I was told the money made was to go to Spanish war orphans. My wife remembers it as in aid of Loyalist refugees in general. I had no interest in the Spanish Loyalists, although like many Americans my sympathies at the time were in their favor on the understanding that they were democrats fighting a dictator. I probably played in one or two games at a probable cost of fifty cents."

¶"You were at one time a subscriber to the Communist newsletter *In Fact,* and you were a subscriber after this publication had been exposed by the press as expressing the view of the Communist party."

"Twelve or thirteen years ago," Goldsmith answered, "someone asked me to join in a group subscription to *In Fact*. As I recall it, I gave the solicitor fifty cents which was to be for one year.

"I looked at the first few issues which came in my mail. There was nothing to indicate to me that it was a Communist sheet. But I thought it sensational, badly written and unreliable. I have subscribed to *Time* magazine for twenty years. The facts of a story printed in *Time* would be so distorted in *In Fact* as to be hardly recognizable. I did not look at it after the first few issues.

"I have never seen any exposure of *In Fact* in the press. I have no reason to doubt that it was exposed, but I missed it, as I am likely to miss anything in the daily press which is not a main headline, or in the sports and comic sections.

"At this time I subscribe to the Washington *Post, Coronet* and *Time* magazine. Fairly regularly I buy the *Saturday Evening Post, Life, Pageant, Reader's Digest,* the Washington *Daily News* and the Washington *Times-Herald. . . .*"

¶"It is also of record that you at one time were a member of the National Lawyers Guild, an organization cited by the House Committee on Un-American Activities as a Communist organization."

Goldsmith replied that he had studied law at night in the early years of his present employment, passed his bar examinations, and then, about 1939 or 1940, had looked for a higher-paying legal job among other Federal agencies.

"At one of them," he said, "and I do not remember which, the General Counsel interviewed me. He told me that he was a member of the National Lawyers Guild and so were practically all the top lawyers in the Government. I inferred that I would not be seriously considered for a legal position unless I filled in an application for membership, which he handed me. I filled in the application then and there and paid him, to the best of my recollection, a dollar, which was the only bill I had with me. I did not get the job.

"That is the complete extent of my connection with the National Lawyers Guild. I never had any interest in it, never went to a meeting and do not know now whether the organization is still in existence."

¶"One Roger Hiram D_____ is known to to have been a regular associate of yours, and it is of record that he was the editor of the *Gazette* [Parkview newspaper] at a time when you and Mrs. Goldsmith were listed as members of the staff of this newspaper as of May, 1940. The *Gazette* was listed as a member of the Washington Bookshop Association . . ."

Goldsmith located D_____, who had moved out of Parkview years ago, and he filed an affidavit commenting on this charge. D_____ said he was himself a Federal employee and had been cleared many times. He described the *Gazette* when he edited it (without pay) as a hand-to-mouth weekly carrying only local Parkview news and said he could not understand how it could have belonged to a "bookshop association." The Goldsmiths had done a little amateur writing for the paper, he said.

Goldsmith attached six issues of the *Gazette* to his formal answer and said he had never heard of the Washington Bookshop Association.

¶"It has been reported that a list of names found on your desk during October, 1952, contained the following, who either are known Communists or suspected of having Communistic tendencies:

"a. Arthur E_____, who was a Chief Defense Attorney in the *Amerasia* case.

"b. Irving F_____, a known Communist and subscriber to the *Morning Freiheit*."

Goldsmith began his answer by noting that the only places on his desk where those two names had ever been listed were his personal telephone book and a scratch-paper strip which wound up on a roller after use. (Presumably, some investigator must have unrolled the strip, taken down all the names on it and in the book, and then checked every name for possible subversive connections. At Fanelli's suggestion Goldsmith unrolled the strip himself one day and counted 407 names on that and in the book.)

As to Arthur E_____, Goldsmith said he had met him only once—and then as opposing counsel in a lawsuit. Goldsmith said he "would not have known whether E_____ was connected with the *Amerasia* case, which to the best of my scanty recollection was concerned with exports."

A Lawyer and His Clients

Fanelli also knew E_____, a respected member of the Washington bar who specializes in business cases, and he decided he ought to tell E_____ about the reference to him. E_____ then filed an affidavit:

"For Mr. Goldsmith's sake, I want to make it clear that my only acquaintance with him was one conference and several telephone calls relating to a libel suit which his client had brought against mine.

"For the sake of my own reputation, I wish to take this occasion to recite the facts of my relationship with the *Amerasia* case.

"By the very nature of his profession a lawyer represents all kinds of people. When he defends a Nazi, a Red, a thief or a murderer, he does not thereby become himself a Nazi, Red, thief or murderer . . . While it is true that I represented Philip Jaffe, the former editor of *Amerasia* Magazine, who has been accused of being a Communist, I have also represented a client who admitted having once been a member of the National Socialist party. Fortunately, from a financial standpoint, most of my clients have been just ordinary prosperous American businessmen, mostly Republicans.

"Mr. Jaffe's attorneys were a leading New York law firm one of whose partners is a former chairman of the Judiciary Committee of the House of Representatives. They needed local counsel because the indictment against Mr. Jaffe had been brought in the District of Columbia. They retained me for this limited local representation. I entered a plea of guilty for Mr. Jaffe in open court. To the best of my knowledge I have never seen him since that day, in 1945.

"I should be pleased if my sworn statements herein can be transmitted to the investigative and security agencies whose correct reporting of a simple and admitted fact led to the absurd non sequitur identifying me with persons 'who are known Communists or suspected of having Communistic tendencies.'"

As to Irving F_____, Goldsmith's written answer said:

"On one occasion in 1947 I represented Irving F_____ in the purchase of a grocery. He retained me on the recommendation of my brother-in-law, who was a grocer himself and knew F_____ from school days.

"Since the purchase of the store I have not seen F_____. However, I have had some indication of his views through one trying incident in the spring of 1950. My brother-in-law was at my home to celebrate my son's Bar Mitzvah [confirmation in the Jewish faith]. He got a phone call from F_____ and told me F_____ was dropping by the house to say hello to him.

"My brother-in-law then volunteered that he had had an argument with F_____ some months previously in which F_____ had talked like a Communist. Although I disliked being ungracious, I wanted no part of a possible Communist. I told my brother-in-law that I would not have F_____ in the house. My wife put chairs in the yard, and F_____ visited with my brother-in-law there while I remained in the house.

"Since then my brother-in-law has told me he became convinced of F_____'s Commie views and is no longer on speaking terms with him. It seems to me, although I am not sure, that I have heard of the *Morning Freiheit* as a Jewish-language newspaper. I have never seen it and know nothing of it."

¶"Several reliable informants have described you as a leader and very active in a radical group in Parkview, Md. Included in this group are those described as ever willing to defend Communism in any discussion of ideology which may occur."

"I am not and never have been," Goldsmith wrote, "a leader or member of any kind of radical group in Parkview or elsewhere. I have not and would not associate with anyone I knew to be disloyal to my country. I have never heard anyone defend Communism in my presence. No one has ever wanted to or dared."

Goldsmith described at length the battle over the sale of Parkview. He pointed out that he was on the conservative side, against continued government ownership. He said he had publicly favored a proposal adopted by Parkview Housing in 1952 requiring every one of the more than one thousand members to take a loyalty oath. (Several affidavits attested to this.) Goldsmith suggested that the broadest charge—and the entire case against him—had been inspired somehow by "disappointed and warm tempered members of the minority."

Any References?

Fanelli wanted Goldsmith to get affidavits covering his whole adult life.

"Go right back as far as you can," he said. "We want to show you've never had any Communist affiliations."

Mrs. Goldsmith did most of the work of asking people for the affidavits.

"That was one of the hard things," she said—"to write or call someone you hadn't seen in years and tell him Bernie was one of those people, a security risk. You couldn't go into long explanations about how he was innocent, you know. I told people: 'All we want to know is what you thought of Bernie when you knew him.'"

Sometimes there were refusals. A fellow employee Goldsmith had gone out of his way to help said he "didn't want to get mixed up in it." A friend at Parkview was afraid because he was a member of the Naval Reserve. One of his closest associates at the office, Goldsmith said, "suddenly was a cold stranger. He wanted to buy back his introduction."

But those were the exceptions. Goldsmith eventually filed ninety-seven affidavits, and he would have had many more if Fanelli had not told him to stop. Many persons volunteered; some were insulted because they had not been asked.

There was one from his former scoutmaster, and one from a man who had first met Goldsmith in his father's candy store in Philadelphia. Every mayor of Parkview during the fourteen years Goldsmith had lived there, except one whom he did not ask, filed an affidavit. So did the city manager and town clerk, a banker, insurance man, minister, librarian.

One affidavit came from the president of the District of Columbia Bar Association. "We used to play ping-pong together," Goldsmith said. "I've hardly seen him in twenty years, but he didn't hesitate a minute."

Three affidavits from Parkview moved Goldsmith particularly.

"One was from a devoutly religious woman. I never knew she liked me especially. One day I met her on the street and she said: 'Bernie, if you're not cleared I'll stop believing in God.'"

The second was from a Parkview man who had opposed Goldsmith's housing plans and once had blocked a proposed increase in his lawyer's fees from Parkview Housing.

"We'd called each other names," Goldsmith said. "I never even thought of asking him. One day he called my wife and said: 'What in the hell are they trying to do to Goldsmith?' "

In his affidavit this man said that, as a Roman Catholic, he "bitterly detests atheistic and Godless" Communism. He said he had often disagreed with Goldsmith and had no particular ties of friendship. Then he said he had found Goldsmith to be "a man of honor and integrity, above reproach in his conduct, his associations and his attitude."

The third affidavit that moved Goldsmith was from his postman. When Mrs. Goldsmith asked him to write one, he said he wasn't sure, that he was certainly in favor of loyalty investigations, and that maybe a few innocent people had to get hurt.

They did not see the postman again until the following Thursday. He said he had waited for his day off, and he gave them this statement, written out by hand:

"To whom it may concern—

"I was greatly surprised when my friend Bernie Goldsmith told me he had been suspended from his job because of alleged Communistic associations. I do not believe Bernie is at all sympathetic with their cause.

"I met Bernie when his son Henry became a member of the Boy Scout Troop of which I was Assistant Scoutmaster. Bernie was always interested in Scouting and willing to help the Troop in its activities. I have been camping with Bernie. We've sat around the campfire talking with other troop leaders and fathers and in discussions he has always impressed me as being 100% American. His son Henry is a swell Scout, and always a credit to the Troop.

"I am a postman, and am the mail carrier who delivers mail to Bernie's home. I am familiar with the type of literature the Communists mail to their sympathizers, and would have noticed if Bernie had received any measure of such literature, and I cannot recall his receiving any at all.

"With all the love in his heart for his family, his God and America, I know there could be no room for communism."

The Evidence Is Weighed

The hearing began on the Goldsmiths' twentieth wedding anniversary—September 21, 1953. It lasted three days.

Security regulations provided that a record of all hearings must be kept and made available to the accused party, but Goldsmith has never seen the record of his hearing. It was taken on a tape recorder that kept breaking down. The chairman later told Fanelli the record was very garbled, and they'd rather not supply it.

As Fanelli and Goldsmith remember the hearing, three aspects of it stand out:

The government produced no witnesses to support the general accusation.

Very little time was spent on the specific written charges.

Most of the time was taken up with discussion of Parkview and of some new names which the government suddenly introduced.

The hearing was held in the conference room of the building where Goldsmith had worked. The three members of the hearing board were government employees—quite high-ranking ones—from another agency of Goldsmith's department. A woman lawyer from Goldsmith's own agency was legal officer for the board; she acted, Goldsmith and Fanelli soon discovered, as an able prosecutor.

The first day was taken up by the five witnesses Fanelli had decided to call, friends and associates of Goldsmith. Fanelli examined each briefly on his opinion of the accused. Then the legal officer tried to impeach the testimony. She asked many questions about Parkview, bringing up names of residents hitherto unmentioned and asking the witness:

"Do you know _____? What do you think about him? Does Mr. Goldsmith know him?"

Most of the names mentioned were those of persons neither Goldsmith nor the witnesses knew or cared for particularly. The Parkview police chief was called and asked to give the names of residents he suspected of being Communists. If he knew any, he answered, he would give them to the FBI.

On the second day Fanelli laboriously entered exhibits—affidavits, copies of the *Gazette,* Goldsmith's high-school yearbook. ("Gee, I hope I get it back. We asked . . .")

At the end of the second day Goldsmith took the stand and answered a few questions by Fanelli. The next day the legal officer cross-examined. By then she had mellowed some, Goldsmith said, and seemed almost friendly. She asked him about the Parkview Housing Board, how often it had met, what the members talked about. And she asked him about his relations with the persons whose names had been brought in during the hearing and whether he thought they were "radical."

When Goldsmith left the stand, the government called as its first witnesses some of his official associates. They were asked their opinion of Goldsmith, and all but one unqualifiedly praised him. The exception was cautious—so cautious that the lawyer and the members of the hearing board eventually gave up trying to question him. Fanelli then asked the man: "Do you think Mr. Goldsmith became more of a security risk as a result of his meeting certain people in his civic activities at Parkview?"

The witness paused, thought, hesitated, and finally said "Yes."

"How long have you worked with Mr. Goldsmith?" Fanelli asked.

"Perhaps a year."

"After associating with Mr. Goldsmith for a year and a half," Fanelli asked, "do you think you are more of a security risk than you were before you met him?"

The witness sat in silence until at last the chairman of the board asked Fanelli whether he would insist on an answer to that question. Fanelli said "No," and the witness said he would rather not answer. He was dismissed.

At the very end of the hearing Goldsmith got a clue to the source of his agony.

The legal officer called as witnesses two Parkview residents who had given Goldsmith affidavits, the town clerk and his insurance agent. Each was offered the choice of appearing in front of Goldsmith or in secret. Both chose to appear before him.

The legal officer asked each his opinion of Goldsmith, and each said it was good. Then she asked, "Didn't an investigator visit you and talk to you about Goldsmith?" Each said "Yes." "And didn't you say he had associated with suspicious persons?" The witnesses said, "Certainly not." "Are you sure?" the legal officer asked. The witnesses said they knew they were under oath, and they were sure.

Then the town clerk volunteered a statement which Goldsmith remembered this way:

"The investigator who saw me was a young man who took no notes at all the whole time we were talking. He seemed to be trying to get me to say that Mr. Goldsmith was associated with some of these people you listed. But I told him just what I told you— that I would not mention Mr. Goldsmith in the same breath with them."

Goldsmith said the members of the hearing board looked surprised.

The legal officer asked Goldsmith if he had any idea who at Parkview might have brought the charges against him. Goldsmith named a few names—members of the minority in the housing dispute—and he got the impression there was a look of recognition on his interrogator's face.

Three weeks later the chairman of the board telephoned Fanelli.

"How would you bet we decided?" he asked.

Fanelli said: "I can't conceive of anything but a clearance."

"That's how we felt," the chairman said. "The decision is ready for mailing. Should it go to you?"

On October 9 the hearing board sent Goldsmith a copy of its memorandum on the written charges against him:

¶ "The evidence did not establish to any degree of certainty that Mr. Goldsmith was associated with Abner and Doris A_____ and Henry and Grace B_____.

¶ "There was evidence that David C_____ was a resident of Parkview and fairly well known to the residents of that community. Opinions of him varied. Mr. Goldsmith's association with Mr. C_____, if any association did exist, was only in connection with civic enterprises and professionally as an attorney.

¶ "The evidence establishes that Mr. Goldsmith was present at a social party sometime during the year 1941. This function was attended by many residents of Parkview, some of whom were reputed to have 'radical' and 'left-wing' tendencies and others whose reputation in the community was unquestioned. It was established that money was raised at this affair for the support of some Spanish relief organization, the exact name of which is not clear. The United Spanish Aid Committee, which allegedly was the recipient, was not placed on the Attorney General's list of subversive organizations until eight (8) years after the party.

¶ "The evidence established that Mr. Goldsmith did subscribe to a publication known as *In Fact* some twelve (12) years ago. There is evidence to indicate that he never renewed his subscription. The evidence does not show that the publishers of this periodical appear on the Attorney General's list.

¶ "The evidence establishes that in 1939 Mr. Goldsmith became a member of the National Lawyers Guild for one (1) year. At that time lawyers of national prominence were members and contributed articles to the quarterly published by the organization. There is no evidence that the National Lawyers Guild was considered a subversive organization when Mr. Goldsmith was a member.

¶ "Mr. Goldsmith, as well as his wife, were connected in some minor capacity with the Parkview Gazette. His connection, like others, was on a voluntary basis. Copies of this newspaper which were received in evidence and perused by the Board failed to reveal 'radical' or 'left-wing' tendencies. Rather, these issues reflected an account of the activities of a small town. No competent evidence was produced to establish that the Gazette was ever a member of the 'Washington Bookshop Association.'

¶ "The evidence indicates that Mr. Goldsmith's association with Arthur E_____ and Irving F_____ was solely in connection with isolated legal matters.

¶ "There is a lack of credible evidence to establish that Mr. Goldsmith was a leader of or active in radical groups in Parkview. In fact, the weight of evidence points to the non-existence in Parkview of 'radical' or 'left-wing' groups, as the words are loosely used.

"The evidence reveals an enlightening and interesting insight into the operations of a cooperative city such as Parkview. Since its inception Parkview has been a subject of controversy.

"From without, it has been eyed suspiciously as a 'queer' experiment. Many believed the Goverment had no business starting it. The extent of the cooperative undertaking was viewed by many as something apart from conventional private enterprise. The result has been that rumor and gossip have given Parkview a 'radical' or 'leftist' reputation.

"Within, management has been characterized by frequent disagreements. The testimony shows heated disputes that often developed into personal animosities. As a result such terms as 'crackpots,' 'radicals,' 'pinkos' and 'Communists' have been bandied about loosely by disgruntled individuals.

"In this environment a civic-minded individual—whether conservative or otherwise—is bound to be exposed to criticism. In the case of Mr. Goldsmith, who took part in many activities, the testimony showed that he was, if anything, a moderating, constructive and conservative influence.

"Based on all the evidence heard by the Board and the reports of investigation furnished by the Government, the Board could reach no other conclusion but that Mr. Goldsmith's employment is clearly consistent with the interest of national security."

Under the Eisenhower security regulations the findings of a hearing board are just recommendations. The final decision in every case must be made by the head of the agency.

At first Goldsmith and Fanelli thought that approval of the board's recommendations would be routine. But on inquiring, Fanelli discovered that the case was before a three-man review board which had just been set up to pass on all security cases. He was told that the board would have to read every item in the record—"and it's a foot thick," an official said.

Four months later, as this account went to press, Goldsmith*
was still suspended from his job.

---

* Goldsmith was, of course, Abraham Chasinow, who was eventually cleared of charges with an apology from the Navy Department.

February 6, 1958

The Cold Wave: *A Reminiscence of Childhood in North Dakota*

By Lois Phillips Hudson

My father and grandfather would often speak of the earlier days in North Dakota—of the strong man who could swing a hundred-pound sack of wheat to his back by flinging it over his shoulder with his teeth, of tornadoes that switched the roofs of barns and houses, and of hailstorms that rained sheep-killing stones, heaping July wheatfields with desolations of ice.

Even more fascinating to me were their stories of the early winters. I would never see any winters like these, they said, for a new and milder weather cycle now prevailed. I would never know the bitter years that built the grim legends of our northern land.

My mother used to tell me how once a prairie wolf had stalked her as she walked home alone from school, over miles of abandoned stubble. I always felt cheated when I looked at the faded photograph of my father sitting on a horse, his hat higher than some telephone wires. He had ridden that horse right to the top of a gigantic snowbank, packed so hard that the horse's hoofs hardly dented its crust. It was true that there was usually a bank in our yard that reached to the top of the clothesline pole, but this was hardly satisfying when I knew what grander things had been. Why couldn't something happen *after* I was born, I wondered.

Yet when the sort of thing I was waiting for finally came, its coming was no natural and casual, so unlike a legend, that I mistook it for a part of the routine of my existence. It was part of my routine, for instance, to run over behind the depot with some of the town kids and slide on the ice by the tracks before I went over to Schlagel's Store to get a ride home with my father. I was almost always the only girl to go sliding, and it was also part of my routine to try to beat the boys to the smoothest patch of ice. On the day I am talking about, the only departure from routine was that there were no contenders for any of the ice.

I didn't slide very long myself, because I began to feel some undefined discomfort that an adult would have easily identified as a deeply pervasive chill. But when an eight-year-old is too cold, he will first feel oddly tired and lonely and deserted, so that he will go to find people. Thus it was that although I began to have the feeling that I had played too long and that surely my father would be waiting for me angrily, when I opened the door to Schlagel's Store, I saw by the big Sessions clock that it was still only a quarter of four and that I would have to wait for him.

Several amorphous large men were warming their hands at the stove in the center of the room and speaking to each other in Russian. Their faces were always very red, and Mr. Buskowski's purplish, large-pored cheeks frightened me a good deal, as did his heavy teasing in a broken English I would make terrified and ineffectual efforts to understand. I managed to sneak past them all to the rear of the store where the harness and great quilted collar pads hung from brass pegs screwed into rough boards. Julius Schlagel's clerk, Irma, was back there shoveling some shingle nails into a brown paper bag. She straightened up from the nail bin, stared at me, and stepped nearer to see my face under the hiss of the gas lamp. "You want to know something? You froze your face, kid."

"How could I? I just came straight over here from school," I lied.

She gave a skeptical glance at the clock and said, "Go get some snow and fetch it in here."

I brought a mittenful of snow and submitted to her harsh

massage. The snow felt hot on my cheeks, so I knew I'd frozen them all right.

"Now don't go out again, hear?"

Except for the candy counter, the store was a dark monotonous jumble of bags and boxes and barrels. I was hungry, so I diverted myself by studying the penny candy and deciding how I would spend a penny if I had one. Since I rarely had the penny, no one paid any attention to me. When I did have one, I would tap it nonchalantly on the grimy glass case—not as though I was impatient to be waited on, for indeed I was not, but just to let Irma and Julius know that I was a potential customer, an individual to be treated with respectful attentiveness when I had finally made up my mind.

Since I had no penny, I was glad to see my father come through the door. He saw that Julius was listening to the radio and he strode brusquely past me to ask him about the weather reports. Julius dispensed about as many weather reports as he did bags of flour and corn meal; in 1935 in drought-ruined North Dakota, radios were a luxury, like candy.

Without speaking, Julius turned up the volume so my father could hear the announcer. ". . . the Canadian cold wave is pressing southward from central Manitoba and is expected to hit northern North Dakota tonight, causing substantial drops in the temperature within the next twenty-four hours. This is KFYR in Bismarck. . . ."

"Forty below in Winnipeg last night," Julius said to my father.

"You been out in the last hour? I bet it's thirty below here right now. The pump's froze solid. We gotta go thaw it out." Directing his last sentence to me, he turned and made his way past the Russians, nodding uncordially.

The sun had set while I was waiting in the store, and a vast gloom in the sky sagged low over the town, weighting the rigid streets with cold. The heat absorbed by my snowsuit was gone instantly, and my thawed-out cheeks stung badly. My father scuffed me up over the brittle heaps of snow at the curb of the wooden sidewalk and hoisted me into the sleigh. The sleigh was a wagon box transferred to runners for the winter. I wanted to stand up, but he made me sit on the old Indian blanket spread on straw. There were hot stones under the straw. Then he draped a cowhide from the high side of the wagon box down over my head.

Though I could see nothing, I could hear my father talking to the horses and I knew he was wiping the frost of their own breathing from their nostrils. Beneath me was the thin scrape of the runners, then the rattle over the railroad tracks and the smoothness of fields of snow. The cow hairs made my nose itch and the straw poked at my legs. It was very dark.

Finally my father stopped the sleigh by our house and lifted me out. "Tell Mother I'll be in directly, soon as I unhitch," he said.

Despite the hot stones, my ankles were numb, and I tripped and fell as I ran to the house. My lip struck the gallon lard pail I used for a lunch bucket and stuck there. I lay tense and still in the snow waiting for it to stop sticking. Once my little sister caught her tongue on the pump handle because she wouldn't believe me when I told her it would stick. She jerked away in fear and tore bleeding skin from the tip of it. So I waited until I could feel the warmth of my breath free my lip before I moved.

The porch timbers creaked with cold, like thin ice. I could hear my mother yelling to me to get the snow off my clothes and to shut the door tight even before I opened it.

The top of the kitchen stove glowed gray-red through its iron lids, and the belly of the big round stove in the living room seemed stretched dangerously thin, as though it would surely melt soon and spill out the flaming coal on the floor. My mother had set the kerosene lamp on the warming-oven doors above the stove so she could see how much salt to put in the potatoes. I could smell the rabbit she was roasting in the oven for the dog.

My father came in the door, stomping snow clear across the kitchen, and demanded a teakettle of boiling water. Seeing that I still didn't have my snowsuit off, he told me to come with him to work the pump handle.

While he poured the boiling water down the pump, the steam rushing up into darkness, I struggled to free the handle, but I couldn't budge it. Even when he grasped it in his large thick leather mitten it didn't move. "Well, it looks like we'll have to melt water for the stock. Take this back to the house." He handed me the teakettle.

I was glad we had to melt snow for water, because then my little sister and I could play a game called Eskimo. We stood on chairs, balancing ourselves imprudently near the searing surface of the stove to lean over the tub. As soon as the dry snow had melted a little, we began to mold the figures for an Eskimo village—Huskies, people, babies, igloos, polar bears, and walruses, just like the ones in the *Book of North American Mammals* my mother had got once in a set of books from the National Geographic Society. We conducted hunts and dog-sled treks and sent the Eskimos into the water to harpoon the seals that were languidly floating there. But as the water warmed, the seals disappeared, and it was death for the harpooners to go into the sea. While the shores of their iceland slipped away into the ocean, the frantic people moved higher and higher on the iceberg mountain. Perched on its slushy sides, they would see a small hole appear in their snow island. Then the sea would gush up through the hole, the island would break in pieces, and the ice people would fall into the fatal warmth. Just as the warm wave washed over my people, the game would become hideously real to me, and I would often have nightmares in which I was climbing, climbing, on an ever-collapsing mountain to escape a hot tide.

After supper my father set out for the barn with two pails of the snow water. I had to spend about a half hour, it seemed, getting my outside clothes on again so I could carry the lantern and open the barn door.

I was well acquainted with the shock of stepping from the warm kitchen into a winter night. But none of the freezing memories of the past could prepare me for the burning air that night. It was like strong hot smoke in my nostrils, so that for one confused instant I thought I was going to suffocate with the cold that was so cold it was hot. I gasped for breathable air, and my father said, "Don't do that! Breathe through your nose—your breath is warmer that way when it gets to your lungs."

We walked carefully down the hill to the barn; then I slithered down the steps chopped in a snowdrift in front of the door and slid it open. The barn was very old, but always before it had been warm with the heat of the animals kept in it all day long. But that night, being inside didn't seem to make any difference. I still had the kind of ache in my temples and cheekbones that I always got when I took too big a mouthful of ice cream. The cows shifted and swung their tails and wouldn't stand still to be milked. My father poured some milk into a pail and told me to feed it to the little new calf in a pen at the rear of the barn.

He had arrived out of season and was not yet two weeks old. Usually by the time the calves came, the mothers were outside all day, and both mothers and calves quickly got used to the idea of being separated. But we had been keeping all the stock inside for nearly a week, and neither cow nor calf was properly weaned. She lowed to him and he cried back to her; he was still determined to nurse. He was still stubbornly bucking and shoving his nose all the way to the bottom of the bucket, and desperately bunting the side of it when he got a noseful of milk. I liked him, though. His hair was almost as fine and soft as a human baby's, and he had a white star on his gleaming black forehead.

Although I had never seen cattle shiver, the little calf looked as though he was shivering as he advanced stiff-legged to our evening battle with the pail. I braced it against my shins and waited for him to begin bunting. At least a winter calf didn't damage you as much as a spring calf did; at the moment I was well padded with long underwear, two pairs of long stockings, and thick pants. I patted him between the ears and he sucked my fingers with his rough, strong tongue.

After the milking was done, we lugged the pails and lantern up the hill and started back for the barn with more water. In two more trips our toes felt numb and thickened, and we both had frostbitten faces. I had the two white spots on my cheeks again and my father's high thin nose stood out bloodless against the chapped red of his face. We took a last look at the stock; there was nothing more we could do. There was no way to heat the barn and the cows were already half covered with straw when they lay down. We rolled the door shut.

In the house we planned for the night ahead. My little sister and I would sleep in one bed, with all the blankets and quilts in the house over us, and my mother and father would use the feather tick we had rolled up in a little storeroom we called the cubbyhole. When we opened the door of that little vault to get the tick, the frigid air pushed out across the living room like a low dark flood against our legs.

It took a long time to warm the tick and blankets from the unheated bedroom at the stove. We would hold them as close as we could to its hot belly, but as soon as the warmed section was moved away it grew cold again. We left the bedroom door open, but though the living room grew instantly colder, the bedroom grew no warmer. While we were making the beds we puffed white clouds at each other across the mattresses. We heated our two sadirons and wrapped them in towels, one for each bed. Then my father stoked both stoves full of coal and we got under the piles of bedding.

My sister and I lay close together, our legs bent and our toes touching the wrapped-up iron. Partly because I couldn't get warm and partly because I was worried about some things, I couldn't get to sleep. I wanted to know what a cold wave was. In the long solitude of prairie childhood I had memorized two sets of books—the set from the National Geographic, and a set called *A Childhood Treasury* that contained legends of many lands, my favorites being those from Scandinavia. How could it possibly be that so many things had happened before I was born? For instance, *The Book of North American Mammals* told of a time when the plains of Russia and of North America had borne glaciers a mile deep. And before the glaciers there had been vast herds of mammoths. There was a drawing of them lifting their shieldlike foreheads against a gray horizon, marching on tall shaggy legs over the frozen tundra—tundra that had once covered our wheatfields. The book told about how before the glacier finally came the weather had gotten colder and colder, so that the mammoths had to grow longer and longer hair.

But even with their long hair and clever trunks and sixteen-foot tusks curved in unlikely tangles of bone, they had been unable to defend themselves. Why? Under the picture it said that a herd of these mammoths evidently had been preserved intact for centuries, and that one of the discoverers had even tried eating the meat of a carcass thousands of years old. Why couldn't the huge and powerful creatures have run away? It must have been some kind of flood, I thought, like the flood we had in our garden after a cloudburst, only different and much bigger—a flood that could race with the speed of liquid one moment and turn completely solid the next, locking forever the great knees bending for another battling step, then the tusks fending off masses of debris, and finally the long trunks flailing above the tide in search of air. A cold wave freezing so fast that the bubbles of their last breathing would be fixed like beads in the ice.

What if some polar impulse was now sending a flood to rise up out of the north, to flow swiftly over our house, becoming ice as the wind touched it, shutting us off from that strangling but precious air above us? I had heard of digging out of a house completely covered with snow—that used to happen in the days before I was born—but did anybody ever dig out of a glacier? I wanted to go and climb in bed with my mother and father and have them tell me that it wouldn't get to us, that it would stop at least as far away as Leeds, twenty miles to the north. But the last time I had tried to climb in with them they had told me not to be such a big baby, that I was a worse baby than my little sister. So I lay there wondering how far the cold had gotten.

Finally the morning came. I could look from my bed across the living room and into the kitchen where my father, in his sheepskin coat, was heating some water saved from the melted snow. The tub, refilled after we had emptied it for the stock, was standing in the corner of the kitchen next to the door. The snow in it was still heaped in a neat cone. It was odd to think of a tub of snow standing inside our house, where we had slept the night, and never feeling the warmth of the stove a few feet away—to think of how the tiny flow of air around the storm-lined door was more powerful than the stove filled with coal.

I felt the excitement of sharing in heroic deeds as I pulled on the second pair of long wool stockings over my underwear and fastened them with the knobs and hooks on my garter belt. I was not going to school because it was too cold to take the horses out, so I was to help with the barn chores again.

The cattle were still huddled together in their one big stall.

My father set down the pails and walked swiftly to the rear of the barn. The little calf was curled quietly against the corner of his pen. The black-and-white hairs over his small ribs did not move. My father climbed into the pen and brushed the straw away from the sleeping eyes, just to make sure.

I stood looking at the soft fine hair that was too fine and the big-kneed legs that were too thin, and it seemed to me that I now understood how it was with the mammoths in the Ice Age. One night they had lain down to sleep, leaning ponderously back to back, legs bent beneath warm bellies, tusks pointing up from the dying tundra. The blood under their incredible hides slowed a little, and the warmth of their bodies ascended in ghostly clouds toward the indifferent moon. There was no rushing, congealing wave; there was only the unalarmed cold sleep of betrayed creatures.

A couple of nights later, over at the store, the men talked of the figures Julius had gotten over the radio. There had been a dozen readings around fifty degrees below zero. Fifty-two at Bismarck, fifty-eight at Leeds, and sixty-one at Portal on the Canadian border.

"My termometer is bust before I see him in the morning!" shouted Mr. Buskowski. "I do not even from Russia remember such a night."

Hopelessly studying the candy counter, I realized that even my father had forgotten the stiff little black-and-white calf in the contemplation of that remarkable number. "Sixty-one below!" they said over and over again. "Sixty-one below!" The men didn't need to make legends any more to comprehend the incomprehensible. They had the miraculous evidence of their thermometers. But for me that little death told what there was to know about the simple workings of immense catastrophe.

PART THREE

The Art

of the Possible

Erratum

The first six paragraphs of the section headed "Birth of a Salesman," which begins on page 221, were the editor's prefatory note. Richard Donovan's article begins on page 222, with the words "When Southern California gave Senator Richard Nixon to the nation. . ."

October 14, 1952

Birth of a Salesman

By Richard Donovan

It seems to be destiny: We keep bumping into Senator Nixon.
Perhaps our thinking about Senators is strongly influenced by
seniority rule, which proves how, at bottom, we are just stuffed
shirts. But certainly we must confess that we never paid any
particular attention to the breezy young Senator from California,
never put him high on the list of those national politicians whose
record we like to watch.

And yet, like fishermen who are after an entirely different
catch, twice we have had our fishing rod rudely tugged, and to
our amazement what has come up has been a big Nixon story.

Our readers certainly remember the first time it happened.
We had a hunch that more than one U.S. Senator had something
to do with the China Lobby, and were rather startled when it
turned out that the connections between that peculiar outfit and
Dick Nixon's campaign were testified to by a reliable witness.
This witness, our readers may remember, was Leo Casey, at that
time an employee of a New York public-relations firm, Allied
Syndicates, Inc. Mr. Casey had been rushed to California by his
employer in the fall of 1950 to organize "Independents for
Nixon," in Nixon's Senate campaign against Helen Gahagan
Douglas. Casey did his job, but Nixon's victory was not the end
of his labors, for he was told by a man who was quite influential
in the firm that he had to go to Washington and "deliver Nixon
to the Major."

The Major was Louis Kung, son of H. H. Kung and nephew of Madame Chiang Kai-shek. Mr. Casey was told that his work in the California election had been done for the "China account." He already knew that his firm was retained by the Bank of China, but was shocked that anyone could brazenly ask him to "deliver" a Senator to a foreign agent. "Soon afterward Mr. Casey left the firm, went to Washington, and told his story to Senator Nixon, who thanked him for the information."

Senator Nixon's thankfulness toward Mr. Casey, plus the fact that he didn't turn out to be one of the most zealous among the Formosa Firsters, led us to conclude that probably the Bank of China had made a rather poor investment and that probably Senator Nixon was not responsible for the assistance he had received. When, last July, he won the Republican Vice-Presidential nomination we were somewhat startled, as everybody was, and in hastily scanning his record we could not find any adequate answer to the question: Why Nixon?

Yet it was our duty to find an answer sooner or later, or at least to satisfy the curiosity in our own and our readers' minds: Who is Nixon, after all? Obviously, there was a job to be done, and we put in charge of it our West Coast staff correspondent, Richard Donovan.

When Southern California gave Senator Richard Nixon to the nation, so to speak, most of his constituents thought he was famous. We all knew him; we'd read all about the Hiss case. But over the mountains to the east, they didn't know him so well. Or so it has seemed from the volume of Nixon biographical material carried by national magazines since he became General Eisenhower's running mate.

As one of Senator Nixon's constituents, I have scrutinized much of this material to see what kind of information outsiders were getting. By early journalistic agreement, the Senator appeared as young (thirty-nine), serious-minded, fast-moving, hardworking, abstemious, honest, poor, bright, ambitious, free of alliances, forward-looking, a "fighting campaigner," a relentless investigator, an individual-firster, a birthright Quaker, and a father of two.

All this was instructive and, we felt, sufficient. But the magazines seemed more anxious than ever to explain Nixon. In an "intimate" story told to Joe Alex Morris by his wife, Patricia Ryan Nixon, the *Saturday Evening Post* undertook to reveal the human side of the Republican candidate in a piece entitled "I Say He's a Wonderful Guy." This story told how Nixon had been "mercilessly heckled by our left-wing foes" in his Senatorial campaign, how Mrs. Nixon and her husband had risked their savings to start him in politics six years ago, and were once so broke Pat wept because she couldn't buy stamps, and what it was like being married to a crusader, helping her husband rise from obscurity to the G.O.P. Vice-Presidential candidacy, and bring up two kids at the same time.

That done, *Look* magazine next took up the explanation in a piece by Victor Lasky, entitled "Why Nixon Was Nominated." Lasky assumed an aggressive tone from the start, as though he anticipated contradiction. He stressed Nixon's youth appeal, and said he favored " 'a return to individual freedom and all that initiative can produce.' " Then he said: "It may surprise the *Daily Worker* that Nixon, 'the tool of Wall Street,' has no income besides his salary."

Well, to be frank with Mr. Lasky, that last is the kind of statement which can only bring unsolicited local contributions into the already overcrowded national Nixon-explanation series, for it greatly surprises many of the Senator's constituents, too.

I'm sure, for instance, that Dana Smith, an able, articulate, well-to-do, and extremely personable Pasadena attorney, was surprised. In the months between Richard Nixon's election to the Senate and his nomination as Vice-President, Smith has dispensed more than $18,000 in personal expense money to the Senator from a large group of his wealthy well-wishers in the Los Angeles area. He said so on September 15, when I visited him in his office, together with two colleagues from the Los Angeles *Daily News* and the New York *Post*. Recalling our conversation, it seems not only a hasty but an ungrateful thing that Victor Lasky wrote about the Nixon income.

Smith, a resoundingly successful tax lawyer and a man of the widest acquaintance among corporation-management officials in Southern California, was glad to talk to us about the Senator.

He had helped persuade Nixon to run for that body, for one thing, and then had handled most of Nixon's campaign finances. Smith had left most of the strategy to others because, as he explained, he was no politician, or even a competent political adviser, but only a private citizen who saw that "The one way to get good government in this country was to line up local people who had no interest in personal gain to take an active part in electing their candidates, and in supporting them after elections."

Smith had had a little previous political experience, of course. In 1948 he had helped gather a few people—Pasadena attorneys Stanley Mullin and David Saunders, Tom Pike of the Pike Drilling Company, Tyler Woodward of the Southern California Petroleum Corporation, Bob and George Rowan, who are in the real-estate and insurance business, Elwood Robinson, a Los Angeles advertising man, and some others—into a group that had backed Stassen, to no avail. By 1950, the Stassen Volunteers had had ample time to evaluate Congressman Richard Nixon, who had not only proved himself a spectacular personality but who also had a "sound" voting record and seemed to have a grasp of original American political and economic principles, among which, said Smith, are constitutional government (Congress, not the President, makes the laws) and the free-enterprise system.

For years, Smith explained, the government had been selling centralized control of all phases of American life so loudly and tirelessly that the individualists had been unable to get a word in and so had been rendered impotent at the polls. "Our thinking," said Smith, "was that we had to fight selling with selling, and for that job Dick Nixon seemed to be the best salesman against socialization available. That's his gift, really—salesmanship.

"But before we could ask a young man with no financial security to risk his career on such a doubtful project as beating Sheridan Downey," Smith went on, "we had to reflect on whether it was worth it to him and to us." (Downey was California's Democratic Senatorial incumbent who retired from the 1950 race before the selection of Helen Douglas in the primaries.) "Finally," said Smith, "we urged Nixon to run for two reasons: He was a Republican with a chance to win, and he was a proved believer in free enterprise."

Someone asked whether Governor Warren did not also have those qualifications.

"Frankly," Smith said, "Warren has too much of the other point of view, and he never has gone out selling the free-enterprise system. But Dick did just what we wanted him to."

What Nixon did, or had done for him, in his 1950 campaign against Helen Douglas was pretty much what he did, or had done for him, in his first (1946) campaign for Representative from California's Twelfth Congressional District. Since most of the recent magazine stories about Nixon have brushed over both campaigns in a sentence or two, perhaps they should be reviewed briefly here.

The Smearing of Voorhis

In 1946, the "Had enough? Vote Republican" year which gave McCarthy, Jenner, Cain, Kem, Bricker, Malone, and Watkins to the Senate, Nixon's opponent was a New Deal Congressman, Jerry Voorhis. Voorhis, the son of a millionaire father, was a ten-year incumbent whose record had caused Washington correspondents to call him "the best Congressman west of the Mississippi," and caused California bankers and oilmen to call him the worst. (Voorhis had voted for Federal control of the tidelands, and had initiated legislation that curtailed the profits of banks dealing in government bonds.)

Sizing up the situation, Nixon, who was picked for Republican nominee by the now famous Whittier, California, "Committee of 100," displayed an understanding of practical politics rare in a neophyte.

In a two-month campaign, hundreds of Twelfth District voters received phone calls from people who refused to identify themselves. "This is a friend of yours," the callers said. "I just want you to know that Jerry Voorhis is a Communist." Other stories were circulated—one that Voorhis had voted to increase the ceilings on Florida oranges but not on California oranges. (Actually, no such legislation had come up in the House.)

In speeches and in debates with Voorhis, Nixon stated that his opponent had the backing of the CIO-PAC, which he charged was Communist-dominated. Thirty of the thirty-one newspapers in Nixon's district supported him, and although he has said again and again that his first campaign was a poverty-stricken affair, voters saw full-page Nixon ads in most of the papers, heard Nixon spot announcements on most local radio stations, and encountered Nixon billboards on an arresting number of vacant lots.

Nixon's pioneering of the fight-Communists-instead-of-your-opponent formula proved so successful that he used it again, with even more brilliant success, in his campaign for the Senate. All this is so well known in California that it seems it must also be known over the mountains. But, like the Senator himself, it probably isn't.

In 1950, with the Hiss case behind him, and with a record of having voted for poll taxes, the Taft-Hartley Act, a $55-million cut in the Mutual Defense Program, the exemption of railroads from the antitrust laws, and the exemption of gas producers from Federal regulations; with a record of voting against extension of social-security coverage, Federal slum clearance and public housing, $60 million for aid to Korea, and domestic rent control, Nixon was once more in search of a campaign theme. He found it when he announced that Mrs. Douglas, who had been for most issues Nixon had opposed and against those he was for, was the political twin of New York's Vito Marcantonio, and, therefore, by implication a Communist sympathizer.

Before the campaign, Nixon had intended to concentrate on the New and Fair Deals. In a speech to a Los Angeles dinner audience, he said: "Believe me, I am well aware of the Communist threat and I do not discount it. But I am convinced that an even greater threat to our free institutions is presented by that group of hypocritical and cynical men who, under the guise of providing political panaceas for certain social and economic problems in our society, are selling the American birthright for a mess of pottage."

But then when the campaign began, Nixon ignored the "cynical men," and instead concentrated on "Mrs. Douglas's friends, the Communists" (by whom, incidentally, she was repeatedly denounced as "a capitalist warmonger").

The Nixon-Douglas campaign may well have been what the Los Angeles *Daily News* called it—"the dirtiest in state history." Candidate Nixon's backers began it with a handbill sent to all registered Democrats. "As one Democrat to another . . . ," the bill began. Since it is often hard for hurried and uninstructed voters to tell a Democratic candidate from a Republican in cross-filing California, this handbill, which never identified Nixon as a Republican, probably went a long way toward achieving its aim.

Later, Nixon headquarters issued its "Pink Sheet," purporting to show that Congresswoman Douglas had voted Marcantonio's way some three hundred times, but neglecting to add that Nixon, and even Congressman Joe Martin, had also gone Marcantonio's way on many of those same votes. In speeches and radio and television appearances, in handbills and handouts to California's overwhelmingly Republican press, in letter campaigns and door-bell-ringing campaigns and mass meetings in the Los Angeles Coliseum, the epithets "left-wing" and "pro-Communist" were thrown at Mrs. Douglas from every direction. Instead of standing by her record, Mrs. Douglas began to concentrate on belaboring Communism too, and then she was lost. She couldn't beat Nixon at his own game.

Money? What Money?

When the election was over and Nixon was in with a 680,947 plurality, attorney Dana Smith, Nixon's campaign finance manager, with whom we were concerned a few paragraphs back, began adding up expenses. In a sworn statement to the California Secretary of State, the Nixon people announced that it had cost $62,899 to elect their man. This figure astonished Helen Douglas, who reported expenses of $156,172, and Governor Warren, who reported expenses of $324,000. It also astonished even certain members of the pro-Nixon press.

First of all, Nixon had had so much billboard space (occupied before and after the campaign by oil companies, railroads, banks, power companies, industrial farms, and so on) that some of it

had run over the border into Mexico. Billboard advertisers estimate that coverage of this kind costs $25,000 a month—and Nixon
had it for four months. The Democratic State Central Committee, a jaundiced source, perhaps, has estimated that newspaper
linage in behalf of Nixon cost $82,000, that his radio and TV
time cost $100,000, that his direct-mail cost was $90,000 and his
printing cost $25,000, and that his general expenses (paid help,
etc.) exceeded $200,000. Total: $637,000. Cut it in half, quarter
it, cut it to one-tenth of that figure, and Nixon's expense account
is still not the $62,899 to which he is legally committed. If you
credit some press estimates of Nixon's expenses (over a million
dollars) or the estimates of such columnists as Drew Pearson
($1.6 million), the confusion of the figurers becomes more under-
standable. Senator Nixon may truthfully say that money may
have been spent in his behalf that he knew nothing about. If so,
were any corporations among the donors of billboard space, for
instance? (Corporations are prohibited from contributing to political campaigns.) How many personal contributions were recovered in tax deductions?

Since Dana Smith was talking warmly about Senator Nixon,
we did not interrupt him.

"Even before Dick announced that he was going to run for
the Senate, we had $10,000 ready to finance him," Smith said.
"That's the first time I ever heard of a candidate having campaign funds before he became a candidate."

We asked whether Smith had handled that embarrassing check
from Senator Owen Brewster via Gruenwald. He said "No," but
that he had signed a $5,000 check, drawn on Nixon's "general
campaign fund" to repay Brewster's loan. Smith made it clear
that the money was a loan, not a contribution.

"After Nixon's election," said Smith, "we did not stop thinking about him. We realized that his salary [$12,500 plus a tax-
free $2,500 for expenses] was pitifully inadequate for a salesman
of free enterprise trying to do a job for his people in California.
We took the position that we had got Dick into this [the Senate]
and that we were going to see him through," Smith went on. "He
told us he needed money for such things as long-distance phone
calls, for ten thousand Christmas cards, for airmail stamps on

thousands of letters that couldn't be franked, for recordings that could be used on free radio time in California but that cost something to make, and for trips to California—he ought to make the trip at least three or four times a year. Well," Smith continued, "between the time of his election to the Senate and his nomination as Vice-President, we gave him between $16,000 and $17,000, which I disbursed." The exact amount turned out to be $18,235.

Smith sat back, beaming.

"Here we had a fine salesman who didn't have enough money to do the kind of selling job we wanted," he said. "So we got together and took care of some of those things. Between fifty and one hundred people put up the money and we put a limit of five hundred dollars per person on the amount anyone could give in a single year." Smith hesitated at this point. "Just so no one could say that we were buying a Senator," he added.

With that cleared up, we asked who some of the contributors were.

"Well, I don't want to throw names around," Smith said.

We asked if the list included any of the people who had honored Nixon with a dinner at the Malibu Beach home of Kyle Palmer, political editor of the Los Angeles *Times,* last August 2. We mentioned some of the names—Al Gock, board chairman of the Bank of America; Leonard Firestone, of the tire company; Joe Schenck, Darryl Zanuck, Harry Cohn, L. B. Mayer, Edward J. Mannix, Mervyn LeRoy and Harry Brand, of the movies; Justin Dart, the Rexall Drug man; William Mullendore, head of the Southern California Edison; Norman Chandler, publisher of the *Times.*

Smith said he had no knowledge of contributions from any of these men.

"It was mostly the same old gang with a few new ones," he said —"the Rowan boys, Mullin, Tom Pike, Earl Adams [an attorney for Southern California Edison], Jack Garland [attorney husband of Helen Chandler, of the Los Angeles *Times* family], Tyler Woodward. Most of the old Stassen Volunteers.

"Any philosophy that throws control of our lives and finances to government is reactionary—a throwback to the Divine Right of Kings," he was saying. "Free opportunity and enterprise is the right theory of progressive living."

We did not argue about that. Instead we asked whether the Stassen Volunteers, who had stumped for Eisenhower even though Warren was the favorite son, had had any say in Nixon's selection as Vice-Presidential candidate.

"We discouraged Dick on that," Smith said. "We thought he should serve out his term in the Senate and then, when he had that under his belt, think about higher offices."

Since Nixon had been picked anyway, Smith and the others had taken it in good grace.

"Actually," Smith said, "there's a great deal Dick can do as Vice-President. He can clean the Communists out of Washington. He can help clean up corruption in government. And, with his Congressional background, he can be the best kind of a liaison between the executive and legislative branches of the government, particularly when it comes to suggesting in initiating sound and desirable legislation. As I say, Dick is a salesman."

Smith thought awhile, and then added: "The whole idea of our Nixon fund is to enable Dick to do a selling job on the American people for the private-enterprise system and integrity in government."

That ended the interview. Before we left, I looked closely at Dana Smith, who had astonished us by saying that he was fifty-four years old and had eight grandchildren, and one more on the way—grandchildren for whom he wanted a decent world. Sitting with his back to a bright window, he looked youthful, open and friendly, strong, honest, and thoroughly sound.

Three days later the Nixon story was broken by the New York *Post,* and the public has been hearing a good deal about it ever since.

On Saturday, September 20, Smith held a press conference at which he gave out the names of contributors to the fund, seventy-six in all, and I was startled to discover that the name of the contributor who had tipped me off about the story was not included.

"I'm glad this story got out," Smith said, "because there wasn't anything wrong about it."

"But, Mr. Smith," I began, "supposing members of a labor union had made a contribution to . . ."

"Oh, that's different," he declared positively. "A labor union is a special interest."

November 27, 1958

Who is Nixon, What is He?

By Douglass Cater

Reporters sensed they were witnessing another "first" at a late October press conference in Minneapolis when the Vice-President blew his top, peremptorily dismissed them, and strode, lips trembling, from the gathering. Covering Nixon over the years, they had seen a number of variations on a theme of anger—sarcasm, scorn, contempt, offended righteousness. But there have been few examples of an uncontrolled reaction from this man who prides himself on his ability to keep a tight control on his emotions.

"The only time to lose your temper . . . is when it's deliberate," he was once quoted in a Sunday magazine feature. Last summer he described his reactions during his harrowing experiences in Peru and Venezuela to Stewart Alsop: "How did I feel? . . . While it is going on, I feel cold, matter-of-fact, analytical. . . . Then when I saw the soft answer would not work, that they wouldn't let me speak, I allowed myself the luxury of showing my temper and called them cowards. It was deliberate, letting my temper show—not that I didn't really feel it . . ."

Having got off the smooth-running Nixon Campaign Special only two days earlier, I was interested to learn the cause of the Minneapolis outburst. Certainly, the tape recording of the press conference gave no obvious clues. In this as in other press conferences, there were no barbs in the questions put to Nixon. It is

a curious fact that reporters tend to take on the semantic characteristics of the officials they cover regularly. With Truman they
were terse and testy. At the Eisenhower press conferences they are
wordy and frequently lose track of syntax. With Nixon they
become glib.

It was Philip Potter's question that touched off the show of anger in Minneapolis. Nixon had declared that he disagreed completely with Southern Democrats on civil rights. Potter, the mild-
mannered correspondent for the Baltimore *Sun,* simply asked
him to spell out his ideas on the subject. Potter referred to a
petition made to the President the preceding week by a civil-
rights group whom Eisenhower declined to receive. Granted, it
was a sensitive subject, but not that sensitive for an old pro like
Nixon. Potter had certainly not made what Nixon called "an
insinuation that I have refused to discuss civil rights."

More likely, Nixon's ire stemmed from an accumulation of
things. He was tired, having got up at six-thirty that morning to
greet the public on the Dave Garroway show; he had a cold
(the sniffle was audible on the tape); he had been dogged by
defeatist polls and divided Republicans all along the campaign
circuit. In New York, a few days earlier, he had been politely
given the leper treatment by Nelson Rockefeller's entourage.
His close friend Hillings's indiscretion and Mrs. Knowland's
magnificent epithet about a fellow Republican were two more
indications of the party's disarray.

But there was more to it than that. For as the 1958 campaign
progressed, Nixon must also have had a foreboding of personal
disaster. Here he was confronted by a crisis not so acute but infinitely more difficult to resolve than the one arising after the
exposure of his "fund" in the midst of the 1952 campaign. Then,
he had been able to salvage the situation with a single television
broadcast and some fancy backstage maneuvers. This time, such
remedies were of little use. As one observer has remarked, "This
time, he is confronted by two years of solid trouble, with a bankrupt party, a weary and disillusioned President, and, for the first
time, a formidable competitor."

Tricky Transformation

The Vice-President had made a calculated decision that proved to be dead wrong. He had no choice, of course, but to wage a tireless campaign if he expected to be his party's nominee in 1960. But the kind of campaign he chose to wage helped stir up again Nixon's peculiar image trouble. After the long and carefully arranged build-up of the new Nixon and, more recently, what might be called the newer Nixon, his campaigning revived the image of the old Nixon. Many noted the old snarl when he labeled the publication of statistics on the State Department's mail concerning Quemoy and Matsu as "the patent and deliberate effort of a State Department subordinate to undercut the Secretary of State and sabotage his policy." When he issued his "clarification" on campaign tactics, newspapers all across the country reproduced a Herblock cartoon depicting Nixon, brickbat in hand, standing in the gutter and telling a passer-by, "Of course, if I had the top job, I'd act differently."

In point of fact, Nixon did not go as far as he had during the 1954 ("Acheson College of Cowardly Communist Containment") campaign. He pointedly declined to identify the "radicals" who were threatening to turn government into a wild spending binge. He didn't even join with Eisenhower in singling out, without actually naming, freshman Senator William Proxmire (D., Wisconsin) as a prize example of the profligate. Early in the campaign, Nixon quoted Acheson as declaring in 1950 that the United States would not defend Korea. Reporter William Lawrence of the New York *Times* pointed out that Acheson had said no such thing. Thereafter, Nixon obligingly quoted Acheson as saying Korea lay outside America's defense perimeter. (Which, of course, was not quite what Acheson said either.)

Throughout the campaign the Vice-President regularly announced, as though his personal reassurance was necessary, that "There is only one party of treason—the Communist Party." He bestowed the loving phrase "gallant warrior" upon his bitter foe Truman. When a reporter quoted Nixon as saying that a "Truman-Acheson policy meant war," a campaign aide irritably corrected him, pointing out that Truman's name was being left off the slogan this year.

Still his moderation failed to get across. Those who have remained skeptical of his advertised growth into a "mature" politician noted the *ad hominems,* the "rotgut" metaphors, and the instinct for the jugular. He refurbished the image of the character once labeled by Democrats, independents, and many Republicans as "Tricky Dick." The image could be as fatal to his future ambitions as the image of "The Man Who Can't Win" was for Robert A. Taft's.

"The Vice-President is a unique official of government," Nixon declared not long ago. "He has access to information in all areas but power in none." This appraisal only tells the half of it. For the advent of Richard M. Nixon to the Vice-Presidency has brought a remarkable transformation to this ancient burial chamber for politicians. Traditionally, the Vice-President has had limited alternatives. He could disappear Throttlebottom-like from public view. He could achieve a certain prominence by his stubborn antagonism to the President, as in the case of Jack Garner. He could use the office to pursue pet projects the way Henry Wallace did. He could become a traveling promoter of good causes in the fashion of Alben Barkley.

But Nixon's arrival in the Vice-Presidency coincided with the full flowering of television, and he has applied many of TV's techniques to develop the potential of his office. He has demonstrated that the Vice-President, if he is skillful, can manipulate the fade-in and the fade-out, the filters and the cropping devices familiar to the cinematographer. In times of crisis, he can even employ television's technique of "going to black"—that is, he can remove the image from the screen altogether for a calculated interval.

William S. White has remarked on this same phenomenon: "[Nixon's] curiously sheltered position—deeply in the Administration but not necessarily or always *of* it, and not directly accountable either to it or for its decisions—has meant that most of his actions have been made known on a leaked or ex-parte basis." It is precisely in this area of journalism by leak that the press in Washington is most vulnerable. The reporter made privy to a confidence feels bound to extract every last ounce of publicity value from it. The same trifling anecdote can ricochet around town, gathering momentum as it moves from news item to Sunday feature page to full-dress magazine article.

Consistency is not necessarily a prime objective of Nixon's public relations. On March 14, Stewart Alsop reported that because of the recession Nixon and Secretary of Labor Mitchell "wanted a $5,000,000,000 tax cut to be announced by the White House at the beginning of the present week." A few days later, the *Christian Science Monitor* correspondent in Chicago reported after an interview, "Mr. Nixon believes that a tax cut is not timely yet." The Vice-President thus reaped publicity benefits as the one dynamic member of the administration, while at the same time maintaining an appearance of strict loyalty to the administration's position. And when campaign time arrived, he could without a qualm denounce those "prophets of disaster" who had proposed "panicky" economic measures.

In such a fashion, the new Nixon has earned encomiums like "far-sighted," "forceful," and "formidable." He has grown, we are told, in all directions at once. Even normally critical reporters have abandoned their customary precision in describing this phenomenon. Richard L. Strout of the *Christian Science Monitor,* who yields to no one as a trenchant commentator, recently described Nixon as "one of the most brilliant and intellectually gifted figures that American politics has produced in half a century."

Another observer has compared Nixon to Churchill as a "real intellectual." As if to bolster the claim to erudition if not to intellectuality, the Vice-President has been quoted by Earl Mazo of the New York *Herald Tribune* as declaring: "I like to examine the lives of public figures, from Caesar, Genghis Khan and Napoleon to Gladstone and Disraeli and the recent ones. I try particularly to find out how they dealt with public problems, how they arrived at decisions, and why they made mistakes." Nixon's recent utterances have contained such learned references as (to a Harvard Business School audience) ". . . The Roman poet said it two thousand years ago . . ." and (to Stewart Alsop) "There's a quotation that expresses what I mean exactly. A German—was it Bismarck? No, I don't think so. . . ."

The refashioning of Nixon certainly goes beyond the reporter's craving for good copy. The reporter in Washington today, much like reporter Henry Adams during Grant's administration, seeks wistfully the sources of creative energy that will enable our government to respond to the tremendous challenge it faces. Adams finally gave up the search and spent his remaining days studying the great cathedral builders of the Middle Ages. The reporter today sometimes takes to building his own cathedrals.

Nixon has furnished blueprints for such construction projects. With the ready consent of the President, he is the first Vice-President in history to become a full-time student in an in-training program for the Presidency. As the popular press tirelessly points out, he sits in the high councils. He has displayed remarkable aptitudes. Those who have had a chance to observe the Vice-President close up have usually come away greatly impressed by his capacity to absorb and to articulate.

In a confused era, Nixon creates a compelling effect. The fair-minded reporter's reaction is not only to be attracted by this persuasive man who speaks such obvious good sense but to grow doubtful about his own recollections of an earlier Nixon. Last spring, the Vice-President invited the British correspondents in Washington to dinner and an off-the-record discussion at his home. Afterward, Max Freedman of the Manchester *Guardian* cabled his impressions of "A hard, disciplined, able, growing mind," and "a generous, constructive and spacious philosophy, akin to the vision which once led Senator Vandenberg." Freedman concluded, "the Democrats . . . really must begin to examine Mr. Nixon and not the malignant myth of their own invention." Since 1955 the same sort of thing has been said by a number of eminent reporters.

The Heir Apart . . .

A short time before this year's elections, a highly placed Republican Party official told this reporter flatly, "I don't care how well Rockefeller does in New York or how bad a beating we take in California. Nixon is the nominee for 1960. Nobody can stop him." A second official in the same headquarters, not quite so highly placed but of longer tenure, also gave a convincing list of reasons why Nixon would get the nomination. Was it impossible to upset him? "Nothing is impossible in this party," he retorted. "I saw Wendell Willkie, the most inept politician of our century, run off with the nomination in 1940. If he could do it, anybody can."

Nixon's prospects do have a clinched look about them. Whatever his impact on the voters, his campaigning this fall renewed his ties with the party professionals all over the country. The defeats suffered by the party may paradoxically have strengthened rather than weakened these ties. For defeat frequently brings the reverse of Lord Acton's axiom into play: power tends to corrupt but being out of power corrupts absolutely. High party affairs are apt to fall into the hands of the hacks. Nixon, through all his difficulties, has had no trouble dealing with the hacks.

But there is an even more persuasive reason for a monolithic unity of the Republican Party behind the Vice-President. He stands, according to the cliché, a single heartbeat from the White House. He is separated from the Presidency only by the brief time it would take an ailing Eisenhower to pen his resignation. If Nixon were to accede to the Presidency by default, the rules of party politics all but foreclose any intraparty challenge to his renomination in 1960. The grave uncertainty that this produces among party leaders may discourage initiatives on Rockefeller's behalf.

But let us examine the other side of the ledger. There are some who are convinced that "if the Lord spares [him] that long"—to use Eisenhower's oft-repeated estimate of his remaining tenure in office—Nixon may never attain the party's nomination, much less the White House. They cite everything from convention statistics to a feeling in their bones to justify their conviction. But their fundamental belief, mingled perhaps with their hopes, is that the Vice-President will fail to sustain the image of a leader able and deserving to be President.

First of all, the business of cutting the Eisenhower apron strings may prove far more difficult than imagined. Judging by his first post-election press conference, the President is dead set on two final years of heels-dug-in economizing. "I think every place we are spending too much money," he declared with the vexation of a man firmly persuaded that he must insert the stopper or the whole nation will go down the drain. And not even the hard reality of the approaching missile age appeared to alter his determination.

Such an interregnum will hardly offer an aspiring Vice-President the platform he needs for 1960, especially when he must deal with a rampant Democratic majority in Congress. Yet in voicing disagreement, Nixon must play a careful game. To move too far out of the shadow would risk an open break with the President, who still holds at least a veto over the selection of the next nominee.

At the same time, Nixon must somehow manage to outperform the most attractive new Republican politician to appear for a long time. Nixon's role is irrevocably cast in the wearisome and strife-ridden drama of Washington. Rockefeller will be able to stage a drama of his own making in Albany. He can maintain the genuine apartness from the declining Eisenhower administration which Nixon can only pretend to.

Viewed in retrospect, the Vice-President endured incredible humiliation by his much-publicized sortie into New York. Both he and the accompanying reporters had been forewarned that Rockefeller would not appear with him in public. He was obliged to outargue Republican State Chairman L. Judson Morhouse in order to keep his scheduled television appearance. All day in the Waldorf Towers, he and his aides remained incommunicado while they waited to learn if there would be any meeting with Rockefeller at all.

Only when his campaign plane was safely headed toward the Middle West did Nixon call a press conference with the reporters on board to explain, "I advised him [Rockefeller]—no, I didn't advise him—I said I thought he should continue his campaign the way he has." Wasn't he upset by Rockefeller's delay until the very last minute to set up the brief breakfast get-together? "I'm not a sensitive fellow," he declared. "I lost that years ago."

Why did he take this humiliation? Simply, one supposes, because the leading Presidential contender could not admit that he was unwelcome in the leading state in the Union. New York and its politicians have played a crucial role in every Republican convention since 1940. Its sources of party financing can make or break a candidate. Though Thomas E. Dewey is in semi-retirement, the power of his well-geared machine to manipulate conventions is still highly respected.

All this Nixon knew. He knows, too, that Rockefeller's overwhelming victory means that his chances of New York backing have practically vanished. It has also endangered the grudging support he had won among the liberal wing of the Republicans in Congress.

"Nixon's got the nomination unless he does something nutty," one Republican professional predicted to me, "and he's too smart to do anything nutty." This belief in the Vice-President's infallibility as a politician is widely held. But it is possible to agree that he has outclassed some rather dreary competition and still to entertain doubts. Was it smart politics, for example, for Nixon to get so deeply involved in the California fratricide this fall? Though he denies it now, he helped thrust Knight out of the gubernatorial into the Senate race. Both Knight and Knowland supporters blame him in part for the resulting catastrophe. A smart politician, too, would have done a better job of winning at least respect among the Democrats in the Senate who will form the majority until 1962 or beyond.

Upstaging from Off Stage

The public-relations job that faces Nixon will be the most difficult one he has yet known. If he is to be convincing to the voters, he must maintain the center stage while not creating the impression of always being on stage. He must achieve the highest form of art—the art that appears artless. He must project the image of the new or newer Nixon (depending on where you're starting from) while not appearing to be tinkering with the slide projector.

He is a talented and durable politician. Yet there was something a little wistful about the huddled airplane press conference when Nixon described his hasty breakfast with candidate Rockefeller. "I ate oatmeal," he told reporters matter-of-factly. "Nelson had eggs. I'm watching my cholesterol count. He isn't."

October 18, 1956

The Loneliest Man in Washington

BY WILLIAM HARLAN HALE

John Foster Dulles's first ninety days in office had barely ended when this most communicative of Secretaries of State reported to the nation on the extent to which he had changed if not reversed signals at the State Department. With satisfaction he announced that a new broom had swept out holdovers from the past. There were already installed ". . . two new Under Secretaries . . . six new Assistant Secretaries . . . a new Legal Adviser, a new Counselor, a new Director of the International Information Administration . . . The whole Policy Planning Staff is to go under new direction . . . We are also bringing fresh vision and new vigor into our United Nations mission and into our Embassies abroad. . . . New ambassadors are installed . . . in . . ." [there followed a long list of places].

Concerning the personnel of the Foreign Service that had come under his direction, Dulles had certain reservations, which he expressed publicly in a kind of reverse English: "There is a tendency in some quarters to feel that confidence cannot be placed in these career officials because in the past . . . they served under Democrat [sic] Presidents and Democrat Secretaries of State." Still, "It is, however, easier than most think" (observe how the "some" has been upgraded to "most") for these officials to adapt themselves to the new leadership. For they were, "with rare exceptions," a splendid and patriotic group.

241

This equivocal praise from the chief was flashed to Foreign Service men around the world. He had already admonished them not only to "loyalty" but to "positive loyalty"—presumably as against something henceforth to be considered mere negative loyalty.

Dulles came into office with a deep desire to disassociate himself from the past, to wipe the slate clean and start afresh according to his own lights. Having declared that the Truman era's policies had "put our nation in the greatest peril it has ever been in the course of its national history . . .," he evidently looked upon the change of Administration as the mandate for an entire change of régime. He mistrusted the particular legacy he had come into, and the Secretary had reasons for not standing in awe of professionals in any case. Dulles was no newcomer: He had moved amid international affairs as long as any of them—in fact, ever since the time he had served at the 1907 Peace Conference at The Hague—and mostly he had moved at the top.

There was another basic element in the incoming Secretary's conditioning. Over the decades—first looking back at the time when his grandfather, John W. Foster, had been Secretary of State, then on the years when his uncle, Robert Lansing, had held the office, and finally on the period when it was filled by Dean Acheson, the man he had served in the heyday of bipartisanship as a Republican consultant—Dulles had observed one constant fact. In a nation many of whose people were traditionally inclined to look on foreign affairs as nothing more than foreigners' affairs, the State Department in general and its chief in particular had never been popular at home. Dulles, his friends agree, had wanted ardently since early manhood to be Secretary of State in the family tradition; but what he had kept to himself was that he didn't want to be one like his Uncle Robert, who had had almost as much trouble with the Republicans on the Hill in his day as Acheson had in his. What good was it to put over your policies abroad unless you could also sell yourself at home?

The Search for a Constituency

"The trouble with the State Department," one of Dulles's chief assistants quotes him as saying, "is that it has no constituency like

Agriculture or Commerce or Labor." Now a constituency means a body of organized support capable of exerting pressure. In Washington's top bureaucracy, a basic rule holds that one's constituency begins in one's own office. Next one seeks to cultivate the press. Then the road—often strewn with traps—leads upward to the Hill and outward toward the voters.

Secretary Dulles, a world-minded lawyer of phenomenal skill, nimbleness of intellect, indestructible stamina, and a confidence in himself fully justified by his attainments, entered upon his duties quite certain that he would be able to overcome the errors, entanglements, and frustrations of his predecessors.

In Dulles's search for constituents, a painful incident before the end of his third month in office taught him a lesson that has stayed with him like Holy Writ. On the eve of taking off for the second of those trips abroad whose pace and number were soon to become legendary, Dulles accepted the advice of his close friend and trusted adviser on public relations, Assistant Secretary Carl W. McCardle, and invited a number of prominent correspondents to dinner to hear, off the record, his views on the state of the world in general and the Far East in particular. Growing expansive, he confided that a time might come when the United States would have to end its support of Formosa and advocate turning it over to the United Nations, while voting also to admit Red China to that body. The story leaked, and Senator William Knowland of California descended upon the White House at the head of a phalanx of aroused legislative friends of Chiang Kai-shek demanding to know what was up. This contretemps brought about a repudiation of Dulles's remarks by White House Secretary James Hagerty.

A bruised Dulles learned not to offend Senator Knowland again. He might disagree privately with Knowland, but still . . . here was a possible constituent. "Dulles's profound respect for the power of the Senate stems in part from his having served in it himself," remarks a Washington correspondent who knows the Secretary well. "The trouble is that he served there only six months—long enough to become impressed, but not enough to learn to discriminate."

Dulles also set out to appease Styles Bridges of New Hampshire, taking in the Senator's protégé and former administrative assistant, R. W. Scott McLeod, as a virtual Grand Inquisitor simultaneously in charge of Security, Personnel, and Foreign Service Inspection—an appointment that helped destroy what was left of Service morale. He even made a public gesture of endorsing Senator McCarthy's investigations into State Department personnel. ("It is a time when exposure through Congressional action is to be expected.") He put up no fight at all when the McCarthy camp tried to block the appointment of career man Charles E. Bohlen as Ambassador to the Soviet Union. He agreed to what later became known as the "book-burning" directives to our overseas libraries, and he made no protest when the incredible team of Cohn and Schine raided and uprooted his information centers abroad.

Dulles's submissiveness was bipartisan: In 1955, when the Democrats had come to power on the Hill, he gave in to the xenophobic Representative Francis E. Walter of Pennsylvania and fired his own top immigration adviser, Edward Corsi of New York, whom he had appointed as a Republican, a personal friend, and also a friend of immigrants.

Meanwhile, again in order to reassure the Knowland wing of his own party, he had replaced his first Under Secretary, General Walter Bedell Smith, who as Chief of Staff of SHAEF had been General Eisenhower's right-hand man in wartime, with an isolationist oilman and follower in Dad's footsteps, Herbert Hoover, Jr.—an appointment that has since led Dulles into troubles he never imagined.

While anxiously pursuing the elusive shape of a constituency outside his department, Secretary Dulles made no attempt to start the job right in his own back yard. The man who for decades had wanted above all things to be Secretary of State found, when the time came, that he didn't really want the responsibilities and burdens of heading the government's senior department at all. According to several sources close to him, he remarked shortly before the inauguration that he wanted to be something higher and freer—a top long-range planner and global adviser close to the President's side, unencumbered by daily routine. His ambition, in short, was to be a sort of updated Colonel House, with a sweeping mandate from the President to trouble-shoot around the world, above and beyond the State Department and not necessarily answerable for all the Department below him.

The ambition was lofty and, as a less ambitious man might have sensed, hardly realistic. For by a long accretion of law and custom supported by Executive order and appropriation, the day-to-day conduct of our basic, peacetime relations abroad *is* lodged in the State Department and the Foreign Service it administers. Together they constitute a vast, sprawling organization of more than twelve thousand permanent officers and civil-service employees who are engaged in activities ranging from representing us in seventy-eight foreign capitals and performing consular chores in 188 posts to coming up with ideas about the future of irrigation in Egypt, the problems of the next decade in Antarctica, the best ways to fight Communist propaganda in Karachi, and the necessities of the whale fishery in Reykjavik.

A Commander Needs Troops

The new Secretary was preoccupied with things that he felt were more important than the Department's immense hierarchy of ranking experts and officeholders, a retinue that today, by the way, is larger than ever before, including at home more than thirty officials of the rank of Deputy Assistant Secretary or better, who in turn are supported by another fourscore Bureau and Office Directors, Executive and Deputy Directors, who in turn are assisted by hundreds of regional and desk officers, coordinators, advisers, special assistants, and *their* staffs—all of whom must be administered by somebody. But if the man entrusted with the seals of the Secretaryship does not want to do all this administering, he at least ought to realize that a commander in the field needs troops. Troops may bungle and fall over each other's feet, but no troops usually means no campaign at all.

In the most elementary sense of all, troops are also constituents. No troops means no immediate followers. Monroe's imperious, lone-eagle Secretary of State John Quincy Adams, in an earlier and much simpler time when America was a minor power at the world's fringe, may have imagined that he could go it alone by force of will or bluff, or both. Dulles's greatest error may have been in trying to play the role of an Adams at a time when our position in the world has been reversed.

Dulles firmly believes in himself and his mission. He also appears to disdain many of his associates, present no less than past, as superfluous to his needs. And there may lie the fatal flaw of a leader who knows a great deal, but not everything, about the world's most demanding and delicate foreign-affairs post.

Shortly after Dulles took office, the surviving veterans of the Policy Planning Staff, once headed by George F. Kennan, offered to brief him with "position papers" on pending subjects. Dulles replied in effect that he didn't need their papers: He was quite well informed already. The Policy Planning Staff thereupon went into a decline from which it has never recovered, dropping into a "kind of secretariat that tries to pick up any pieces the Secretary has dropped," as one member has put it privately. Nevertheless, its director, Robert R. Bowie, an exceptionally articulate and vigorous advocate even in dissent, is one of the few men in the present State Department who do have the ear and direct confidence of the Secretary, although he is himself a holdover. This is one of the paradoxes of Dulles's régime.

Otherwise "communications upward" largely broke down when Dulles took over—even communications from his own appointees. The usual departmental custom of having the desk officer for any country present in the Secretary's office when the envoy of that country calls fell into the discard: The new Secretary had little need of expert advice.

When in town, the Secretary does maintain a rule of presiding over an early-morning half-hour staff session at which his Assistant Secretaries and several of their deputies are present. But this brief run-through in the presence of perhaps a dozen men, as one of them puts it, "is pretty much a classroom exercise—you wait until maybe teacher calls you." Of the Assistant Secretaries responsible for vital geographic areas abroad, only one, the brilliant and durable Livingston T. Merchant of European Affairs, can be said to have held the immediate confidence of the Secretary. (Mr. Merchant has since been transferred as Ambassador to Canada.) Another, Walter S. Robertson of Far Eastern Affairs, a holdover sustained by his enthusiasm for the cause of Chiang Kai-shek, at least has the confidence of the Knowland wing and thereby enjoys an irremovable place in the department—another paradox of the Dulles régime, since the Secretary himself does not think highly of Chiang, and furthermore Mr. Robertson is a Democrat. A third Assistant Secretary, George V. Allen, was in charge of Near Eastern Affairs until his recent transfer to Athens, but it is common knowledge at the department that in many of the negotiations that led up to the present crisis with Arab leadership, he stood not at the center but at the periphery.

The new chief soon confessed in private a certain irritation with the ways of his second in command, Under Secretary Smith, for trying to serve as a sort of departmental Chief of Staff with the job of harmonizing views down below for presentation to the head man for a simple yes-or-no decision. That technique might have been all right for someone like General Marshall, Dulles let it be known; but as for himself, he had too many ideas of his own about foreign policy to want it. He had lived in this field all his life, and he wanted to get his thinking in at the start and not just at the end of the process. He cited what had been done at the Caracas conference in getting an agreement for common action against Communist subversion, which he considered a tremendous accomplishment. The agreement was all his idea, he said, and nothing would have happened if he had just sat and waited for position papers. (The Secretary's insistence on his own initiative at Caracas has since been slightly modified by his assertion during the present campaign that Dr. Milton Eisenhower also played a leading role.)

Perhaps Dulles does not actually feel, as he is reported to have remarked once, that he doesn't know whom he can really trust in the Department. But he has certainly acted as if he felt that way. He has stood apart in a world of strangers. Although he had doubts about the veterans, he brought along to make up his own "team" only a handful of men whom he himself knew at first hand. He arrived on the scene almost alone, except for an incongruous personal entourage composed of Herman Phleger, a San Francisco lawyer; Carl McCardle, a hearty Philadelphia newspaperman without experience in the public-affairs and propaganda field he was to head; and Roderic L. O'Connor, a personal assistant. Dulles's own new Under Secretary for Administration, Donald B. Lourie of the Quaker Oats Company, was almost unknown to him. "All I can tell you about him," the new Secretary informed the staff gathered in the plaza behind the State Department Building to hear him make introductions, "is that a few years ago he was an All America quarterback." And when it came to choosing an Assistant Secretary for the vital post of Economic Affairs—a subject Dulles is known to view with a distaste matching Carlyle's stricture on "the dismal science"—he had no candidates at all, and it was left to Paul H. Nitze, a holdover then leaving the directorship of the Policy Planning Staff, to propose and recruit the Nebraska banker Samuel C. Waugh.

When a Washington reporter asked Dulles why he had taken the unprecedented step of appointing one man, namely Scott McLeod, to the joint posts of security officer and personnel chief —functions hitherto kept rigidly separate in the Federal bureaucracy in order not to let security run personnel—he answered with a shrug, "I leave these things to Smith."

When Dulles was confronted by his Foreign Service people with arguments that to dismiss career officer John Carter Vincent simply on the ground of "failure" in his reports from wartime China might intimidate and stultify future official reporting, he dismissed those objections too. It seemed that the new Secretary, charged with the over-all conduct of foreign relations, was not particularly interested in precisely who was going to be working for him, since he'd be doing all the really important work himself.

When one asks in Washington or of officials abroad how well Dulles has run the State Department, the most typical answer is that he actually hasn't run it at all. While busying himself at top levels around the world and chalking up almost 350,000 miles of travel, he has left others to run an institution that he apparently neither likes nor trusts. Some of those others are people who in turn don't fully share his views. The President delegated to his friend Dulles the stewardship of Foreign Affairs, and Dulles in turn has delegated a great part of the trust—abdicated it, some critics would say—to his present Under Secretary, Herbert Hoover, Jr., an Old Guard conservative who opposes many of Dulles's best ideas.

Dulles's Right-Hand Man

The second Herbert Hoover was brought in as a Great Engineer who had won success in the international oil business, just as his father had in mining before him. A silent, shy, and guarded man, he had first come to public notice as the expert who mediated the British-Iranian impasse over oil resources in 1954. He was then catapulted into the role of Under Secretary and day-to-day administrator of the world's most demanding foreign office.

In addition to giving Hoover the broad run of departmental administrative affairs, the chief also deeded over to him the whole broad field of economic affairs. In this field, at least, Hoover held strong views, and if the Secretary hadn't troubled to find out in advance what they were, he soon learned.

Hoover belongs to the school led by Secretary of the Treasury George Humphrey which holds that American aid abroad should be strictly limited and based only on security interests. This runs directly counter to Dulles's own call last winter for a dynamic new approach to eastern peoples in the form of large-scale, long-range aid projects, and to his assertion that we might have to spend some $4 billion annually on aid for a long time to come. Hoover supports Humphrey in the latter's insistence on keeping long-term foreign aid down to $100 million a year—and since Humphrey, with his control of purse strings and his personal allies, is just about the most powerful figure in the Administration, there is not much Dulles can do about it.

Hoover is for high tariffs, while his own chief is not. Dulles favors the exchange of scientific visits with the Soviet Union, but Hoover opposes them, fearing for our security. It was Hoover who during the Secretary's absence last year turned down Chou En-lai's bid for bilateral talks—a move Dulles disavowed on his return. It was Hoover who had the Department issue a gratuitous statement last year on the "success" of Chancellor Adenauer's humiliating talks in Moscow and who performed the famous off-again, on-again bobble over the shipment of tanks to Saudi Arabia—both again in the Secretary's absence. If it is true that Dulles has ingrained doubts as to the caliber or dependability of the officials about him, he may have had occasion by now to confirm them in the case of his hostage to Old Guard fortunes, Herbert Hoover, Jr.

A function to which Under Secretary Hoover gives several hours each week is that of chairing the inter-departmental Operations Coordinating Board—a mushrooming new Washington growth that proliferates into every agency concerned with Foreign Affairs. In essence, OCB is a follow-up body charged by the President with ensuring that decisions reached by the National Security Council are properly carried out—"implemented" is the word—by the several agencies concerned. It is also supposed to initiate new proposals, which then make their way to the NSC's Planning Board and so from there on up to the NSC itself, and then back down again.

Today, however, in addition to providing a get-together near the top, OCB has erupted into some forty-odd sub-boards or "working groups" that are supposed to provide co-ordination across agency lines all the way down to the desk levels of the various departments. OCB itself meets once a week with Hoover in the chair and a membership made up of Jackson (now the President's Special Assistant for security affairs and psychological problems), Director Allen W. Dulles of the Central Intelligence Agency, Deputy Secretary of Defense Reuben B. Robertson, Jr., Director Theodore G. Streibert of the U.S. Information Agency, and foreign-aid chief Hollister. But that is only the beginning. OCB is served by an executive secretariat of twenty, and subordinate liaison officers of the various agencies "liaise" with *it*. Twoscore or more lesser officers of each agency sit on the subgroups also busily co-ordinating below decks. "We just keep ourselves busy co-ordinating sideways," remarked one disgruntled desk officer deep in the heap below Dulles, "because we can't co-ordinate upward—or rather, the Secretary himself doesn't co-ordinate down."

"I'm sure OCB made sense at the start," says one career veteran, the geographic director for a key area of Europe. "But now it has become a device for diluting and dividing responsibility down the line so that all semblance of initiative and leadership is lost. Down here, we find ourselves having to spend days every month reconciling our views with those of the military before anything can go upstairs. The sources of new thinking of foreign policy have been muddied."

Will There Be a Super-Dulles?

In establishing an aura of apartness and departmental aloofness about himself, Secretary Dulles has only succeeded in creating what he surely never planned—a power vacuum where other men with other ideas have been able to move in. Some of the White House staff, particularly, criticize him for having absented himself so much from his country and his department that vital decisions have been reached in the NSC without him. They argue that if Dulles didn't know in advance last year about the proposal of the chairman of the Joint Chiefs of Staff, Admiral Arthur Radford, to slash our overseas ground forces by 800,000 men—as he says he didn't—the fault is largely his, for the proposal involves essential relations with the entire Allied world. They charge also that a whole string of NSC emergency decisions affecting the Middle East had to be taken last fall while he was off at Geneva and only in intermittent communication. They say there is no point in trying to strengthen Dulles's hand on Asian-aid projects so long as he simply refers the whole thing back to co-ordinator Hoover—and then flies off to Karachi.

Today at the White House, after almost four years of watching co-ordinators galore move in where Dulles himself has been too preoccupied to tread, there is a feeling that even more co-ordination may be needed. An idea now going about in the President's immediate entourage is that of providing the Chief Executive with a new top-level assistant who would have the same mandate in foreign affairs as that bestowed on Sherman Adams in domestic affairs. The President rather likes the idea, says an inner-circle adviser who should know. But this poses a question: If the White House needs a super-Dulles, then why Dulles?

All this confusion might have been avoided if Eisenhower's Secretary of State had recognized at the start that the job to which he was appointed was actually to be Secretary of State, in fact as well as in name—and if the President, upon finding some reservations in his Secretary's mind on this score, had called him in and told him in effect, "Foster, I want you to get hold of that Department, use it, and *run* it."

For lack of that, we have had the spectacle of a brilliant one-man operator and peripatetic energizer stopping occasionally at a suite of rooms on the fifth floor of the new State Department Building but occupied chiefly with his own flow of ideas—a super-abundant flow but not a particularly continuous one. This situation leaves everyone hard put to keep up with Dulles, including the President himself.

To his technique of diplomacy by visitation, aimed at producing effects abroad, Dulles has added the technique of diplomacy by press conference, aimed at producing effects at home. This makes the position of everybody in the department in general and of Public Affairs man Carl McCardle in particular somewhat difficult, since no one can predict just what the Secretary is going to say, and thus give advance guidance to the Voice of America or our embassies abroad.

Dulles has come out both for and against Nasser, against the immorality of neutralism and (amending himself) against his own pronouncement, for "massive" and "instant" retaliation and (also amending himself) for the notion that he didn't really mean "instant" or "massive" at all. "Our line will be to follow that set by the Secretary's latest remarks, which should be used *in full*," is the substance of the instruction that repeatedly goes from McCardle's office to the U.S. Information Agency. That, as one USIA official put it, often leaves the man at the propaganda desk asking, "Which line?"

In 1953, Dulles talked of liberating the Soviet World's captive peoples. That idea was quickly forgotten. Next there was "agonizing reappraisal"—a threat as unfortunate to our relations with France as his off-the-cuff statement that a defeat of Chancellor Adenauer in the German elections would be "disastrous" was to our relations with Germany. Then, after the "unleashing-Chiang" line in the Far East, came the "no-more-retreats" line—after which we agreed to the partition of Vietnam.

There was the expansive talk of "dynamic new approaches" to eastern peoples, at which point, since it involved money, Under Secretary Hoover and Secretary Humphrey took over against dynamism. There were the extraordinary statements on Goa (a Portuguese "province") and on the merits of the Cyprus controversy—against both of which Dulles's own Office of Near Eastern and South Asian Affairs had protested in advance, only to be overruled. There was the line of giving Israel at least some assistance, preceded by the line of giving it none. There was the line of grim "foreboding" about Communist intentions in early 1955, followed by the line in early 1956 that the Soviets were on the run—a conclusion Dulles's own Russian experts by no means share.

There was the policy of building a "Northern Tier" alliance of Arab states to hold the line against Communism, followed by a refusal to join the resulting Baghdad Pact when Egypt's new dictator, Nasser, didn't want to play. There was the line of building up Nasser as the leader of the western Arab world, followed by the present line of building him down. There was the line of giving Nasser almost any aid he wanted, including the Aswan High Dam, followed by the line of withholding aid, including the dam, after Nasser had approached the Soviets for aid, too. The turnabout as history already knows, gave Nasser his golden opportunity to grab the Suez Canal and thereby produce a general crisis with and within the West.

The Dulles revolution at the State Department has been a personal one, the result of one man's desire to divest himself of advice he didn't particularly want and of a staff whose routine thinking he thought he could do without. But since even Dulles has some of the personal limitations of a human being, the revolution has backfired on him—and on the American people and on the democratic world as a whole. The immensely gifted man who thought he could do without advisers—under whom such crack veterans as Freeman Matthews, James Riddleberger, and Livingston Merchant have been relegated to the outer circle abroad—finds himself the prisoner of men like Herbert Hoover, Jr., with the jovial newspaperman Carl McCardle his closest confidant.

Never perhaps has a Foreign Affairs chief been so cut off from his own authority, his colleagues, and his duties.

December 20, 1949

Kansas City . . . Twelfth Street

By Llewellyn White

Twelfth, or Sin, Street in Kansas City, Missouri, really begins at its western terminus, a hundred and some feet down in the flat valley of the Kaw, or Kansas, River. For a long time this was called the West Bottoms; now it is known as the Central Industrial District, but transcontinental Pullman occupants still identify it readily by the mournful bellowing of steers and the ceaseless olfactory duel between the glue factories and Loose-Wiles's cookie bakery.

From a bluff not high enough to escape such humble but profitable smells, Twelfth Street runs due east (roughly parallel to the Missouri River and never more than ten blocks from it) for a dozen miles, until it almost hits the muddy Missouri's second tributary, the Blue. At right angles to Sin Street, just south of its westernmost thirty blocks or so, lies a rectangle filled with a jumble of factories, shops, office buildings, and parking lots, ending at, say, Twenty-eighth, where a fifteen-mile-long rectangle of handsome houses and boulevards begins.

In the 1900's, the six blocks between Broadway and Grand—then as now a double row of nondescript buildings better seen at night and from the inside, or, better still, in terms of the people in them—were the center of society, from tailcoats to tarts. They are still the center of the hotel, shopping, and business-office districts, though both white ties and white slaves have vanished,

254

and Karmel Korn and jimcrack souvenir shops have taken over many a spot where strong rye and strong language once flowed. Like the snow goose, life has flown south, leaving a deserted backwash where, at night, historic Twelfth Street echoes only to the croaking of an occasional bum.

Twelfth Street was nothing at all—just an undrawn line through the forbidding hills—when the town of Kansas was founded in 1838 on the Missouri levee. It was still nothing in 1845, when Senator Thomas Hart Benton of Missouri, great-uncle of the artist who paints there today, watched the stern-wheelers steam westward up the Missouri to meet the wagon trains of the Oregon Trail, and rumbled, "Gentlemen, there is the gateway to India."

Kansas City began to realize its destiny at the close of the War Between the States, when the interrupted flow of homesteaders and prospectors swelled to floodtide, and Colonel Kersey Coates snatched the first trans-Missouri rail link away from St. Joe and Leavenworth. Soon cattle-poor Texas began driving its steers to Kansas City, which rapidly became the biggest market. Saloons, brothels, hotels, and boardinghouses sprouted from the red clay like March crocuses. Fists and greenbacks became the currency of masculine prowess, and variety-show girls who doubled as waitresses saw to it that no one carried too much of the latter away.

In 1880 Big Jim Pendergast arrived from Ireland via the effete East, threaded his way through a corridor of touts, pimps, and pickpockets at the cupolaed new depot, found a convenient boardinghouse, and went to work as an iron puddler. The roaring frontier era was drawing to a close. In 1881 open gambling was banned by the Missouri Legislature, and Bob Potee, the best faro dealer east of the Barbary Coast, walked out into the Missouri until his iron hat floated gently downstream. So much the better for Jim Pendergast, a big fellow with enormous drooping mustaches, who never forgot a man's face, name, or problem, and who felt strongly that any wage earner should be able to hold his liquor and take the bulk of his pay home to the missus.

Big Jim's first tangible contribution to the law and order in which he believed was The American Inn, a high-class "tabble doat" boardinghouse. In premises safely guarded from lady guests, he opened a saloon, and the solidest citizens of the town soon came to nurse the two drinks to which Jim rigorously limited them, and to seek advice from a natural-born leader.

By 1886 the West Bottoms had become so industrial that the very poor were being squeezed onto the levee and south up the tortuous slits that were Broadway and Wyandotte, Delaware, Main, and Grand. With no thought of deserting his Kaw Valley parishioners, Jim opened a second saloon on North Main, and thereafter became father-confessor to the Second Ward as well.

So that was where and how and when Twelfth Street and Jim Pendergast, Sr. began. A half-mile-long viaduct 110 feet above Bluff Street was built in 1914 to take the long lines of factory-feeding trucks down to streets where nobody lived any more, and where nobody got off the cars of Kansas City's seventeen railroads any more, either; for that same year they unveiled the stunning new Union Station, still the handsomest passenger depot in the world, out on Twenty-fourth Street between Main and Broadway.

On a brilliant late Indian-summer day I stare down at the western terminus of Twelfth Street, and try to remember if that gray building under the mammoth Macy billboard was the old Blossom House, so long an oasis of middle-class respectability in a shimmering desert of rich and poor shame. Macy's is absolutely the newest thing in Kansas City. The spot down there beneath the tangle of crisscross freight tracks where I heard my first breathless string of fascinating four-letter words must surely be one of the oldest landmarks.

Now, after the decades (thirty-nine years since I heard the four-letter words, twenty-four since I lived and worked here), I feel the need of reorientation. There are eight or nine miles of Twelfth Street stretching out before me straight as a royal flush to Blue Valley and beyond.

One house here at Washington Street stands on the city's highest peak, old Quality Hill. Whoever built it is no longer remembered. But as late as the early 1900's it was Doc Carson's crutchlined Temple of Health, and only a year or so ago it flourished briefly as an expensive restaurant with (so everybody imagined) dice and card tables upstairs. Now it is nothing again, an empty hull smelling of burned cooking fat and almost vanished scent, although the neon sign says "Sammy's Bar-B-Q." The shadow of the Cathedral of the Immaculate Conception still juts across from Eleventh Street, for the priests and sisters, like the Pendergasts, have stoutly resisted the temptation to desert the needy, leaving it to the fashionable Methodists and Presbyterians to leapfrog one depressed area after another in the mad rush to the Elysian Fields.

On down near Central, one long, low building has a familiar look. The Missouri Hotel, it says. On one side of the narrow lobby is a novelty shop featuring a special on packaged whiskey. On the other is a Greek beanery, and beyond it at the corner the Folly, which describes itself as a burlesque-vaudeville house. Heaven knows, the full-length photographs of half-clothed females are no fit advertisements for burlesque or vaudeville, or sex, or anything but the poignancy of unwanted old age. Shades of Ann Pennington, I mutter. Then it all comes back with a rush: This is where the Golden Age of Twelfth Street began.

To this very corner, in 1900, came Joe Donegan, protégé of Ed Butler, the St. Louis saloonkeeper-politician. Ed had fallen heir to the old Century Hotel, had sent Joe there to see if it could be made into anything. Joe made it, for nearly two decades, the center of theatrical, sporting, political, and masculine social life, a Mecca for every male who had the good sense to break his trip at the edge of the Kansas desert.

Joe remodeled and swanked the place up in 1911, renaming it the Edward in honor of its owner. Thereafter the Edward Grill, in the basement, and the Edward Cabaret, upstairs, became world-renowned. On New Year's Eve the top hats shone in the swirling snowflakes as big Tom Mason, Joe's ex-cop bouncer, restrained the eager crowds that stretched down to Main.

The cabaret was a cozy place, gayer, in its baby-blue pastel, than the oak-lined grill. Three times nightly its walls shook to the blasts of singing the like of which has not been heard for ages. That was Emma Weston, Big Emma, the Female Barytone, flame-haired, whiskey-husky, and endowed with those subtle powers which make mild little men dream beyond their means. It was here in this tiny room that Ernie Burnett, Joe's pianist-

maestro, working off a spirituous and romantic hangover late one
bilious morning, picked out, with a listless right hand, the melody
of "Melancholy Baby." Here, too, Ernie taught Edith Baker how
to club the keys in the three-note variation that came to be known
as the "Twelfth Street Blues"; and his pupil went on to become
Edyth Baker of the Ziegfeld Follies, take her own show to London, teach the then Prince of Wales the Black Bottom, marry a
title, and stay.

At the supper hour the dimly-lighted grill swarmed with the
great and near-great: Fireman Jim Flynn, Frank Gotch, Ad Wol-
gast, Packy McFarland, Eva Tanguay, Ann Pennington, Eddie
Foy, Sr., Bat Nelson, Jack Dempsey, and Jack Johnson, who, with
his white wife, occupied Ed Butler's royal suite above Joe's
Century Theater.

Everything came and went easily with Joe Donegan. Throughout his career he served free drinks to newsmen. No out-of-luck
comedian, hoofer, horseplayer, or fight manager was known to be
refused a loan. And the poor of the neighborhood got theirs, for
Joe was a power in the First Ward, presiding over his little empire, meeting, greeting, dispensing political wisdom and food
baskets, coal and cash, forever puffing away at one of the Century
Maiden cigars that profitably stank up his burlesque house.

And then came the Eighteenth Amendment. Some of the important men of the town said the hell with it, but most of those
who continued to drink the Edward's liquor began prudently to
vote and talk dry. The paradox confused Joe, an essentially simple man. He took to betting heavily on the bangtails, lost consistently, gulped his first drink of hard stuff, lost more, drank
more, finally gave up in 1923, and, before his death in 1930, was
on the receiving end of more than one touch.

Prohibition ended Twelfth Street's Golden Age, but while it
lasted there was much more to it than the northwest corner of
Central. Steeply downhill past Wyandotte, past the spot where
Billy Watson's Gaiety and its female Beef Trust ran in lively competition with the Century, past the six-and-a-half-million-dollar
Municipal Auditorium, past the slightly stuffy Muehlbach Hotel,
where the First Baptist Church stood until 1915, was the Baltimore Hotel.

It is not there any more; its north end is a parking lot, its south a row of one-story shops fronting on Twelfth. When it was opened in 1898 it was a showplace of red brick and white limestone, scarcely to be matched between coasts, one of the few Twelfth Street structures of that or any day that looked imposing from the outside.

The Baltimore Grill was a breath-taking thing of shining mahogany and of low crystal chandeliers, whose light flattered the bare shoulders of feminine first-nighters, who arrived at the hotel from the old Willis Wood Theatre, an exact replica of the Paris Odéon, through a marvelous underground passage.

On première nights everybody came through the passage, presumably for food and refreshment, or just possibly to catch sight of Tom Finnigan, the Mayor of Twelfth Street.

Thomas J. Finnigan came to Twelfth Street before the turn of the century, and for thirty years he never left it. For more than half of those thirty years, he sold the Harvard Classics for the P. F. Collier & Son Distributing Company, serving on the side as the social confidant of actors, the sartorial adviser of sports figures, and the political Gallup-Roper of Jim and Tom Pendergast. For twenty years he lived in Room 503 of the Baltimore, and to this chamber came Otis Skinner, Bert Wheeler, and many another to pay respects. Everyone esteemed it a rare privilege to be invited, for Tom talked like Damon Runyon wrote.

But Prohibition and the First World War did something to Tom, as they did to so many up and down his street. He saw the doughboys converge on the drab six-story Dixon and Sexton Hotels across the street, bellowing for whiskey and women, and getting both. During the 1920's and 1930's no one imagined these two hostelries had ever been used just for sleeping; though when the Sexton went up in 1903, at the amazing cost of $85,000, it was much favored by visiting Methodist bishops and presiding elders. Tom saw the lawless era, too, the see-you-and-raise decade when hoodlums were heroes everywhere, and Johnny Lazia, Kansas City's number one hood, forced T. J. Pendergast, Big Jim's younger brother and heir, to take him on as a political ally. That was the period when a nearby club offered four strip-tease acts, stark-naked waitresses, and the blue-plate, all for a buck; when the basements of the Sexton and Dixon were laid out in elaborate dice, card, roulette, and horse rooms, with football and baseball pools on the side, and window-cards up and down Twelfth Street directed the boobs to their slaughter.

Not that Tom Finnigan objected to gambling; he objected to gambling in anything but white tie and tails. Accustomed to distinguished male companionship, to temperate and discriminating conversation mixed with drinking of the same order, he regarded the spectacle of painted schoolgirls being sick in the gutter as a profanation. He stayed on in Room 503 until they tore it down around him, stayed on in Twelfth Street until the reformers in 1938 shut everything up tight, the good with the bad; and then, in 1941, his old friend Leo Fitzpatrick came and took him away to die of a broken heart in Detroit.

Twelfth Street was always "uptown" to Jim Pendergast; and although he was well aware that the center of political gravity was slipping southward, he stuck to North Main and continued to minister to the North End have-nots about whom the Republicans made speeches but did nothing, having perhaps what Gladstone Harvey, the local Spinoza, called "a Presbyterian idea of heaven: everyone else in jail, and them holding the keys."

Sometimes at Jim Pendergast's quarters, as it was to be later at T. J.'s, three hundred little people would arrive in a day: an Italian mother wanting a light sentence for a boy caught in his first scrape, a newly-arrived Greek needing a job, someone reporting a hungry family of Mexicans down on the levee—all going to the kindly man with sprawling brown mustaches who mastered the brother's-keeper routine decades before Alcoholics Anonymous was even thought of.

William Rockhill Nelson railed publicly at Jim, just as his present-day successor at the patrician *Star*, Falstaffian Roy Roberts, was to rail at Brother Tom, and, ultimately, at Tom's boy Jim (until, just this past year, he had to backpedal furiously to save young Jim from an upstart challenger named Charlie Binaggio). But then as now, it was sometimes difficult to say where honest indignation left off and journalistic opportunism began; for the *Star* has always had to be the impeccable bible of

Christian Kansas, and until the late 1920's it had to scrounge for circulation with whatever weapons came easiest to hand.

The *Star* knew lots of things about Big Jim and Tom it did not choose to ballyhoo: that it was Jim who in 1902 came out for the direct primary; that under his goading the city in 1908 set up the first Public Welfare Department in the United States; that the Municipal Auditorium and the magnificent new courthouse, city hall, and police buildings between Oak and Locust were Tom's handiwork, as surely as Union Station was, to borrow Nelson's phrase, "Jim's monument"; that without the Pendergasts' bought-with-kindness (and a sprinkling of two-dollar bills) votes, the *Star's* ceaseless campaign that has given Kansas City the finest park, boulevard, and residential layout in the country would still be blueprint talk; that without the Pendergasts' personal largesse, the Community Chest drives would have fallen many thousands further below their yearly goals.

But what about Lazia and his sort? What about the rows on rows of wide-open cat houses of the early 1930's on Thirteenth, Fourteenth, and Fifteenth, with naked women sitting in life-sized picture frames in the windows rapping at passersby, until every schoolboy knew what a "woodpecker" was?

As I keep walking, past Cherry, Holmes, Charlotte, Campbell, Harrison, Troost, I think the air might clear my brain. No, not this air. Not these cheap bazaars and pawnshops, these miserable fleabag hotels, these stinking saloons, jukebox after jukebox grinding out cowboy laments to drown the caterwauling of drunken trulls. The signs in the window dutifully warn all under twenty-one to stay out. But there is no youth here, only creeping death; the abandoned picnic grounds of two generations that feasted here and had their fill and went away to greener pastures, leaving their banana skins and wax-paper sandwich wrappings strewn all around.

On across Forest and Tracy. One thing has to be admitted about Kansas City's slum dwellers: They are not packed in tight, after the fashion of Harlem or West Philly; the push south left most of the little one-family houses intact, and time and stingy property owners have supplied a plentiful sprinkling of weed-choked vacant lots between.

Virginia, Lydia, the Paseo—these are the streets where the Negroes live: the girls and children shrieking with unknowing laughter; the men swaggering in and out of their tiny saloons and snooker parlors, rank with stale beer and rib drippings; the women darkly silent. It might be Beale Street, Memphis, or any other Southern Negro street; which seems strange, because this was the line between North and South, only more North than South, and these people are the direct descendants of Underground refugees once greeted with open arms and fervent oratory. There on the left are the new low-rent bungalows: shacks with a little white paint on them, and with the bathrooms wealthy taxpayers "just knew these people wouldn't know how to use properly." Ninety years of Republican oratory, and now these painted shanties, and still the Negroes vote Democratic. Why? Mostly because they could always see a Pendergast, see one and get help from him.

But why measure out this *via dolorosa* to its bitter end? It is much the same for all those five miles more, except that the Negroes end at Prospect, where the Italians begin, trickling south from the river, always moving, always multiplying, until now, as in so many cities, their bright young Binaggios can challenge the traditional Irish grip.

Now, suddenly, I am back on Baltimore, in front of the hotel. I stand there a moment, not minding the sharp chill, wondering how it is that, starting out to write a nostalgic little piece about a street's past, I wind up worrying about its future.

The thing keeps turning in my mind and won't stop. When the "best" people decentralize a city by fanning out to the suburbs, they leave behind a sort of power vacuum. And if they're very lucky, a relatively decent boss like Big Jim Pendergast comes along to take care of the orphans the "best" people don't want to see or know about or have any trouble with; and sees to it that the Pharisees get their boulevards and sewers and fine public buildings, to boot. Only when the saloons go, there have to be new physical power-centers, and other professions at which the bosses can earn their livings; and if they choose something like sand, gravel, and cement, as Tom Pendergast did, that makes the business of new boulevards and sewers a little sticky.

Maybe the new-style contractor-political boss, no longer tied downtown by a saloon, builds himself a palace out south and becomes one of the fashionable refugees, at least after dinner; and the vacuum starts all over again. And then if the son, who's never lived anywhere but out south, proves to be sensitive to the odors of the unwashed, you get a Charlie Binaggio. And if it happens to be the home county of the President of the United States and the Chairman of the Democratic National Committee, you get a grand jury to thumb Binaggio out of there—perhaps with an assist from the newspaper, which doesn't want power, only a compatible whipping-boy to scold when the world and national news is slack; all of which takes care of Binaggio, but does it dispose of the vacuum?

And then suddenly I realize that this isn't just a Kansas City problem. How about the Cincinnati Basin? Or Cleveland's East Ninth Street? How about any modern American city?

PART FOUR

Portrait

Gallery

January 13, 1955

Some Negative Thinking
About Norman Vincent Peale

By William Lee Miller

I've been thinking negative thoughts, which Dr. Norman Vincent Peale, America's most successful Protestant minister, says we should never think. What's worse, my negative thoughts have been about Dr. Peale himself.

Dr. Peale believes in the Power of Positive Thinking. He says "only positive thoughts get results." What results? you ask. Success, happiness, money, health, friends, relaxation, peace of mind, power, self-confidence, vacations on Waikiki Beach, and, what is to me a truly frightening prospect, "Constant energy."

The results Dr. Peale himself has achieved by following the "Magic Formula" of Positive Thinking are impressive indeed. His weekly network TV show, "What's Your Trouble?" gets upwards of five thousand letters a week; his articles, such as the famous "Let the Church Speak Up for Capitalism" in the *Reader's Digest,* appear in popular magazines by the dozen; his own magazine, *Guideposts,* is one of the "fastest-growing inspirational publications in the country"; he himself has been the subject of many lyrical articles, including a cover story in *Newsweek* and "The Power of Norman Vincent Peale" in *McCall's;* his printed sermons ("How to Stop Being Tense," "No More Gloomy Thoughts") and his self-help booklets ("Spirit-Lifters," "Thought-

Conditioners") are mailed around the world by his own publishing outlet, Sermon Publications, Inc., of Pawling, New York; he speaks regularly to large national gatherings, especially of business groups; he has a regular network radio show, "The Art of Living," and appears often on radio and TV in such special appearances as a one-night substitution for his Pawling neighbor, Lowell Thomas; Christmas cards bearing a cheery message from him are sold throughout the land; he has a weekly syndicated newspaper column carried "in nearly one hundred dailies"; and now he has a regular question-and-answer page in *Look*. Of the *Look* feature, the press release said, "Norman Vincent Peale will add new millions . . . to his already colossal audience. . . . He will answer the questions of *Look* readers on social and moral problems. In his first article, Dr. Peale gives *Look* readers his advice on such problems as debt, falling in love with someone else's husband and the H-bomb."

Somewhere in between Dr. Peale finds time to preach in the Marble Collegiate Church of New York City, where there are overflow crowds at two services each Sunday. The worship bulletins of the church dutifully record, in column after column, the far-flung enterprises of the minister, with dates, times, and prices. And the "lounge" of the church serves as a salesroom: thirteen of Dr. Peale's sermons on LP records, $4.50; a subscription to *Guideposts*, $2; "maroon, gold-lettered binders" made to hold "a year's supply" of Dr. Peale's sermons, $3.

The Book

And then there is his book *The Power of Positive Thinking* (Prentice-Hall, $2.95). This product of Dr. Peale's constant energy has already sold nearly a million copies, and the publishers are said to have a goal of two million; it is available on records in an RCA album ("You can hear the inspiring talks of Dr. Norman Vincent Peale *right in your own home!*") and now there is an edition for young people ("Your market—every parent among the millions who have read this inspirational best seller. . . . Specially rewritten by Dr. Peale and adapted to the needs and interests of young people. . . . Backed by major national advertising, special juvenile market advertising, and all-out Christmas advertising"). For 112 weeks, as of this writing, *The Power of Positive Thinking* has been on the *Times's* best-seller list, a far longer time than any other current book, and for most of that time it has been the nonfiction leader.

I have just read *The Power of Positive Thinking*. In addition, I have read Dr. Peale's other books: *A Guide to Confident Living* ($2.95), *You Can Win* ($1.50), *The Art of Living* ($1.50), and those of which he is co-author, *Faith Is the Answer* ($2.95) and *The Art of Real Happiness* ($2.95). Let me say, in the unlikely event that anyone else would undertake this redundant inspirational feat, that it isn't necessary. If you have read one, you have read them all. There are no surprises in Dr. Peale. The chapters of his books could easily be transposed from the beginning to the middle, or from the end to the beginning, or from one book to another. The paragraphs could be shuffled and rearranged in any order. The swarms of examples, which alternate successful business executives and successful athletes, with successful military figures thrown in for variety, could be transposed to support one point or another interchangeably.

As a result of reading Dr. Peale's one point in every simple, easy book, chapter, and paragraph, I am so full of "confidence-concepts," "faith-attitudes," and "energy-producing thoughts," of "thought-conditioners" and "spirit-lifters," of "10 simple, workable rules," "8 practical formulas," "7 simple steps," "2 fifteen-minute formulas," and a "3 point program," of "proven secrets," "true stories," and "actual examples," of "healing words" ("tranquillity," "serenity") and "magic words" ("Faith Power Works Wonders"), so adept at "Imagineering" and "Mind-drainage" (also "grievance-drainage") that I have the Confidence, Faith, Vigor, Belief, Energy, Efficiency, and Power to write an article criticizing Dr. Peale. Believe me, Dr. Peale, without you I never could have done it.

"The secret of a better and more successful life," according to Dr. Peale, "is to cast out those old dead, unhealthy thoughts." "To make your mind healthy," says Dr. Peale, "you must feed it nourishing, wholesome thoughts." The trouble with a fellow like me, he claims, is that my "mind is literally saturated with apprehension, defeat thoughts, gloomy thoughts." But my prob-

lem is not only that I find that there are real things in the world
about which we legitimately can be apprehensive, negative, un-
hopeful, and even gloomy from time to time, but that one of the
surest causes of such negative thinking, in me, is Dr. Peale's own
kind of "Religion."

The key to the immense success of that "Religion" is its message. In this, Dr. Peale differs from other heroes of the current
popular religious revival. In a way Dr. Peale is the rich man's
Billy Graham, furnishing the successful and those who yearn to
be so something of the same excitement, direction, and reassurance with which Mr. Graham supplies his somewhat less prosperous and more fundamentalist followers. But there is an important
distinction to be made. As Mr. Graham surely would admit, his
own message is essentially similar to that of hundreds of other
evangelists, past and present, rising from a fundamentalist background; the key to Mr. Graham's special success is not in any
distinctive message but in his personality and his virtuosity as a
performer. But Dr. Peale's attraction lies somewhat less in personal charism than in his constantly reiterated single theme. Mr.
Graham's success depends almost entirely upon his personal
presence, but Dr. Peale has been as successful with the written as
with the spoken word.

This is not to say that Dr. Peale's personality and speaking
ability are unimportant. He is an effective master of an audience,
full of jokes and anecdotes, buoyant and confident. But it is his
message that explains his unique success. One comes away from
Billy Graham impressed not so much with anything that has
been said as with Billy Graham; from Dr. Peale, one comes away
with a vivid awareness of the one thing he said. It is an idea that
has made Dr. Peale.

The idea is that affirmative attitudes help to make their own
affirmations come true. Dr. Peale takes the obvious but partial
truth in this idea and builds it into an absolute law; he erects
on it a complete and infallible philosophy, psychology, and religion, so that he can solve every problem just by denying it really
exists and promise that every wish can be fulfilled just by "thinking" it: "Expect the Best and Get It"; "I don't believe in defeat";

death is "not Death at all"; "Change your thoughts and you change Everything."

All this is hard on the truth, but it is good for the preacher's popularity. It enables him to say exactly what his hearers want to hear. He can say it constantly, confidently, simply, without qualification and with the blessing of God. He need say nothing that might cut across his hearers' expectations, challenge the adequacy of their goals, or make demands of them.

Dr. Peale's idea thus allows him to go completely over into that situation of which liberal Protestantism always is in danger, where the desires and notions of a traditionless congregation determine absolutely what gospel shall be preached. In this again, Dr. Peale differs from other leaders of the popular religious revival. Someone like Bishop Fulton J. Sheen has obligations to Catholic dogmas that prevent him from fashioning his message entirely according to popular preference; Billy Graham, too, has some restraint upon him from the more or less fundamentalist gospel to which he is committed. But Dr. Peale is apparently free of obligation to any intellectual tradition or framework of interpretation antecedent to that which he works out to correspond exactly to the climate of opinion and desire in which he preaches.

Though I have said that Dr. Peale's books are all alike, yet there is this one qualification: The later books are worse. The earlier ones, in which Confident Living and Positive Thinking were plainly foreshadowed, nevertheless spoke the message in something nearer to the ordinary preacher's tones. The word was already self-help, but the voice was more like that of an ordinary liberal pastor, with his three points, usually in alliteration, with homely examples, some passages from the Bible, a rhetorical flight or two, a few quotes from Tennyson or Shakespeare, and some spaces through which a word greater than any words of the preacher might manage to make its way to some hearer. But in *The Power of Positive Thinking* such spaces are pretty well sealed; every quotation from the Bible is cut, clipped, and interpreted to make just Dr. Peale's point; the rhetoric of the sermon has been replaced by the short punchy sentences and atrocious jargon of the advertisement; the three points of the preacher have been supplanted by the Five Things You Can Do of popular psychology; and Tennyson's place has been taken by Eddie Rickenbacker.

Dr. Peale is good at what he does. He has the ability—and the nerve—to fit his message precisely to the exacting requirements of mass popularity. His discoveries parallel those of the composers of singing commercials. For example, he extols, and assiduously practices, "repetitious emphasis." He is willing to use without flinching the most blatant appeals and to promise without stint. The advertisements of his book explain, with remarkable candor, the basis of its appeal: "ARE *YOU* MISSING THE LIFE OF SUCCESS? Norman Vincent Peale's great best seller . . . is GUARANTEED to bring it to you! Make people like you. . . . Increase your earnings. . . ."

Like other success salesmen, Dr. Peale numbers his points and fixes them in the mind with memorable new words; his "formula" for solving problems through the power of prayer, for example, is "(1) PRAYERIZE, (2) PICTURIZE, (3) ACTUALIZE." He is careful to avoid the slightest hint of anything that would be definite, determinate, or different enough to offend anyone; and above all he requires not the slightest effort either to understand or to act upon his message. As Dr. Peale says elsewhere, "Don't doubt. Doubt closes the Power flow."

Dr. Peale's idea and his ability to present it might enable him to be popular in any place at any time, but it seems to work especially well in America now. The importance of studying Dr. Peale lies in what his enormous success means about our present situation in this country.

The American roots of Positive Thinking are not hard to find. They include most of those characteristics which observers are always identifying as typically American: our self-confidence and optimism, our worldly practicality, and our individualism and striving for success, concerned more with private career than public problems. They include, more particularly, that special combination of these characteristics which places its practical, individual confidence in the triumphant power of "mind" or "faith" over all external limits. This combination appears in the peculiarly American religion of Christian Science, in the "mind-cure" movement of the turn of the century, which William

James discusses in *The Varieties of Religious Experience,* and in many a "mental science" type of religion since. Perhaps these themes, especially the last, are characteristic more of middle- and upper-class American than of the nation as a whole, but they do seem to appear both in our serious literature and in our popular culture, as in the Horatio Alger stories of another day and the "How to" books and newsstand self-help of today. What Dr. Peale has done is to take these themes, which represent much of what is sound and also much of what is not so sound in American life, and reduce them to a unity, stating them in their simplest, baldest, extremest form. What was sound has pretty well been lost in the process.

It's Personalized!

But Dr. Peale's statement of his simplified version of these old American themes may be extremely popular right now just because they no longer seem self-evident. His success may be partly explained, ironically, by the fact that we no longer automatically believe what he is saying; we need to be reassured. Disturbing events have intervened, and so we listen a bit desperately to this voice which insists, more confidently than ever, that what we always believed is still true and that things *will* turn out all right, they will, they will. Just write it on a card and repeat it ten times a day.

The absolute power that Dr. Peale's followers insist on granting to their Positive Thinking may betray, however, a note of desperation. The optimism is no longer the healthy-minded kind, looking at life whole and seeing it good, but an optimism arranged by a very careful and very anxious selection of the particular bits and pieces of reality one is willing to acknowledge.

The success striving is different, too. The Horatio Alger type seems to have had a simple, clear confidence in getting ahead by mastering a craft, by inventing something out in the barn, or by doing an outstanding job as office boy. The Peale fan has no such confidence and trusts less in such solid realities as ability and work and talent than in the ritual repetition of spirit lifters and thought conditioners written on cards and on the determined refusal to think gloomy thoughts.

The "individualism" of the message is of that "personalized" kind which, having lost a genuinely personal relation, tries now to recapture it by contrivance, which thinks it overcomes standardization by stamping the buyer's initials on the product, or which, by adding "and I do mean YOU," pretends to be speaking to an individual instead of to a microphone and a Hooper rating. Dr. Peale's works are "personalized" with the same insistent YOU the Uncle Sam on the recruiting poster used, sternly pointing his finger at the YOU, who is everybody and nobody. The drugstore I went to this morning had a new sign tacked to the screen door: "Norman Vincent Peale Solves YOUR Personal Problems —in Look Magazine." *My* personal problems? In *Look* magazine? No, thank you.

The effort to regain by devices what cannot be regained by devices is especially evident in Dr. Peale's "power," "energy," and "vitality." The feeling of the loss of those powers must be very deep. Every chapter seems to promise "power": prayer power, creative mind power, faith power. This "power" is not control over the world so much as over oneself. That which should be natural—vitality, vigor, animal energy—is here the subject of "spiritual" manipulation. Human powers are not evoked by revealing some true center of interest and excitement in the world outside, but are exhorted to rise by the sheer mesmerism of "repetitious emphasis." There is no real *content* to Dr. Peale's preaching, in the sense of some vivid objective interest: a job to be done, a cause to be joined, a truth to be understood. The transaction is entirely within the reader. There is a complete absence of any really concretely interesting and exciting world, which might bring out the reader's vital responses and overcome his boredom, which must be immense. There is no such world because to see it, to be interested and excited by it, and to respond to it would require effort, and Dr. Peale's "amazing results" never require any effort.

This is a striking difference between Dr. Peale's themes and those in the American heritage to which his are related: His optimism and practicality are "easy" and "simple." There is never the suggestion that hard work might be involved in achievement. There are no demands upon the reader. This is not the sturdy practical guide whose maxims have to do with the shoulder and the wheel, the nose and the grindstone; there is no pushing and grinding to be done.

Many of Dr. Peale's techniques come from the famous and successful men with whom he is intimate. In Dr. Peale's books these men turn out to talk just like Dr. Peale. There is a continually recurring episode in the books that goes like this: Peale meets Great Man; Peale humbly asks Great Man for his secret (his formula, technique); Great Man tells Peale strikingly Peale-like secret (formula, technique) upon which Peale then expatiates. Something like this occurs in *The Power of Positive Thinking* on page 105 ("dynamic man at the height of his power"—secret is to repeat Mark 9:23), page 117 ("outstanding newspaper editor, an inspiring personality"—secret is card in wallet with words to effect that successful man is successful), pages 150-151 (Howard Chandler Christy, artist—secret is spending fifteen minutes filling mind full of God), page 229 (a Member of Congress—secret is to be relaxed), page 212 ("outstanding man in his line"—secret is don't think defeat), page 223 ("a famous businessman who handles important affairs and varied interests"—secret is quiet period in living room with wife after breakfast).

Everything in this maze of formulas and techniques is "workable," even the teachings of Jesus. We are referred to "competent spiritual experts" and to Dr. Peale's own "How Cards." Dr. Peale takes all of our worship of the practical and the technical unabashedly into the realm of the spirit. But nothing much that could be called spiritual remains. In place of any Holy of Holies there is the bathroom mirror, on which you are to paste the latest slogan.

Like Hot Cakes

About the current book there is a faintly blasphemous promise, for a religious book, of a money-back guarantee. The message is endorsed throughout by satisfied users; it is PROVED, it has WORKED, it is TESTED. In fact, Dr. Peale's book is not much else than an extension of the advertisements of that same book, telling again between the covers, with further testimonials, what we have already been told, with testimonials, on the jacket and in the ads: This method WORKS. One might give prospective buyers of the book the tip that since the book is "repetitious emphasis" of positive thinking, one can achieve exactly the same effect—and save money—simply by reading and rereading the advertisements.

But to do that might be to miss what is beyond doubt the most remarkable of all the multitudinous examples of the power of Positive Thinking that appear in Dr. Peale's best seller, the incredible story of the Mustard Seed Remembrancers. For those who are too busy, or too negative, to read the book I now pass on this truly heart-warming story.

A couple named Flint were failing, broke, and full of negative thinking. They read a condensation of Dr. Peale's *A Guide to Confident Living*. The Flints, on reading Dr. Peale, were particularly impressed with the section on "Mustard Seed Faith." Though living in Philadelphia, they drove each Sunday to New York to hear Dr. Peale and continued to do so, says Dr. Peale, "even in the most inclement weather."

In an interview, Dr. Peale told Mr. Flint that if he would "utilize the technique of faith, all his problems could be solved."

One day Mr. Flint said to his wife that his powerful recommendation would be easier to follow if he had some tangible reminder of faith. They looked for a mustard seed. His wife fished something out of a pickle jar and he carried it around with him. But the seed was small and he lost it, and, since he had already begun to think positively, he got the idea that it might be put in a plastic ball. Mr. Flint asked Dr. Peale if he thought the resulting object could be merchandised, and after consulting a businessman ("one of the greatest executives in the country"), the gadgets went on sale in a department store in New York. The initial ad said: "symbol of faith—a genuine mustard seed enclosed in sparkling glass: makes a bracelet with real meaning." Dr. Peale adds, with the glint of Positive Thinking in his eye, "These articles sold like hot cakes."

The Flints now have a factory in a Midwestern city producing Mustard Seed Remembrancers, the perfect ending to the story of Positive Thinking. However, there is one unfortunate negative note at the end of Dr. Peale's account: "So popular and effective is it that others have copied it, but the Flint Mustard Seed Remembrancer is the original." That's the trouble with Positive Thinking; other Positive Thinkers come along and try to cut into your territory.

The suspicion that there is danger in all this is strengthened by a look at what Positive Thinking means in specific areas like psychology and politics.

Dr. Peale has been concerned with psychology and psychiatry throughout his career. He was one of the first ministers really to take seriously the contributions of these studies, before the relation of religion and psychiatry became the fad it is now. He joined in founding the American Foundation for Religion and Psychiatry, and his church continues to provide its chief financial support.

Some of Dr. Peale's early books were written in collaboration with psychiatrist Smiley Blanton. Dr. Peale has gone on, independently, to use a few words and ideas of popular psychology for his own easy, simple, and successful operation. Men who are working to relate psychiatry to pastoral counseling say he has set their work back many years. The heart of the criticism is that Dr. Peale short-circuits the difficult processes of psychological healing; he promises quick, painless, and complete "solutions" to problems which may be deep and complex, and which may require real discipline and professional treatment. Moreover, he tends to encourage the weak, sick, and confused to depend not upon the agencies of their own local community but upon himself and his books.

The basis for the criticism that serious counselors make of Dr. Peale becomes obvious in this episode from his TV program: A child has been frightened by the stories of the new bombs, and worries and loses sleep. Dr. Peale, scarcely waiting for the problem to be voiced, pats the child on the head and says, Don't be afraid; God will take care of you; no H-bomb will fall on New York.

This is Positive Thinking, all right, following the counsel of his book: "Never mention the worst. Never think of it." But how long does it last, to repress those worries on the affable assurance of the preacher? And what does it do to one's maturity? And what happens if an H-bomb *does* fall on New York?

A woman with a real problem, once a fan of Dr. Peale's, now says in disgust, "He told me I didn't have any problem." Certainly Positive Thinking can help when a problem rests in some unjustified pessimism or lack of confidence. But sometimes our problems are real, aren't they? And then Dr. Peale's message is a dangerous counsel that we not face them. Dr. Peale's rejection of "negative thinking" may be a rejection of any real thinking at all, for serious thought necessarily involves the confrontation of all the elements of problems. Dr. Peale's message tends to reinforce the anti-intellectualism of the times, for any serious thought is bound to appear somewhat negative to the bland outlook of the Peale follower.

The social and political meaning of this message is clear in its immense admiration of power figures and big names. These admired persons are all successful in the most immediate and worldly sense: military men like Douglas MacArthur, for whose faith book Dr. Peale wrote an introduction, businessmen, and athletes. No professors, no serious writers or serious artists, no thinkers or critics, no one whose life enterprise has a different goal than success.

"Executives" as a class are special favorites of Dr. Peale's. As the comedian Henry Morgan once said of *The Power,* "This book isn't for me, I'm not an executive; nobody in this book but executives." What the book can mean to executives is made plain in this advertisement: "EXECUTIVES: Give this book to employees. It pays dividends!" The most unsettling part of this proposal is not just that this "religious" book is justified at the cash register ("It really pays off in dollars and cents!" says William A. Cole of Toms River, New Jersey) but that the profits are obtained by the executive buying the book in lots to use on his employees, quieting their complaints, making them enthusiastic for their firm, and increasing sales. Salesmen are said to have "Renewed faith in what they sell and in their organization" (apparently regardless of what the product or the organization may be). The book brings "Greater efficiency from the *office staff.* Marked reductions in clock-watching. . . ."

Positive Thinking also makes politics much easier and more efficient. In 1952 Dr. Peale proposed a "prayer plan" to select the President, a plan which seemed to encourage its users to regard their choice as an absolute and divinely inspired selection of *the* man God wanted.

God seems regularly to answer Dr. Peale's own prayers with the Republican candidates. His (Dr. Peale's, that is) most startling political act was his letter to ministers in New York State suggesting that they support Joe Hanley for Lieutenant Governor because he had once been an ordained clergyman. In 1952 he said that though ordinarily ministers should stay out of politics, when there was a *moral* issue involved they should speak up, in this case for Eisenhower and Nixon.

And so what does the Peale phenomenon mean? It means that an old, wrong answer to our new American problems is very popular, and that we have a hard choice to make. We are a people accustomed to simplicity and success and unprepared for tragedy, suddenly thrust into mammoth responsibilities in a complex world and a tragic time. In the face of hard and unexpected facts we can rise to a new maturity, or we can turn instead to those who pat us on the head and say it isn't so at all, like the Reverend Doctor Norman Vincent Peale.

July 20, 1954

Senator Styles Bridges and His
Far-flung Constituents

By Douglass Cater

On the thirteenth of November, 1953 (which happened to fall on a Friday), the Concord (N.H.) *Daily Monitor* carried a startling item on its front page. Beneath a two-column photograph of Senator Styles Bridges, Republican of New Hampshire, were the words "Top United States Official." Noting that President Eisenhower was in Canada, Vice-President Nixon in Korea, and Speaker of the House Martin in Europe, the *Monitor* pointed out that the mantle of *de jure* Presidential power had fallen temporarily on Bridges, the president pro tem. of the Senate. It was a sober reminder of the fact that in the event of catastrophe to America's top elected leaders, Congress, under its Constitutional mandate, provides a successor to the President and that, party seniority being what it is, Styles Bridges is now third in line for the White House.

Bridges indeed once told a Congressional committee that when he took his oath as Senator he undertook to look after the welfare of the entire United States. In pursuing this perfectly laudable aim, however, the Senator has chosen to interest himself in the causes and cases of an extraordinarily varied assortment of people. He has, in fact, served probably as motley a collection of non-New Hampshire constituents as ever passed through the doors of the Senate Office Building. When he made the above-mentioned declaration, for instance, he was attempting to explain to the committee why he had interceded time and again with the Internal Revenue Bureau to settle the tax case of a Baltimore liquor dealer Bridges claimed he had never met, and who in turn claimed that he had never met Bridges.

In addition to making him a somewhat remote heir presumptive, Bridges's Senate seniority makes him chairman of the Senate Appropriations Committee and ranking majority member of the Armed Services Committee. It is doubtful whether there are two better positions for providing that readily negotiable Washington currency called influence.

It is somewhat surprising that a man so powerful should be almost an unknown. In the seventeen years he has served, no major legislation has borne the name of Bridges. Though the New Hampshire Senator proudly occupies the desk of Daniel Webster, few words that are likely to enter the history books have been heard from behind that desk in recent years. Senator Bridges, a handsome man grown somewhat fleshy of face and figure, is not inclined to waste much time in colloquy on the Senate floor. Despite an otherwise savvy manner, his attempts at oratory are strangely faltering.

Direct heir to the progressive "Sons of the Wild Jackass" tradition in the Republican Party, Bridges has defended rank conservatism as blindly as any member of the Old Guard. A lonely Republican internationalist before the outbreak of the Second World War, he has in the main voted silently for the major post-war foreign-policy programs while at the same time endorsing nearly every crippling amendment dreamed up by such Senators as Kem, Jenner, Dirksen, Welker—and by himself. He has regularly voiced deep discontent with some of America's Allies in Europe, but has pledged undying support to the exiled government of Chiang Kai-shek.

Bridges remained outwardly neutral when the Eisenhower forces scored their great victory in the 1952 New Hampshire primary, though his sidekicks were ardently pro-Taft. After the election, he says, he issued a plea for party unity, but soon joined Senators McCarthy and Dirksen in the fight against the nomination of Charles Bohlen as Ambassador to Moscow—the first Senate cabal aimed at undermining the new President's authority. For a new Administration desperately in need for leadership in Congress, he has been a slender reed.

Probably the main reason for the obscure character that Bridges has retained during his many years in the Senate lies in the nature of the specialized political field in which he has achieved his greatest eminence. The repute of a manipulator of political influence is not susceptible to standard publicity gimmicks. Such a man must pursue hidden paths, conduct his negotiations in inner rooms, speak in the halftones of suasion and threat. There must be an aloof, secondhand quality to all his transactions.

Bridges has mastered these patterns. He has stymied the decision of a great department of government without uttering a word for the public record. He has shoved a manufacturer out of the aircraft business with a few swift raps of a committee gavel. And throughout, the Senator has proved himself capable of discretion far above and beyond the call of Senatorial duty.

Contrary to widespread belief, such adept handling of the levers of influence depends by no means on whether one's own party is in power. The printed hearings of a House investigating subcommittee refer to an occasion in 1949 when a Democratic Commissioner of Internal Revenue called in a subordinate, told him that Bridges had made inquiry about a case, and then added significantly, according to the later testimony of the subordinate, that "The Senator was about the only or certainly one of the few Republican friends that the Bureau of Internal Revenue had on the Appropriations Committee." That same year a Democratic Secretary of the Air Force, Stuart Symington, reportedly affirmed the Air Force's appreciation for Bridges by promising that "if there is to be a new air base in the eastern part of the United States, I want it placed in New Hampshire."

To this reporter, Senator Bridges pointed out the particular problem that arose during the long period of Democratic dominance when a Republican citizen found his state represented by two Democratic Senators. A Republican Senator from another state would have had to be "an utterly cold bird," he remarked, to turn down a request from such a person. No cold bird, Bridges admitted that he had frequently been haunted by such out-of-state constituents. The late Senator Taft, he added, had been equally beset.

Senator Taft, however, was considerably more choosy about whose interests he served. Taft, for example, never was shown to have as a constituent a man such as Henry ("The Dutchman") Grunewald, who was a Democrat himself and the friend of high-placed Democrats.

The Grunewald Constituency

Actually, Henry Grunewald was not a mere constituent, but a broker for widely variegated constituents and clients who had particular problems to be ironed out in Washington. Though highly successful at this, Grunewald was comparatively unknown to the public at large until recent years. Certainly former Federal Judge William Clark of Princeton, New Jersey, had never heard of Grunewald in the summer of 1947 when he came to Washington still hopeful of regaining the judgeship that he had lost due to a political mischance while in military service during the war. Clark's old Harvard classmate, Representative W. Kingsland Macy (R., New York), suggested that Senator Bridges, then Chairman of the Appropriations Committee during the Eightieth Congress, might be able to help. But instead of arranging a direct introduction to his fellow Republican, Macy, somewhat to Clark's surprise, called in Grunewald, whom he described as "a very good friend of Bridges." It was Grunewald, in turn, who escorted Clark to the Capitol, through an antechamber where, Clark recalls, at least one or two Senators were waiting, and into the New Hampshire Senator's presence.

Bridges agreed to place some remarks in the Congressional Record on Clark's behalf. Nothing came of the Judge's request. Clark heard no more from Bridges or Grunewald until nearly a year later. At that time his son, Blair Clark, who was publishing a weekly paper in New Hampshire, turned up a scandal involving large-scale embezzlement by a prominent contractor and the state comptroller. Thinking that the corruption might go further, young Clark was also looking, among other things, into a possible tie-up between Bridges and the contractor, who had recently done a major renovation job on Bridges's East Concord home. Suddenly Judge Clark, then serving as legal consultant to General Lucius Clay in Germany, received a transatlantic telephone call from Macy and Grunewald. Recalling Bridges's earlier "assistance" to the Judge, they suggested that Clark direct his son to drop his inquiry. Judge Clark abruptly rejected the suggestion.

It turned out that such solicitude was needless, for neither Blair Clark nor the special state's attorney who subsequently prosecuted and sent to prison the contractor and the comptroller found evidence of any collusion on Bridges's part. But it was through such precise attention to all possible contingencies that the energetic Grunewald managed to build his reputation and solidify his friendships among the politically powerful.

Born of German parents in South Africa, Henry Grunewald came to this country when he was about sixteen. Without benefit of wealth, much formal education, pretense of culture, or even citizenship until 1942, he climbed the ladder of success in Washington, finally toppling off and landing in jail in 1953. Before he arrived in the nation's capital in 1930, Grunewald had served variously as a Navy seaman, during which time he became a champion boxer; as an undercover man during the First World War; as a prohibition agent, from which job he was fired as a result of his own difficulties with the Volstead Act; and finally as a private investigator. It was a wealthy and eccentric retired insurance executive, Henry Marsh, who sent Grunewald to Washington at a nice salary with the simple mission of keeping tabs on what was going on. Before many years, Grunewald knew so much of what was going on that he became an independent operator.

In fact, so successful was Grunewald that at various times he has drawn large fees from such diverse enterprises as Pan American Airways, the American Broadcasting Company, the General Cable Corporation, the United Mine Workers, and the Nationalist Government of China. Though Grunewald professes to be a liberal Democrat, an examination of his receipts by a Congressional committee a few years ago turned up $5,000 from Senator

Owen Brewster, then Chairman of the Republican Senatorial Campaign Committee. It seems that Grunewald had been serving as a "conduit" for the Republicans to pass along these funds to certain primary candidates who could not be granted them officially.

The wiretap, the shakedown, and the fix were all part of the services Grunewald could and did offer to his clients. He displayed extraordinary resourcefulness in probing into the hidden facets of men's lives and was skillful in making others realize how potentially useful—or dangerous—such probing could be. Though neither a lawyer nor an accountant, he handled tax problems with proficiency, winning dubious recognition from a House committee investigating the Internal Revenue Bureau as the person who "personifies the decay of the Federal tax system during the period following World War II." Grunewald loved to take up difficult tax cases at the point where reputable lawyers left off.

A number of prominent Senators are known to have been on friendly terms with Grunewald. None besides Bridges, however, has ever been reported as working so closely with him on what must rank as the most peculiar constituency problem of all times. This was the tax case of a Baltimore liquor dealer named Hyman Harvey Klein.

Klein's story might be entitled "The Case of the Mystified Constituent," for Klein subsequently insisted that he had never heard of Grunewald and knew Bridges only by reputation. Yet in December, 1951, Klein was suddenly to learn that these two had been interceding with top officials in the Internal Revenue Bureau on his behalf over a period of several years. Bridges later testified that he was acting at the request of a friend who was helping out a legal associate who in turn was trying to do Klein a good turn. Apparently nobody ever bothered to tell Klein or his attorneys.

Klein's troubles stemmed from a wartime enterprise that had involved shipping whiskey from Canada into the United States while carrying the transactions on the books of several dummy Cuban and Panamanian corporations. In this way Klein had been able to justify a considerable price mark-up on the liquor.

The mark-up, the House committee later concluded, was in direct violation of U.S. ceiling-price regulations. But the scheme worked so well that in two years' time Klein and three associates realized a profit of approximately $20 million on their original four-thousand-dollar investment.

Such a windfall presented some problems. The Alcohol Tax Unit of the Internal Revenue Bureau began to probe Klein's operations. In 1947, when Klein sold his share of the Cuban corporations for $5 million and paid capital-gains instead of income tax, the Intelligence Division of the Bureau began to look for tax fraud. In early March, 1948, receiving word that Klein had booked passage out of the country, the Bureau slapped jeopardy assessments totaling nearly $7 million on him and his wife.

Three weeks later, according to the office diary kept by Charles Oliphant, the Bureau's general counsel, he and Commissioner George A. Schoeneman received a visit from Henry Grunewald. Grunewald stated, Oliphant later testified, that he was representing Senator Bridges in the matter of the Klein case. Bridges has subsequently denied it.

Before the intervention of Grunewald, as many as two hundred agents had been assigned to probe the Klein empire. It would have been logical, following the laying down of jeopardy assessments, to intensify that investigation preparatory to indictment. Strangely, after the Grunewald visit the investigation lagged remarkably. Only one agent from the New York office was assigned to the case full time between April and August, 1949, and for two of those five months he was otherwise occupied. At the end of the summer, Daniel Bolich, who as Special Agent in Charge in New York had responsibility for supervising the case, was promoted to Assistant Commissioner of the Bureau. On his final day as special agent he ordered the discontinuance of the Intelligence Unit investigations of Klein; the next day, under his new authority, he ordered the Alcohol Tax Unit investigation stopped.

Bolich's impartiality was challenged when the House committee investigators produced evidence that subsequently he lived for a year and a half in a Washington hotel suite maintained by

Grunewald, drove a new Chrysler paid for by Grunewald, and over the period 1946-1950, when he was dealing with Grunewald on Klein's case and several others, spent at least $115,000 while reporting an income of less than half that amount. Bolich is currently under indictment for income-tax evasion.

Despite Bolich's assistance, Klein still needed to get his assets freed. According to statute, this could not be done administratively unless a bond was posted or the tax was paid. Klein evidently didn't want to do either. The attempts to help him were persistent but unrewarding. In January, 1949, Bridges paid a visit to the Bureau after which its three top officials in rapid succession summoned Aubrey Marrs, head of the technical staff, to report the Senator's interest. Commissioner Schoeneman, according to Marrs's testimony before the King Committee, was a model of discretion. He cautioned that nothing improper should be done but that one should not forget Bridges's friendship for the Bureau. Assistant Commissioner Bolich, on the other hand, was more direct: "My impression from what he said to me," Marrs later testified, "was that 'You have got your orders. Now, you find some way to do it.' "

Whether coincidentally or not, both Bridges and Grunewald subsequently gave thorough evidence of their friendship for officials of the Bureau. That September Bridges introduced a Senate measure specifying a pay raise for Counsel Oliphant. This, however, was defeated by his economy-minded colleagues. (Earlier that year Bridges had opposed an increase for cancer research with the admonitory words, "We must decide between what is desirable and what is absolutely necessary.") The following spring, Grunewald took both Schoeneman and Oliphant on vacation with him at his Miami estate.

Shortly before their departure, on March 22, 1950, Bridges conferred again with these two, and a day or so later Grunewald was on the phone to Oliphant, announcing, "What he [Bridges] can't get away from, they slapped a jeopardy assessment on these people and put them through all this trouble and he is a little peeved about that, see? . . . He asked if I could find out from you how long it will be before the thing is wound up?"

Evidently the law was inflexible and certain Bureau officials, like Marrs, refused to be pushed around. Bureau records show a telephone call over a year later between Schoeneman and Oliphant discussing a pending visit from Bridges to discuss the Klein case. In July, 1951, the records contain transcripts of several phone calls in which Bridges discussed plans for a settlement conference on the Klein case.

A few months later, members of the King Committee, plowing through the interesting and detailed office log of Charles Oliphant, were startled to discover the evidence of this curious teamwork between Bridges and Grunewald. Although the Committee was never able to get the full details of the case, its investigations had several impressive results. Grunewald served a short term in jail for contempt rather than give frank answers to the Committee's questions. Daniel Bolich is under indictment, and both Schoeneman and Oliphant have resigned from the Internal Revenue Bureau. The testimony of William Power Maloney, the tiny, blustery lawyer who, according to Bridges, asked his assistance in Klein's behalf, was sent to the Justice Department by the Committee to be examined for evidence of perjury. Hyman Harvey Klein was indicted by a grand jury in May, 1954, for income-tax evasion.

Such are the niceties of Congressional etiquette, however, that when the Committee, by this time Republican-controlled, made its final report on the case last fall, the name of Styles Bridges was not even mentioned, despite the frequency with which it had cropped up during the hearings. There had been brief embarrassment for Senator Bridges when he appeared on March 27, 1952, to explain his interest in the Klein case. "I represent the State of New Hampshire," Bridges said, "but when I took my oath of office as a United States Senator I became a Senator of the United States, and my first obligation is to serve the welfare of the country . . . Sometimes it is a terrific burden but it is one of the things that Senators and Congressmen do, if they intend to stay in Congress."

Bridges declared that he had acted to help out his old friend, William Maloney. (Presumably Maloney, a Democrat who had served in the Justice Department for many years, was incapable of finding his own way around the Revenue Bureau.) Bridges said he had never authorized Grunewald to speak for him and that he would never have intervened in the case had he known that fraud charges were involved. His recollection was extremely vague about what inquiries he had made in Klein's behalf or what he had done with the information gained.

Bridges lost some of his composure when the committee counsel, Adrian DeWind, led him through the mass of diary notations, telephone transcripts, and other evidence documenting his intercession. At one point he burst out angrily, ". . . I have always heard it was illegal to record telephone conversations . . ." Then, catching himself, he added quickly, "but I have no objection to this thing, because those telephone conversations probably are helpful now." His composure vanished completely when Congressman Thomas J. O'Brien (D., Illinois) asked the question that was in the minds of all those present: "Senator Bridges . . . can you tell us of any other cases where you have taken action at the Bureau of Internal Revenue on behalf of people who were not from New Hampshire?"

The printed record of the hearings reveals an answer that could scarcely be described as lucid. "I cannot, right offhand, but undoubtedly probably I have, but I do not know. I could not answer you right offhand on that but my assumption is—and when anybody asked me anything from New Hampshire, I have always done it, if I thought it was proper; and if anybody who was a friend—if you came to me Congressman O'Brien, and said—and I knew you—and you said, 'Will you make an inquiry for me of the Bureau of Internal Revenue on a matter,' or the Department of Commerce, or anybody else, of course I would, and I think every Congressman or Senator would."

No one reminded the Senator that he didn't know Hyman Harvey Klein, didn't even know his case had been under investigation for tax fraud. Chairman Cecil King did, however, express a sense of disquiet that the life-and-death power of the Senate Appropriations Committee might have played a part in influencing the Bureau's actions. King told Bridges that his friends Grunewald and Maloney had taken deliberate advantage of him. "I think down deep inside you, you are going to welcome the first opportunity or you should, to meet both of them and let them have the benefit of your thinking."

When interviewed recently, Senator Bridges was decidedly cautious in giving this reporter the benefit of his thinking about Grunewald. Bridges remarked that he had known Grunewald for many years, first having met him through Grunewald's boss, Henry Marsh, but that sometimes two or three years would go by between Grunewald's appearances in his office. He considered him neither an aide nor a social acquaintance.

The Path of Glory

Bridges's career reveals both the challenge and the perplexities of the American dream that an ambitious young man can rise to the top in politics no matter what his birth or circumstances. The eldest child of a poor Maine tenant farmer, young Henry Styles (he was ultimately to drop the Henry for fear of confusion with the leftist West Coast labor leader Harry Bridges) was forced to work hard to support the family and put himself through the agricultural course at the University of Maine. A brief, unhappy marriage in his youth only added to his financial burdens and left him with a son to support. He was still a young man when he crossed into New Hampshire to work on the agricultural extension staff of the state university there, and later for the State Farm Bureau Federation. Via this route, Bridges had before many years entered the hazardous field of politics.

Poverty was not Bridges's only handicap in this pursuit. Not being a lawyer, he could not enjoy the lawyer's penchant for moving in and out of public life with continued opportunities for enhancement of his professional career. Indeed, it is doubtful whether Bridges would ever have gotten into politics but for a benefactor of immense prestige and integrity, ex-Governor Robert P. Bass. During the 1920's Bridges was private secretary to the wealthy Bass, who led a vigorous group of New Hampshire progressive Republicans against the Old Guard forces of Senator George Moses. (It was Moses who had joined with the elder Senator Henry Cabot Lodge to frustrate America's entry into the League of Nations and who sneeringly coined the phrase "Sons of the Wild Jackass" to describe his progressive Republican colleagues.) Bass's group, including a number of eminent New Hampshire men like John Winant, John McLane, and Charles Tobey, wielded a powerful idealistic force in the state's political life, battling such vested interests as the utility holding companies that sought to dominate it.

Not long ago, Bridges recalled in the presence of this reporter his early crusading days. "You'd be amazed," he said, "but when I first got into politics in New Hampshire I got in actively fighting the top holding companies—Insull and the rest. It was one of the chief issues. Nowadays, because I believe in private power, people say I am a conservative."

Others who remember those times tell a slightly different story. It was in 1930, according to one version, that Bridges first entered public life—as Governor Charles Tobey's appointee to the New Hampshire Public Service Commission. The Governor's Council, an archaic elective body in New Hampshire that used to reflect the desires of the vested-interest groups, at first turned thumbs down on Bridges. Tobey stuck to his nominee, however, re-submitting Bridges's name at session after session of the Council. Suddenly, one day, the nomination went through without opposition.

Nothing in Bridges's subsequent career apparently caused the utility representatives to regret his appointment. The Senator has been a relentless and bitter foe of TVA and every other public power enterprise. Old-timers in the Senate still recall the afternoon the elderly Senator George Norris (R., Nebraska) pointed a finger at Bridges and described him as "the one Member outstanding in the Senate of the United States who does just exactly what the Power Trust of America wants done."

The first forebodings of disillusionment came to the Bass group during Bridges's gubernatorial campaign in 1934, when its members got word that Bridges was receiving financial support from the Rockingham Race Track interests. Confronted with the rumor, Bridges denied it, but defiantly added, according to the recollection of one of those present, that better men than he had accepted such support.

In the main Bridges was adjudged a good and progressive governor. The No. 1 enemy remained old George Moses, grown more and more cantankerous during his long years in the Senate. When, in 1936, Bridges decided to contest Moses's effort to return to the Senate (Moses had lost to a Democrat in 1932), there was no question as to whom Bass and his friends would support. They were for "Little Boy Blue"—the sobriquet Moses had sarcastically given the natty young governor. Bridges could in turn reassure his friends and rebuke Moses with the solemn promise: "When I go to Washington, I shall go with clean hands. . . . No one will be able to tap on my shoulder and demand my vote by reason of any obligation incurred." In January, 1937, Senator Bridges went to Washington.

A former friend of the Senator wrote this reporter not long ago: "You ask why he changed from a reasonably promising young liberal into what he has become. That question has always fascinated me. Knowing him as I do quite intimately, I can say that he is essentially a weak man, easily influenced by other more dominant people who may be close to him at the time. When he was a young man he was a liberal and was very much under the influence of the liberal Republican group. His second wife, Sally Clement, was a very fine woman, and had she not died in the middle '30's, the story might have been quite different."

A shrewd Washington reporter who has observed Bridges closely for a number of years provides a slightly different assessment. He points out that the ambitious young man arrived in the nation's capital to find himself pretty well blocked from further advancement. He represented a state with four electoral votes, hardly enough to cut much ice at the national conventions. He lacked the personal wealth that would allow a Member of Congress to enjoy independent status. Finally, he was a member of a skeleton Republican crew destined to endure sixteen more years of Democratic rule. Bridges made his final serious bid for national stature as a favorite-son candidate in the 1940 Republican Convention.

The Constituency of John L. Lewis

It may be counted a rare occasion indeed when a Senator claims as a constituent a bitterly denounced political foe. In 1937, young Senator Bridges had declared: "The Republican

National Committee does not owe John L. Lewis or his CIO affiliates any money and I thank God for that." In 1939, he told a Republican gathering that "Republicans will be wasting their time in seeking compromises with John L. Lewis, Harry Bridges, and the like." In 1941, he took the floor of the Senate to denounce " 'Steam-roller' Lewis . . . attempting to stampede government representatives into giving him control over the destinies of workers. . . ."

Yet in 1946, according to one of the rare bits of Henry Grunewald's testimony before the House committee, Bridges's attitude toward Lewis must have mellowed. That year Lewis staged a crippling Mine Workers' strike and tried to defy a court order issued by Federal Judge T. Alan Goldsborough. Goldsborough responded by slapping a $3,500,000 fine on the Mine Workers and a $10,000 fine on Lewis personally. Amid the fracas, Grunewald was hired by Lowell Mayberry, a disbarred Boston lawyer working for Lewis, to investigate Goldsborough's personal life. Grunewald and an associate received approximately $15,000 for this unsavory and unfruitful piece of research.

Grunewald's testimony before a closed executive session of the committee, which was later read into the public record by Congressman Hale Boggs (D., Louisiana), was that Senator Bridges introduced him to Mayberry and was present during the discussion of the proposed private investigation of Goldsborough. Later, in a public hearing, Grunewald amended his testimony, saying that Bridges had recommended him to Mayberry for investigative work but had not participated in the Goldsborough discussion.

When asked about this recently, Senator Bridges remarked that the newspapers had never printed the executive testimony of Mayberry, in which he denied Grunewald's testimony. Bridges conceded that newspapers cannot publish executive testimony until it is released (which Mayberry's never was), but added, "I have chosen to keep silent on the whole thing." Why then had Grunewald dragged him into the picture? Bridges said he thought Grunewald had been "confused."

In 1948 Lewis was once again staging a Mine Workers' strike in contempt of a court order. The trouble this time stemmed from the Mine Workers' pension fund, set up in 1947, which was supposed to be administered by Lewis for the Mine Workers, Ezra Van Horn for the mine owners, and a "neutral" third trustee. Early in 1948, the neutral trustee had resigned and the other two were deadlocked, Trustee Van Horn arguing that Trustee Lewis was trying to pay out such large benefits for retired miners that the fund would soon be bankrupt.

On Saturday morning, April 10, 1948, at eleven, House Speaker Martin called the two recalcitrant trustees to his office in the Capitol, and minutes later had achieved a remarkable agreement. The record of the meeting relates that "The Honorable Joseph W. Martin, Jr. proceeded forthwith, and while the two trustees were present, to engage the Honorable Styles Bridges by telephone in order to ascertain as to whether he would accept the trusteeship of the United Mine Workers Welfare and Retirement Fund, and at that time, approximately 11:13 A.M. on Saturday, April 10, the Honorable Styles Bridges so acquiesced . . ."

A few sour notes were sounded amid the general huzzahs for Bridges and Martin. Enterprising reporters sniffed around and discovered that Van Horn had been the only participant in the agreement at Martin's office who had not been forewarned. Equally curious was the fact that Bridges, Martin, and a big Philadelphia oil man, Joseph Pew, had dined together the evening prior to the remarkable compact. A coal operator voiced to Joseph Loftus of the New York *Times* the bewilderment that was felt by many about this turn of affairs: "I don't know what it is or how it happened, but it has an awful strong smell."

Not even the disgruntled, however, knew whether it smelled of oil or politics or of something else. It was nearly sixteen months later that a Senate Banking subcommittee, conducting routine hearings on "The Economic Power of Labor Organizations" chanced to discover that Bridges was collecting $35,000 per annum for his services as a trustee of the Mine Workers' fund.

When this fact hit the headlines, Bridges's response was immediate. In answer to a query from the publisher of the Portsmouth (N.H.) *Herald,* he wired the following explanation: AS YOU KNOW I AM NOT A MAN OF PERSONAL MEANS AND UNDER SUCH CIRCUM-

STANCES IT WOULD BE IMPOSSIBLE FOR ME TO SERVE IN THE CAPACITY OF NEUTRAL TRUSTEE MEETING THE COST INVOLVED OF PERSONAL ACTUARIAL AND LEGAL COUNSEL TO MAKE MY WORK AS TRUSTEE PRUDENT AND LEGAL. THEREFORE I AM ACCEPTING MONTHLY PAYMENTS FROM THE FUND AT THE RATE REFERRED TO AND FROM THOSE PAYMENTS WILL MEET THE COST OF EXPERT ACTUARIAL AND LEGAL COUNSEL RENDERED ME PERSONALLY.

Senatorial courtesy might have closed in to conceal the embarrassment, except for the curiosity of Senator Glen Taylor, that strange maverick from Idaho who had served as the Progressive Party's Vice-Presidential candidate in 1948. After that fiasco, Taylor didn't care much about etiquette. He wrote to the counsel of the Banking Committee requesting further clarification. Had Bridges in fact been obliged, he asked, to deduct actuarial and legal expenses from his salary? Had the job demanded a great amount of time and travel expense? Finally, Taylor wanted to know how successful Bridges had been in maintaining "neutrality" as the third trustee?

Committee Counsel Robert L'Heureux, himself a New Hampshire man and a protégé of Senator Charles Tobey, provided a very fully documented answer. Letters and minutes of trustee meetings revealed that shortly after Bridges had become a trustee he demanded that the cost of independent advice should be borne by the Fund. The other trustees had agreed, and on one occasion there was a record of $12,000 paid out to an independent actuary hired by Trustee Bridges. On the matter of work and travel burdens, Bridges had attended a total of nine meetings, each lasting between forty minutes and three hours, and all taking place in Washington.

On the subject of the Senator's neutrality, L'Heureux listed all twenty-nine disagreements among the trustees; in every case, Trustee Bridges and Trustee Lewis sided together against Trustee Van Horn. On August 18, 1949, after L'Heureux's report had been made public, Bridges told reporters that it was simply an effort of Henry Wallace's former running mate to cause political embarrassment. He promised to tell the "full story" and to identify the experts he had paid from his own salary after he left the Fund, which he said he planned to do in the near future.

By the following month it had become evident that the pension policy adopted by Lewis and Bridges had gotten the Fund into trouble, and Van Horn bitterly castigated the other two trustees. For the first time Bridges sided with Van Horn against Lewis, voting to suspend temporarily all pension payments as well as trustee salaries. A mine pensioner filed suit against the trustees for suspending his pension. Finally in April, 1950, Bridges announced that he was quitting.

Not long afterward, a reporter for the Claremont (N.H.) *Daily Eagle* called on Bridges in Washington to get the accounting that had been promised. The Senator, while refusing to give details, admitted that he had gotten some "compensation" above expenses. The reporter, basing his estimate on the per annum rate, filed a story that the Mine Workers' fund had paid Bridges "more than $45,000 plus expenses" during his tenure.

A few days later, the Concord *Monitor* reported that Bridges was threatening to sue the *Daily Eagle* for having published that figure. "When I get home this summer," the Senator was quoted in a telephone interview, "I'm going into the home town of every one of these cheap b . . . . s and tell my side of the story."

Up in Claremont, five summers have rolled round since then, but no one has yet had an opportunity to hear the senior Senator's side of the story. The publisher of the *Daily Eagle* no longer worries about a libel suit.

A New Kind of Pork

Besides his hegemony as senior Republican and as Chairman of the Appropriations Committee, Senator Bridges also is ranking Republican on the Senate Armed Services Committee, which maintains surveillance over the one department of the government far exceeding all the rest in dollar expenditures. Because of this, the Defense Department has in recent years been the object of anxious scrutiny by many thoughtful people who fear the enormous political power accruing from such vast disbursements. Last year the editor of the Concord *Daily Monitor* concluded gloomily: "In the old days of relative peace and smaller budgets, river and harbor bills used to be the principal pork barrel legislation for members of Congress. There is increasing evidence that defense spending has taken the place of river and harbor improvements in such grabs."

The Concord editor was voicing concern over the way the site for the $45-million Portsmouth-Newington (New Hampshire) strategic bomber base had been chosen. In 1950, William Loeb, owner and editor of the Manchester *Union Leader* and a close political supporter of Bridges, had been called down to Washington by Air Force Secretary Stuart Symington, who told him, according to Loeb's later recollection, "I appreciate all the things Styles Bridges has done for the Air Force during these dangerous days, and if there is to be a new air base in the eastern part of the United States, I want it placed in New Hampshire."

A year and a half later, Loeb announced joyously in a front-page editorial, "Bridges Brings Back the Bacon!" Only Bridges among New Hampshire's elected leaders deserved credit for getting the air base, Loeb's paper reported.

For a time it looked as if the Republican Administration would undo what a Democratic one had done, for in the spring of 1953 Defense Secretary Wilson announced that Air Force economies would oblige deferment on construction of the base. A few days later Bridges made a cryptic remark to the effect that "the air base cutback could lead to other major reductions in defense spending by a Senate Appropriations Committee." Not long after that, the Pentagon again reversed its course and decided to go ahead on a limited scale on the Portsmouth-Newington base for "stand-by" purposes.

This evidently was still not satisfactory to the New Hampshire Senator, who told reporters during a visit to Portsmouth in August that he was in telephonic communication with Air Secretary Talbott on the matter almost every other day. On August 31, 1953, a victory communiqué was handed out from Bridges's Washington office and confirmed a half hour later by the Pentagon: Work would proceed at full speed on a fully activated base with an annual payroll of $27 million. Fletcher Knebel commented later in *Look* that it was the one time the new Pentagon economizers had beat "an open political retreat."

An interesting postscript is provided by the fact that certain lawyers in Manchester, New Hampshire, have recently discovered that old clients are now paying retainers to attorney Wesley Powell, Bridges's former administrative assistant, in hopes of getting construction contracts for work on the base. Powell has already demonstrated his prowess by forming an architects' syndicate that has secured the contract for planning work at the base.

The Hammer Constituency

Congress itself, leery of favoritism in the letting of defense contracts, in September, 1951, passed Public Law 155, giving the two Armed Services Committees veto power over military decisions on the acquisition or disposition of property valued at more than $25,000. In the very first decision to come under committee purview following the passage of the law, Senator Bridges demonstrated how the Act could be used as an instrument of favoritism.

Bridges's favored constituent in this instance was a New Jersey businessman named Dr. Armand Hammer, who is the owner of United Distillers, Inc. Bridges's friendship with Hammer dated back to the early war years, when Hammer for a time owned a small distillery in New Hampshire. In 1948, Bridges and his wife accompanied Hammer on a Caribbean cruise in Hammer's private yacht. In 1949, one of Bridges's assistants made inquiries with the New York State Liquor Authority when one of Hammer's companies was having trouble over a license violation.

In 1951, the Army announced its intention of leasing the huge Morgantown Ordnance Works in New Jersey for the private production of fertilizer nitrates, of which there was a shortage at the time. Hammer came forward as a potential lessor, but from the Army's point of view there were at least two strikes against him. For one thing, United Distillers did not have the experience that would qualify it to operate the nation's largest single plant of this type. Secondly, Hammer himself, though showing no present signs of Communist sympathy, had lived in the Soviet Union during the 1920's and collaborated with the Communists on large-scale business activities. He had written a book in 1932 that contained glowing praise of Lenin, as well as messages from that Soviet leader addressed to "Comrade Hammer."

Senate investigators, including Bridges himself, have been

known to have a field day on much less provocation than this. After due consideration, Under Secretary of the Army Archibald Alexander decided to reject Hammer's bid and to lease Morgantown to the Mathieson Chemical Corporation.

In doing so, Alexander was not unaware of a lively degree of political interest in Hammer's case, that of Senator Bridges being among the liveliest. Before the Army's decision to lease Morgantown had even been announced, Bridges had requested Alexander to give consideration to Hammer's bid. On subsequent occasions, the Senator again spoke personally on Hammer's behalf. Other Members of Congress were also active.

Amid the chorus of political support for Hammer, a crass note crept in. An assistant to Alexander received a telephone call one day in midsummer of 1951 from a fairly prominent New Jersey politician. The caller emphasized that Hammer's company was incorporated in New Jersey and that it might be advantageous all around if Hammer were to receive the Morgantown contract. He then said it would be worth $100,000 to Alexander's campaign [Alexander was considering entering the gubernatorial campaign in New Jersey] if the Morgantown award went to Hammer. There was no indication that Hammer knew of this attempted bribe. He actually contributed to Alexander's Republican opponent when the Under Secretary ran unsuccessfully for the Senate in 1952.

Friendly intercession from Capitol Hill turned to furious opposition in September, 1951, when the Army announced its decision in favor of Mathieson. In the House Armed Services Committee, Congressman L. Gary Clemente (D., New York) demanded and got a full-scale hearing under the provisions of Public Law 155. In spite of a warning from an Assistant Secretary of Agriculture that a delay would seriously reduce the fertilizer supply for 1952 crops, the House committee proceeded to summon Army witnesses from the Under Secretary on down, but finally approved the lease in early December.

In the Senate committee, only Bridges continued to balk, but Senatorial privilege entitled a single member to hold up approval. A call from Under Secretary Alexander to Bridges, who was at a vacation spot, brought polite evasion. Finally on December 20, as the Army's option with Mathieson was due to expire, thus invalidating the contract, a committee staff member took matters into his own hands. He placed a long-distance call to Bridges and put the decision squarely up to him, saying that either the Senator must permit the contract to go through or he must be prepared to accept the blame. Bridges replied that he would reluctantly yield. The Army had managed to uphold its decision under all the pressure, but, as one official commented afterward, it could not afford many such victories.

Today Bridges's memory of the case is cloudy. He recalled in talking to this reporter that Hammer had once told him that he was the highest bidder for Morgantown, but, he said, "I never paid much attention to it. My association with it was relatively slight."

The Kaisers Face the Music

The Hammer story indicates that it is sometimes extremely difficult for even the most baronial Senator to force an affirmative decision upon a government agency against its will. It is not quite so difficult to compel an agency to back down from one of its own decisions, as Henry J. Kaiser was to learn in 1953 when he was tossed right out of the aircraft production business overnight.

Somehow Kaiser has never managed an entree into the circle of Bridges constituents, although he would seem to possess very adequate qualifications. Periodically since 1946, Bridges has leveled one attack or another against the Kaiser enterprises. His speeches on the subject, in contrast to his usually fairly colorless utterances, ring with such supercharged phrases as "dimpled darling of the New Deal" and "Miss Democracy's best kept boy friend."

Kaiser kept going in spite of Bridges's protests. Then, in late 1950, the Air Force awarded him a contract to build Fairchild Flying Boxcar cargo planes at his Willow Run plant, as a secondary source of supply to the parent Fairchild Corporation. Later, the Air Force phased out Kaiser's Boxcar production but awarded him a contract for assault transports. For the Air Force, it meant broadening the industrial base as a preparedness measure. For Kaiser it meant a chance to establish himself in the aircraft-production field, which idea aroused no enthusiasm on the part of Fairchild.

There is conflicting opinion about how well Kaiser handled his opportunity. His unit cost for the first planes was very large compared to Fairchild's; there were experts, however, who argued that his "learning curve" was not excessively steep and that his costs would be comparable to Fairchild's when he had reached a similar volume of production.

The argument soon became academic. On June 2, 1953, Senator Bridges, as chairman of a Senate Armed Services subcommittee, opened hearings on what was announced as a broad inquiry into "Aircraft Procurement." Before many minutes it became clear that the Kaiser contract was the only thing on the agenda. On the fourth day of ruthless interrogation, the Air Force capitulated. Lieutenant General Orval Cook, Deputy Chief of Staff for Materiel, announced to the subcommittee, "The Air Force is disappointed . . . in the performance of the Kaiser-Frazer operation."

Vainly, the Kaisers, father and son, tried to come in and defend themselves. They brought detailed statistics to document their case, but it was useless. On the morning of June 24, while the Kaisers were testifying in the Armed Services Committee room, a messenger arrived from the Pentagon. The Air Force had canceled Kaiser's contracts.

Minutes later, Chairman Bridges recessed the subcommittee *sine die*. It has neither met nor filed a report in the nearly thirteen months since then.

China Lobby: New Hampshire Div.

Senator Bridges has served one constituent with a zeal surpassing that which he has displayed toward all others. This is the China Lobby. In early 1950, Bridges announced to the Senate, in line with his apparent belief that the alliance with Chiang is to be cherished above almost any other: "Mr. President, I propose this policy for the United States. I propose that our government give the Nationalist Government of China its unqualified assurance that whatever assistance is needed to insure its continued existence will be furnished."

Unlike many other constituents, the China Lobby has sought to acquire a legitimate relationship of sorts by putting down roots in Bridges's state. Such are Oriental finesse and discretion, however, that many old-time residents will be surprised to learn that Nationalist representatives now maintain a sumptuous summer residence on the shores of Lake Winnipesaukee, and that both the senior Senator and the state attorney general, a Bridges protégé and former aide, have set up vacation cottages on land adjoining and partially carved from this estate.

Bridges has expressed a high degree of unconcern about the existence of a China Lobby, having announced at one time that he didn't know of any such outfit, "but if there is one . . . [and] they are not doing anything illegal, they are certainly helping to carry out the policy of the United States of America today." On another occasion, he explained a munificent campaign contribution from Alfred Kohlberg by remarking that he had been interested in the cause of Nationalist China a long time before he knew the gentleman in question.

Bridges was among the first to blame the developing tragedy in China on the U.S. State Department, when after the resignation of Ambassador Pat Hurley in 1945, he called for a housecleaning of that institution. In 1946, William Loeb, president of the American China Policy Association, the strong right arm of the Lobby, bought the late Colonel Frank Knox's excellent newspaper, the Manchester *Union Leader,* the only New Hampshire paper with statewide circulation, and proceeded to turn it into a propaganda organ for the Lobby. Loeb, a close friend of Bridges, has filled the *Union Leader's* news and editorial columns with violent abuse of America's chief foreign policymakers, and has continued to do so without letup even after the change in Administrations. On July 4, 1953, for example, he dispatched from his Nevada home (Loeb until recently at least had never bothered to establish a permanent residence in New Hampshire) a telegram to President Eisenhower which was duly reprinted as a front-page *Union Leader* editorial: SUGGEST THAT IF YOU WANT PEACE AT ANY PRICE IN KOREA, YOU AND THE JOINT CHIEFS

OF STAFF CELEBRATE THIS FOURTH OF JULY BY CRAWLING ON YOUR
COLLECTIVE BELLIES BEFORE THE COMMUNISTS. . . . NO PRESIDENT
IN THIS NATION'S HISTORY HAS SO DISHONORED THE UNITED STATES
AS YOU HAVE. . . ."

A second pillar of the Lobby who has been attracted to the
New Hampshire Senator's circle is the aforementioned Alfred
Kohlberg. Though not a resident of New Hampshire, Kohlberg
was listed as second-largest contributor to the Bridges campaign
in 1948—his $2,000 covering more than forty per cent of the listed
cost of a campaign in which there was no opposition in the primary and only a token Democratic candidate in November.

Winnipesaukee Pleasure Dome

The most fascinating example of the China Lobby's attraction
for the New Hampshire Senator, if only because it is the most
devious, has to do with the bona fide Chinese members of the
Lobby. The story begins shortly after the Second World War
when Arthur Beaumont Rothwell, a Britisher who had spent a
great deal of time in the Far East, came to this country and set up
operations. Rothwell prospered noticeably during the ensuing
years, but remained tight-lipped about the nature of his business
activities. Even the close neighbors of his various residences on
Long Island, Park Avenue, and in Panama could never learn
what it was he did; some even suspected, quite wrongly, that he
was a British secret agent.

In reality, Rothwell was confidential financial agent for the
prominent family of H. H. Kung, brother-in-law of Generalissimo
Chiang Kai-shek, operating genius of the Bank of China in the
United States and officer emeritus of the China Lobby. H. H.'s
son Louis figured as political strategist and Congressional liaison
man for the Lobby during the 1950 Congressional elections.

Rothwell served as a front for the Kungs in a wide variety of
business and other activities. In 1950, for example, he quietly
bought a partnership in David Charnay's public-relations firm,
Allied Syndicates, after the Kungs had selected it to handle the
Bank of China account. This partnership, by the way, was
never listed as required under the Foreign Agents Registration
Act; it became known when Charnay, testifying in executive

session before the Kefauver Committee, identified Rothwell as a silent partner and as the man who had brought an ex-convict into the organization.

Charnay, though professedly a Democrat, has felt no qualms about helping out Republicans. In particular, he, like a number of Democrats already mentioned, has found a friend in the New Hampshire Republican Senator. They shared, so to speak, the same constituencies, for besides the $75,000 China account Charnay was handling John L. Lewis's UMW Welfare Fund.

Arthur Rothwell appeared to have a penchant for seeking out those who were close to the New Hampshire Senator. Another was Louis Wyman, onetime secretary to Bridges and presently attorney general of New Hampshire. Only a few months after Wyman left Washington in 1949, his wife, Virginia, became a director of the Franconia Trading Corporation, of which Rothwell was president.

Franconia Trading and another of Rothwell's companies, the aptly named Oriental Fine Arts, suggest something of the character of his activities. Both companies were listed by the Commodity Exchange Authority of the Department of Agriculture among the "Chinese traders" that speculated heavily in soybean futures just prior to the outbreak of the Korean War, a bit of dealing in the lucrative side of disaster that Congress never got around to probing. The Chinese traders, apparently acting on intelligence from the mainland about a late June invasion of South Korea, had bought up vast speculative holdings of July soybean futures and almost succeeded in cornering the market.

When Mrs. Wyman left Franconia's board of directors in 1950, Burbeck Gilchrist, who had worked for Louis Wyman on a Senate campaign-investigations committee under Bridges's sponsorship, took her place. At about this time Wyman himself was retained to represent Rothwell and Kung interests in New Hampshire. In 1951, Gilchrist went to Panama to serve as secretary and director of three companies managed by Rothwell—Compañía Pacífico, Compañia Canal, and Compañia Polar, S.A.—which, according to a reliable banking source in Panama, do no business there but represent large holdings of "Asiatic capital."

The setting up of the China Lobby's elaborate enclave in New

Hampshire was handled in a typically circuitous and circumspect way. Some time during the fall of 1950, at a breakfast party given by Charnay and attended by, among others, Louis Kung and Senator Bridges, young Kung announced that he was looking for a safe asylum to which the family could retreat when the third world war should break out. He said he had been told by a military expert in whom he had great confidence that this would occur in 1954. Bridges reportedly suggested New Hampshire as ideal for such a purpose.

It was not long after this that Harry Hopewell, of Wolfeboro on Lake Winnipesaukee, which proudly claims to be the oldest resort community in the United States, excitedly told neighbors that the Chinese were planning to buy his old family estate, Spruce Acres, on Wolfeboro Neck. A short time later, Hopewell grew strangely uncommunicative. He announced that the deal with the Chinese was off. Then in February, 1951, he reported that the estate had been sold to a New York businessman by the name of Arthur B. Rothwell.

For the old-time Yankee residents of Wolfeboro the new ownership of Spruce Acres became a subject of much gossip. There was a report that Senator Bridges and his wife had spent a week at Spruce Acres during the summer of 1951. According to rumor, which was later confirmed, Madame Chiang Kai-shek came up for a visit during one of her trips to this country. A gentleman who owns a summer home adjoining the road leading into Spruce Acres relates that one afternoon he was working in old clothes in his garden when a long black limousine passed with three formally dressed Chinese sitting in the back. They turned and bowed stiffly to him, "like Chinese warlords greeting a small landowner," he recalls.

The greatest mystery of all shrouded the movements of Arthur B. Rothwell. Those who worked at redecorating the estate were kept from contact with him. An elderly woman who owned land next to Spruce Acres was highly desirous of selling some of it to the new owner. She was told at various times that Rothwell was in Europe, Panama, and Alaska. She has yet to meet him.

In fact, Bridges and Bridges's protégés seemed to be the only ones who had the faintest idea of what was happening at Spruce

Acres. Louis Wyman's brother Eliot, who became counsel to Bridges's Appropriations Committee in 1953, served as agent in charge of the extensive modernization of the estate, with his wife, Polly, handling all relations with local contractors. On October 13, 1951, the office of the recorder of deeds in Wolfeboro accepted a deed of sale transferring a portion of the lakefront property from Rothwell to Louis Wyman. On September 26, 1952, a second chunk of Rothwell's land was deeded to Wyman who, three days later, deeded a portion of this chunk to Mrs. Styles Bridges. Today, both the Wymans and the Bridgeses have built attractive summer cottages on the lakefront adjoining Spruce Acres. According to a reliable source, they quite frequently enjoy the hospitality of the big house, which is staffed with servants from New York and often filled to overflowing on summer weekends with friends of Louis Kung.

The mystery surrounding Spruce Acres has grown all out of proportion to the facts of the story, but neither Rothwell nor his friends have helped much to stop speculation. When two representatives of *The Reporter* paid a visit to Spruce Acres last Labor Day weekend in search of the elusive owner, they were met on the entrance drive by Attorney General Wyman, clad in a bathing suit, were told brusquely that Rothwell was not there, and were turned away. Next day, Wyman reported that he had telephoned Rothwell and that a request to take pictures had been refused.

When Rothwell himself was finally tracked down by a *Reporter* representative in Panama, he angrily responded to all queries about Spruce Acres and about his past relationship with Charnay, Wyman, Bridges, and the Kungs with "No comment," and soon broke off the interview by walking away. Later, in his lawyer's office in Panama, he told a representative of *The Reporter* "You can't investigate me or my business."

Burbeck B. Gilchrist, erstwhile officer and director of the Panamanian corporations, is one member of the team who has apparently not fared too well. He was finally located last winter at a service station he now runs just outside Boston. He was adamant about not answering questions. "My mother always told me to keep my own counsel," he said.

The main question was, why all the mystery, anyway? Attorney General Wyman, in a later interview, tried to be helpful. Wyman said that he didn't know much about Rothwell except that Rothwell was a trusted friend of Louis Kung, whom Wyman said that he himself had met in Bridges's office. As a lawyer, Wyman represented both Kung and Rothwell interests in New Hampshire; but whether these interests include anything other than Spruce Acres he declined to say. Wyman knew very little about the Franconia Trading Corporation; he said that Rothwell had suggested that his wife become a director.

Mrs. Wyman had, in fact, never even attended a directors' meeting, though she had received a thousand-dollar "director's fee" in late 1950. Neither he nor his wife, according to Wyman, had ever heard of Franconia's soybean speculation that year. Wyman admitted that in retrospect it had been a mistake to allow his wife to take such a position without knowing more about it. He insisted, however, that he would never be party to anything of a dubious nature.

He attributed the aura of secrecy that pervaded Spruce Acres, as well as all of the Kung-Rothwell activities, to fear on the Kungs' part of the Communists who had driven them out of their native land and who threatened to requisition Nationalist Chinese holdings abroad should Red China ever be recognized by this country. He was horrified at the suggestion that this secrecy might be a cloak to conceal trading activities with the Communist mainland. When asked if he had been aware, for example, that Kung money had been heavily invested in the Yangtze Trading Corporation (Yangtze's export license privileges were suspended by the Department of Commerce in June, 1951, because of irregularities connected with the firm's shipments of strategic tin to the Chinese Communists), Wyman replied that he had questioned Louis Kung about this when *The Reporter's* China Lobby articles came out and had been informed that Louis was terribly angry with his brother, David Kung, for having gotten involved in that enterprise. Wyman felt certain that Louis Kung would have nothing to do with such trade. "As for David Kung," he remarked, "he is a big black mystery to me."

Everywhere from the shores of Lake Winnipesaukee to Roth-well's handsome residence in Ancon in the Canal Zone, attempts to discover something about this strange New Hampshire division of the China Lobby had been met with evasion and silence. But probably the most baffling experience of all was the interview with the New Hampshire Senator himself. It was baffling, first of all, because it was so difficult to get to talk to Bridges, and then because the Senator declared that he could throw absolutely no light upon the great mystery of Rothwell and Wolfeboro Neck.

For nearly two months this reporter's requests for an interview were put off by Bridges's office for one reason or another, but never finally rejected. Finally, pressed for a definite answer one way or the other, Bridges consented to the interview.

One afternoon in late May, this reporter was escorted into the Senator's office. The next hour and a half resembled a kind of diplomatic negotiation more than an interview. Throughout, Bridges's administrative assistant and his executive secretary flanked the Senator. In relays his stenographers entered the room to keep a verbatim transcript of the conversations.

The discussion roamed over the wide field of Bridges's associations, finally coming to the Britisher of the mysterious business interests, Arthur B. Rothwell. There was no surprise on the Senator's face when the name was mentioned. "I have never met him in my life, don't know him, never had any association with him," said the Senator. The reporter in turn registered surprise. Had the Senator never met Rothwell when he was a partner of David Charnay? The Senator said that he hadn't. Did he not know anything of Rothwell's other business enterprises, including the one involving Mrs. Wyman? Nothing, the Senator said. Had he never been entertained in Rothwell's home, Spruce Acres? "I have never stayed there but have been there for a meal, a visit, or a swim from the shore. I did it when Major Kung, whom I have met on various occasions, was occupying the place. I understand he was a friend of Rothwell's."

Finally the reporter asked, did the Senator not own a piece of land that had been part of Rothwell's Spruce Acres? The Senator answered quickly that the land on which his summer place was built had been bought from George Carpenter. Rapidly he drew a piece of paper out of his desk drawer and started to sketch a triangle of land. This, he said, was what he had bought from Wyman in order to gain access to the main road. Since then an access road had been cut through the Carpenter property. He didn't need the Wyman land any more.

The interview was drawing to a close. Bridges said he could not recall the breakfast party with Kung and Charnay in the course of which he had volunteered to help Kung locate a New Hampshire retreat. The reporter had failed to stir the Senator's memory. To Bridges, the name of Rothwell, like those of Hyman Harvey Klein, Armand Hammer, and Henry Grunewald, was but a hazy feature of some distant landscape.

February 23, 1956

The Lady of Villa Taverna

BY CLAIRE STERLING AND MAX ASCOLI

Clare Boothe Luce, U.S. ambassador to Italy for three years, will soon be coming home. She will be returning with the glow of success that usually surrounds this remarkable woman to face a public that has heard more about her than any ambassador in recent American history. She has frequently complained, during these three years, that Americans have been told too much about her and not enough, that she has been written about almost always as a woman, rarely as a serious diplomat. Since it is on her record as a diplomat that the public may soon be asked to judge her—for a Senatorship, a Cabinet post, possibly even the Republican Vice-Presidential nomination—an account of that record is given here.

The new ambassador got the full Neapolitan treatment for visiting celebrities when she stepped off the gangplank on April 22, 1953—flowers, guitars, boisterous crowds cheering under the warm sun of Naples. The Italian Foreign Ministry gave her an unctuous welcome in Rome. But it was no secret that the Italians resented her appointment.

What bothered the Italians was not simply that she was a woman. Accomplished as she was in many ways, everybody knew that she was coming to Italy not because she was peculiarly qualified for the post but because her husband had contributed powerfully to General Eisenhower's nomination and election.

The appointment, it is said, had been offered first to Henry Luce himself. If he turned it down in favor of his wife, the decision was reached after both had carefully considered her handicaps, which were many. Among them was the fact that she was his wife. While some Italians might cherish the prospect that the three big Luce magazines would acquire a vested interest in featuring Italy, many had qualms. "Luce once adopted China," a reporter in Italy remarked, "and look what happened to China." Apart from that, Mrs. Luce was beautiful—beautiful enough, even at the age of fifty, to infuriate other women and embarrass her diplomatic colleagues. It might have been different had she looked like Gertrude Stein.

Also, she was a recently converted Catholic, too unrelaxed for Italy's ancient, comfortable Catholicism, too combative for a population which, if Catholic in religion, has a long tradition of anti-clericalism in politics. She was an easy target for the Communists: rich, Republican, well known in leftist circles for "hating Communism with an African passion," as *Pravda* put it— this in a country whose Communist strength represents one-quarter of the voters.

She was to find other handicaps as she went along. Her sharp tongue and wit did not suit her temperamentally for a diplomatic world peopled by the Stuffed Shirts she had once lampooned in a popular book of that name. Moreover, if she was untrained as a diplomat, she was well trained as a journalist. For a journalist, news has no value until it is published, while for a diplomat it is the other way around. Mrs. Luce is annoyed by the charge that she talks too much. "I don't really talk too much," she says, "but I'm widely misquoted." (Nevertheless, she has talked too much.) Furthermore, her appointment was political in intent as well as origin. Where a professional ambassador might have no greater dream than a bigger and better ambassadorship, her ambition has been frankly to "dramatize the dynamic new Eisenhower Administration."

She has worked enormously hard, driven, as always, by a determination to prove herself on a man's level. "I come from a world," she had Miriam say in her celebrated Broadway hit, *The Women*, "where a woman's got to come out on top—or it's just too damned bad."

She has filled forty-three bound volumes with press clippings, some favorable, others not, but all testifying to her tireless energy. She has traveled thousands of miles up and down the peninsula, posed for thousands of photographs, made hundreds of speeches, and entertained almost everybody—not everybody, unfortunately —in the handsome Renaissance residence, Villa Taverna, provided by the U.S. government. In her first year, more than seven thousand people signed the Villa Taverna's guest book; and during 1955 alone, she received several hundred Members of Congress. (Some might have driven her to despair if they had not provided her with priceless stories for conversational use. One wanted to know how Garibaldi got his elephants across the Alps, another what the Russians were doing behind the Rurals, while a third once instructed her secretary to "Call me a plane.")

At times her sense of public relations has been superb. When an Italian LAI plane crashed at Idlewild a few days before she was to go home on leave, she canceled her flight with an American line and booked with LAI. When Prime Minister Alcide De Gasperi died in 1954, she rushed back from a summer vacation in the States for the funeral, causing the British Ambassador grudgingly to do likewise. When the Amalfi coast was struck by a flash flood, she flew to the scene to make a round of the hospitals, beating the President of the Republic by twenty-four hours.

Millions of Italians have come to know and admire her for these activities. But all this proves how vigorously she has applied herself to her ambassadorial job, not how successful she has been at it.

Mrs. Luce started out without the biggest advantage her predecessors had had; she could not promise the Italians much money. Where the United States had given Italy $2.8 billion in direct economic aid before she came, Italy got a net of $105 million in fiscal 1954, $45 million in 1955, and $5 million in the first quarter of 1956: and where mutual defense assistance off-shore-procurement contracts had reached a total of $383 million during her first summer, they had slackened off to $91 million the next year, and $39.5 million the year after.

In effect, this meant a fast passage from proconsular to inter-allied diplomacy between two nations that in various degrees needed each other. More precisely, it meant trying to convince the Italians, using other means of persuasion than money, to do what the State Department was anxious for them to do: attain political and economic stability, support the Atlantic Alliance and the European Defense Community, roll back the biggest Communist Party this side of the Iron Curtain. Since most government leaders were already at least verbally inclined to do these things, it meant keeping them on the right path by exerting a discreet influence in Parliament and among the voters. Quite an undertaking for even a seasoned politician-diplomat, irrespective of sex.

She began badly. A month after her arrival and two weeks before the difficult elections of June 7, 1953, the Communist newspaper *L'Unità* triumphantly caught her giving out crucifixes to a group of southern peasants during the inauguration of a land-reform village called La Martella. Crucifixes are customarily distributed in Italy on such occasions, but not by a U.S. ambassador. A week later she got into worse trouble by saying publicly in Milan that any electoral victory for the extreme Right or Left would have "grave consequences for the intimate and friendly co-operation between Italy and the United States." Several Italian and American newspapers claimed later that the speech cost the center parties the election.

The charge was unfair. In saying what everyone knew, she probably did not change many votes, let alone the 57,600 by which the government coalition fell short of the total necessary to get the bonus seats the recent election law provided for. But the speech hurt her personally. She was making her maiden address as ambassador, at a decisive moment in Italian politics, in the most politically literate city in Italy, before people who were waiting for her to fall on her face. (She told an Italian paper recently that she had not written the speech herself and that of the two aides who did, one is now stationed in Singapore and the other in South Korea. The disclosure may help explain away her first big mistake; it has not improved her staff relations.)

The elections that June opened a difficult era in Italy. Under De Gasperi's leadership for the five preceding years, the Christian Democrats and their minor partners—Republicans, Social Democrats, Liberals—had governed with a safe majority and comparative stability. After June 7, the center coalition had a margin of sixteen seats in the Chamber of Deputies. On the Left there was a bloc of 143 Communists and 75 left-wing Socialists. On the Right there were 40 Monarchists and 29 Neo-Fascists. Short of holding new elections, which, as De Gasperi said, were "absolutely necessary and utterly impossible," the center parties had a choice of trying to carry on as they were or making a deal with either the Left or Right. While the politicians debated the question, the country had four different Prime Ministers within eight months.

The idea of moving to the right, if not all the way to the Fascists then at least as far as their Monarchist allies, was being pushed hard during those months by several influential Italians: Luigi Gedda of Catholic Action; Don Luigi Sturzo, founder of the first Catholic popular party; Giuseppe Pella, who headed a Christian Democratic caretaker Cabinet at the time. The conclusion that a coalition of the Right—eventually leading to some sort of constitutional monarchy—would turn popular opinion toward the Left was finally reached by the most influential Christian Democratic leaders.

But not by the American ambassador. She had made up her mind: Only by enlisting the Monarchists and strengthening the right wing of the Christian Democratic Party could Italy ever have a strong, stable government.

Although a newcomer to Italy, Mrs. Luce was neither unsympathetic nor unfamiliar with the outlook of the Right. But she only knew the political Right in her own country, the Republican Party that had just returned to power, and she had little notion of how weak, Bourbonic, and thoroughly unpopular the Italian Right is. It is a haven not only for groups of jittery businessmen and landowners but also for unregenerate feudal barons, as well as former Fascist goons, crackpot young bomb-throwers, fetish worshipers who once kidnaped Mussolini's corpse and sophomoric nationalists who want to retrace the late Duce's military steps over the long African route to Ethiopia. Incidentally, it also includes many who despise Britain and hate the United States.

The ambassador may not have liked all these people—her anti-Mussolini record was clearly established before the war—but she could never understand why the same reason of expediency that brought the United States to accept Franco as an ally could not apply also to Italian internal politics. Indeed, she had only scorn for those Italian democrats—and there are many of them—who, if forced to choose between the Right and the Communist Left, would not hesitate to choose the Communists. Nor could she make out why the mere fact that she dealt with even the least objectionable Rightists would render her objectionable herself. Mrs Luce believed that only a firm anchorage to the Right could stop the drift of Italian politics.

It was primarily in the hope of winning the rightist-nationalist support that Mrs. Luce worked so strenuously all during the summer of 1953 to get a settlement in Trieste. Italy's quarrel with Yugoslavia over this tiny Free Territory had offered both Right and Left a chance to discredit the Christian Democrats' western-minded régime. If Italy were to get at least Zone A, which included the port of Trieste—so she argued—the Monarchists might be induced to rally around Pella's government.

The solution was announced on October 8, 1953, in the form of a joint American-British declaration giving Zone A to Italy and Zone B to Yugoslavia. It came after Mrs. Luce had wrangled with the British for months and gone over the State Department's head by sending her husband to the White House three days earlier. (The Secretary of State, more interested in Tito's military strength than Italy's political weakness, had said only a month earlier that he was open-minded about alternatives to the Big Three's 1948 pledge to give Italy all of Trieste. As Mrs. Luce was to observe after several similar experiences, "Every time I open my mouth, Dulles puts his foot in it.")

The plan might have worked if Marshal Tito had not been left in the dark about it—because of American impatience to make the announcement, according to the British; because of a deliberate British oversight, according to our ambassador. As it was, Tito moved his troops up to the Zone A border and threatened war; Italy replied with angry demonstrations in nearly all its major cities; in Trieste itself, rioting left six dead. It was not until a year later, after Pella had fallen and Mr. Dulles had sent Robert D. Murphy as a special emissary to Rome and Belgrade, that a solution much like the original one was accepted by both sides.

Opinions differ as to how much credit Mrs. Luce deserves for this settlement. There are those, among them the authoritative *Corriere della Sera* of Milan, who give her most of the credit for the belated agreement. "No one will ever know," said the *Corriere* when the Italian flag went up over Trieste, "how much Italy owes to this fragile blonde creature." Others, including members of her staff, say that the settlement had been maturing for some years and that the October 8 declaration delayed it, if anything.

Whoever is right, Trieste did not bring the results she had hoped for. In fact, the end of the Trieste crisis deflated the nationalist boom, and from then on the Rightists started losing ground. Even before the settlement came, Pella, who was thriving on that boom, had gone so far to the right that all of Italy's democratic forces compelled him to resign. For two things are clear about Italian postwar politics: First, the trend is to the left although not necessarily to the Communist left; second, all attempts to consolidate the Right have failed. Unfortunately, the U.S. ambassador could never quite manage to recognize the leftward trend of Italian politics and come to terms with it.

It had been a bumpy eight months for the ambassador when she came home for her first Christmas holiday, and the stories in the American press soon after she arrived led her into even greater trouble. On January 7, 1954, the New York *Herald Tribune* reported that the Italian Christian Democrats had actually won the bonus seats in the June elections, as revealed by a recount of most of the million voided ballots. It claimed the Rome politicians would publicly deny the facts, went on to question the constitutionality of all Italian Cabinets since that election, and declared that "Italy is now undergoing a dangerous political crisis . . . which need never have happened . . . " The same story, more or less embroidered with the notion that the Communists would take over in two or three years, was carried by nearly every major American newspaper, several syndicated columns, *Newsweek,* and *Time* over the next few weeks, with particular emphasis on the recount (though no recount has been completed or officially reported).

There could be no question about the source. Mrs. Luce herself told a press conference in New York that the "democratic and republican forces" in Italy could still stop the Communist Party "when and if they want to," thereby attributing to Italian statesmen like De Gasperi a lack both of vision and of will.

(Almost three months later, Mrs. Luce was accused of having inspired all these stories by the pro-government Italian weekly *L'Europeo,* which published a purported account of her off-the-record talk with Washington correspondents at the Hotel Mayflower on January 5. She denied the account.)

It is hard to see what Mrs. Luce expected to gain from her alarmist campaign. *La Stampa* described it as a "shock tactic . . . needed by the U.S. Republicans for the forthcoming election" of 1954, and it may have served that purpose. In Italy, however, it caused bedlam. Assuming it were true, for instance, that the Christian Democrats had really won the majority necessary for the bonus seats—a claim never proved—what would they have gotten by holding a complete recount and claiming victory? Probably a civil war, since nothing less would be likely to unseat some sixty-three leftist Deputies in Parliament at that late date. Assuming also that the Communists were on the verge of power and the center parties were too flabby to hold them back, who would have been likely to gain by the ambassador's revelations? Only the Communists. Certainly not the Christian Democrats, who, even as Mrs. Luce was talking at the Mayflower, were trying desperately to find a way out of the crisis brought about by Pella's fall.

Pella's resignation caused Mrs. Luce to cut her holiday short by ten days and return to Rome. Shortly afterward, she invited leaders of the Republican, Social Democratic, Liberal, and Monarchist Parties to Villa Taverna for separate talks on the crisis. She had evidently hoped to line up these parties behind the new Christian Democratic candidate for the Premiership, Interior Minister Amintore Fanfani. The effort not only failed but exposed her to unprecedented attack, since consultations of this kind are the prerogative of the Italian Chief of State. The Communist leader, Palmiro Togliatti described Mrs. Luce suavely in Parliament as an "old lady who brings bad luck to everything she touches."

While all this was going on, the New York *Times* broke the story that the United States had authorized its ambassador to Italy to cancel all offshore-procurement contracts with plants where Communist workers were in the majority, which was the case in most big Italian factories at the time. The announcement caused a furor. A spokesman for CISI, the predominantly Catholic labor federation, described the policy as "brutal blackmail"; the secretary of the other anti-Communist federation, UIL, added, "The point is not to punish workers by denying them work but to encourage them by providing it."

By the time Mario Scelba was confirmed as Prime Minister at the beginning of March, 1954, Italo-American relations were scraping bottom. Mrs. Luce had no confidence in the center coalition that Scelba had pulled together again, and Italian politicians were criticizing her so openly that the State Department was reported by one press association as wondering "whether it is in the United States' interest to have an ambassador who is the object of so much public debate."

The Scelba experiment, however, opened a better year for Mrs. Luce. With only the most lukewarm support from his own party, Scelba needed a friend badly, and the anti-Communist program he announced the month he became Premier met most of the objections Mrs. Luce had been raising all winter. His Cabinet, he said, would crack down on the Communists in the civil service, throw them out of the government-owned buildings and printing plants, prosecute them for slandering the government, and curb the Communist-owned or -controlled export firms that were trading with Red China. Since the Communists were too solidly embedded in Italy to be dug out so easily, only the easiest parts of this program were ever carried out. But as a token of intentions, the effort was appreciated in our embassy. Slowly Scelba was gaining favor.

There were other onslaughts against the Communists during that year, which, to say the least, did not displease the embassy. Prominent among them was a movement called Pace e Libertà (Peace and Liberty), led by Edgardo Sogno, a Foreign Office official who had been a hero of the Resistance. The movement's purpose, as Sogno told the readers of his magazine, was to rally Italians around a National Anti-Communist Front; and it pursued this aim by publishing a string of shocking revelations about top Communist leaders—offering documentary evidence that many of them were once informers for Mussolini, that party bureaucrats rode to work in expensive custom-built cars, and that Togliatti, among others, kept a "concubine" draped in costly furs and jewels. The movement, which for a while was quite lively, has now petered out. As Ignazio Silone said, "The question isn't whether party leaders are scoundrels, but whether they are capable and effective scoundrels."

This question reveals why the Communist Party started to show the first signs of an erosion that is still going on. Mrs. Luce feels, and some people agree with her, that the psychological atmosphere created by Scelba, Sogno, and the American embassy in 1954 was a major factor leading to the Communists' loss of Fiat in March, 1955, and most big northern factories thereafter. While all three may have played some part, none of them could even remotely be compared to the part played by the Communists' own leaders, who had pressed too many workers too long to go out on too many protest strikes in obedience to Cominform *diktats*.

This is not to say that the offshore-procurement policy, one of the ambassador's most publicized endeavors at home, was insignificant. While anti-Communist union leaders have disowned the policy and still don't like it, they admit privately now that by canceling $25 million worth of contracts in two Communist-dominated plants the United States persuaded thousands of Italian workers to vote against the Communist-controlled CGIL (General Confederation of Italian Labor) in order to keep their jobs. Nobody will know until the next elections whether or not the political opinions of these workers have changed.

The ratification early in 1955 of the Paris pacts that replaced the ill-fated EDC was a genuine victory for Mrs. Luce, though it is hardly imaginable that Italy could have held out alone. But the really major achievement of the American embassy was to have kept Mario Scelba in office fifteen months. (One of the more painful things Mrs. Luce has suffered is the ingratitude of the politicians whom sooner or later she has come to befriend. If the ambassador had not gone far beyond the call of duty to prop him up, Scelba would have fallen months before he did; yet he says now that "after all, a male ambassador would have been better.")

Scelba's trip to Washington surely contributed to prolong his tenure in office. The invitation was extracted from a State Department made reluctant by its awareness that Scelba's Cabinet was beginning to spring leaks at every seam. But there was not even a hint of the irrepressible crisis in the American press when the ambassador started home after Christmas. There has been "a remarkable improvement in the Italian picture" she told reporters. "Now there is a stable government . . . Italy has clarified its whole situation." Three months later, on the eve of Scelba's departure for the United States, he was to be humiliated by the proposal of a parliamentary injunction to limit his actions in the United States, forcing a ninth vote of confidence.

The problem of Italian oil had become a stormy political issue by that time. Promising deposits had been found, first in Sicily, then in the Abruzzi, and an antiquated Fascist law still on the books was keeping most of the oil underground. The draft of a new law, written several years earlier by lawyers of American oil concerns in collaboration with the then Minister of Industry, Malvestiti, which offered considerable advantages to foreign companies, had been bottled up in parliamentary committee; and the group opposing it, led by the head of the state natural-gas monopoly, Enrico Mattei, was becoming stronger with every new sign that the deposits were very substantial indeed.

The American oil companies quarrel with Mattei had taken an ugly turn that summer when *Fortune* magazine, followed later by *Time,* pointed a finger at him as the biggest single obstacle to large-scale American investment in Italy. Apart from the merits of the case—and there were many on both sides—the fact that the publisher of *Fortune* and *Time* was also the U.S. ambassador's consort led many Italians to consider this as semi-official American pressure. They were already suspicious because of persistent rumors leaking from government headquarters to the effect that the State Department was holding out on any further financial aid to Italy "until this oil business is settled."

Then Mrs. Luce herself entered the picture. Her first statement in the New York *Times* in January, 1955, did not attract much notice. She repeated it in essence a few weeks later, however, in an interview given to *Il Globo,* the financial daily owned by Confindustria (the Confederation of Italian Manufacturers). Pointing out that "capital comes where the profit is greatest," and that "political security is associated with economic convenience," she went on to say: "Much depends on the oil policy of the Italian government. It is known that oil investments are a good index of the security and profitable nature of the market. Many private companies can be led to invest their capital here if they see the oil companies doing it."

Her interview brought the long-smoldering dispute to an uproarious blaze. Shortly thereafter, the Socialist Party introduced a motion in Parliament requiring Scelba's pledge that he would not discuss oil on his American visit. The motion did not pass. But the Christian Democrats forced the Premier to give Parliament a moral commitment along the same lines. What Scelba talked about in Washington is still, and probably will remain forever, a deep secret, but certainly he kept mum about oil.

As everybody in Italy knew, Scelba had gone to Washington mostly for the ride. He brought back the promise of ten tons of heavy water for atomic experiment, a routine agreement ending double taxation of American businesses in Italy and vice versa, five honorary degrees, and a model of the Empire State Building in silver. But that was not enough to bring him past the last deadline his party had set: the election of a new Chief of State.

The Gronchi Enigma

The election of Giovanni Gronchi as President of the Republic at the end of April, 1955, was the final blow for Scelba, and Mrs. Luce's most bitter personal defeat. As a left-wing Christian Democrat and an uncompromising enemy of Scelba and Fanfani, Gronchi was opposed vigorously by both, and it was partly but not exclusively because these two men opposed him that more than a hundred disaffected Christian Democratic Members of Parliament joined in a weird coalition with the Right and extreme Left to elect him.

Mrs. Luce, who had met Gronchi only once, considered him a pro-Communist who would steer Italy toward a neutralist foreign policy and bring the fellow-traveling Nenni Socialists into the government. Only from his behavior in office will we ever learn whether, or to what extent, Mrs. Luce's judgment was correct. But certainly her behavior during the Presidential contest can scarcely be called correct or wise. The American correspondents who were summoned to lunch at Villa Taverna the day before the fourth and final ballot came away thoroughly persuaded that Gronchi's election would mean disaster.

The same conviction was expressed by Lodovico Benvenuti, then Under Secretary for Foreign Affairs, on whom the ambassador had evidently borne down with all the influence of the government she represented. Before the fourth ballot, Benvenuti told a packed and riotous Christian Democratic caucus that Gronchi's election "would end a ten-year friendship with the United States and force the State Department to review Italy's role in the whole network of European defense." An angry roar answered him and on the fourth ballot Gronchi was elected. A prominent cabinet minister called Gronchi's election "the American embassy's masterpiece."

The ambassador was in the diplomatic gallery when the vote on the final ballot was being counted. As it became apparent that Gronchi had won, but before the result was announced, she walked out.

It was three weeks before Mrs. Luce paid her first courtesy call on the new President—the British ambassador had made his the day after the election. In the meantime, the American press showed how deeply her apprehension had affected U.S. reports from Italy. On May 17, the New York *Times* in a dispatch from Rome said: "Recent political developments in Italy have convinced U.S. military authorities of the need for a review of Italy's position regarding the West, particularly NATO. . . ." The dispatch added: "Doubts about Italy's present attitude have been created by the election of Giovanni Gronchi . . . and by events since. President Gronchi has always inclined toward neutralism and never shown any enthusiasm for the Atlantic alliance. . . . In his inaugural speech he made no secret of his belief that room should be made in the Government for fellow-traveling Left-Wing Socialists if not for the Communists themselves." There were no quotes to back up this statement.

On the same day and in the same paper, however, a dispatch from Washington said: "Officials of the State Department . . . saw no particular need for a review of U.S. policy toward Italy"; and the same dispatch quoted a Pentagon spokesman as saying "he had heard nothing suggesting [such] a review. . . ."

Several more weeks were to pass before the *Times's* and other papers' Rome correspondents came around to a more temperate view, and it was six months before the State Department in a move toward reconciliation invited the new President to visit America.

Things have changed in Italy since the events of May 1956. Scelba's successor as Premier, Antonio Segni, is as pro-Western as the Premiers before him. But his relations with the American embassy are cool, and his Cabinet has come to rely more on leftist support than any in the last eight years. His two major accomplishments since being sworn in—the establishment of a constitutional court and the reform of the tax system—would have been impossible without Communist and Socialist votes. Embassy officials do not blame Gronchi for this situation, or Segni himself, who is the most moderate of Christian Democratic left-wingers. The responsibility lies mostly with the secretariat of the Christian Democratic Party, which has not yet succeeded in providing the party machine it is supposed to run with adequate discipline, purposefulness, and money.

There is a strange limpness in Italian politics today which affects both the Christian Democrats and the Communists, while the minor parties, right or left of Center, are getting increasingly feeble. Among the political leaders the only one whose stock keeps rising is Pietro Nenni, who registers the uninterrupted leftward drift of the nation.

This, by and large, is the record of what has happened in Italy in the three years since Mrs. Luce arrived to carry out the dynamic policies of the Republican Administration.

Of course nothing could be more absurd than to hold Mrs. Luce responsible for everything that has gone wrong with Italian democracy during the last three years. She could not have foreseen the weakening of Alcide De Gasperi's hold on his party after the 1953 election, not to speak of his death a year later. Even so, it would have been the better part of wisdom to consider that De Gasperi's matchless skill in keeping an ever-changing, precarious balance within his party as well as within the democratic coalition could some day run into a very serious snag, and that—after all—he was not immortal. And how can Mrs. Luce be blamed for having failed to foresee that the vaunted relaxation of international tension would ultimately, under Communist management, result in a relaxation of tension between the Communist and anti-Communist forces in the internal politics of the major European democracies?

But it is not unfair to hold Mrs. Luce responsible for having stubbornly held her rightward course, and for having guessed wrong too many times. For a politician, that is the capital sin. A politician she was before going to Italy, and a politician she will most probably be again when she comes home. A politician she was in all her persistent concern with Italian domestic affairs. There is nothing reprehensible about this concern: In our day and age a U.S. ambassador must play a sustained yet discreet role in the domestic policies of an allied country. What *is* reprehensible is to have backed those among the democratic politicians who because of their rightist inclinations were bound to lose ground. Either luck or skill failed Mrs. Luce.

To her credit, she never spared herself, never was slack in her job, never shunned taking chances and assuming responsibilities. She drove herself and her embassy at a merciless pace, with an energy that few could rival, let alone surpass.

Most of her mistakes came from overdoing, from showing her hand and playing it too heavily in many cases where she might have succeeded had she been firm and discreet. Frequently she chose to be shrill and hard, while she could easily have achieved her goal just by quietly turning on a little bit of that charm with which she is so eminently endowed.

For instance, like many other people, American or non-American, she may have had good reason to dislike "The Blackboard Jungle," and to eliminate that controversial movie from the Venice Film Festival. But this was no excuse for her being so carried away by anger as to tell Ottavio Croze, the director of the Festival, that if there was juvenile delinquency in America, it could be blamed largely on narcotics that came from Italy.

On other occasions, she preferred to exhibit a sort of girlish pettiness rather than face with quiet forbearance situations not to her liking. So, for instance, when Eleanor Roosevelt spent four days in Rome last spring, the U.S. ambassador invited about forty guests to meet her at an elaborate luncheon. All but a few were from the embassy. Not a single Italian of the many eager to pay their respects to that truly great American woman was invited or, for that matter, offered a chance to meet her.

According to people present, however, the luncheon turned out to be a triumph for Mrs. Roosevelt. The guests, particularly the younger ones, were so taken with her, so anxious to hear her talk, that the ambassador had no choice but to let the party go on and on, while looking nervously at her watch.

Her fretful impatience and poor judgment contributed heavily to the failure of Mrs. Luce's mission to Rome. Perhaps part of the responsibility should go to Mr. Luce, who has spent half his time in Rome, working strenuously to make his wife's mission a success. His circle of friends was made up of the most typical representatives of Italian big business, men who can scarcely voice Italian feelings and needs. As things turned out, it was not advantageous to have two ambassadors for the price of one. Both Mrs. and Mr. Luce found it difficult, if not altogether impossible, to realize—hardened by success as they are—that the fight against Communism just cannot be conducted on the Seven Hills the way it is conducted from Rockefeller Center.

In fact, on more than one occasion Mr. Luce did not conceal his dismay at what seemed to him the Vatican's softness toward Italian and international Communism. His wife has been more reserved, and has managed to avoid too close contacts with the Catholic hierarchy, as she promised to do before going to Italy. She has been ambassador to the Italian Republic, not to the Vatican.

At least once her fretfulness got on the nerves of the highest Vatican officials. This was last summer, when that saintly and rather erratic man, Mayor Giorgio La Pira of Florence, attended the World Mayors' Conference in Rome. Photographs of Elia Cardinal Dalla Costa, Archbishop of Florence, bowing over the hand of Moscow's mayor greatly incensed the U.S. ambassador. She let it be known at the Vatican's Secretariat of State that the Vatican's failure to curb La Pira, whom she held responsible, made the U.S. ambassador wonder whether the Church could still be considered an effective bulwark against Communism; perhaps the United States was the only bulwark left. The Papal Secretariat of State did not find this outburst to its liking. The Vatican has lost none of its centuries-old skill in handling its saints, and it knows how to wait for the fall of great empires, be they secular or journalistic.

Perhaps Mrs. Luce's mission to Rome would have achieved different results if this extraordinary woman whose public relations are usually matchless were equally adept at human relations. She certainly could have made better use of her staff if she had not so overawed the Foreign Service people under her command as to lead too many of them into thinking that the thing to do was to tell her what she wanted to hear. (Her embassy became known as "the snake pit.")

She might have been spared many costly errors if she had had the patience to listen—particularly to those Italians who are friends of the United States rather than panderers to it. But somehow she has failed to surround herself with a large and representative Italian constituency. She certainly has met many kinds of Italians, but, at least at present, her most familiar milieu is a small coterie of professional wits and punsters. She got bored with the old aristocracy and disillusioned by the many Italian politicians panting after subsidies for their hard-pressed factions or parties. The heavily earnest and moralistic men who are striving to keep some integrity in the maze of Italian politics may occasionally offer pearls of wisdom, but in general they are not fun to be with.

The punsters who have become habitués of the Villa Taverna *are* fun. They write in a magazine, *Il Borghese,* that never mentions democracy without a chuckle or a sneer. Their wit, well appreciated not so long ago at the courts of Mussolini and Ciano, has lost none of its sharpness in the change of political régime, and it is not likely to be dulled by moralism ever.

After all, not so long ago Ambassador Luce was a playwright and an editor of *Vanity Fair*. Political success has not spoiled her wit, just as the passing of time has not altered her looks. She is as sprightly as ever, with a kind of inexhaustible vitality, constantly wound up. There is a sort of a strident, metallic quality about her, revealed in the high pitch of her voice.

Perhaps she has failed in Italy precisely because of her strong points—brightness and shrewdness and dash. The fact is that all these flowers, some bright and innocent, some sweetly poisonous, and all of them beautiful, have been growing on Italian soil for centuries and centuries. In Italy they are a drug on the market.

December 30, 1954

Elizam—a Reminiscence of
Childhood in Ceylon

By T. Tambimuttu

Elizam had no choice in the matter. Her wishes, her own decision to dispose of her future as she wanted, if she had thought about it at all, had not been given a moment's thought by anybody. I was only a child, but people were always asking me what I wanted to be when I grew up, and they seemed to be very much interested when I replied "a doctor" or "an engineer." I had that freedom of choice, but Elizam had not, and it made me furious.

Although she was ten years older than I was, I felt that I understood her, and I was sure that Elizam did not wish to leave us. But the fate that had seemingly blessed her two elder sisters had now overtaken her, and she looked miserable on the morning she was married. Her big eyes, framed by long lashes, had lost their usual brilliance.

She was dressed as I had never seen her before. A gay wedding sari had replaced the simple bodice and sarong she had worn ever since I could remember. Rubies set in gold hung from her ears. Gold bangles tinkled at her wrists. Around her neck she wore the traditional gold ornaments—a choker with pendant, a triple gold chain, and the *thali* or wedding necklace. The jewelry had been given as a dowry by my mother. Elizam would have been given more if she had been married off in our village like her sisters. They had received cottages on Grandfather-with-the-Beard's es-

328

tate for as long as it belonged to our family, as well as the right to farm a bit of the land.

For Elizam Mother provided only clothes and jewelry. It was sufficient that Mother had found her a husband who could support her and her children. Elizam's chocolate complexion was not popular in the marriage market, so that even a poor farmer was a "catch" on which Mother congratulated herself. But Elizam did not seem grateful.

I hated the bridegroom as soon as I set eyes on him. He was a *chuvvalai,* or fair-complexioned man, not much taller than Elizam, who was big for a Ceylonese girl. He arrived in his bullock cart from his farm at Kantalai, about twenty miles from Trincomalee, to have a look at Elizam before giving his consent. I could tell from the way Elizam hid in the kitchen and refused to come out that she didn't want to get married.

Mother called to the girl several times as if she had some household task for her, but Elizam knew there was a suitor around the place and wouldn't emerge. Then Mother asked me to call her, but Elizam knew that I had been put up to it.

When it was time for tea, it was her cousin Sita who served it. Elizam still hid in the kitchen, and no amount of threats from Mother could make her come out. But Mother was not really angry. She was hugely amused at Elizam's shyness, a natural and proper attribute of a bride-to-be. But Elizam was not just being coy. She didn't want to get married at all. She had been with us most of her life—in Atchuvely, in Singapore, and in Malaya—and she wanted to stay on.

The farmer could have peeped into the kitchen, but that would have been undignified. It is not really necessary to see a bride before marriage. If she is seen at all, it is only by accident—at most an accident that had been staged by one of the parties. The farmer waited patiently, however, chewing his betel leaf and tobacco as if he belonged to the house.

I can't remember what eventually brought Elizam out. It may have been the arrival of the vegetable or oil seller. Anyway the farmer saw her full, strapping figure by the kitchen door—the kitchen was a separate building—and he went away well content, having given his promise. He may not even have noticed the beautiful molding of her oval face.

When Elizam got married she was saying good-by to her childhood. Like her sisters and cousins, she must have joined us when she was two or three. Her parents and the parents of her cousins lived in cottages on Grandfather-with-the-Beard's estate in Atchuvely village. Their children were sent into the service of my grandfather or that of his children up in Trincomalee. If they received any pay at all, it was sent to their parents, but they had a comfortable home and as soon as they reached the age of seventeen or eighteen were married off with a small dowry. That was one duty we had toward them.

Elizam called us by our own names, which was forbidden our other servants. Though she did not attend school, as we did, it was she who dressed us for school. She saw to it that we got there safe and was always there by the school gates at four to see us home again. In the mornings, between classes, she or her cousin Sita brought our glasses of milk.

She rubbed our bodies with sesame oil on Saturdays and then bathed us after we had run about under the morning sun for an hour or two. Earlier in the day she had boiled limes, *cheekakai* pods, and bassia meal. She shampooed our hair with the mixture and then rubbed in the limes. The rinses left our hair softer and glossier than any patent shampoo could have done. It was she who arranged our visits to the harbor and the various beaches of Trincomalee. Once a year when we camped in the jungle at Madhu or Paalai Oothu, it was she who slept with us beside the campfire. When the wild boar was brought in, it was Elizam who broiled the first pieces, though she was not the regular cook, and she always gave me the largest piece. She packed parcels of the meat to send to relatives and dried the rest under the sun. When we brought back birds from our shoots she cooked them for us, or when we brought green mangoes that we had stoned down from a nearby grove she secretly dressed them with salt and chili for a relish which we loved dearly but which was forbidden by Mother.

She was always preparing surprises for us. As we dug into our dinner of rice and several curries, with her fond voice coaxing us on, we would come across all kinds of delicacies hidden under the rice—eggs, chicken legs, fried shrimps, cuttlefish or roe, soft-shelled crabs, stuffed bitter gourd, fried wild boar, fish baked in ashes, meat wrapped in leaves, or a quail so tiny that you could eat its wafer-thin bones.

Elizam was the household expert on the preparation of that king of soups we called *kool,* whose only occidental equivalent I can think of is Provençal bouillabaisse. This main-dish soup is a north Ceylon specialty, and Elizam knew all its village mysteries.

On our family's *kool* day, a day to which we looked forward because there were no tiresome solid chunks of meat and vegetable to eat, Elizam superintended all the stages of its preparation, from the buying of fish to its eating. It was her special day in the kitchen. The matrix of the soup was made of a flour ground from the plumules of palmyra seeds. In it floated grains of rice and bright red stars of chili. Into the pot went tiny dried and fresh fish, medium pink fish and medium blue fish, small crabs, large crabs quartered, fillets of more fish along with their heads, the chestnuts of the jack fruit, the crisp fleshy jacket of jack seeds, tiny immature jack fruit cut into wedges, large "double shrimps," and the leaves of a certain creeper with red fruit that had a special rough texture which was delightful to chew.

In Trincomalee we always ate the soup out of bowls, but the way Elizam served it back in Atchuvely village was out of individual cups made of the glaucous jack leaf. Elizam herself took charge of the pot, ladling it out with her long shapely arm, her blue-black hair done into a very large bun at the back. Even mother, who often superintended our dinners, left the *kool* ceremony to Elizam.

Another village ritual perpetuated by Elizam in our urban surroundings was eating the pulp off the large palmyra seeds after they had been dipped in a weak solution of tamarind. It is a messy but delightful business. For the poor of the village it was sufficient dinner. When we went on hikes with the Boy Scouts she gave us parcels of *kattu choru.* Cooked eggs, meats, fish, vegetables, and rice were wrapped and pinned with a palm sliver in banana leaf and placed in a palm-leaf basket. The banana leaf, which cooked in the slow heat of the food inside it, flavored everything delicately. We also loved her *palanchoru,* which is cooked rice left overnight in water and made into balls filled with delicacies like shrimp or turtle meat. The proper way to eat it is off a small banana leaf held in the right hand.

Then there were Elizam's *pattchadis*. Between her cousin Sita and herself, all the *pattchadis* of Atchuvely were made available for our table. *Pattchadi* of bananas, *pattchadi* of eggplants, *pattchadi* of dried fish or shrimps, all baked in ashes, *pattchadis* of green ginger, neem flowers, lotus roots, banana inflorescences and their purple spathes, hibiscus blooms, heart of banana stem, portulacas, edible leaves of weeds, and tender stems of *pirandaithandu* creepers.

All this was now about to end. Elizam's younger sister Innesu, who had been brought up in Grandfather-with-the-Beard's household, had come up to take her place, but things would never be the same again without Elizam. Her father, who had come up from the village, was hilarious with the many guests. He was tipsy on arrack. But her mother was crying quietly, and I could see that Elizam would cry too before long. She was a wife now, this was her going-away party, but she looked very upset.

As is usual in Ceylonese weddings, the men were in the drawing room and the women in another part of the house. Being only eight, I was allowed to wander from one part of the house to the other. The men who liked a drink took trips to the small bar almost hidden away in a corner. That is also a tradition—to do the drinking away from the general company so as not to give offense.

The whole house was reeking with the pungent odor of black Jaffna cheroots. Many of the guests were hardened smokers from the north, including Elizam's mother, who smoked her own homegrown in a clay pipe. The teetotalers dug into the plates of tidbits and slaked their thirst with quantities of lime juice and carbonated water.

The time was drawing near for Elizam's departure. The *koorai,* or special wedding sari (which would become an heirloom), was carried in on a brass tray by my mother and offered to each guest in turn, who touched it with the right hand for good luck.

After I touched Elizam's sari I went to the study room and opened my desk. I wrote in Tamil on a sheet of paper: "Dear Elizam, Come back to see us soon. Thurairajah." I went to my mother's room and saw the *koorai* sari on the brass tray on the side table. I took a pin out of the sewing box and pinned my note on one of the inside folds. Elizam was bound to find it the first time she wore the sari.

The bridegroom had now drawn up his cart and two bullocks in front of the house. Accompanied by the women, Elizam came out and got into the front seat. There were tears in her eyes.

The bridegroom cracked his stick and the bullock cart creaked up the rose-pink gravel road on which the sun lay like golden coins. My brothers and I and our neighbors the Wambeek boys ran behind the rattling cart as far as the first crossroads. Through the thatch roof of the cart we saw Elizam turn around to have a last look at us. She did not wave.

I can't even remember whether we lit Chinese firecrackers at Elizam's wedding. Maybe we did.

I think I may have gone to bed with a book and no lunch that afternoon, as I usually did when I wished to protest against anything. That was a last resort to have my own way, and somehow it usually improved matters. If I did do this on Elizam's wedding day, I feel sure that I did it with no other motive than to mark the occasion with personal regret, as on the day our dog Luxmi died.

On the following Sunday, the second day after Elizam's wedding, there was the rumble of cartwheels outside our house at lunch time. When I went to the front door to see who it could be, Elizam rushed up and folded me in her arms and kissed me, a thing I can never remember her doing before. Her husband was standing by the cart smiling sheepishly.

There was tremendous excitement in the house at Elizam's return, with all of us tumbling around her and her sister Innesu full of smiles. Mother looked puzzled and she asked Elizam's husband what the matter was.

Apparently Elizam had found my note when she was dressing in her *koorai* sari to pay her first visit to the local church. She had burst into tears, and nothing would console her. She wanted to return to Trincomalee at once. Her husband had no choice but to drive her down at once the twenty miles in his bullock cart. That was how we happened to see Elizam in her *koorai* sari. She looked wonderful.

Elizam spent that day with us and promised to return to see us, which she did often. We were even taken one day to see her at her home in Kantalai near the famous irrigation tank built by King Aggabodhi II in A.D. 601. It was full of crocodiles. All the birds of creation seemed to be at Kantalai—teals, cormorants, Indian darters, and flights of terns, snipe, flycatchers, flamingoes, wild duck, waterfowl, minivets, peacocks, gay-colored jungle fowl, the solitary pelican, sunbirds, tailorbirds, golden orioles, bluejays, jungle crows, coucals, hawks of all sizes, bee-eaters, *buttagoias,* and all the kingfishers—river, giant, pied, and stork-billed. Truly it was a beautiful place to live in.

That day Elizam cooked for us her famous *kool* in her tidy thatched cottage, with jack fruit from her own tree, palmyra shoots from her own beds, and rice from her own fields, but we did not know then it would be our last. She died soon after in childbirth.

Elizam's sister, who looked very much like her, grew more dear to us as the years passed. Today we are as fond of her as we were of Elizam. She too was married off at the age of eighteen. But at that time we were much older and better able to appreciate the festivity of the occasion.

I distinctly remember that we did light Chinese firecrackers at Innesu's wedding.

PART FIVE

Grand

Tour

March 20, 1958

Mattei the Condottiere

By CLAIRE STERLING

ROME

Enrico Mattei has been fighting his own war against the world's biggest oil companies for thirteen years. It used to be a limited one, largely confined to the Italian mainland. But now Mattei has carried it to Egypt, Iran, Pakistan, Yugoslavia, Spain, France, Somaliland, Libya, Tunisia, and Morocco, and has said recently that he plans to go still further. He has announced, in fact, that he intends to expand Italy's oil interests "wherever and whenever" the occasion arises; and there is a very good chance that he will.

These forays abroad should be none of Mattei's business. As head of an Italian government authority called ENI (Ente Nazionale Idrocarburi), he is supposed officially to be exploring Italy's own subsoil for any petroleum that might add to its slender fuel resources. But Mattei has none of the bureaucrat's reverence for the letter of the law. Having looked for oil in Italy and not found very much, he has simply decided to look elsewhere. "Crude oil," he says, "must be searched for wherever there is the greatest possibility of finding it under economically advantageous conditions."

Inasmuch as this happens also to be the viewpoint of companies like Standard Oil, Gulf, British Petroleum, and Royal Dutch-Shell, Mattei has found the field fully occupied. He has, however, devised a wonderful way of making an entrance.

Early last year, he persuaded the Shah of Iran to give him three highly promising concessions, covering an area of 8,800 square miles, on terms that shocked the international consortium there (BP, Royal Dutch-Shell, Standard of New Jersey and of California, Gulf, Socony, and Texas, together with nine American independents and the Compagnie Française des Pétroles), but delighted the Shah. The fifty-fifty royalties split traditional in the Middle East was formally maintained. But Mattei guaranteed an additional fifty-fifty split in profits to the Iranians by undertaking to bring their government into equal partnership with him if he found oil. He also agreed to pay all the costs of exploration, with the Iranian government repaying half the investment only when and if he found the oil.

This agreement wasn't the first of its kind, since Mattei himself had made one very much like it with Nasser a few months earlier. But only a trickle of oil has yet been found in Egypt, whereas Iran produced thirty-five million tons last year. The Egyptian deal, therefore, was only a dress rehearsal for a sensational debut in Iran.

The violation of the fifty-fifty principle wasn't really new. New Jersey Standard's subsidiary in Venezuela, Creole Petroleum, holds to the fifty-fifty principle, but the inclusion of the American independent companies brings the average arrangement up to 56-44. Furthermore, the oil companies, taken together, have actually been paying a much higher percentage than that in the form of huge entrance bonuses for new concessions—a system that brought $700 million into the Venezuelan treasury in the high-mark period of 1956-1957, and is also very much in use throughout the Middle East. Mattei paid no such bonus in Iran. He was asked for one at the beginning: $35 million, he says, as against a reported 40-million bid from the consortium for the same concessions. But the Shah soon dropped the question. What Mattei had to offer was evidently more tempting than cash.

The alluring aspect of Mattei's deal was the prospect of equal partnership, which no oil-producing Middle Eastern state has ever had before. That alone would be enough to alarm the consortium members. An arrangement that went beyond the fifty-fifty royalties split and included equal participation in profits was a most serious menace not only to their holdings in Iran—ten times the size of Mattei's—but to all their other holdings in the Arab States, where nationalism is running high and where the Big Seven's combined profits yielded enough to pay $216.7 million in royalties to Iran last year.

Had it been possible to keep Mattei in a kind of Iranian quarantine, the consortium might not have been so concerned. But the ink was hardly dry on his Teheran contract when he was off traveling around the Mediterranean with copies of it in his briefcase. He may have missed some potential oil-producing country en route, but the news of his Iranian contract didn't. It was evident, therefore—and still is—that Mattei's move might change the *status quo* in the Middle East as drastically as Standard Oil and other American companies themselves changed it in December, 1950, when they accepted the fifty-fifty principle in Saudi Arabia while the British were paying far lower royalties to Iraq.

Inasmuch as the British had been done in the eye by the Americans in Iraq and also in Iran a little later, they were not by any means as hostile as their American colleagues toward Mattei during this crisis. Indeed, they seemed to take a certain quiet satisfaction in his behavior, as they have on other occasions before and since. They were even prepared to offer him a compromise, in the form of a five per cent membership in the consortium. There is reason to believe that he might have accepted the offer if it had been made soon enough. He himself says that he hinted as much to U.S. Ambassador James Zellerbach in Rome. "I told him the Americans were annoying me in Teheran, but that we might still find a way to get together." The ambassador didn't take the hint, however; and by the time the British got around to making the proposal, it was too late.

No doubt Mattei turned the compromise down partly through pique. Standard Oil and Gulf have been his bitterest enemies in Italy for years—particularly since last year, when he finally succeeded in driving the major foreign oil prospectors off the Italian mainland. Both tried so strenuously to keep him out of Iran that the Shah, in a rare display of royal temper, attacked them publicly for their "open, constant, and heavy-handed interference."

The Big Seven maintain that no oil company could operate on

a sound commercial basis under Mattei's 75-25 division. British Petroleum, however, whose share in the consortium is forty per cent, earned a net $60 million in Iran last year. Petroleum experts admit that once Mattei finds oil, he can expect a profit of forty cents on the dollar. The point, of course, is whether he can find it and how much he will have to spend in the process. On both counts, the consortium naturally hopes he will fall on his face. A few years ago he might have. But by now he has developed a corps of eight hundred highly trained petroleum technicians, and his new Pignone factory near Florence is turning out some of the best drills in the world. As for capital, it comes far more readily to his hand than to that of any private industrialist in Italy—or anywhere else on the Continent.

In his Iranian agreement, Mattei undertook to spend $6 million in the first four years for exploration. That is a paltry sum for a man who, for the same purpose, has perhaps spent $10 million in Egypt in less than two years. Even fifty times that amount would probably not faze him. Indeed, he talked freely of putting up half a billion dollars for a thousand-mile pipeline going from the newly discovered Qum oil fields in Iran to the Mediterranean. All he asked in exchange was a fifty per cent share in these oil fields, and the Shah was on the verge of agreeing until an American investment firm, Allen & Co., made a tentative offer.

One might ask, and Mattei's enemies at home frequently do, how the manager of an Italian government-owned authority can conceivably lay his hands on so much money.

No one has ever accused Mattei of being personally acquisitive. He lives modestly, even ascetically, has no expensive hobbies, and turns over most of his salary to an orphan asylum in his home town. He is, however, decidedly elusive in accounting to the government for the financial workings of ENI, and rarely informs the cabinet of what he's doing until he has already done it—if then. Since he controls a block of fifty Christian Democratic deputies and contributes more than generously to their party treasury, the government tends to leave him alone.

He has done spectacularly well with ENI under these circumstances. When he took over its predecessor, AGIP, in 1945, the entire property of that defunct Mussolini agency was on sale for a million dollars, with no takers. Today, ENI is a state holding company with fifty-three subsidiaries and $2 billion. Its biggest asset is natural gas, which Mattei's engineers discovered while prospecting for oil in the Po Valley, and which, produced now at an annual rate of nearly five billion cubic meters, covers thirteen per cent of Italy's fuel needs, saves the nation more than $100 million annually in foreign exchange, provides industrial energy for two thousand factories, and cooks the meals of 2,500,000 Italian families.

Among the other enterprises that ENI owns wholly or in part are metal works, iron and steel works, natural-steam works, chemical factories, oil wells and refineries, a soap factory, an electric power station, a string of service stations and slick new motels, an entire new state highway, a tanker fleet, and the third biggest network of natural-gas pipelines in the world. It is also on the point of completing a $150-million, five-hundred-acre industrial complex at Ravenna—the only one of its size and kind in Europe, and the only important new one to be built in Italy since the war—that will produce fifty-five thousand tons of artificial rubber and 650,-000 tons of nitrate fertilizer a year. Furthermore, Mattei expects before this year is out to begin construction of a $75-million Calder Hall-type reactor, with a capacity of 200,000 kilowatts—the largest atomic-energy plant yet on the drawing boards anywhere—with patents, equipment, information, technical assistance, and substantial credits furnished by the British Atomic Energy Authority. Although he has plans for another atomic plant built to American designs, it seems unlikely that he can get U.S. loans for that one while investing his own capital so arrogantly in Iran and elsewhere.

There are few businessmen in Europe, and surely none in Italy, who started with so little and built so much. What's more, Mattei has managed it with no financial help from the government beyond an initial $48-million sinking fund, part of which represented the value of AGIP's assets. To be sure, he has benefited from extraordinary governmental indulgences. Between 1956 and 1958, for instance, ENI was permitted to float $144 million worth of bond issues, six times the ceiling set for Fiat, the biggest private industry in the country. Since Mattei says he will invest more than that during the current year alone, however, he evidently must have some other sources of capital somewhere, no one knows exactly where. These sources certainly don't leap to the eye in ENI's annual report, which listed a net profit for all its subsidiaries last year of only $7.5 million—of which two-thirds was turned over to the government. But somewhere between ENI's net and gross income lies what must be a formidable sum accumulated by selling natural gas at from two to three times its cost of production.

This artificially high price has brought Mattei more withering criticism than anything else he has done. He argues that it is the most painless way to finance his oil explorations; that he couldn't lower it anyway without putting many factories still beyond the reach of his pipelines at an unfair disadvantage; and that if he did lower it, the savings "would not be passed on to the consumer, but would merely increase the industrialists' profits, whereas a state enterprise can use the profits for an investment policy in the most backward zones of the country, like the south."

If Mattei had used his particular state enterprise that way, he would not be where he is. Actually, he has invested very little in the poverty-ridden Italian south. Like the industrialists he talks about, he has gone where the profits are highest, charged what the market will bear, and plowed the dividends back into business investments that will bring in more.

Indeed, he has been a more forward-looking industrialist than most. With the counsel of an American management firm, he has streamlined ENI's every operation, introduced efficiency experts, adopted a progressive labor-management policy, and is even talking enthusiastically of eliminating the standard sleep-inducing Italian lunch of *pasta* and wine in his mess halls in favor of salads and Coca-Cola. Commendable as this aggressiveness on the part of an Italian civil servant may be, it is not, of course, what the government hired him for, which was to venture where private business would not go, in order to discover and exploit Italy's natural resources to the fullest. Nevertheless, this improbable and, some say, intolerably arrogant civil servant can make a good case for what he is doing.

Italy needs the equivalent of 52 million tons of coal a year now, and will need 76 million in 1965 and 110 million in 1975. At present it produces only 22 million tons of coal equivalent, or 42 per cent of current needs, of which Mattei's natural gas accounts for nearly a third. On a long-term basis, its most urgent problem is to build atomic-energy plants—an estimated thirty-five as large as the two that Mattei is planning—by 1975. Meanwhile, the big problem is to find oil. So far, Gulf has found enough of it in Sicily to produce about a million tons a year, and Mattei claims to have found enough near Gulf's reserve to produce another million by and by. But Italy consumes 11 million tons a year, which will go up to 15 million by 1960; and promising as the mainland has looked to geologists for years, no one since Gulf has found any significant deposits there.

The Big Seven blame this almost wholly on Mattei, who has exclusive rights to 21,000 square miles in the Po Valley—the most promising area of all—and who has recently pushed through a new petroleum law that in effect makes the whole Italian Peninsula his exclusive domain. Mattei himself will not say precisely how intensive a search he has made for oil, as distinct from natural gas, in the Po Valley. But he does claim to have drilled a great many wells there in search of both—some of them deeper than any drilled outside the United States; and he strongly suggests that if he hasn't made an important strike in the area by now, no one else would be likely to. On the other hand, a consortium in which he holds a substantial interest has found oil in Egypt, not very good in quality but enough to give Italy an extra 700,000 tons a year. Why not, then, go exploring abroad on a more extensive scale, where the prospects are better, the costs are lower, and the massive capital accumulated by ENI through the years might easily bring in quick and lush returns?

Mattei's opponents point out that there are several pressing economic, political, and diplomatic reasons why not. In the first place, oil exploration is a terribly expensive game of chance, even where the prospects are best. Four-fifths of all the exploratory wells dug in the world are dry; only six in a hundred pay the cost of drilling; and only one in a thousand reveals a really big deposit. Mattei may be reasonably hopeful of finding oil in Iran, Tunisia, or Morocco, but he can't be certain. Meanwhile, he will be risking enormous sums of money belonging to the Italian state, at a time when Italy is looking desperately for capital to develop its domestic economy. Furthermore, assuming he should find oil in quantity in the Middle East, he would not necessarily be ensuring Italy's supply by that means. The Suez crisis was so instructive in this regard that most western nations are now making extravagant efforts to find and develop fuel resources as far from that troubled area as possible. The fact that Mattei signed his partnership contract with Nasser only three months after the Sinai invasion—when all other western investors were trying frantically to get their money out of Egypt—suggests he is not overly sensitive to the peculiar political dangers of the Arab world. The fact, too, that he undertook to protect an older ENI oil well in the Sinai Desert during the invasion by sending fifteen Italians with machine guns to guard it suggests, among other things, a buccaneering spirit more attuned to a past age than to postwar Italy.

Mattei may even be appreciably increasing the very turmoil he so casually creates by making his appearance at the time and in the way he has done in Iran. The repercussions of his move may not be felt for some time. But it can hardly fail to feed the nationalist currents running against all western countries, including, in the long run, his own.

While he argues that any other shrewd businessman might have made the same move, his critics point out that he isn't merely a businessman but the head of a government agency, though such an influential one that wherever he goes, the Italian Foreign Office is bound to follow.

He is not in the habit of consulting the Foreign Office beforehand. When, for example, he negotiated an exploration treaty with Tito in Belgrade last December, the Italian Foreign Minister, Prime Minister, and President of the Republic had to wait until their ambassador told them what had really happened. Accordingly, Italy is finding itself more deeply embroiled every day in Middle Eastern politics, not in the role of impartial arbitrator it has tried to be during the past eighteen months but as an interested party.

The effects are already discernible in Italian foreign policy, which has begun to veer off in one direction toward a new position called Neo-Atlanticism, and in another toward a very old one called *Mare Nostrum*. Neo-Atlanticism, which is not quite heartily pro-western, includes a policy of active friendship with Nasser, as well as a proposal for an international diplomatic consortium, including both the United States and Russia, to preside over the Middle East. *Mare Nostrum* means literally that the Mediterranean is an essentially Italian sea, and that Italy should consequently develop a zone of influence around it. The phrase has a most unpleasant ring to Italians who hated Mussolini during his two decades of imperial expansion. But Mattei, who first emerged as a Resistance leader, says today that he sees "nothing wrong with the idea, except for Mussolini's use of force in applying it."

When Standard Oil and Gulf were feuding with Mattei inside Italy—with an eye on the lucrative Po Valley and an arrogance at least equal to his own—he was a vastly popular national hero. He is somewhat less so today. Many thoughtful Italians are very much distressed by his extravagant success in driving all foreign oil prospectors and their millions of useful dollars off the mainland, by his new international role and its disagreeable effects on Italian foreign policy, and by his cool disregard for the government he is supposed to be serving. "Mattei has become a prime example of what's wrong with Italian democracy," says Professor Ernesto Rossi, an outstanding economist who was once among his stoutest defenders. "He could not be so strong if our government were not so weak."

No one seems to be in a position to stop him. Aside from his transcendent influence in the ruling Christian Democratic Party, he has the solid backing of countless independents, who still think of him as Italy's closest thing to a trust buster—to say nothing of the Communists and Nenni Socialists, for whom he is a cornucopia of anti-western propaganda at the moment. He also has the support of the country's most influential newspapers, whose commercial sections are regularly filled with ENI advertising. (One national daily called *Il Giorno,* recently taken over outright by an intermediary of Mattei's, occupies three pages in the Milan telephone directory because it installed telephones gratis in every newspaper kiosk in the city.) Above all, he has been fortified by a close personal friendship with Giovanni Gronchi, whom he helped elect President.

With almost complete security, therefore, Mattei is going ahead with his plans to penetrate the petroleum world from the Persian Gulf to the Moroccan end of the Sahara Desert. He has been checked in Libya, where, under what must have been fearsome pressure from the Big Seven, King Idris tore up an Iranian-type contract with ENI that was awaiting his signature. But Mattei is now negotiating an even more far-reaching contract with Morocco, on the invitation of King Mohammed V; he is either already drilling, or is in private partnerships, or in preliminary discussion stages in all the other countries listed at the beginning of this article; he is completing a geological survey in Iran, where he hopes to begin drilling next summer; and he is building his first offshore platform for underwater exploration in the Persian Gulf off the coast of Iran. Moreover, since last year shipments of Egyptian crude are already unloading in Italian ports; and while he has had some difficulty about getting it into those refineries he owns jointly with Standard Oil and British Petroleum—who evidently prefer to refine their own crude—he does not expect this to be an enduring obstacle. "If Standard and BP don't change their minds," says one of his top aides, "we'll simply nationalize them."

Nevertheless, his security is not quite complete. Last December, the Italian government announced its intention of opening up part of the Po Valley to private—and foreign—exploration. "The new phase of ENI's activities abroad," said Minister of Industry Silvio Gava, "the uncertainty of supplies from the Middle East, the growing need of energy resources for the Italian economy, the development of new energy sources which suggest using the time left to consume our existing sources, are all circumstances showing the need to accelerate the exploration of our national territory, including the Po Valley."

Maybe this is just another attempt to stop Mattei. Loss of the Po Valley or any part of it would be a severe blow to him, for his career began in that rich demesne and his greatest source of strength, natural gas, lies under its surface. He may parry the blow and probably will. Yet the government's announcement was a pointed warning. An increasing number of influential Italians are made uneasy by the near sovereign status that Enrico Mattei has acquired.

This head of a state agency exerts too much power over the state, and even President Gronchi, once one of Mattei's closest friends and supporters, has shown his concern.

June 26, 1958

Once More the Heart of Europe

By Max Ascoli

Home again from Europe, much of what I thought and heard there seems to recede into comparative unimportance. But some feelings I had in Paris one day, the day of May 26, haunt me, and I don't know whether, if ever, I will be relieved of their poignancy.

In Italy anti-clericalism is rampant, I found, and yet the electoral process does not provide it with even remotely adequate expression. A formidable number of Italians want no part in the existing political order and keep voting Communist just because the Communist Party has no chance of sharing power with the Christian Democrats.

In London I found a strange political lassitude, a tiredness with both major parties, and that bitter mixture of anger at each other and concern with seemingly unendurable national difficulties that only a few years ago seemed to be the monopoly of Paris. But all these and many more troubles that I found in Italy and in Great Britain I had known before and, I am sure, will be awaiting me next time.

In Paris I saw that lurid thing that is a nation without institutions. The actual reality of anarchy hits you and paralyzes your thinking. You only know that you are lonely and miserable.

Are the gendarmes in the guardrooms of the ministries the protectors or the keepers of the men in power? Perhaps they themselves don't know and, you are told, it all depends. Depends on what? you ask. Anything may happen.

Gendarmes and Gardes Mobiles are grouped in front of many buildings on the Champs Elysées and in strategic squares, clustered around their Black Marias. Near them are harmless onlookers and obvious thugs. The movies of René Clair have taught all of us to recognize the Parisian thug. If the killers run loose, what will the police do? You look at a gendarme and wonder. When the moment comes—as it may any minute—to take the pistol from its holster, whom is he going to fire at, poor little man? He is no longer an agent of the law. He *is* the law—all that's left of it. Everybody, gendarme or thug, is the law when he has a gun.

That morning, I had been told that the Pflimlin cabinet could not count on the loyalty of the armed services. It was not a revolt —or not yet. It was simply that the levers of command did not respond, or could not be counted upon to respond. Yet no new cabinet was in sight, and moreover, what was fast coming to an end was not just a cabinet but that constitutional form of government called the Fourth Republic.

Between the Fourth and a Fifth Republic, there could be civil war. True, the Communists were expected to put up only a token fight, if any. But if shooting starts, if people in the street drop dead, then there is not such a thing as limited civil war. The extreme right wing certainly was readier than the Communists to start the killing, you were told by some left-of-center leaders who, it was said, had been marked for extinction.

The Fourth Republic is dying and the sooner we start the civil war the better, I heard people say. I could not find any reason to mourn the Fourth Republic, and yet I could not help feeling that the death of a legal order, even that of the Fourth Republic, was a horrid thing to behold. Those are the moments when you realize to what an extent men are dependent on their laws. The sovereign individual, when all the legal ties are loosened, turns out to be a rather incongruous lump.

In all revolutions there has been that spell of void, that hiatus between two orders, which I felt in Paris. Yet even then I could not help sensing something peculiar in that particular revolution.

Or was it a revolution? Violence was in the air. It had been in the air for several days before I reached Paris, and remained for several days after I left. True, violence could explode at any moment because of someone's schemes, or trigger-happiness. The paratroopers were expected to land. But even in Algeria, where open rebellion had occurred, not one drop of blood had been spilled.

The cause for that restraint, in Algeria as well as in Paris, had a name: de Gaulle. Maybe it was nothing more than a name. Yet it was toward the man with that name that all minds were turning, and on whose actions—if and when he cared to act—everyone's reactions depended. It was as if de Gaulle had already unified France, at least in the sense that the policies of the various parties and factions were determined by the various expectations of what he would do, or by different interpretations of the way his mind was working. Was he becoming once more France's man of destiny —maybe on borrowed time, perhaps borrowing the time of his own past?

There was something both formidable and eerie in de Gaulle's sudden return to France's political stage. He had spent years making himself into the monumental statue of General de Gaulle. Now the statue, like the Commendatore in the last act of *Don Giovanni,* had stepped down from the pedestal.

But who is de Gaulle? In Paris and in London I kept asking this question of people who had known him, and of political thinkers at large. I don't care to list all the answers I received, for by now they can be found in print everywhere. That he is an egomaniac though an honest one, that he cares above all about re-establishing his country's lost grandeur, that he may turn out to be a Kerensky, thereby paving the way for a dictatorship of the Right or of the Left—all this I have heard, along with, of course, the names of Napoleon III, Boulanger, Mussolini, Franco, and all the rest. Whenever the history we happen to live is disturbed by the occurrence of a new event, the attempt is invariably made to dismiss it as the more or less literal repetition of something that has already happened.

In the case of de Gaulle this is particularly shocking, since we are dealing here with a historic personality, who has taken the utmost pains to give a detailed account of himself and of the role he has played in history. So much has been said about his being a sphinx, although usually sphinxes don't write books.

I was familiar enough with de Gaulle's *Mémoires de Guerre* to know that the book is a masterpiece, written with the religious care for each word and the tireless literary craftsmanship that are already a mark of greatness. Rather than go on inquiring about de Gaulle, I decided to read him. Maybe against the background of the events in Paris I could find in de Gaulle's *Mémoires* the measure both of his greatness and of his limitations.

Perhaps all of de Gaulle is in one paragraph of the first volume of his *Mémoires,* the one that has been somewhat translated into English. When he went to London after the fall of France, he knew the staggering magnitude of his self-imposed task. In the worst moment of France's history, he, Brigadier General Charles de Gaulle, had to be France. "As for me," he writes, "at the beginning, I was nothing. At my side, not a shadow of military power or political organization. In France, no following and no reputation. Abroad, neither credit nor standing. But my very lack of everything dictated the line I had to follow. It was only by uncompromisingly pursuing the cause of national salvation that I could find the authority I needed. It was by acting as an inflexible champion of the nation and of the state that I could gain consent, even enthusiasm, among the French, and that I could win respect and recognition from the outside world. The people who throughout this drama were offended by this intransigence refused to realize that, for me, straining as I was to beat back countless conflicting pressures, the slightest wavering would have brought disaster. In fact, limited and lonely as I was, and just because of this, I had to gain the highest peaks, and never again descend."

Was any one of our wartime leaders subjected to any comparable test? Is there any memory of comparable achievements in the history of free men? De Gaulle remade France, literally as he said, starting from nothing. He wanted to keep France within the alliance, and to do this he had to defend from the Allies the France that he was reassembling piece by piece. Helped only by his faith and by the enthusiasm he was generating, he shouldered his way among the leaders of the Grand Alliance, who all resented him, and some of whom treated him shabbily—worst of all, Franklin Roosevelt.

Perhaps it was difficult for democratic politicians to understand this man who just could not make compromises. Yet in his *Mémoires* he is singularly lenient with the Allied leaders. He doesn't justify them; neither does he refrain from describing the clashes he had with them. But in the sober reflection of the historian, he succeeds in understanding why they acted toward him the way they did. For actually, after the defeat, what was left of France if not a motley collection of real estate—and most of it in the heart of Dark Africa?

For de Gaulle, the rallying of Dark Africa round his movement was the beginning of the awakening both of Africa and of France. The way ahead was clear to him from that time: the French empire must be transformed into a Union Française, or French commonwealth.

The notion that Metropolitan France is just one part of the French commonwealth—a commonwealth of free, self-ruling peoples equal before the laws that the revolution had given the Republic—this notion is to be found, expressed with the utmost clarity, throughout de Gaulle's *Mémoires*.

So is his republicanism. In fact, his conception of the government France should have, far from being even remotely Napoleonic or plebiscitarian, is that of a classic Jacobin. True, the democratic institution that he likes the least is the party system. But he certainly does not go as far in his condemnation of party politics as did Jean-Jacques Rousseau, the arch-Jacobin of them all.

When France was being reconstructed, first in Algiers and then after the Liberation in Paris, de Gaulle's aim was to harness partisanship, not to suppress it. He failed in his effort, as he failed even more miserably when he, of all people, tried to enter party politics and established the Rassemblement du Peuple Français. The Rassemblement was not supposed to act like other political parties, and when de Gaulle realized that in fact it did, he hurried back to Colombey-les-Deux-Eglises.

This man who seems to be enigmatic is actually outspoken and punctiliously clear in the expression of his thinking. He has been worrying about politics or, in the broader sense of the term, he has been in politics most of his adult life. Yet he never ran for office. He is not an enemy of the politicians—indeed he knows that there can be no freedom without politicians. But he is alien to them, and they to him.

He is only good at making France, but is unwilling and unfitted to run it. When the institutions collapse because of external attack, internal rebellion, or political mismanagement, when France is reduced to the bare idea of France, then de Gaulle knows how to become the embodiment of that idea. He has done so twice. It must also be added, however, that he failed after his triumph to prevent the return of the political habits that so greatly contributed to the wartime collapse.

Now he is engaged in a second attempt at remaking France. The difficulties he faces are appalling, yet they are not greater than those he had to face when he went to London, all alone, and, before the mike of the BBC, told his countrymen that France was still fighting.

This time, he must act on Algeria while laying down the foundation for a Fifth Republic, and for a French commonwealth. He will certainly also give new direction to European initiatives within the Atlantic Community. The man who during the war resented so bitterly the fact that France was not treated as an equal by the major powers, certainly knows now that the coalition has grown into a community from which France cannot secede. It is equally certain that de Gaulle will make the full weight of his country felt within the Atlantic Community, for there is no community without Europe, and France is the heart of Europe.

De Gaulle must tackle all his formidable problems concurrently and find solutions for them in an appallingly short time. There is nothing he will do for his country that will not affect the alliance as a whole—not even his reforms of the French constitution, and his attempt to put a brake on partisanship. For it so happens that a certain lassitude toward politics is to be found in a number of European democracies, from Italy to Britain. In the same way, it happens that criticism and resentment of American leadership of the coalition is more acute than ever. This restlessness was bound to find its European leader.

De Gaulle has taken a portentous gamble—and not with France alone. If he fails, if fascists or Communists try to get hold of France, then the civil war will not be limited to France alone. Then the violence that I felt imminent in Paris will have no restraint.

Strangely enough, the fate of western democracy, at least on the European continent, maybe even the survival of the western coalition, largely depends on the success of this extraordinary Frenchman, Charles de Gaulle.

July 8, 1952

The Tragic Life of a
Polrugarian Minister

By Isaac Deutscher

Polrugaria need not be exactly located on the map. Enough that it lies somewhere in the dark eastern reaches of Europe. Nor need the name of Vincent Adriano, a high Polrugarian official, be looked up in any *Who's Who,* for he is a half-real and half-imaginary character. Adriano's features and traits can be found in some of the people who now rule the Russian satellite countries, and not a single one of his experiences related here has been invented. It need not be specified what post Vincent Adriano holds in his Government. He may be the President or the Prime Minister or the Vice-Premier, or he may be only the Minister of the Interior or the Minister of Education. In all likelihood he is a member of the Politburo, and is known as one of the pillars of the People's Democracy in Polrugaria. His words and doings are reported in newspapers all over the world.

It is common to refer to men of Adriano's kind as "Stalin's henchmen," "Russian puppets," and "leaders of the Cominform fifth column." If any of these labels described him adequately, Adriano would not be worth any special attention. To be sure, he is unavoidably something of a puppet and an agent of a foreign power, but he is much more than that.

355

Vincent Adriano is in either his late forties or early fifties—he may be just fifty. His age is significant because his formative years were those of the revolutionary aftermath of the First World War. He came from a middle-class family that before 1914 had enjoyed a measure of prosperity and believed in the stability of dynasties, governments, currencies, and moral principles. In his middle or late teens, Adriano saw three vast empires crumble with hardly anybody shedding a tear. Then he watched many governments leap into and tumble out of existence in so rapid and breathtaking a succession that it was almost impossible to keep account of them. On the average, there were a dozen or a score of them every year. The advent of each was hailed as an epoch-making event; each successive Prime Minister was greeted as a savior. After a few weeks or days, he was booed and hissed out of office as a misfit, scoundrel, and nincompoop.

The currency of Polrugaria, like the currencies of all neighboring countries, lost its value from month to month, then from day to day, and finally from hour to hour. Adriano's father sold his house at the beginning of one year; with the money he received he could buy only two boxes of matches at the end of that year. No political combination, no institution, no established custom, no inherited idea seemed capable of survival. Moral principles, too, were in flux. Reality seemed to lose clear-cut outline, and this was reflected in the new poetry, painting, and sculpture.

The young man was easily convinced that he was witnessing the decay of a social order, that before his very eyes capitalism was succumbing to the attack of its own deep-seated insanity. He was aroused by the fiery manifestoes of the Communist International signed by Lenin and Trotsky. Soon he became a member of the Communist Party. Since in Polrugaria the party was savagely persecuted—the penalties for membership ranged from five years' imprisonment to death—the people who joined it did not do so, in those days, for selfish or careerist motives.

Adriano, at any rate, gave up without hesitation the prospect of a secure career in the academic field to become a professional revolutionary. He was prompted by idealistic sympathy with the underdog and by something he called "scientific conviction." Studying the classics of Marxism, he became firmly convinced that private ownership of the means of production and the concept of the nation-state had outlived their day, and further, that they were certain to be replaced by an international socialist society which could be promoted only by a proletarian dictatorship.

This proletarian dictatorship meant not the dictatorial rule of a clique, let alone of a single leader, but the social and political predominance of the working classes, "the dictatorship of an over-whelming majority of the people over a handful of exploiters, semi-feudal landlords, and big capitalists." Far from disowning democracy, the proletarian dictatorship, so he thought, would represent its consummation. It would fill the empty shell of formal equality, which was all that bourgeois democracy could offer, with the content of social equality. With this vision of the future he plunged into the conspiratorial struggle of the revolutionary underground.

We need not relate in detail Adriano's revolutionary career—its pattern was, up to a point, typical. There were the years of his dangerous work in the underground, when he lived the life of a hunted man without name or address. He organized strikes, wrote for clandestine papers, and traveled all over the country studying social conditions and setting up organizations. Then came the years of prison and torture and of longing in solitude. The vision of the future that had inspired him had to be somewhat adulterated with expedients, tactical games, and tricks of organization—the daily business of every politician, even of one who serves a revolution. For all that, his idealism and enthusiasm had not yet begun to evaporate.

Even while imprisoned he helped sustain in his comrades their conviction, their hope, and their pride in their own sacrifices. Once he led several hundred political prisoners in a hunger strike. The strike, lasting six or seven weeks, was one of the longest ever known. The governor of the prison knew that in order to break it he had first to break Vincent Adriano. Guards dragged the emaciated man by his legs from a cell on the sixth floor down the iron staircase, banging his head against the hard and rusty edges of the steps until he lost consciousness. Vincent Adriano became a legendary hero.

With some of his comrades, he at last managed to escape from prison and make his way to Russia. Inasmuch as he spent several years in Moscow, it is now often said and written about him that he belongs to that "hard core of Moscow-trained agents who control Polrugaria." Such words, when he happens to read them, bring a sadly ironical smile to his lips.

When Adriano arrived in Moscow in the early 1930's, he was not among the chief leaders of the Polrugarian party. Nor was he greatly concerned with his place in the hierarchy. He was more preoccupied with the confusion in his own mind that arose when he first compared his vision of the society of the future with life in the Soviet Union under Stalin. He hardly dared admit, even to himself, the extent of his disillusionment. This, too, has been so typical in the experiences of men of his kind that we need not dwell on it. Typical, too, were the truisms, the half-truths, and the self-delusions with which he tried to soothe his disturbed Communist conscience. Russia's inherited poverty, its isolation in a capitalist world, the dangers threatening it from outside, the illiteracy of its masses, their laziness and lack of civic responsibility— all this and more he used to explain to himself why life in Russia fell appallingly short of the ideal.

"Oh," he sighed, "if only the revolution had first been victorious in a more civilized and advanced country! But history has to be taken as it is, and Russia is at least entitled to the respect and gratitude due the pioneer, whatever that pioneer's faults and vices." He did his utmost not to see the realities of life around him.

Then came the great purges of 1936-1939. Most leaders of the Polrugarian party who had lived as exiles in Moscow were shot as spies, saboteurs, and agents of the Polrugarian political police. Before they died, they (and even their wives, brothers, and sisters) were made to bear witness against one another. Among the dishonored and the executed was one who more than anybody else had aroused Adriano's enthusiasm and sustained his courage, who had initiated him into the most difficult problems of Marxist theory, and to whom Adriano had looked up as a friend and spiritual guide.

Adriano, too, was confronted with the usual charges. By a freak of fortune, however, or perhaps by the whim of the chief of the GPU, N. I. Yezhov, or of one of Yezhov's underlings, he was not made to face a firing squad. Instead, he was deported to a forced-labor camp somewhere in the subpolar north. With many others —Trotskyites, Zinovievites, Bukharinites, kulaks, Ukrainian nationalists, bandits and thieves, former generals, former university professors and party organizers—he was employed in felling trees and transporting them from the forest to a depot. Frost, hunger, and disease took their toll of the deportees, but the ranks were constantly filled with newcomers.

Adriano saw how people around him were first reduced to an animal-like struggle for survival, how they next lost the will to struggle and survive, and how finally they collapsed and died like flies. Somehow his own vitality did not sag. He went on wielding the ax with his frostbitten fingers. Every third or fourth day it was his turn to harness himself, along with fellow prisoners, to the cart loaded with timber and to drag it across the snow- and ice-covered plain to the depot several miles away. These were the worst hours. He could not reconcile himself to the fact that he, the proud revolutionary, was being used as a beast of burden in the country of his dream.

Even now he still feels a piercing pain in his heart whenever he thinks of those days—and that is why he reads with a melancholy smile the stories about the mysterious "training in fifth-column activity" he received in Russia.

With a shred of his mind he tried to penetrate the tangle of circumstances behind his extraordinary degradation. At night he argued about this with the other deportees. The problem was vast and confused beyond comprehension. Some of the deported Communists said that Stalin had carried out a counter-revolution in which every achievement of Lenin's revolution had been destroyed.

Others held that the foundations of the revolution—public ownership and a collectivist economy—had remained intact, but that instead of a free socialist society, a terrifying combination of socialism and slavery was being erected on those foundations. The outlook was therefore more difficult than anything they could have

imagined, but there was perhaps some hope, if not for this generation then for the next. Stalinism, it was true, was casting grave
discredit upon the ideal of socialism, but perhaps what was left of
socialism might still be salvaged from the wreckage. Adriano could
not quite make up his mind, but he was inclined to adopt this
latter view.

Events now took a turn so fantastic that even the most fertile
imagination could not have conceived it. One day, toward the end
of 1941 (Hitler's armies had just been repulsed from the gates of
the Russian capital), Adriano was freed from the concentration
camp and taken with great honors straight to Moscow. The Kremlin urgently needed east and central European Communists capable of broadcasting to the Nazi-occupied lands and of establishing liaison with the underground movements behind the enemy
lines. Because of their country's strategic importance, Polrugarians
were especially wanted. But not a single one of the chief leaders of
the Polrugarian party was alive. The few less prominent ones who
had been dispersed in various places of deportation were hurriedly
brought back to Moscow, rehabilitated, and put to work. The re-
habilitation took the form of an apology from the Security Police
to the effect that the deportation of Comrade So-and-So had been
a regrettable mistake.

Several times a week, Adriano, facing the microphone, shouted
into the ether his confidence in the Land of Socialism, extolled
Stalin and his achievements, and called on the Polrugarians to
rise behind the enemy lines and prepare for their liberation.

He sensed sharply the incongruity of his situation. He was now
a propaganda agent for his jailers and torturers, for those who had
denigrated and destroyed the leaders of Polrugarian Communism,
his dear friend and guide among them. At heart he could neither
forget nor forgive the agony and the shame of the purges. And
with a part of his mind he could never detach himself from the
people he had left behind in the north.

But he could not refuse the assignment. Refusal would have
amounted to sabotage of the war effort, and the penalty would
have been death or deportation. Yet it was not merely from cow-

ardice that he was doing his job. He was eager to help defeat the Nazis, and for this, he felt, it was right to join hands "with the devil and his grandmother"—and with Stalin.

Nor was this merely a matter of defeating Nazism. Despite all he had gone through, he clung to his old ideas and hopes. He was still a Communist. He looked forward to the revolutionary ferment that would spread over the capitalist world after the war. The more severe his disillusionment with the Soviet Union, the more intense was his hope that the victory of Communism in other countries would regenerate the movement and free it from the Kremlin's faithless tutelage.

The same motives prompted him to agree to a proposal, which Stalin personally made to him a few months later, that he should organize a Polrugarian Committee of Liberation and become its secretary. It was certain that the Red Army would cross into Polrugaria sooner or later. The Committee of Liberation was to follow in its wake and to become the nucleus of a provisional government.

Adriano's hands were full of work. He was now in charge of liaison with the Polrugarian Resistance. He issued instructions to the emissaries who penetrated the enemy lines or were parachuted behind them. He received reports from the guerrillas in the occupied country and transmitted them higher up. He arranged that leaders of the non-Communist and even anti-Communist parties be smuggled out of the country and brought to Moscow. And he induced some of them to join the Committee of Liberation.

The sequel is known. The Committee of Liberation became the provisional government, and then the actual government of Polrugaria. The non-Communist parties were squeezed out one by one and suppressed. Polrugaria became a People's Democracy. Adriano is one of the pillars of the new government, and so far nothing seems to foreshadow his eclipse. He has not found the way out of the trap; neither has he been crushed in it.

There are two Vincent Adrianos now. One seems never to have known a moment of doubt or hesitation. His Stalinist orthodoxy has never been questioned, his devotion to the party has never flagged, and his virtues as leader and statesman are held to be unsurpassed. The other Adriano is almost constantly tormented by his Communist conscience, a prey to scruple and fear, to illusion and disillusionment. The former is expansive and eloquent, the latter broods in silence and hides even from his oldest friends. The former acts, the latter never ceases to ponder.

From 1945 to 1947 the two Adrianos were almost reconciled with each other. In those years the Polrugarian party carried out some of the root-and-branch reforms that for decades had been inscribed in its program. It attacked the problem of Polrugarian landlordism. It divided the large semi-feudal estates among the land-hungry peasants. It established public ownership of large-scale industry. It initiated impressive plans for the further indus-trial development of a sadly under-developed country. It sponsored a great deal of progressive social legislation and an ambitious edu-cational reform. These achievements filled Adriano with real joy and pride. It was, after all, for these things that he had languished in Polrugarian prisons.

In those years, too, Moscow, for its own reasons, was telling the Polrugarians that they should not look too much to Russia as their model, that they ought to find and follow their own "Polrugarian road to socialism." To Adriano this meant that Polrugaria would be spared the experience of purges and concentration camps, of abject subservience and fear. Communism, intense industrial and educational development, and a measure of real freedom to argue with one's fellow and to criticize the powers that be—this seemed to be the achievement of an ideal.

What disturbed him even then was that the people of Polrug-aria were showing little enthusiasm for the revolution. To be sure, they saw the advantages and on the whole approved them. But they resented the revolution that was being carried out over their heads by people whom they had not chosen and who did not often bother to consult them and who looked like stooges of a foreign power.

Adriano knew to what extent the presence of the Red Army in Polrugaria had facilitated the revolution. Without it, the forces of the counter-revolution, with the assistance of the western bour-geois democracies, might have reasserted themselves in bloody civil war, as they had done after the First World War. But he reflected that a revolution without genuine popular enthusiasm behind it is half defeated. It is inclined to distrust the people whom it should serve. And distrust may breed dark fear and terror as it had done in Russia.

Yet, although he saw these dangers, he hoped that through honest and devoted work for the masses, the new Polrugarian government could eventually win their confidence and arouse their enthusiasm. Then the new social order would stand on its own feet. Sooner or later the Russian armies would go back to Russia. Surely, he thought, there must be another road to socialism, perhaps not exactly a Polrugarian one, but not a Russian and a Stalinist road either.

In the meantime, Vincent Adriano did a few things that were understood only by the initiated. He sponsored in Polrugaria a cult to glorify the memory of his old friend and guide who had perished in Russia, although Moscow had not officially rehabilitated the latter's memory. The biography of the dead leader can even now be seen displayed in Polrugarian bookshops, side by side with the official life of Stalin. Since the circumstances of the martyr's death are not mentioned in the biography, only the older Communists are aware of the hidden implications of this homage.

Adriano has also set up a special institute that looks after the families of all the Polrugarian Communists who perished in Moscow as "spies and traitors." The institute is called the Foundation of the Veterans and Martyrs of the Revolution. Such gestures give Adriano a measure of moral satisfaction, but he knows that politically they are irrelevant.

As the two camps, East and West, began to marshal their forces and as the leaders on both sides, each in their own ways, confronted everybody with a categorical "who-is-not-with-me-is-against-me," Adriano's prospects darkened. If he could have had his way, Adriano's answer would have been a hearty "plague o' both your houses." He who has been an outcast in Stalin's Russia, a beast of burden in one of its concentration camps, he to whom every copy of *Pravda*, with its demented hymns to Stalin, gives an acute sensation of nausea, has watched with a shudder as his "Polrugarian road to socialism" has become more and more the Soviet road. Yet he does not see how he can depart from it.

He takes it for granted that all the West can offer to east and central Europe is counterrevolution. The West may extol freedom and the dignity of man (and who has explored the meaning of these ideals as tragically and thoroughly as Adriano?), but his gaze is fixed on the gulf he sees between western promise and fulfillment. He is convinced that in his part of the world every new upheaval will bring more rather than less oppression, more rather than less degradation of man.

He is willing to concede that those who speak for the West may be quite sincere in their promises, but he adds that he has retained his old Marxist habit of disregarding the wishes and promises of statesmen and of keeping his eyes on social and political realities. Who among the Polrugarians, he asks, are ready to rally to the banners of the West? There may be a few well-meaning people among them, but these will be the dupes.

The most active and energetic allies of the West in Polrugaria are those who have had a stake in the old social order, the privileged men of the pre-war dictatorship, the old *soldateska,* the expropriated landlords and their like. These, should the West win, will form the new government, and, in the name of freedom and of the dignity of man, let loose a White terror the like of which has never been seen. Adriano had known *their* terror once, also. But that was at a time when the old ruling class believed that their rule would last forever, and when their self-confidence prevented their terror from becoming altogether insane. Now, if they came back, they would be mad with fear and revenge. The real choice, as he sees it, is not between tyranny and freedom, but between Stalinist tyranny, which is in part redeemed by economic and social progress, and a reactionary tyranny which would not be redeemed by anything.

At times Adriano would be happy to give up his high office and withdraw into obscurity. But the world has become too small. He cannot seek asylum in the West. This, in his eyes, would be not much better than treason—not to Russia, but to his ideal of Communism. Nor can he withdraw into obscurity. Resignation and withdrawal on his part would be a gesture of opposition and defiance, and this the régime he has helped to build would not allow.

How much is there in common between the young man who once set out with Promethean ardor to conquer history's insanity as it manifested itself in capitalism and the middle-aged Cabinet Minister who vaguely feels that history's irrational forces have overpowered the camp of the revolution and, incidentally, driven him into a trap? He does his best to bolster his own self-respect and to persuade himself that as statesman, dignitary, and leader he is still the same man he was when he championed the cause of the oppressed and suffered for it in the prisons of his native land. But sometimes, while he solemnly receives delegations of peasants or salutes a colorful parade, a familiar sharp pain pierces his heart. Suddenly he feels that he is, even now, being used as a beast of burden.

July 11, 1957

Notes on Israel

BY MAX ASCOLI

A visit to Israel is no joy ride for a political analyst—particularly when it happens to be the first visit. There is too much that cries to be seen, and too much that is hidden; too much that is admirable, indeed exalting; too much that is bewildering and, at first, shocking. But most of what is shocking turns out to be caused by the fact that the Israelis have given a peculiar content to ideas so familiar to us that we have come to think of them as endowed with unquestionable, abiding significance. This is the case with political parties, trade unions, government, and even nation. Sometimes I had the feeling that this applies even to what over here we consider a fact of the type William James called stubborn and irreducible.

This does not necessarily mean that we—or the Israelis—are wrong, or that it is just a question of semantics. But it does mean that an effort is required to correlate our values and those of the Israelis. In these days of summer traveling, you can see ads in the papers about simple pocketable gadgets that tell you quickly how much a given amount of foreign currency is worth in dollars. But there are no such gadgets for the ideological rates of exchange.

Yet the difference between our standards of political and ideological values and those of the other democracies is increasing, just as the number of new and different experiments with democracy all over the world is increasing. Perhaps we are paying the price for having had our revolution well before everybody else.

It is distressing for one who flies across the Atlantic every year to realize that the less the number of hours it takes to cross the ocean, the fewer are the points of reference that the American traveler finds he has in common with his European friends. The more comfortable the crossing, the more uncomfortable the stay. Worries and doubts start haunting the traveler's mind abroad and don't leave him even when he is back home.

In my own case, one particular obsession stayed with me: the fear that America's leadership of the free world may become something very similar to the U.S. supremacy in baseball, evidenced every year by the fact that an American team wins what we still call—of all things—the World Series.

The need could not be more urgent: We ought to follow as closely as we can what old and new democracies have done to values that in our country we do not bother to re-examine or maybe to understand. This is why our diplomats, our economists —even our political analysts—had better keep on the road as much as they can and endure the acute discomfort of traveling.

Israel, as a very new and very old country, is a particularly intriguing and bothersome place to visit. It has troubled me deeply, both when I was there and since I came back. But I don't know whether I ever had a more rewarding time. I am deeply grateful to Israel for being the country it is, and for the trouble it has given me.

The Ingathering of the Exiles

The first shock in Israel was to realize how misleading is the notion that the country is small—in fact, approximately the size of Massachusetts. The distance from Dan to Beersheba is 175 miles, a five-hour drive. From Tel Aviv to Haifa is sixty miles. If from Beersheba the traveler wants to venture to Elath, he can do it by jeep in four hours or by air in one hour from the Lydda airport. But Israel is not a country to fly over or to speed through. If you look at the map from north to south, you see

such names as Tiberias, Nazareth, Armageddon. You see where
the hills of Samaria are and the Carmel Range and the hills of
Ephraim. Israel has excellent roads, and more are being built all
the time, partly for strategic reasons, partly for unemployment
relief. But there is too much history all along those roads, and
you don't know how to take in enough of what you see, or to
connect it with what you remember.

Yet even the legacy of time past, the somewhat obsessive sense
that distance is multiplied by time, was not half as stirring to
me as the faces of the people I saw in the crowded streets of
Tel Aviv and its suburbs. You can never drive slowly enough,
or, for that matter, walk slowly enough. The color of the hair
and of the skin, the bearing, the light in the eyes of the people
around you are so astonishingly different and varied that only by
stopping and talking to each one of them, and asking how, and
from where, and when did they or their parents come to Israel
—only that way can you do justice to the men and women you
see. You feel somewhat swamped and lost. There may or may
not be an Israeli people. But all those people in Israel are an
amazing assortment of samples from all the countries and civilizations of the earth.

You can guess the national origin of some of them. The lean,
brown bearded man you see must be from Yemen; that sturdy
peasant from Kurdistan. Certainly that young woman with close-
cropped hair and an air of ruthless determination must be an intellectual from Germany. The slender, slant-eyed kids marching
after that stocky, blond girl in shorts must be from North Africa.

All those men and women moving past you have been called—
or cursed—by the same name. As long as they were scattered all
over the world, the sameness of that name, plus a few common
traditions and religious practices, seemed to be enough to
identify world Jewry. In Israel, the land where many of them
have ended their Diaspora, the fantastic heterogeneity of what is
called world Jewry hits you between the eyes.

The language most of them talk is Hebrew. Their own faith
or other peoples' hate has uprooted them from the lands where
most of them were born. Or else they have been brought into
Israel by immemorial fear or Biblical hope. Those born in Israel

are a sort of race apart, and have a name of their own—Sabras. Most of the old people who have worked the hardest to set the nation going, who have fought underground and aboveground against the British and the Arabs, are now at the head of the nation. All those men and women you see may be Sabras or old pioneers or recent immigrants. Yet they all go about as if in the grip of a relentless destiny that has caught up with them.

"Israel is not a melting pot. It's a pressure cooker." I first heard this said a few hours after I arrived. Later on, so many other English-speaking Israelis repeated it that I could hardly stand it. At first I thought there might be something to it, for I sensed that an overwhelming pressure was being brought to bear on these people, but I could scarcely know the nature of the forces pressing hard on them. Later, when I started meeting people I had known in Europe long before they became Israelis, I realized that the pressure is, to an astonishing degree, self-willed. These people not only lend themselves to the forces that remold them, but they want these forces to operate quickly, and they help them along with all their will power.

The first new Israelis I met belonged to the intellectual or professional classes. But among many people I became acquainted with later—intellectuals or nonintellectuals—I found the same eagerness to do away with the past, to speak only Hebrew, to become thoroughly Israeli in habits, inclinations, and instincts. I was amazed when I realized how people from a European country, all friends or business associates who came to Israel at approximately the same time, stick to Hebrew even when they are among themselves. If the presence of someone who is not Hebrew-speaking obliges them to relapse into their native language, at the moment of parting they never fail to say "shalom" to each other, as if in atonement.

There are, of course, exceptions—lumps of old habits that resist the furious energy of the pressure cooker. But not for long. By and large, the immigrants are grimly, tirelessly determined to become self-made Israelis. Toward this goal they are driving hard, and to this goal they are driven. This makes communication with them rather difficult sometimes, for their inflexible determination to lose whatever of the non-Israeli self may have remained in them renders them rather self-centered and touchy. You quickly learn not to ask how they have managed to remake themselves so thoroughly, for you get the same stereotyped Pollyanna story. In the same way you quickly learn that it is not good manners to ask a Sabra where his folks came from. A Sabra is a Sabra—and everybody wants to behave like one.

Just at the outskirts of Tel Aviv, there are large patches of cultivated land where the soil has been almost literally man-made: swamps that were reclaimed by the pioneers, or rocky hills terraced with clods of earth the pioneers carried on their backs and shaped with their own hands. You see miles of orange groves, blossoming now because rocks have been carried away and water piped in.

A relentless energy went into this work. The men and women who did it were self-made agriculturists, for whom work on the land, no matter how hard and risky, was a means to an end. The end was that of giving to anti-Semitism an answer that would last for all time.

These men and women were Zionists. They believed that what two thousand years had done to people called Jews could be undone. Anti-Semitism, by shaking or breaking in many a land the ties that link the Jews to their fellow countrymen, set large groups of Jews once more on the move. For the Zionists, the move could lead only to Zion.

Zionism quickly learned how to shepherd the victims of anti-Semitism toward Zion. Sometimes it arrived too late, when only a remnant of what had been huge Jewish national communities was left to be rescued. It had little or no chance in those countries where anti-Semitism had been latent or mild and the roots of the Jews in the land of their birth could not be broken. The two extremes of massive annihilation and of peaceful, gradual assimilation left Zionism with a large intermediate zone where it could operate. It did operate—and the results can be seen in Israel.

Which did more to bring immigrants to Israel—Zionism or anti-Semitism? This question is not welcome to those men who laid down the foundations of Israel during the British mandate and who still lead it. One day I was telling a prominent Israeli leader that in his country I had realized, as never before, the horrid power of anti-Semitism in so many parts of the world. He answered angrily that in Israel I could see the evidence of a faith, not of a hatred. "Zionism and anti-Semitism," he said, "have nothing to do with each other."

I told him that after all there must have been some relation between the two, since Theodor Herzl, the founder of the Zionist movement, discovered the way to Zion at the time of the Dreyfus Affair, when he saw "Death to the Jews" scribbled over the walls of Paris. I couldn't have been any more wrong, I was told, and then I listened to an angry tirade, the gist of which was that Herzl had not discovered Zionism; he had been discovered by Zionism.

This attitude is representative of Israeli leadership today. The tendency is to date back the origin of Zionism—and therefore of Israel—to the series of events, approximately two thousand years ago, that forced the Jews to move away from the land then called Judaea. The Israeli leaders want to redress the wrongs the Jewish people suffered at the hands of Greek kinglets and Roman emperors.

These leaders are a formidable lot. With trenchant relentlessness, secretiveness, and unending inventiveness, they have gotten around all obstacles, and have made their interpretation of destiny into the destiny that rules the lives of nearly two million human beings—as of now.

Zionism, this man-made destiny for people called Jews, has succeeded in making Israel—a nation dedicated to what they call the Ingathering of the Exiles. The survivors of the German concentration camps came, masses of them, nearly 150,000 of them, people who absolutely and literally had nowhere else to go. Others came, particularly after the foundation of the state— people who though in no immediate danger in their native countries were induced to migrate to Israel by prospects of a new life or by old Messianic dreams.

Actually, it is quite difficult to single out among the immigrants those for whom life out of Israel had the bitterness of exile, the D.P.s who had nowhere else to go, and those who left their native lands following the inducements of Zionism. Moreover, there are countless subcategories, and there is not much use in categorizing. The pressure cooker is well sealed, and it works fast.

As far as the Israeli state is concerned, they are all "ingathered exiles," and they are all treated accordingly. One can still find in the immigrant camps, now scattered all over Israel, Moroccans or Algerians or Iraqis who left their countries when they were facing no other danger than the continuation of their immemorial misery. The North Africans have proved to be particularly hard to assimilate. Many of them who came to Israel seven or eight years ago have not yet mastered the Hebrew language—particularly the women. Many of the men hold no steady jobs. Some of them still complain of discrimination in favor of the European Jews. But they all have enough to eat, get medical care, and their children are treated like all other children in Israel. The schools, youth organizations, and the army see to it that every boy and girl has a chance to get an education and grow strong.

When you talk to these half-assimilated refugees from the ghettos of the Middle East, you still hear plenty of gripes, but few if any expressions of regret at having come. Perhaps, they say, it was a good idea, considering the trouble the Middle East is in right now. And then it is good to have gained some seniority as Israeli citizens. Many of them who for years have lived in temporary housing or in huts have been recently moved to better quarters. Quite a number of the old huts have been torn down, but luckily enough of them were left to be patched up in a hurry. For new immigrants are coming, practically every day.

From May 15 to December 31, 1948, 101,819 immigrants arrived. The following year, 239,076. Then immigration started going down until in 1953 it reached a low of 10,347. In fact, in that year a slightly larger number left Israel. In 1956, immigration reached 54,925. During the first two months of 1957, there were 12,839 immigrants, and the prospect is about one hundred thousand for the year.

Israelis constantly remind you of what this figure means: In terms of our own population, they say, it would be the equivalent of ten million new immigrants to the United States.

Yet the same people who give you these frightening figures are far from frightened. This is all as it should be. Isn't it for this that the state of Israel was born? The new immigrants, you are told, come from Egypt, North Africa, and eastern Europe.

You see them now, scattered all over the country from the moment they disembark, huddled in the huts from which the immigrants of previous waves have been vacated. Some look scared. There are so many things unfamiliar to them—Hebrew inscriptions, for instance, and all the evidences of a refugee camp's dreariness. But if anything, there are even too many representatives of organizations that want to help them. Social workers are busy questioning the immigrants and filling out long questionnaires.

It is obvious that quite a number of the immigrants need radical retraining. A professional interpreter from Egypt is told that his skill is of no use in Israel, where there are already too many people with a good command of all his languages. A man from eastern Europe seems to be greatly excited, and the commotion quickly spreads to his family and friends: They don't want to work or live where there is anything of a communal nature—certainly not in a kibbutz and not even on a co-operative farm. Communism has made them intractable individualists.

You don't know whether you feel more sorry for the immigrants, those people whose only guilt is their race, or for the social workers who have to play God to all these pitiful human beings.

Part of what you see is the usual routinized tragedy of all refugee camps. In Israel, however, one thing is unique: These people are not refugees, not immigrants; they are all "ingathered exiles." No matter whether they are Zionists who at long last reach the country of their dream or Zionists by default, they are all Israelis from the moment they land. Indeed, their birth entitled them to Israeli citizenship. The Israeli political parties have been competing for their vote ever since their journey to Israel started.

I could not help being shaken by the fantastic disproportions between that majestic phrase—"the Ingathering of the Exiles"—and the human beings before my eyes to whom it is applied.

Those people, aside from getting settled in a new land, have to erase two thousand years of history. The leaders of the state of Israel, for that matter all those who have made themselves into Israelis, are in deadly earnest when they welcome the new immigrant with that majestic phrase. The newcomers will be driven hard, soon will start driving themselves hard, so that some time they can start feeling that they have come home after an exile of two thousand years.

Or, if not they, their children.

The Israeli declaration of independence says it: "The State of Israel will be open to the immigration of Jews from all countries of their dispersion."

During the first three or four years this law was lived up to in the most literal sense, with no exception on grounds of age or sickness or previous record. Israel has been paying very dearly for those first few years of thoroughly unselective immigration.

Now, while the general principle remains in full force, immigration of people who are hopelessly sick or insane or have no way of becoming self-supporting is somehow discouraged. To a limited extent, the discouraging is done by the Israeli consulates abroad, and more directly by the Jewish Agency, which pays the passage and provides assistance for the immigrants.

Yet the Israeli authorities usually become self-conscious and evasive when you ask them about the criteria of selectivity—as if there were something both illegal and immoral in keeping away any Jew who wants to come to Israel.

There are still situations where immigration is perforce entirely unselective, as when large numbers of Jews are suddenly expelled from a country—Egypt's recent action is an instance.

Such situations and, in general, the current wave of immigration find Israeli leaders both concerned and prepared. There is a gleam of pride in their eyes when they talk to you about the prospects of new immigration. Or I should say a gleam of fanaticism.

The discussions about immigration are the most unforgettable among the many I had in Israel, for invariably, even among the most congenial friends, at a certain moment I saw that gleam of fanaticism. I learned to expect it, and it never failed. Invariably it also happened that when they asked me, "Where else could they go?" I had no answer. The fanatics were right.

Giants in the Earth

On my first morning, I took a drive through Tel Aviv to get a first feel of that singularly unplanned and oppressively unattractive city. It was quite clear that it just grew, with two or three main streets and without a center to which its growth could be anchored. It must have taken some effort, I thought, to build such an ugly city on such a beautiful Mediterranean coastline. But then I remembered that frenetic improvisation is evidenced in the way many other Mediterranean cities have grown—Naples included. On the outskirts, the long rows of tin and wooden shacks, with washing hanging out in the wind and swarms of poorly dressed children—all that was thoroughly Mediterranean.

I inquired about some fairly well-built apartment houses. They belong to a political party, I was told. That was my first jolt. "Are political parties in the housing business?" I asked. The answer was that they all were. Some days later, talking to a man prominent in Mapai, the right-wing socialist party and the most powerful in the nation, I asked whether Mapai too has its housing projects. "Mapai has none," I was told. The same day, I put the question to somebody else: "Is Mapai in the housing business?" The answer was "yes and no." I was to hear that answer many times during my stay in Israel.

In Israel political parties either own or control, directly or indirectly, housing projects and assorted businesses that over here could not possibly be considered as integral parts of a political machine. But then over here the organization of party politics, particularly on the national level, is a desultory affair. In Europe things are already different, since a political party, if it is to carry any weight, must have a nation-wide network of full-time paid party workers. Israel is like Europe, only much more so. For in Israel, political parties, to stay alive, must deliver something concrete, aside from patronage, to the party faithful.

There was a time when the Jewish political parties had their own school systems and even their own armies. Since the formation of the state, the army belongs to the nation, and the schools can, at the utmost, be controlled or influenced by parties—particularly by religious ones. Still, the management of kibbutzim, co-operatives, and other business activities is the object of lively party competition. Each party must offer some measure of social assistance to its members, and therefore must have in its coffers more funds than the membership dues can contribute.

Having learned this much about the parties, I started to inquire about the party label not only of individuals and municipalities but also of factories, kibbutzim, co-operatives, local and national public services, and so on. I got to know a number of things. One was that all Israeli parties, officially or unofficially, have their network of business establishments and public services for the benefit of the faithful. Second, I did not hear of any politician who had got fat at the expense of the party faithful or the public at large: Austerity is still the rule in Israeli public life. Third, I learned that while the struggle between parties can be exceedingly bitter when it comes to conquering the management of a kibbutz or a branch of local government, on the national level the fight is not too venomous, and is seldom waged on basic issues.

As all the parties are made more or less of the same stuff and indulge in the same practices, they have a great deal to keep silent about. Moreover, they are all minority parties and their interests, of necessity, become interrelated and interdependent. Even the Herut, which is not in coalition with any party at any level, is not very obstreperous.

The parties in Israel, I came to realize, are not primarily designed to provide the voters with alternative sets of leaders for local and national government. Rather each one of them is a little government in being. In some ways they are closer to our states than to our parties, and the very active defense of party rights is the Israeli equivalent of our perennial fight for states' rights.

The national government, which is only nine years old, has taken over all those functions that could not possibly be left to parties without courting chaos—like defense, national finances, and foreign relations. On this last point, however, there is a zone of "yes and no," for each party cultivates its friends abroad.

The singular cohesiveness of each party structure and the essential similarity among these structures give the state, as of now, a somewhat federal nature. Some of the most wide-awake national leaders are not too happy about this state of affairs. Ben Gurion himself is credited with having frequently warned against the dangers of "party totalitarianism." Indeed, he went so far as to propose the abolition of proportional representation. He wants to have the politicians freer of their party's bureaucracy and more responsible to new geographic constituencies. Should he have his way, the present party system would be shaken to its foundations, and the reputation Ben Gurion has already gained as a founder of the new Israel would be further enhanced by that of a miracle maker.

While we wait for the miracle it is only fair to recognize that the peculiar party system still prevailing in that peculiar country has some positive things to its credit. It has not prevented sizable shifts of popular opinion, as the last elections proved, when Mapai, Ben Gurion's party, received 32.2 per cent of the popular vote, as compared to 37.3 per cent in the previous election. Moreover, the party system has contributed to the stability of the country by establishing a multiple system of ties: The ties of the citizen with his party and of the parties among themselves have tightened the ties between the citizens and their state. With the single exception of the insignificant Communist Party, all parties are intensely patriotic and bring their pressures to bear on the new immigrant in order to strengthen his will to become a full-fledged Israeli.

The political parties are by no means the only nuclei of semi-governmental power, nor are they the only states in being to be found in the state of Israel today. All these nuclei of power—political parties included—have been deliberately, assiduously constructed by that extraordinary group of men and women who made the last half century of what has now become Israeli history. There is no way of understanding what has been going on in the nine years since the state was founded unless we focus our attention on what Zionist leaders did in Palestine during the four previous decades—and particularly the last two.

These men and women wanted a Jewish state in Palestine, and everything they did, no matter how called or disguised, was aimed at making the state inevitable. At first during the Ottoman rule, later with vastly increased vigor under the British mandate which recognized the establishment of a Jewish national home, every Zionist undertaking in Palestine was conceived and carried out as a center of political power.

Or maybe one can say of sovereign power. This was eminently the case with the kibbutzim. Each of these was much more than a farming unit designed to retrain Jews in the cultivation of the land. They were rural city-states, complete with their own system of self-government and of education, and with bastions that, if not visible, were certainly well guarded. A communal way of life, socialist ideologies apart, was mandatory for these tiny city-states. The pioneers in the kibbutzim, men and women, had no time for frills or privacy. They had to cultivate the land, to remake themselves, and to defend their ramparts.

It was during the British mandate that the Histadrut was founded. In 1920, when it was established, it had less than five thousand members, and its name in English was General Federation of Jewish Labor. Actually, trade-unionism played about the same role in the Histadrut as did production of agricultural commodities in the kibbutzim. Its aim was statehood.

The Histadrut had to fight at first against Jewish employers, who preferred the cheaper Arab labor. Once that hurdle was cleared, it started creating revenue-producing businesses that could keep its members at work. It succeeded thanks to the austerity of the workers themselves and to contributions from abroad. Labor and foreign contributions created capital that could be reinvested to create more labor.

For the most part, the leaders of Histadrut were socialists from eastern Europe. Quite a few called themselves Marxists, while some of them were followers of French syndicalism. But the theories of Marx or of Sorel or of Proudhon, no matter how feverishly discussed in the Histadrut's bull sessions, were somewhat incongruous, and certainly rather difficult to carry through. For there was not a state to be conquered, but a state to be made. The same applied to capital: The Histadrut had to create it.

The so-called General Federation of Jewish Labor had to take

care of more than wages and conditions of employment. It had to
extend its assistance to meet all the worker's needs—whether he
happened to be a wage earner of a capitalistic entrepreneur or,
for that matter, of the Histadrut. This meant medical, political,
and spiritual assistance. Membership in the Histadrut became
citizenship in a workers' welfare state. The unofficial, somewhat
underground government of the Histadrut had also to take care
of foreign affairs: It needed financial assistance from non-Pales-
tinian Jews, and it had to do its share in taking care of the immigrants who, lawfully or unlawfully, were coming into
Palestine.

Finally, the Histadrut had to take care of fighting—and not just
around the bargaining table. It had very much to do with the
Haganah, the secret army of the not yet born Jewish state. Most
of the Histadrut's activities grew one on top of the other, and
one because of the other. During the years of the British mandate
it had to act somewhat secretly and without too much publicity
as to aims, costs, and results.

At the beginning of the Second World War, that so-called federation of labor had under its wing not only a group of federated
trade unions but also a health service for all its members—
including those who were self-employed—a central co-operative
marketing society, fishing settlements, the largest contracting
firm in the Middle East, an educational system, banks, credit
corporations, insurance funds, et cetera. The "et cetera" should
be underlined, for it included, among other things, a private
system of justice for the settlement of disputes among Histadrut
members, who did not like to bring their litigation to regular
courts.

Even the most pro-Zionist among the British leaders could not
help recognizing that there was something quite peculiar about
Histadrut—something very much like a state. Yet even today you
find Israeli leaders who still bristle with anger when they
remember that in 1930 Sidney Webb, by that time Lord Passfield
—that British imperialist, they call him—had the nerve to write
in a British White Paper that the Histadrut was a state within
the state. Incidentally, this definition was not too appropriate con-

sidering that under the British mandate Palestine was not much of a state.

When war came, however, the Histadrut's giant contracting firm, Solel Boneh, was of considerable help to the British government. It undertook large, dangerous public works in Iran, Iraq, Cyprus, in fact all through the Middle East. When Rommel was on the rampage and nearly broke through at El Alamein, Solel Boneh was in Egypt building fortifications very close to the fighting line. During the war, the underground soldiers of the Haganah came out into the open and joined up with the British Army. A strong unit was formed, the Jewish Brigade, that fought well for the liberation of Italy.

Another organization with rather transparently sovereign attributes was working in Palestine: the Jewish Agency. But the Agency was never frowned upon by the British, who considered it as the responsible representative of world Jewry. The Agency came into existence in 1929 as a result of an agreement between Zionist and not-so-Zionist Jews all over the world, and its principal aim, according to the 1937 Royal Commission on Palestine, was "to secure the admission into Palestine of as many Jews as the country can absorb from the economic point of view." This was quite a big order and left considerable room for bargaining with the British on the "economic point of view." The Agency concerned itself with industrial and town development, and made its influence felt on many issues, including tariff protection. "In fact," the Royal Commission stated, "there is no branch of the Administration with which the Agency does not concern itself. . . . Speaking generally, it may be said that the Jewish Agency has used to the fullest extent the position conferred on it by the Mandate. In the course of time it has created a complete administrative apparatus. This powerful and efficient organization amounts, in fact, to a Government existing side by side with the Mandatory Government."

All in all, thanks to the work done by the Histadrut, by the Agency, by the pioneers in the kibbutzim and in the co-operatives, by private capitalists and by philanthropists, the economic growth of Jewish Palestine proved a momentous achievement.

Between 1922 and 1947, the number of factories increased more than ninefold, from 270 to 2,445. There were 71 Jewish settlements in 1922, covering a total of 1.4 million acres. In 1945, the settlements were 265, and the acreage 2.8 million. The Jewish population in Palestine was 83,790 in 1922 and 563,829 in 1945.

Figures, however, can give only an inaccurate indication of the growth in power. The same men had been directing the growth of all the centers of self-regulating, self-expanding power, and the men at the top, the leaders of Zionism, never had any doubt about the nature and the goal of the power they had tirelessly contributed to generate. The power they always wanted for Jewish Palestine was political, the goal was sovereignty.

The two main centers of power, of course, were the Histadrut and the Agency. In 1933, Ben Gurion, who had been until then one of the guiding spirits of Histadrut, moved to the Agency, although he never ceased to concern himself with the Histadrut. A game of musical chairs started between the top men of the two organizations.

On May 14, 1948, Jewish Palestine achieved sovereignty, and Israel was born.

A State In the Making

In 1957, all the centers of self-regulating authority whose combined pressures brought the state into being in 1948—political parties, Histadrut, Agency, kibbutzim—all are still in existence. The power of each of them and the balance of forces among them has, to be sure, greatly changed, for since 1948 there has been a national government that has had its capacity to rule tested by two wars, one in 1948-1949, the other in the fall of 1956.

The political relevance of the kibbutzim has greatly diminished. The authority of the national government, with its 49,000 civilian employees, has established itself in the fields of defense, foreign policy, national taxation and expenditures, education— briefly, in all areas a western state takes under its formal jurisdiction. Still, this Israeli state that has been since its inception under socialist leadership, and is dedicated to the austere ideal of the welfare state, has put itself in charge of austerity and has left most of the welfare activities and the socialized enterprises to the Histadrut. The Histadrut is still entrusted with extraordinarily varied functions in Israel and abroad, but not all citizens belong to it. It is not the state, but neither is it under it.

The state, as its declaration of independence formally proclaims, is dedicated to the Ingathering of the Exiles, but it has delegated a large share of the "ingathering" to the Agency. True, the state could scarcely do otherwise, since the Agency is uniquely equipped to bring in from all over the world not only "ingathereds" but also the means for their migration and succor. Still, the state contributes heavily to make the immigrants into gainfully employed, self-supporting citizens. The Histadrut itself is largely dedicated to the same purpose.

Three interlocking bureaucracies are at work. A measure of unity is provided at the upper layers by a flourish of co-ordinating committees. Israel must be a dreamland for co-ordinators and a nightmare for accountants.

Planners, too, both indigenous and imported from abroad, have been hard at work on Israel's economic problems, even before the state was born. One of the difficulties I had to overcome when I was in Israel was to reconcile all the planning I was being told about with all the improvisations that were pointed out to me.

Shortly after I arrived I was taken, like every visitor, to see Operation Lachish. The Lachish settlement project was officially launched in May, 1955. The idea, I was told, had been Ben Gurion's, at the time when he had retired from the government and was living in a remote desert kibbutz. At present, it is well beyond the blueprint stage, and one can see how the area is being developed into a single economic unit. It is designed to be an integrated agricultural and industrial community, with scattered urban hubs where all the essential administrative, shopping, and schooling facilities are to be found. There have been many such experiments all over the world in what may be called rural urbanism, or balanced development of agricultural and industrial resources.

I greatly admired Ben Gurion's inspiration, the planners who had brought it to the blueprint stage, and the Jewish Agency, which together with the Ministry of Agriculture had provided the means. But I could not help asking how come it had taken the Israeli leaders so long to get around to the Lachish idea. I put this question to five or six people, and I got five or six different answers, ranging from lack of available water to lack of funds.

Then it occured to me that one of the reasons might have been the particular mystical mood prevailing in Israel after 1948. It took some time for the old resistance leaders to realize that the new immigrants were something quite different from the pioneers they themselves had been. The ideas of land and home had still a magic power. Of course, they thought, "ingathered exiles" would naturally and happily come to live in houses provided for them in the land of their forefathers and would happily cultivate that land. The magic did not always work and many of the houses remained empty. It was at that point that planning of the Lachish type had to be thought out. But the curious interplay between planning and improvisation goes on. In people of great faith, belief in magic dies hard.

The Private Governments

One frequently hears in Israel that democracy and feudalism somehow manage to live side by side. All the basic democratic freedoms are there: The press enjoys great freedom, the people vote and talk as they please, the courts protect the citizen's rights. On these three scores I heard few if any dissenting opinions. Yet people whom I had reason to trust gave me persuasive bills of particulars proving that a number of private governments or feudal baronies share with the national government the power of running the nation's affairs.

I must also add that some of the critics of Israeli affairs were men high in the nation's councils. There are quite a number of such men, called by the rather trite name Young Turks. Some of them are in the Knesset and in the very party of Ben Gurion, Mapai. These men do not only talk. Respect for the Great Old Man may sometimes make them cautious, but they are certainly alert and active.

When I inquired how the various baronies happened to be

carved out, the answer was nearly invariably the same: They date from the time of the resistance, when the various segments of the Israeli state were shaped and assembled underground. The coagulation of existing interests that may or may not be parasitical today, the ingrained habits that may not make for efficiency or order, are all left over from the hard, sometimes heroic struggle at the time of the mandate. The anomalies of today have, if not their justification, their origin in great services rendered in the past.

Take the Haifa longshoremen, for instance. They seem to be a rather aggressive breed, ready to muscle in wherever their bosses think their strong-arm arguments may be persuasive. Yet it was by using strong-arm methods that the longshoremen gained their stronghold on the waterfront, at the time the British wanted to keep illegal immigration away from the shores of Israel.

A co-operative organization for the distribution and marketing of food, you are told, has succeeded in preventing the establishment of supermarkets that could substantially lower the cost of staple foods. But you also hear that the same organization did yeoman work at the time of the war of liberation in providing people with enough food to keep alive.

The waving of bloody shirts seems to be a fairly well-established practice, and sometimes the stain may not stand chemical analysis. But much more frequently the evidences of real blood are unmistakable.

From the moment the state of Israel was born it had to carry a heavy burden of past achievements and of vested interests. Or perhaps one can say of that birthday what can be said of a solemn wedding which makes unobjectionably legitimate a long, successful, and prolific common-law ménage. The Israelis are right to celebrate the anniversary of May 14, 1948, with all pomp and ceremony. But the wisest among them know it well: Their state was in existence long before that date and, as of now, is still in the making.

This does not mean that there is anything tentative or weak about this state or that it is a house divided against itself. But it does mean that the structure of the state is being built from the roof down and from the foundation up. People have different ideas as to the shape of the intermediate floors, or of the use that can be made of the superabundant cornerstones.

The state, as it has been frequently proclaimed, is a socialist one. Some of the most prominent among its leaders at the time it was founded were bold enough to announce that complete socialism—whatever this may mean—was going to come in a matter of months.

Certainly the adherence to rigorous dogmas of socialist austerity has imposed a number of shackles on the Israeli economy. The tax structure, which is a complicated mixture of direct and indirect levies, is exceedingly heavy. It is, so I heard, an exceptionally crude and inelastic system that discourages saving and the accumulations of private capital. That complaint I have heard before in a few other countries.

Israeli authorities are proud of the small difference that exists between the lowest and the highest rates of pay. They talked about a ratio of four to one, but I found out that the ratio between professionals and laborers is less than two to one.

According to the July, 1956, statistics of the Bank of Israel, the daily pay of an unskilled agricultural worker in Israeli pounds is 6.2, of a civil servant 7.7, and of a highly skilled construction worker 10.3. This principle has been followed with uncomfortable consistency—uncomfortable particularly for the salaried classes. Some categories of wage earners, like the longshoremen in Haifa and the bus drivers all over the country, have managed to go higher than the average for skilled workers. Those on the high echelons of the three main bureaucracies are helped, it is said, by expense accounts and by the time-honored habit of wearing several hats. The professional classes, however—teachers, doctors, and the like—have been very hard hit. There was a strike of the intellectuals last year, but whatever the hard-pressed intellectuals have gained out of it has been lost by the increased cost of living.

The government is by no means alone in fostering social equalitarianism and economic austerity. The Histadrut, in spite of the fact that it is the biggest employer of labor, and sometimes finds itself in the embarrassing predicament of having to break the strikes of its own employees, is still primarily concerned with the welfare and job security of the wage earners. The parties that make up the government harbor different interpretations of the socialist idea, but are united in fostering socialism. And here we go back to the plurality of centers of power, and to what is called the Israeli feudal system.

Having frequently written on our own American feudal system and on the private governments of Big Capital, Big Labor, and great independent authorities, I was keenly interested in finding out what kind of feudalism, if any, had grown up in Israel. The Israeli variety, I quickly came to learn, is well ahead of ours and is endowed with peculiar features of its own. The major centers of self-regulating authority are equally anxious to maintain their own sphere of jurisdiction and to go into partnership with each other and with the government. Partnership was one of the pet ideas of the first Eisenhower administration. The advocates of that idea should go to Israel, where partnership is running riot.

Israeli capitalism, too, has caught up with the trend. The habit of partnership between business concerns and the Histadrut is widespread, although the interpretation of what makes for the singular habit are at a great variance. Some say that the capitalists cannot help it and that partnership is the price they have to pay for labor peace. Histadrut sources tell you that they are sick of collecting lame ducks, and that for every business concern they go into partnership with, they turn down ten. The same goes for the concerns that are begging to be taken over by the Histadrut. Israeli capitalists don't care much for long-range, productive ventures, since loans and assorted other investments can bring in profits of twenty-five per cent or more.

Independent critics both of the Histadrut and of capitalistic habits tell you that the reason for the partnership arrangements is that the employees gain higher wages plus unmolested featherbedding, and that the employer is guaranteed against the danger of bankruptcy. As to business concerns taken over by the Histadrut—well, it is said, that's just the European habit of socializing losses.

Relations between the Histadrut and the manufacturers' association are supposed to be quite chummy. A recent strike in Haifa attracted wide national attention because the head of a large company with seventeen hundred employees refused to follow the practices of the manufacturers' association and stood firm against the Histadrut.

Yet one must think twice before passing judgment on that extraordinary Israeli capital-labor-welfare combine that is the Histadrut. There is no doubt that the interests of the workers are its overriding concern. Its leaders are still ruggedly labor people. The most controversial among them are frequently accused of recklessly seeking power. But even their critics admit that those American labor chiefs who lately became infamous as seekers after personal enrichment have no counterpart in Israel.

The Histadrut is tireless in its efforts to keep workers on payrolls and to see to it that the unemployed get jobs. This may not always coincide with the interests of the national economy. It may ultimately not even coincide with the interests of the workers. But certainly this is the same line of action the Histadrut has followed ever since the days of old: It wants to take care of all sides of the workers' lives as best it can and as it sees fit. True, it is acquiring more power than its top men can handle, but it is not its fault if it was already powerful and far-flung to start with, when the new state came into existence.

In the same spirit, driven by the same motives, the Histadrut is in partnership with the government in many projects of agricultural development and urban planning that have to do with the absorption of immigrants into the labor force. So is the Jewish Agency. And the political parties push hard in the same direction.

This state in the making is today a system of concurrent governments, or concurrent federations. It may not be a particularly efficient or rational system but it works, and the nation is, if anything, even too tightly held together.

The government could certainly take over some of the activities that are at present run by the Histadrut—particularly, health insurance. In due time it may. Or the government might take over some of the Histadrut's deficit-laden business enterprises or holding companies. In fact, some of the Histadrut's leaders seem to be anxious to have this happen. Should it happen, the government would be enriched with a whole stable of Trojan horses.

But there is no great danger that things will move in this direction too fast. Old habits die hard. When I was in Israel I was told by any number of people in positions of importance that the government had taken over the labor exchanges, or was going to—it never was quite clear in my mind. Somebody else told me that it would not make much difference anyway, since the same Histadrut people would have gone on running the labor exchanges under government auspices. Only later did I learn that while the discussion about the transfer had been going on for a long time, the law had not yet been passed by the Knesset.

Moreover, one should never forget what the load of new immigrants—most of them unskilled or in need of retraining—means. It certainly does not make for a more functional reorganization of the state and of its various dependent or independent branches. It does make for slow motion in the process of state building.

Is Israel a viable state? This question is frequently—too frequently—asked in this country and elsewhere. I never could understand exactly what it means, for if a state to be viable has to be solvent, with a sound balance of trade and a balanced budget, then how many of the new ones that have come into existence since the end of the war, or indeed how many of the old ones, can be considered viable? To be sure, the economic difficulties of Israel are of a very serious nature. Exports have increased from $29.7 million in 1949 to $108 million in 1956, but as of last year imports amounted to $364 million.

An equally serious fact is the maldistribution of the working population in Israel: Less than half the national income is earned by workers employed in agriculture and industry. In Israel, it's not automation that makes for the large percentage of the working population that is not engaged in the production of goods.

Ben Gurion is reputed to have said that the laws of economics do not apply to Israel. Maybe this is not among his most original statements, for I wonder whether these laws apply even in our country. Certainly our farming population is well sheltered from them.

As far as Israel is concerned, its people have well proved their will and their capacity to do the utmost with the manpower and the resources they have. Moreover, no matter what responsibility Zionism and anti-Semitism may share for having brought the Israeli state into existence, certainly that state deserves, to say the least, the support of all civilized nations. No other sustained effort has ever been made in history to give a new chance to the victims of a most abominable persecution.

Assistance to Israel, at least on the present scale, may not be required for too long. A new generation is growing up there— a generation that is fiercely independent, infinitely less burdened by memories of past achievement or of past glories. It is only when this generation takes over that the work of state-making can be finished, for its men and women will not suffer like their fathers the tortures of divided allegiances. They will not have to decide whether their loyalty goes first to the state they have brought into being or to the erstwhile underground in which they worked so hard to make the coming of the state inevitable.

The men and women of the old generation, and above all their leaders, should be proud of what they have achieved. Their state is probably not the tidiest in existence. Some of its practices may be against the standards of democratic behavior, just as they may violate some of the so-called laws of economics. But that state of theirs has a superabundance of energy.

In fact, its leaders could afford to be somewhat more relaxed, less eager to gain universal approval for what they have done. Largely thanks to them, there is no longer any doubt that Israel is here to stay. Or maybe what seems to be worrying them and sometimes making them act as if they were insecure is that they are still not clear in their minds about what Israel is here for.

Quo Vadis, Israel?

There are those in Israel who date the origin of their state back to the day when God made his compact with Abraham. There are those who think the state had its start when, at the beginning of the century, the second wave of Jewish immigrants settled in the Holy Land. And there are those who think Israel was born on Independence Day—May 14, 1948.

Ben Gurion belongs to all these three groups—and to many more. Ben Gurion is a socialist and a nationalist. He is also a man who practiced his socialism as a tradeunion leader, worked prodigiously for the establishment of Israel, and has tried to bridge the gap of two thousand years and find in the Old Testament the rightful title for what he has done as a statesman and a politician.

Yet overwhelmingly absorbed as he is in the intricacies of foreign affairs and defense, he still has an uncanny sensitivity to what's wrong with his nation. He still acts as the spokesman for the Biblical past, for the makers of the new Israel, and for the young Sabra generation. But he is not a Sabra and he is not young.

The fact that he is not young is evidenced not only by the halo of white hair and by the visible burden of his years—seventy-one—but by his growing tendency to withdraw more and more from the present and from his own personal past into the great old book—the Bible. Perhaps it is modesty that leads him to find only one cause for his own and for his nation's achievements. That cause is in The Book. In The Book is a power no human will can thwart, and that has made inevitable everything that has happened to Israel during his stewardship—like the rebirth of the Hebrew language, the Ingathering of the Exiles, and the victories of the Israeli army.

There is something unique in this man. Nowhere else but in Jerusalem can one find the extraordinarily active head of a government willing to plunge at the slightest provocation into a long discourse on the relationship between matter and spirit, and on the perception we mortals have of God.

But Ben Gurion does not happen to be the head of all those who believe in God and are searching after God. He is the leader of a small nation, glorious to be sure, but very much in need of a somewhat narrower definition of its identity.

Yet Ben Gurion cannot think of Israel in any other terms than those of Biblical eternity. Israel for him is a nation based on a national faith; but this goes beyond sheer nationalism into a realm whose definition can be found in The Book. Israel is a culture, but not just a culture. It is an ideal of social justice that goes well beyond Marxism or the doctrine of any social reformer. The original source and the ultimate destination of all these "beyonds" is, of course, The Book.

To many a visitor this passionate inclination on the part of the prime minister to refer everything to The Book leads to the conclusion that they have been admitted to the presence of the latest Jewish prophet. This is quite strange, considering that the prophets might have excelled in foreseeing things to come but did not much care for statesmanship or politics. But proofs of Ben Gurion's statesmanship are to be seen all over Israel, and his politician's skill can be easily detected even in his uncanny ability to keep away from issues he doesn't want to talk about— by plunging into issues related to The Book.

Yet with most of the people who have had the privilege of talking to him his Biblical discourses have gone over quite well. In my own case, I was somewhat bewildered. I have the greatest respect for the man, but I like my Bible straight.

The Great Old Man is certainly the most representative leader of his country in all respects but one: his attitude toward the Bible. In Israel today, while the most orthodox and extreme forms of Judaism are to be found, for a very large number of people, particularly young people, religion plays a rather limited role—or no role at all.

There is, of course, in the heart of Jerusalem that much-described center of tourist attraction called Mea Shaarim. The approximately three thousand super-orthodox Jews who live there refuse to recognize the state of Israel. These people see no reason why there should be a Jewish government, with police and soldiers and tax officials—a government like any other government that, in their opinion, defiles the language of the Holy Scriptures by making it into everyday language.

The men and women of Mea Shaarim speak Yiddish, pray in Hebrew, and don't go into the army. The men, most of them with long beards and earlocks, wear black and brown cassocks of the Polish or Lithuanian ghettos; the women long, dark woolen stockings, the shaven heads of the married women always carefully covered. The men spend most of their time praying in the synagogues.

In Jerusalem but not in Mea Shaarim, I met a man who represents in purest form the spirit of Mea Shaarim, but expresses it in terms of western, twentieth-century thinking. I had known him in Europe as a leader of Zionism, but in Jerusalem he wasn't a Zionist any longer. He was just an inhabitant of Israel, too removed from the Israel state even to denounce it. I could guess his thought from the little he said, and from the despair I could read in his eyes. Yet he did not talk like a man who is hopeless for, according to his faith, a Jew is not allowed to be hopeless.

He thought, I gathered, that the Jewish people in Israel were no longer living up to the compact God had made with the sons of Abraham. In the old land of Judea all the idols that keep the world divided and enslaved are now being worshiped—like nationalism and socialism and statism, and all the other beastly isms. How could God rescue the people He had chosen among all others, once they turned out to be just like all the others? And how then could mankind be saved?

That man, ever since I had known him had been the living evidence of how crushing are the outward and inward commitments of the Jewish faith. He had lived that faith to perfection. Now he was—in Jerusalem—not hopeless and not even bitter, but just alone, unspeakably alone.

Ben Gurion and all the literal and not-so-literal believers in the Old Testament are not the only ones in Israel who think the new nation stems from The Book and lives—or should live—by it. But the Old Testament, in all its majesty and glory, is an ancient book, where quite a number of layers of Jewish history can be found. To which of these layers can the new state relate itself, so as to find there both its origin and its guidance or, in the truest sense of the term, its foundation?

This is one of the reasons why archaeology has become the craze in Israel. Yigael Yadin, the man who was the chief of operations during the war of liberation in 1948 and 1949, is now

Lecturer in Archaeology at the Hebrew University of Jerusalem. He has become the greatest Israeli authority on the Dead Sea scrolls.

The Israelis, literally, have fallen in love with their soil. They, or their fathers, have toiled on it. But this is not enough. They are searching for the roots that have been broken centuries ago. Can the new nation grow closer to these roots, can it become linked to them?

The Dead Sea scrolls have opened new vistas to the Israelis in search of their antiquity. Biblical scholars have been busy for years interpreting the scrolls or disputing about them. For the Israelis, what seems to be most important is the information the scrolls provide on the Essenes, a pre-Christian and near-Christian Jewish sect. This evidence, in turn, seems to prove how completely early Christian thought and practices derive from Jewish thinking, with little or no contribution from Hellenistic sources.

Even the most self-controlled among the professional or amateur Dead Sea scrolls experts can scarcely restrain their fervor when they tell you about the new evidences that have now come to light about the Essenes. It is proved now, they tell you, that Christianity was not a new departure from Judaism and that Christ was representative of a religious trend, not its originator.

There were occasions when, in talking to Israeli philosophers as well as scrolls experts, I somehow sensed an eagerness to accentuate the Jewishness of Christ, to reduce Him to the level of one of the many Jewish prophets and, in that way, to get close to Him. It was as if they were trying to recapture Christ and to find in Christ a new link both with their past and with the outside world. The urge to "ingather" in Israel all the exiles may reach very far into the past. "The first centuries of Christianity are part of our history," an old Israeli scholar told me.

The Young Army

At the other extreme, there are those who show very little concern with history or religion, and no interest in bridging the two-thousand-year gap. Most of these people, of course, are Sabras. The talk about the Sabras creates about as much excitement in Israel as the discussion about the time when Christianity branched off.

A great deal has been written, and not only in Israel, about the stolid, unintellectual, un-neurotic quality of the Sabras—the first kind of Jews, so it seems, who can afford not to be too intelligent. Once I was talking to an eminent psychoanalyst, who had, he said, too many patients, too many people in need of readjustment. I told him not to worry, for the Sabras would certainly force him into a sort of technological unemployment. "Oh, no," he answered, "quite a number of my patients are Sabras." He knew what I had in mind, smiled, and said, "You know, every situation creates its own neurosis."

Another day I was talking to a young Sabra who happens to be a high officer in the army, and the conversation turned to that perennial theme: Where will the Sabra generation go? That young man was precise in his talk, and unverbose. His face was deeply tanned, as is so frequently the case with army people, and most of the time expressionless. Only occasionally his thin lips would curl in a restrained and disciplined smile, and his extraordinarily luminous eyes would flash. "Perhaps," he told me, "we Sabras will turn out to be a breed of men a bit closer to the Gentiles. Ours is a durable race."

Of course we came to talk about the Arabs. "There is a new Moslem upsurge, and the West is not aware of it," he said. "There have been several other upsurges like this that have been beaten down or coalesced. We know the Arabs. We are skin to skin with them. We don't get alarmed, we don't waste our energies. It will be all right." Then he proceeded, his eyes flashing, "We Israelis are holding the outpost of western civilization. If you want, you may call it of Christian civilization."

That amazing young army, where even the highest officers are in their middle thirties, is the best thing that Israel has produced. There are no dissenting voices among foreign observers: Israeli politics may be an extraordinarily complex thing, and the state is still in the making. But the army is made.

It's a people's army, always ready to go to work wherever and whenever the citizens—and particularly the new ones—can be helped by the example of spontaneous and inventive teamwork. This example the army is invariably happy to offer, no matter whether the obstacles come from the vagaries of nature or from incompatibilities among people of different national origins.

Israeli soldiers, men and women, can march smartly in a parade, but one could never accuse them of being overaddicted to military polish. Some of the pictures I saw of the Sinai campaign made me think that Bill Mauldin's characters, Willie and Joe, had joined the Israeli army. Sometimes, looking at the officers, I thought that by some miracle Willie and Joe had got some brass.

As in the case of every resistance movement that has come to power, some of the men at the head may have become somewhat flabby. But not the army. The Haganah could never be disbanded. The muscles could never become flabby, for Israel has never had peace. Certainly, if the army of today is the Israel of tomorrow, the nation has nothing to fear.

It is horrid to think of that country and of that region that cannot have peace. This feeling is particularly unbearable in Jerusalem.

There is a belt of green that divides the city between the Israeli and the Jordanian section. From the Israeli side, early in the morning, you hear the Christian bells and the crowing of the cocks from the rural belt—the no man's land that is in the heart of Jerusalem. There is a sense of unearthly peace, and you forget that on both sides of the rural belt there are armed men permanently on guard.

Yet it is difficult to keep one's mind on the unending, even if not shooting, war. The landscape of that city has a character of sublimity, and sometimes one wants to forget its history, the names of some of those hills, or of the few man-made landmarks, for fear of being hypnotized by the past. Particularly toward sunset the extraordinarily pure light of the sky seems to bless the earth.

But, when the thought of the unending war comes back, and you think of the Arabs who have been pushed away and of the Israelis who have struggled so hard to remake themselves and their country, then the prospect of this thing going on and on becomes truly unbearable.

Perhaps the tide has already turned. That vanguard of the West, Israel, as definitely unwilling to be cut off from the whole East—Near, Middle, and Far. Israeli diplomatic and commercial envoys are actively engaged in seeking trade and fostering friendly relations with African and Asian countries.

The Sinai campaign proved, first of all, that the Israeli army could wage a perfect, one could almost say a classic, limited war. Since Nasser did not bomb any Israeli city, neither did Dayan bomb Egypt. Ben Gurion did not ask for Nasser's unconditional surrender. At the same time, the Sinai campaign proved how concerned the whole world is with the Arab-Israeli conflict. New military campaigns or new harassments have become rather unlikely.

The prospect is for less tension on the Arab as well as on the Israeli side. The new Sabra generation, according to all evidence, seems to be infinitely more poised, at peace with itself than that of its predecessors. In fact, I was told that there is a trend among young people to debunk a lot of old dogmas or slogans—including the "Ingathering of the Exiles."

On these and on many other subjects—indeed, every time I needed help in understanding Israeli matters—I wished Chaim Weizmann had been still alive. Truly, I felt his absence as a personal loss. Quietly, unrhetorically, he had managed to bridge the two-thousand-year chasm and could look far beyond it, for he had the profundity of the scholar and the imagination of a great scientist. He is buried now in the ground where the institute he created stands—one of the greatest and freest centers of scientific research in the world.

I remembered something I had talked about with Weizmann in New York in the days when he was working for the recognition of his state. I had asked him whether Israel would not result in a sort of collective bargain with assimilation. On an individual basis, of course, assimilation means dispersal into the Gentile world. A Jew then becomes a spent Jew. Probably the world needs both spent Jews and a mass reservoir of Jewry.

How I would have loved to pursue this conversation after having taken a close look at Israel. Again I thought of Weizmann when my plane was leaving the Lydda airport. He and Ben Gurion and all the others had done a stupendous job in bringing into existence the reservoir of Jewry. The only thing that was needed now was some peace, so that the "ingathering" might be balanced by "exgathering." The world can benefit from both.

March 16, 1954

The Trial of Jomo Kenyatta

By Santha Rama Rau

A dark, infinitely foreign face from the mountains of Kenya stared out at Americans from their newspapers a few weeks ago. The man's hair was ragged, the eyes flat, the expression altogether uncomprehending—an obscure Mau Mau terrorist, condemned to death by a British court, standing beside an English soldier in a neat uniform with bright buttons, gazing with that wild look into the camera.

It was all supposed to be over by now: the terrorism, Mau Mau, the military outposts in the forests and hills of Kenya. It was supposed to have ended a year ago with the trial and sentence of Jomo Kenyatta. As I looked at the newspaper picture the other day, I remembered again that extraordinary trial, what it had taught me about Africa, and how it has been the beginning, not the end, of one of the most turbulent problems in the world.

The trial of Jomo Kenyatta, the only African to emerge as anything approaching a national leader in that curious association of colonies, trust territories, and protectorates that makes up British East Africa, began with a certain degree of local interest in an obscure village in a wilderness on December 3, 1952. It ended four months later in a flurry of world-wide publicity, in the wake of a massacre, with the conviction and seven-year sentence of Kenyatta on charges of leading and managing the secret society of African terrorists known as Mau Mau.

To the people who were following with fascination the progress of the trial—the foreign journalists, the white settlers in Africa, the Labour Members of Parliament in England, the representatives of the Colonial Office both in Britain and in Kenya, and of course the Africans—the outcome was never in very much doubt. But the issues held such enormous interest and importance for Kenyans, whatever their race, that the circulation of the chief newspaper reporting the trial in Swahili (the closest thing to a vernacular *lingua franca* for Africans) more than doubled during those weeks; and as the tension grew through the months of the equatorial summer and autumn, both the weather and the Royal Family were superseded in the Englishman's small talk by details of the Kenyatta trial.

Perhaps to the outside observer most of all, the Kenyatta trial seemed an extraordinary, bizarre, and ominous affair, exposing as it did many elements of magic, witchcraft, Christian fervor, atrocities, politics, and, even more horrifying, the chasm of misunderstanding, fantasy, and ignorance between the races.

The Charges

On October 21, 1952, Jomo Kenyatta was arrested in Nairobi, the capital of Kenya, and detained under the emergency regulations that had come into force to deal with the disturbed conditions in the colony as a result of Mau Mau activity. Specifically Kenyatta was charged with "management of an unlawful society, Mau Mau, which is dangerous to the good government of the Colony." With him were charged five other Africans, all members of the Kenya African Union.

These six men were all charged with conspiracy "by use of physical force or by threat or intimidation, to compel persons in Kenya to take an oath, or engagement in the nature of an oath, purporting to bind those taking it to act, or not to act, in any particular way." To the layman these charges are inclined to seem vague—which is not altogether surprising since Mau Mau itself is so ill defined. The one clear point was that they referred to Mau Mau procedure and organization. This conspiracy, the government claimed, was intended to promote disaffection and discontent in Kenya, and to cause friction between the races.

The Europeans in the colony put it more simply and more catchily—if less accurately. To them Mau Mau was an anti-European movement designed to kick the British out of Kenya by terrorism, murder of human beings, slaughter of livestock, and possibly, in the end, a scorched-earth policy. They called it "the African Stern Gang," or sometimes a "Ku Klux Klan in reverse."

The felonious activities for which the six men were arrested were supposed to have taken place between January 1, 1950, and the date of Jomo Kenyatta's detention on October 21, 1952. Actually, the secret society called Mau Mau has been known as a functioning if elusive organization since 1942. For ten years the authorities saw no reason to worry about Mau Mau. Sir Philip Mitchell, Governor of Kenya until 1952, declared about three months before Kenyatta's arrest, "You will even see it reported that East Africa is seething with African unrest—of all inexplicable nonsense!"

Relatively little was at first known about Mau Mau beyond the fact that it was confined to the Kikuyu tribe, one of the most advanced of East Africa's 220 tribes; that its members seemed to be mostly in the Rift Valley, the vast geological fault that runs like a monstrous trench through the plateaus of Kenya; and that its membership, enrolled by oath, was confined to men. Even now, after the murders and massacres attributed to Mau Mau, after the extensive publicity it has received, after the committees, officials, policemen, soldiers, and journalists have all inquired into it, Mau Mau still retains most of its original mystery. Nobody (not even the majority of the members themselves) even knows what the name means. Various guesses have included the possibility that Mau Mau was evolved from the initials of Member of the African Union, and a more fanciful idea that Mau Mau is a corruption of "miaow-miaow" because the terrorists sometimes left a strangled cat at the scene of an atrocity as a symbol of their society.

The most logical suggestion is that Mau Mau is an anagram of *Uma Uma*, which in the Kikuyu language means "Get out! Get out!" But even this has never been confirmed authoritatively. Jomo Kenyatta answered the question when it was put to him in the witness box by saying that he had "no idea what Mau Mau means." Nobody really knows the extent of Mau Mau membership. Estimates vary from ninety-five per cent of the Kikuyu tribe —which would amount to more than a million people—to only five per cent.

The purposes of Mau Mau have remained almost as obscure as the name. It has come to be pretty generally accepted (except by the more diehard of the white settlers) that one of the reasons for the rise of Mau Mau was the Kikuyu land hunger. The huge productive plateau straddling the equator in the middle of Kenya is known as the White Highlands because here the Englishmen who arrived around the turn of the century to establish Kenya as a colony ruled that no Africans or Asians might own land, and that the Highlands remain White in the racial sense.

In the last fifty years the population of the Kikuyu tribe has grown enormously, largely because the white man, in a way, brought his own destruction with him. Epidemics and tribal wars, which had previously kept the population pressures at a perilous equilibrium, were extensively controlled by the newly arrived foreigners. The land set aside for the Kikuyu tribal reserves can no longer contain them. Even on the land that they have, they are forbidden to grow the better-paying crops such as coffee, sisal, and pyrethrum (a variety of marguerite from which is extracted an essential component of most insecticides).

Finally, as Dr. L. S. B. Leakey, the most distinguished authority on the Kikuyu and their customs, claims, it is firmly established in Kikuyu tradition that the White Highlands were leased, not sold, by the tribe to the foreigners. Now the Kikuyu want them back. Mau Mau was supposed to force land concessions from the British.

To the average white settler who has bought his farm in good faith with all the right legal documents, developed the land far beyond its previous state, invested his money, and made his home in the Highlands, this whole argument seems, naturally, to be the outrageous nonsense of socialists or malcontents.

Another version of the purpose of Mau Mau that is quite often advanced is that it is a strong and sudden return to magic and the old beliefs of the power of tribal chiefs and witch doctors. This is supposed to have come about as a reaction to the work and preaching of missionaries and the teaching the Africans have received in mission schools. Here, it is claimed, the encroaching foreigner broke down the security of the African in the rigid structure of his tribe and the compulsive fears and confidence in his religion of magic and terror without providing an alternative society that was close enough or comprehensible enough to the African, and without substituting a religion that he could understand.

Certainly to the average African, even if he can sort out in his own mind the conflicting sects and contradictory creeds of the different varieties of missionary in his country, the contrast between Christian teaching and ethics and the African place in the new Christian society that has evolved in Kenya must be disturbing and embittering.

A more cynical explanation of Mau Mau is that it was conceived largely as a money-making concern. With the rise of the cost of living in Africa the compulsory Mau Mau entrance fee has risen from seven shillings to sixty-two shillings and fifty cents— about nine dollars, or six weeks' wages for an African. Somebody must be getting all this money for a relatively small output. Mau Mau in this case would be only a sort of gangsterism, an extensive protection racket.

The most idealistic version of Mau Mau is that it is a genuine nationalistic movement designed to get self-government for Kenya Africans, and that its terrorist aspects are an unfortunate by-product that grew up—against the wishes of the leaders—among the impatient elements who felt that there was no chance of receiving a just settlement from the British by peaceful means.

Still other explanations are that the present outbreak is an inevitable race war; that it is the revolt of the intellectual African against the British and their discrimination against the colored races; that it is the revolt of the primitive and savage African against the intellectual African, and only incidentally against the British; that it is a Communist or Communist-directed upheaval; that it is an anti-Christian movement, that the whole thing has been hysterically exaggerated and that Mau Mau is really no force at all.

When Jomo Kenyatta was tried, there was a good deal of evidence to back up every one of these conflicting theories. For each there was also a good deal of discrediting proof. Altogether it was rather difficult for the outsider to make out precisely what—in the broad sense—Kenyatta was accused of.

Defenders of the African cause were quick to claim that Kenyatta's arrest was simply an excuse to ban the Kenya African Union, the first organized and politically aware group of East Africans to flourish and gain support for their work. The other extreme felt that unless Mau Mau leaders were dealt with firmly, Africans would lose respect for British sovereignty and government.

Only this much at least was certain, out of all the conflicting theories and explanations: that Mau Mau contained elements of blind superstition, intimidation, and political aspiration accompanied with savagery, brigandage, and murder of the most horrifying sort. Because of these the Europeans' anger against Kenyatta from the time of his arrest rose sharply.

When Kenyatta was first detained it would have been possible under the emergency regulations for the British authorities simply to exile or intern him without any trial at all. During the more explosive moments of the trial, and as the list of European murders mounted to a total of eight in those weeks, a good many of the people involved wished that the authorities had done just that, for the Kenyatta trial quickly grew into much more than the exile of a troublemaker.

D. N. Pritt, Q.C.

Kenyatta was arrested in Nairobi, but because the police felt that there was danger of public uprisings and trouble in the capital if the trial were held there, he was taken up to the Northern Province. This is a vast desolate frontier region of Kenya where the tribes are supposed to be particularly primitive. It is a "restricted area," where nobody is allowed in or out without a police pass. It was to this area that troublemakers, Communists, and various political and criminal prisoners were exiled or held in detention. And it was in Kapenguria, a tiny village there, that the trial of Jomo Kenyatta was held.

The point at which world attention suddenly focused on Kenyatta was when no European lawyer in Kenya would handle his defense. It would have ruined his practice. D. N. Pritt, a lawyer of considerable distinction, a Queen's Counsel, a Labour M.P. for fifteen years, a man who made his reputation on political trials and who is perhaps best known in the United States for his successful defense of Gerhart Eisler when he jumped ship in England, announced that he would take the case and became the chief counsel for the defense of Kenyatta and his five colleagues. Pritt, a red-complexioned man of medium height with an off-hand manner, flew to Kenya and plunged at once into the tangle of misunderstandings and the great gap between cultures that would characterize the trial. Pritt was met by an enthusiastic crowd of Africans, many of whom, it turned out, had heard his title "Queen's Counsel" and assumed that Elizabeth II had so taken Kenyatta's cause to heart that she was sending her personal lawyer to defend him. The next few days, however, made it clear that Pritt brought no such overwhelming authority.

Pritt's very first act resulted in an antagonism that quickly grew to fury among the white settlers as the trial progressed. He appeared before the Kenyas Supreme Court to declare with angry bluntness that indictments against his clients were "the vaguest allegations of conspiracy I have ever seen in forty-three years' experience" and to demand that the venue of the trial be changed to Nairobi, where he would have access to libraries, essential documents, and witnesses.

Pritt's fireworks made the Kenyatta trial news for most of the world and such a *cause célèbre* in Asia and Africa that several lawyers from India and West Africa joined the defense team. This, in turn, raised a number of complications. It became clear that the trial was no longer a private Kenya affair. Inevitably the position of all Africans was going to be discussed. Probably the presence of the British in Kenya, even in all East Africa, would be considered. A number of vaguely discreditable and definitely disturbing facts about life in Kenya were going to get an uncomfortably public airing.

The various defense lawyers ran immediately into one of the bitterest issues between the races. They met it first in the matter of living quarters. All of them except Pritt were, in the Kenya sense, colored. They could not therefore stay in hotels, in clubs, or in wayside inns. They couldn't eat their meals in European restaurants, or travel first class in trains, or get a drink in a bar. Eventually they all crowded into the home of an obliging Indian businessman.

Kapenguria itself is too small a village to have any public accommodation. All the people involved in the trial lived twenty-four miles away in the nearest town, Kitale. There, the one hotel and one residential club were exclusively for Europeans, and the color bar (or the "culture bar," a genteel phrase some of the Europeans insist on using) excluded all the defense team except Pritt.

The Kenya Supreme Court turned down Pritt's request for a change of venue, and in an atmosphere of growing tension and hard feelings the trial opened in Kapenguria on December 3, 1952. The setting itself added uncomfortably to the drama of the occasion. Kapenguria has no courtroom, so a little red schoolhouse, normally used for government-sponsored classes in agriculture, was requisitioned for the purpose, and the only large classroom was arranged as a court. The immediate grounds of the schoolhouse were surrounded by barbed-wire fences and enclosures to which Jomo and his five fellow prisoners retired for their luncheon recess. The spectators from the nearby farms and counsel, as if at a picnic, sat on the grass munching sandwiches and bananas and drinking coffee or warm Coca-Cola. The surrounding area and the roads leading to Kapenguria were patrolled by armored cars and by special details of police.

The Courtroom

Inside the cheerful, humdrum little room the antagonisms, the loyalties, the tensions, and the rancor were so vital as to change the quality of the air one breathed. About fifty spectators could be seated comfortably in the room at the scratched school desks with the scribbled figures of old calculations on them, the carved initials, the doodles. In front sat the prosecutor, A. G.

Somerhough, large, round-faced, balding, with the cultivated Englishman's sense of humor and sarcasm, a popular man in Kenya for his distinguished war record, his work on the trial of the war criminals in Germany, and, more recently, for the ability he had displayed as the second-in-command to the Attorney-General of the colony. Both he and his blond, handsome assistant wore the conventional formal black coats and striped trousers—startling and incongruous in the equatorial sunlight.

Next to them at the defense tables the lawyers were more informally dressed in tweeds and lounge suits. In front of them and to their right was the witness box. At the end of the room was the low dais where R. S. Thacker, the magistrate, sat in his robes and wig with his back to a blackboard and under a colored print of the young and smiling face of the Queen. To the left of the audience, on a long narrow bench set against the wall, guarded by two tall askaris in their uniforms of navy blue sweaters, khaki shorts, and red Moslem fezzes, observed by several English CID men both inside the room and from the veranda, sat the six prisoners, looking unexpectedly short and shabby. Through the windows, across the barbed wire and the patrol cars, you could see the tall silver eucalyptus trees, the blue air of the high country, and the incredibly beautiful foothills of Mount Eglon.

The Principal Defendant

Naturally most interest centered on Kenyatta himself. Throughout the trial, except for moments of intense emotion in the witness box, he seemed entirely at ease, sometimes amused. In the weeks that followed, his corduroy golf jacket, suede shoes, and colored shirt all became a familiar part of the trappings of the court. He is a stocky man with an ugly, powerful face. As the magazines and newspapers were soon to prove, he can be photographed to look either like a frog or like one of the more impressive and saintly Biblical prophets. He has a short, sparse beard and a big, curving mouth which shows uneven yellow teeth when he smiles. His nose is broad and his hairline receding. It is his eyes that transform his face, his admirers claim, into the dedicated countenance of a righteous leader. They have been described variously as hypnotic, flashing, brilliant, mesmeric, cunning, and blank. An Englishman once described him as "part mountebank, part Hampstead intellectual," but all the same he is just about the only African whose name is known throughout East Africa and who has devoted friends and followers among the most educated and the most backward of the Africans. Perhaps his most famous asset is a formidable gift of oratory.

When he spoke in public he drew audiences of thirty to fifty thousand. Throughout Kenya people knew his voice, his speeches, and his mannerisms—so much so that one story ran that a sort of code had been established between him and his audiences. He always carried a stick with an ivory handle carved to resemble an elephant head. Another prop was a large ring in which was set a white stone about an inch in diameter. The rumor went that he used these props to indicate to his audience whether he meant his words to be taken seriously or as the exact reverse of what he was saying. In the course of his trial this question of his sincerity in his public speeches became one of the more important aspects of the case for the Crown.

Even the "facts" of his life allow for so much guesswork and interpretation that a baffling amount of contradiction exists. He doesn't, for example, know when he was born. His passport, based presumably on how old he seemed at the time he got it, makes him fifty-nine. He is by blood a Kikuyu, and was educated in one of the Church of Scotland mission schools, but beyond that, he says, he was "self-educated." Certainly his formal education was interrupted for a considerable period, for right after he left school in 1914 he went to work as a laborer on a farm in the White Highlands. In 1922 he began the political work which so consumed his interest that by 1928 he was devoting almost his full time to it. He earned a living by working as a meter reader for the municipal water board of Nairobi. In 1929 he went to Europe on money raised for him by the Kikuyu tribe. Already they recognized him as an important force.

Europe changed Kenyatta's life radically, although just what he did in the seventeen years he was there remains for the most part obscure. By his own admission he visited Moscow twice and

spent altogether nearly two years at the Moscow University. He
also spent some time at the London School of Economics, where
he, like so many other students from various colonies and parts
of the British Empire, fell under the influence of Harold Laski.
He received a postgraduate diploma in anthropology in London
and wrote as his thesis the semi-autobiography that was published as a book, *Facing Mount Kenya*. During this period he
married an Englishwoman and had a son by her. He already had
a Kikuyu wife.

In 1946 Kenyatta returned to Kenya. To all black Africans educated abroad, the return home is a disheartening experience. In
Europe they have been treated as equals, if not actually lionized
by the people they have met and worked with. Back home they
are again thrown back to the irritations and insults of the color
bar, and the more concrete grievances of lower pay and lesser
jobs and virtually no possibility of economic advance, all counte-
nanced by law and jurisprudence.

I suppose it must be assumed, in the light of Kenyatta's conviction, that he returned from England and immediately became
the manager of Mau Mau. It is also assumed that the extensive
job of founding African schools independent of the foreign missions—to which, ostensibly, he gave all his time that was not taken
by the semi-political activities of the Kenya African Union—was
really an elaborate way of establishing underground channels for
spreading Mau Mau propaganda. When he was arrested these
schools were either closed down or had been placed under strict
supervision to purge their staff of Mau Mau teachers, and the
Kenya African Union, already suspect as an organization, virtually ceased to function. Kenyatta's friends announced hotly that
its suppression, not Mau Mau terrorism, was the purpose of his
arrest.

To the spectators in the court, almost every day there was some
new excitement, usually of a melodramatic sort. The prosecution's case, however, was entirely concerned with Mau Mau and
fell into three broad sections. The first was intended to show that
Kenyatta had taken and administered the Mau Mau oath; the
second that on the occasions when he had denounced Mau Mau

he was insincere and that his real policy, along with the policy of the organization of which he was president (the Kenya African Union), was anti-European and pro-Mau Mau; and the last that he had allowed himself to be idolized, with his name blasphemously substituted for Jesus Christ's in hymns; and that these actions were consistent only with his role as manager of Mau Mau.

The first few prosecution witnesses—all of them Africans—set the mood for mystery, magic, and barbaric rites. They were the ones who claimed to have seen Kenyatta take the Mau Mau oath himself and administer it to others. All begged Thacker to withhold their names from the press because they were afraid of reprisals. They were all kept in a specially guarded encampment, for it was not considered safe to allow them to live in their villages. To a question of whether these witnesses needed such elaborate protection because they were committing perjury, Somerhough replied acidly and with considerable effect, "It isn't a question of witnesses committing perjury but of committing suicide."

Among them the witnesses established what became the classic description of the ceremony of the Mau Mau oath taking: the walk through the banana-leaf arch, the eating of the sheep's meat, the touching of the mucus and liquid from the sheep's eye to the lips, the payment of sixty-two shillings and fifty cents. It was brought out that the oath-takers were told that "If you ever sell our land to Europeans, you will die."

It must have occurred to a good many people who saw the trial or read about it that this whole question of oath taking and the government stand on it could create considerable confusion in the minds of the average uneducated Kikuyu tribesmen. Clearly the government considered the articles of the Mau Mau oath described by the witnesses wicked and worthy of punishment, though, to reverse the situation, an Englishman commits himself to many of the same things. An Englishman, for instance, cannot sell land in the White Highlands to anyone of another race; he too would be considered a traitor were he to "sell his country or his people"; and presumably he too lives under the threat both of punishment and of social ostracism.

Besides the commandments to which a Kikuyu was sworn under the Mau Mau oath, the manner of his swearing apparently aroused considerable disgust deepening to utter revulsion among the Europeans. Yet, fantastically enough, even more drastic ceremonies were condoned or initiated by the government authorities. In a ritual that undertook to release Kikuyu from their Mau Mau promises, which was officially called a "cleansing ceremony" but which became more popularly known as a "de-oathing," the authorities were looking for a ceremony so powerful that it would undo even the terrifying Mau Mau oath.

The procedure was, accordingly, intensified. Instead of simply touching the mucus of the sheep's eye to the lips, in the de-oathing one had to eat the eye, the theory being that a stronger witchcraft would destroy the weaker magic. This routine so upset Members of Parliament in England, who deplored the using of barbarism to defeat barbarism, that the more extreme forms of the de-oathing had to be suppressed. However, the ritual of de-oathing continued in a milder way.

One such ceremony that I saw was officially sponsored in a part of the Kikuyu tribal reserve where there was supposed to be an extremely high incidence of Mau Mau influence and membership. It was conducted by a fully qualified witch doctor wearing his regalia of ostrich plumes and scarlet jacket over rather patched and worn clothes. He was decorated with safety pins and carried the traditional quiver full of arrows. He performed the de-oathing ceremony with one of the magic *ithikari*—sacred stones which have seven holes in them to represent the seven orifices of the body. The man who was being cleansed placed the end of a sliver of bamboo in each hole. Holding the ends of the seven sticks, he repeated the oath of loyalty to the British government. The oath followed very closely the pattern of the Mau Mau's. It must be puzzling for the ordinary Kikuyu to decide just where foreigners stand on the question of witchcraft.

Soon after the opening of the trial an African acquaintance of mine pointed out to me a news item in a magazine. It described a Mau Mau "court" which was discovered while it was in session by some of the members of the Kenya African Rifles, a regiment that had been called up to help maintain law and order, and a few administrative officials. Thirteen Kikuyu members of the "court" were arrested, and among their confiscated paraphernalia were a rhinoceros whip and a white furry cap worn by the judge. "Look," said the African, "here in the Nyeri district it is a white cap and a whip. In Kapenguria it is a wig and a gavel. One is magic and one is British justice. Who should tell the African the difference?"

There must have been yet another source of confusion for many people in the fact that all the prisoners and many of the early witnesses who were in the box for having taken an oath were immediately put on oath again. To those of them who had accepted Christianity, possibly there was no doubt of which was the higher oath. To others who had felt betrayed by Christianity and who had specifically renounced its conventional form before they ever came to trial, the issue was less lucid. What in such cases constituted perjury? Which oath or loyalty should a Kikuyu abide by? What, in the end, is the power of an oath beyond the willingness to be bound by it or the threat of what will happen to you if you aren't? In most of Kenya there isn't even a social stigma attached to going to jail—it is popularly known as "visiting King George's Hoteli." The work is light, and there are the advantages of fairly good food and secure shelter.

To the stranger in Kenya the puzzling point is, which of all the laws that seem to surround the African does he consider binding? I asked this of an African friend of mine and received the answer, "The law with the biggest stick behind it." This in turn left me—as possibly a good many Africans are left—with a tricky question of judgment. Who has the bigger stick? Mau Mau or the British government? Missionaries or witch doctors? One's neighbor in an African village or the European on a big farm or in a distant town?

These objections may well seem specious to the Englishmen accustomed to the truism that a court does not administer justice, it administers the law. To the African without the great tradition of British justice to comfort him, I imagine that this seems at best arbitrary and at worst complete chaos. In either case it is certainly open to the political interpretation that the British, having established themselves in Kenya and wishing to preserve their position there, have enacted laws to protect that position and enforce them to ensure that it remains protected.

The Mau Mau, in any case, were apparently following a similar pattern. By whatever means they established their power, once it was established they too enacted their laws and enforced them. Their actions too were deeply motivated by political exigencies, however inchoate. Early in the trial the whole question of the political significance of Mau Mau and the involvement of the Kenya African Union came to the surface when Prosecutor Somerhough put into the witness box three deviationists, officials of one of the branch offices of the Kenya African Union who testified that Jomo Kenyatta had appeared to speak at a public meeting in their part of the country. They asked him why in his speech he had not openly denounced Mau Mau. Kenyatta, they said, had evaded the question, and eventually they were forced to close their branch of K.A.U.—presumably for being unwilling to support pro-Mau Mau policies.

Here was the direct implication that East Africa's only large, serious, well-organized, and actively functioning native political organization was not only deeply sympathetic with the aims of Mau Mau (whatever they might be), but was actually the main channel for the spreading of subversive propaganda and a front for its wilder methods. Kenyatta himself, of course, made the flat assertion from the witness box, "I say that K.A.U. has no connection with Mau Mau."

It might occur to the observer that there is something deeply unhealthy about a situation in which all the African politicians of stature are concerned with Mau Mau, and, further, that the solution has to be more fundamental and more searching than simply the imprisonment of such political leaders. The Europeans could answer with justification that no political rapprochement was possible until Mau Mau and its leaders were destroyed, that Mau Mau itself was the clearest indication of the African's political immaturity and the continuing need for British government in Kenya.

The Kenya Independent Schools—Kenyatta's special baby and one of the chief branches of activity of the K.A.U.—also came heavily under attack. These schools were designed to meet the African's enormous enthusiasm for education, which needed more outlets than the missions or the government could provide. (The European and Indian schools were not open to Africans.)

Now it was suggested that these schools, too, were used as channels for propaganda, that many of the hymns that were soon to become famous in the emerging testimony were first taught and sung to the schoolchildren. These hymns substituted the name "Jomo" for "Jesus" and "white people" or "the British" for "the wicked"; they spoke of Kenyatta as "the Saviour." All this was blasphemous—that is, if you happened to be a Christian. The hymnbooks that were produced over and over again in evidence contained passages like "The hearts that are brave were made brave by Jomo" and, more ominously, "The judgment will be delivered by Jomo." When Somerhough read from one of the hymns an extract that ran, "The love of Jomo Kenyatta is very great, he gave himself to become an agitator for our land," the prisoner interrupted fiercely and banged his fist on the edge of the witness box. "You are after my blood, my friend," he said. "I am not an agitator. The word means a fighter with words and demands." Somerhough represented a large part of Kenya's European opinion when he replied, "There is not much difference."

One of the early witnesses, a girl who had overheard a Mau Mau ceremony, established the connection between the atheistic sentiments of the hymns and Mau Mau. Among the fragments of conversation that she had overheard at the ceremony were, "I know there is no God," and "Jesus Christ they talk about is an Englishman." Her uneasy comment in the witness box was, "To my mind Jesus Christ is the son of God and right to the end of the meeting I had no joy in my heart because of this."

Why Aren't They Grateful?

Sitting in that classroom, looking out at the sunlit hills, at the farms which are ordered and productive only because some Englishman has fought the forest, cleared the land, set up his homestead, and adopted Kenya as his country, it is easy to understand the bitterness the settler now feels at the suggestion that he is a wicked imperialist exploiting the native and should now go home.

Kenya, these Englishmen had always thought, was different. It wasn't a colony in the usual sense of the word. The men who followed Lord Delamere to Kenya considered themselves genuine pioneers. They made farms out of the wilderness; they made a nation out of scattered, warring tribes; they created a country in which they planned to live and which they hoped to bequeath to their children. Apart from their loyalty to the Crown, they considered themselves entirely separate from the Englishmen in other parts of the Empire who performed their tour of duty—even if it lasted twenty-five years—but then returned to England. Those people were colonists. Here, in Kenya, they were settlers.

Without them, they felt, the young Masai warriors, their bodies smeared with red ocher, living off fresh milk and cow blood drunk from a reed inserted in the vein, would still be raiding the Kikuyu villages, stealing the women and cattle and slaughtering the men. Without the settlers, East African agriculture would still be a primitive scratching of the soil, for they are the ones who had made Kenya a smiling and a lavish country. There would be no written language, no schools, hospitals, or roads. No central government ever existed before them, no public services, no towns, no police force.

"It may sound patronizing," an English friend told me, "to people who haven't lived here, but we *are* better for the Africans than the Africans are for each other."

Some settlers call the anger and ferment that have resulted in Mau Mau "ingratitude"; others simply accept it as an instance of the savagery that is so close to the surface of the East African character.

I think that nobody who travels in Kenya can help being impressed by the good intentions of the government, and if he visits the countryside, by the magnificence of the achievement of the pioneer white settlers, however outdated their opinions and their way of life may seem. But like nearly all the Englishmen I met in Kenya, these settlers lacked only the quality that is chron-

ically lacking in whatever one means by the English character—
an understanding and compassion for the other person's sensi-
tivities.

Kenyatta on the Stand

The prosecution called Kenyatta himself as the last witness on
its list. He was questioned for ten days. During this long, frustrat-
ing examination, when Somerhough tried to establish that he
had never openly denounced Mau Mau, the accused replied that
he had. "The curse," Somerhough said, "was not a strong one
and it had a double meaning."

Kenyatta replied that as far as he was concerned there was no
longer or stronger curse.

Somerhough said that he understood that the earth was one of
the most sacred things on which a Kikuyu could take a curse.

Kenyatta looked puzzled and pointed out that the fifty thousand people he had been addressing at the time could not put a
single piece of earth to their lips, and further that the earth oath
was an oath to deny or accept something, not a curse. The strong
curse, the one that he had used, had been handed down among
the Kikuyu for countless generations.

Somerhough, at the end of his patience, asked, "That is the
strongest thing you could have done? Translated in *Baraza* [the
official Swahili paper] as 'Let Mau Mau go and be hanged'?"

"The translation has not the same meaning as the Kikuyu
words to the Kikuyu people," Kenyatta answered, making perhaps a larger generalization than he realized about the state of
affairs in Kenya.

Again, after denouncing Mau Mau in a public speech, Kenyatta was supposed to have said, "Now let us all take a pinch of
snuff." Again, in a fog of semantics and half-understood psychology, there was a fruitless exchange about whether or not Kenyatta had made such a comment, and if he had whether it meant
the same to the Kikuyu tribesman as "Take all this with a pinch
of salt" would mean to an Englishman.

Certainly the whole world of curses and their ritual was foreign to the foreigners there. It was rather more surprising that
even the language was foreign to Kenyans. But most frightening

of all was the chasm between the two minds, the two races, and the two worlds.

Yet again, in questioning Kenyatta about an inflammatory anti-British speech he had made, Somerhough asked him, "Did you say the English had relieved you of the slavery of the Arabs and then ask who purchased the slaves from the Arabs?"

"Yes, I did."

"Did you say that before the English relieved you of Arab slavery, they themselves used to carry away slaves in a ship called *Jesus?*"

In effect, Kenyatta answered that he had.

"Do you know [Somerhough was getting angrier] when the English abolished the slave trade in East Africa?"

"Whether they did or did not, did not prevent me relating a historical account of the slave trade.

"Even if they abolished Arab slavery we were put into worse slavery. Our land was taken away and we were put to forced labor."

Somerhough protested: "This is not an answer; it is a speech."

"The wages given to our people were so low that we lived in a sort of serfdom." The intensity of Kenyatta's voice rose. "Formerly a man could walk and feel like a man. All that was changed and we were subjected to the color bar and all kinds of humiliations. . . . If slavery was abolished, a new kind of slavery was introduced. When you have taken somebody's land . . ." He stumbled over his words. "Leaving him . . ." His voice broke off. "I can't go on."

"Go on," Somerhough said with infinite sarcasm, "I am hanging on your lips."

Briskly Kenyatta recovered his composure, "I hope you do not fall," he said in a cool voice. "If you had to change places with an African and live like him for a week—or even two days—I bet you would not stay there. You think they are happy but they are not."

Meanwhile, tensions built alarmingly between the Englishmen themselves and continually exploded in quarrels in the courtroom and in the jeers and anger of the spectators. Pritt claimed that he was working in "Cloud Kikuyuland" where the normal laws of evidence have no meaning. After one of Pritt's half-audible insults, Somerhough protested furiously, "How dare you, sir! It is intolerable and impossible! I cannot go on."

Pritt had his own grievances. "I have been exasperated in this case but I have tried to go on."

Thacker, the magistrate, deeply distressed and caught between the two, plaintively made his statement. "I am not used to dealing with abuse and have little training in it. . . . There have been occasions during this trial when I have felt it almost impossible to go on, and this is one of them."

In a way he was the most pitiable figure of all, trying the last case of his career, suffering from toothache, flying to his dentist five hundred miles away on weekends and during recesses, guarded night and day by English bodyguards because, as an acquaintance of his put it, "If he convicts them the Mau Mau get him." Laboriously he took longhand notes on the interrogations, asking counsel or witnesses to repeat things occasionally that he didn't catch, exhausted from the long strain of the trial and of the steamy atmosphere of conflict.

In the little Kapenguria courtroom the trial had become an abortive and unsatisfactory political battle in which few points were made but everybody's bitterness deepened. The rift between the races grew wider. The testimony at the trial seemed to be clarifying no issues and demolishing no barriers. Near the end of his days on the stand Kenyatta said, "The disease of the heart cannot be cut out with a knife."

The Defense

After the long succession of witnesses and the special drama of Kenyatta in the box, after all the turbulent questions that had been raised, Pritt's defense seemed short and relatively flat. It consisted mostly of contradictions of what the prosecution witnesses had claimed. Witnesses who were supposed to have been at oath-taking ceremonies described earlier in the trial appeared to testify that Kenyatta had not been present. For the one prosecution witness who testified he had been present to see Kenyatta administer the Mau Mau oath, Pritt produced ten to say he was lying. To refute the prosecution witness who had connected Kenyatta with the Mau Mau initiation ceremony, Pritt produced eight men with contradictory evidence.

One woman whom Pritt called to the box was obviously rattled by the whole procedure. She claimed that the statement she had made for the prosecution had been extracted by threats and force. A police officer, she said, had threatened to take her up in a plane and drop her out.

Why, if the statement was false, had she allowed her thumbprint to be put to it? (But that she should feel that a thumbprint should have any authority was open to question.) Well, her hand had been held by force. To her, clearly it all seemed quite reasonable. "I wanted to be released and go away," she said. "I wanted to be returned to the place where I lived." But most of the spectators must have sympathized with Thacker when he said it was a very peculiar position. "I cannot follow the African mind, I'm afraid," he added sadly.

"The question," an English lawyer who had practiced for some years in Kenya remarked to me, "should be, 'Does the African mind follow Thacker?' In court," he continued, "as you watch these solemn black faces listening to English questions, translations, interpretations, the whole elaborate business of English court procedure, what on earth do you suppose they make of it?"

I asked him what is the biggest stumbling block in legal forms to most of the Africans. "The laws of evidence, I think," he answered. "Especially what is hearsay and what isn't. You ask a man how he knows something, and he says, 'The Chief told me—how else would I know?' You tell him, 'But in that case you don't *know*, you *heard*.' He doesn't understand at all and says, 'But I just explained, I know because the Chief told me.' Of course," he added, "when you reach philosophic concepts like 'a reasonable doubt' you're really lost." Most Africans, he assured me, think in terms of testing innocence by ordeal.

How, I asked him, would they react to the Kenyatta trial—surely they didn't see it as an elaborate ordeal to test him.

"The purpose of a trial like this wouldn't, in their minds, be to establish guilt or innocence. Everyone would know that Kenyatta was Mau Mau. To them the only remaining thing is to settle how much he has to pay—how many goats or cattle."

However it may have appeared to the Africans, the Europeans for the most part didn't seem too surprised by all the shifts and contradictions of testimony. Such, apparently, was only to be expected from Africans, and only added another sort of mistiness to an already obscure situation.

Pritt, in his final address to the court, which he read in a monotone at breathtaking speed, used the general obscurity to claim that there was never a real case against his clients at all. In fact, he said, the prosecution had never really decided just what the charges against Kenyatta were. He flung a series of questions calculated to disturb almost anyone in Kenya. If Kenyatta was charged with managing Mau Mau, then the prosecution's job should be to show just what it was that he was managing. Why, and in what fashion? In what office? With what policy or with what documents? Was he the sole manager? Was he just one of a number of members of the management? And, of course, at the heart of all these questions was a problem of very long standing: What was Mau Mau?

Not only, Pritt continued, were the charges "vague and woolly," but the evidence produced by the prosecution was designed to show that Kenyatta was sympathetic to Mau Mau, that he had not denounced it forcibly enough, that he was anti-European, or even, to push it to its furthest limits, that he had taken the Mau Mau oath. Of course, Pritt said, the defense claimed that most of this was untrue, but even if it were true, ". . . the charge is not of being friendly to Mau Mau or of lacking in zeal in discouraging Mau Mau. The charge is of managing Mau Mau."

As to the political aspects of the case, Pritt insisted that Kenyatta had never said or written anything in contradiction of the published statements of the moderate and constitutional policy of the Kenya African Union. Obviously, he indicated, the answer was that the government did not wish these Africans to carry on propaganda of the sort demanding "more land for the Africans," as this would tend to be embarrassing to the British.

One by one Pritt checked off the points made against his client in the prosecution's case: the points about the oath taking which he felt had been refuted by the testimony of his witnesses, then the evidence of the three deviationist K.A.U. officials, who, he said, were "almost as obsessed with Mau Mau as a Washington politician is with Communism." These men had demanded that Kenyatta denounce Mau Mau, which he had done; the rest of their evidence could not be credited.

On the various occasions that Kenyatta had spoken in public against Mau Mau there was no evidence that he was not sincere. And as for the various songbooks, hymnbooks, and exercise books that had contained verses in praise of Kenyatta, well, the accused could not be held responsible for anything that anybody thought fit to write about him, and the fact that some of the documents were found in his house certainly did not prove either that they were his property or that he had any connection with them.

That, said Pritt, was the whole of the case against Kenyatta in this "very important political prosecution." Clearly, he concluded, Kenyatta and the other five accused should be acquitted.

Somerhough's Summation

Somerhough, immediately on beginning his final address, protested that Kenyatta's trial and prosecution were certainly not "political"; however, "it would be a fair retort to say that the court had heard a political defense."

But it was when Somerhough began to reply to Pritt's "Where?" "Why?" and "How?" that the true and very broad political aspects of the case emerged. The answer to "Where is Mau Mau?" was simple, said the prosecution counsel. Mau Mau was in Kenya. This was, of course, altogether too simple for some of the observers of the trial to swallow without any mental chewing. It stated a fact without either answering the question or accepting its real, and to Kenyans extremely important, meaning.

The answer to "Why?" wa slightly more complicated. "If the Crown were asked why it has suggested that these people should have managed and controlled Mau Mau, the answer would be 'the lust for power.' It must be that, and can't really be anything else." (Of course it could be something else. It could be several other things ranging from nationalist fervor to gangsterism.) "It has increased their prestige and increased their hold on the people so that they could exercise more power."

Possibly unintentionally, Somerhough by this statement made it clear that this was, after all, a political trial. Possibly unintentionally, he had suggested that the danger of Kenyatta and the other five accused lay in their increased prestige. If participation in Mau Mau had given them greater standing with their own people, then the political strength and use of such an organization became obvious, and Mau Mau appeared as much more than the amorphous and inexplicable thing that Somerhough himself later described as "a purely barbaric movement accompanied by circumstances of revolting savagery."

The answer to "How?" was, again, Somerhough continued, fairly simple. Mau Mau was run largely by propaganda. Africans were told that they had been robbed of their land. They were encouraged to drive out the Europeans, and in the hymnbooks designed to spread the propaganda there were "fantastic allegations about slavery and that sort of thing." But the real damage was done to the "simple African" who was being taught to feel he had grievances.

Immediately after this, Somerhough tacitly accepted the political and emotional power of those grievances—imaginary or otherwise—in his comment that if you can find people "to follow their leaders and do as they are told, obey the orders of the leaders and to come when they are called, then you are building up an army of persons who are bound to you by a strong sanction. This sanction appears to have reached a strength which it is very difficult for a European to comprehend." To the foreigner the striking point was that it is a sanction that for the Kikuyu, at least, superseded both their previous emotional ties of loyalty or affection to the Europeans and their political ties to the government.

Kenyatta, Somerhough concluded from his replies to Pritt's queries, was the only man with the "personality and the education" to manage an organization of the scope of Mau Mau.

Later in his speech, Somerhough came to the heart of the tangled situation in Kenya that had made the trial such an extraordinarily bewildering series of cross purposes and muddles, and in a way diagnosed the sickness of most of Africa. "We maintain that Mau Mau can only flourish in an atmosphere of hatred between the races. It is no good telling Africans to drive out

Europeans, or to tell Europeans to do likewise if they like each other. Neither party will listen to you. The only soil in which Mau Mau could flourish would be in soil poisoned by racial hatred."

Among the Africans of various shades of political opinion to whom I talked in Kenya, certainly none would have disagreed with Somerhough. They might, however, have wondered where the poisoning of the soil had begun. In colonization or in Kikuyu land hunger? In economic grievances or in anti-European propaganda? In the color bar or in Mau Mau?

The Verdict

During the month that Thacker spent considering the evidence and the cases of the defense and the prosecution, Kenyatta's case remained in the news and in the horrified conversation of Kenyans. New Mau Mau conspiracies were discovered. Some of the remaining African leaders who were Members of the Kenya Parliament and had always been represented as moderates were imprisoned after a dramatic night raid in Nairobi. This inevitably emphasized the political ill-health of the entire colony. Some days before Thacker gave his verdict, Mau Mau's biggest and most senseless atrocity took place. A hundred and fifty Kikuyu were killed in one night in one of the African locations called Lari. Their villages were burned to the ground, and the people who tried to escape from the blazing huts were chopped to death with the *pangas, simis,* and *rungus*—the three typical varieties of knife—of the waiting terrorists. One story said that the massacre had been planned in protest against Kenyatta's conviction and sentence, which the Africans had anticipated, but something had slipped up and the timing had been entirely misjudged. Another rumor said that Thacker had delayed giving his verdict because he was afraid, if the mistimed massacre was any sample, of the carnage that might result.

Another news item in the month before the verdict concerned Pritt's departure from Kenya with the honors given him by the Nairobi Africans—a stool, a robe of colobus monkey skins, and a fly whisk—the traditional equipment of an African tribal elder. Most of the Europeans of Kenya seemed to feel that Pritt had only contributed to the worsening of the situation; that he had so played up the race war and political angles of the trial that he had really done the Africans a disservice and made it much harder for them to deal in a friendly and equitable way with the Europeans in the future. But I think an African I talked to about this spoke for many of his countrymen when he said, "It is very wonderful for us to see an Englishman fight so bravely on the side of an African."

Eventually, protected by soldiers and Sten guns, Thacker gave his verdict in the Kapenguria schoolroom. For Kenyatta and the other five accused, the sentence was seven years' hard labor—the maximum he had the authority to impose, though even that, he said in the course of his speech, was "quite inadequate" for what Kenyatta had done.

Kenyatta replied that he and his colleagues were not guilty and did not accept the magistrate's ruling. In his opinion the purpose of the trial was simply to strangle the K.A.U., "the only African political organization which fights for the rights of African people." The world, he said, was meant for human beings to live in happily. Consequently he would continue to object to racial discrimination and would continue to demand—in a constitutional way—the return of African land and eventual self-government. "I am not," he said, "asking for mercy, but that justice might be done and that injustice against the African people should be righted."

Thacker, apparently despairing of any solution for Kenya's problems, said, "I am sorry to say I don't believe you."

PART SIX

Views

and Reviews

April 17, 1951

"Scott in Thorns"

BY JAMES THURBER

As a writer who occasionally does pieces requiring research, I am familiar, on a minor scale, with the kind of problems that must have confronted F. Scott Fitzgerald's biographer when he began, some years ago, to try "to make Scott clear," as Hemingway puts it in one of the notes in Arthur Mizener's *The Far Side of Paradise*. The researcher lives a new life, more complicated than his old one. Interviews with informed sources, male and female, lead to hangover or friendship, both of which take up time; important clippings in scrapbooks have been torn in two by somebody's little niece; the person you most want to talk to is on a West Indies cruise, or hunting in Africa, or mute with laryngitis; the gentleman who gave you the item or anecdote you prize above all others calls up and pleads with you not to use it; the most fascinating notes and letters turn out to be as hard to get your hands on as the private papers of Geoffrey Aspern; and at least one man wants to sock you, and one woman threatens to sue you and your publisher if you mention her—or if you don't.

Mr. Mizener must have gone through a lot of things like this in his long labor of love, but his interest remained remarkably fresh and intense, and I am impressed by that, and by his skillful organization of a mountain of data and details. If there sometimes seems to be almost too much material, so that it becomes hard to tell the facts from the truth, I am sure the author threw out twice as much stuff as he finally included, in a book that is not only biography and criticism but what amounts to an exciting and fast-moving novel about the most colorful and crowded marriage of the Crazy Twenties, a period many of us once prayed we might survive, and to which we would now gladly return, as if it were a warm and serene womb of time. It is this feeling, natural enough in an era of desperation, that probably accounts for the fact that the Mizener book soon began to move like a fictional best seller. People have a nostalgia for a decade in which a man could freely make fun of the kind of Congressman that now scares him to death.

I say "crowded" marriage, because there were four or five Zeldas and at least eight Scotts, so that their living room was forever tense with the presence of a dozen disparate personalities, even when they were alone in it. Some of these Fitzgeralds were characters out of a play or a novel, which made the lives of the multiple pair always theatrical, sometimes unreal, and often badly overacted. They had a flair for destructive wit and exhausting extravaganza, but they were rarely relaxed enough for true comedy or comfortable enough for genuine humor, and they seemed to move dramatically, from the beginning, in settings designed for tragedy. In even their most carefree moments and their most abandoned moods there was scarcely ever, from this book's report, the casual ring of authentic gaiety. The "dead-earnest" husband and the frantic wife, to name only two of them, did not know how to invite gaiety. They twisted its arm, got it down, and sat on its chest.

Mr. Mizener has brought to his study of Fitzgerald the sensibility, taste, and discretion of a devoted admirer, but "to make Scott clear" he had to report, I suppose, many of the old familiar eccentricities and violences of his subject. These stick out like the peaks of icebergs, more startling than significant, indicating, but never fully revealing, the complex, submerged personality that impulsively thrust them into view. Scott Fitzgerald will be remembered, I am afraid, as The Great Drinker of the Jazz Era, but he was not, I stubbornly insist, a natural alcoholic in the same way, for example, that Joe DiMaggio is a natural ball

player. He began to use liquor for posture and gesture, like almost any other writer of the 1920's but by the time he was forty,
he had found or invented ten or twelve reasons for keeping it
up. (Most writers have only four or five.) The most persistent of
these was that his creative vitality demanded stimulation if it
was to continue to operate. His earlier tendency to turn to alcohol because of Zelda's tragedy, his constant financial worries,
his conviction that he was a failure, his disillusionment about
The Kingdom of the Very Rich, and his sorrow over the swift
passing of youth and romantic love was not pathologically compulsive, and I think he could have overcome it. But when Fitzgerald began to drink because he thought he had to, in order to
write, he was lost. At the very end, however, he gave it up to
work, slowly and painfully but surely and brilliantly, on the
novel that many critics believe would have been his finest.

I can think of no genuine alcoholic who could have gone as
far as he did and ever have found his way back. To him Ring
Lardner was The Great Drinker, and he seemed ruefully surprised that Hemingway insisted on viewing him in the same
light. Hemingway once wrote him a letter in which he said, "of
course you're a rummy. But you're no more of a rummy than
Joyce is and most good writers are. . . ." The saga of Fitzgerald's
bats and benders runs all through the Mizener book, but I doubt
if we know enough about drinking and drinkers to classify or
define Fitzgerald with absolute certainty. To prove to myself how
hard it is to classify drinkers, I dashed off, one afternoon, my
own personal definitions of a few of the more famous categories
of bibulous men. Nobody, I imagine, will agree with me, but
here they are, anyway.

The Rummy. He has several suits, but always puts the brown
one back on when he gets up in the afternoon. (Fitzgerald was
neat and fastidious.) He is inclined to be friendly rather than
obnoxious, and likes to tell you that he gets more done and feels
better than he did in his sober years. He is given to humming.

The Drunk. He is the stranger who annoys your party as you're
leaving "21." He has no name. He appears from nowhere and
reels off in the direction of nothing. He talks to himself.

The Drunken Bum. Same as The Drunk, except that he asks for money, or falls down, or both. He curses.

The Souse. He drinks the way other men play cards or bet on the horses. He always stands at the bar, and will not sit in a booth. He has the lowdown on everything, and loves to talk about his wife, and sports. The more he drinks the shrewder he becomes, and he is a hard man to roll, to cheat at cards, or to lure into the badger game. He could find his way home blindfolded on the darkest night of the year. He loves to sing in a male quartet.

The Sot. He always sits alone at a table in a corner, doesn't know where he is or who you are, and doesn't want to be told. He has had the prettiest girls and the toughest luck of anybody in the world. He calls everybody Jack. He likes to play one song on the juke box over and over, as many as thirty times.

The Inebriate. He calls The Drunk "My man," and tells him to "be off." He has gray hair, half a dozen topcoats and canes, and a silk hat. He has invented a fancy mixed drink of his own and sticks to it. He likes to tell how he got the better of some eminent official in Washington. He enjoys only classical music.

I met Scott Fitzgerald only once, but it was a long meeting that began at ten o'clock in the evening and lasted until after seven the following morning. I think it was early April, and I know it was 1934, because *Tender Is the Night* was just about to be published, and Zelda was having a show of her paintings in New York, and Mizener's book says that it was held during April of that year. Scott was going on forty then, and my first glimpse of him was when he stepped up to the bar in Tony's famous kitchen on Fifty-second Street and ordered a drink. The collar of his topcoat was turned up rakishly on one side and his hat, which he kept on, was pulled down jauntily over one eye. It was an almost studied effect, but it was oddly contradicted by Fitzgerald's curious air of self-disapproval. He seemed to stare at himself in the mirror behind the bar as if he were the awkward "peasant" from the Middle West that he used to claim to be when he talked about the Very Rich.

I had always wanted to meet him—most writers of the 1920's had, and still have, a strong affection for F. Scott Fitzgerald, whether they knew him or not. When Tony brought him to where I was sitting, and mumbled my name, Fitzgerald said, flatly, "Why should I talk to you?" I explained that I was a Middle Western writer hammering briskly away in my tiny corner of literature, and he snarled at Tony, "Why don't you get names right?" and sat down. He was, during the next five hours, witty, forlorn, pathetic, romantic, worried, hopeful, and despondent, but the Scott Fitzgerald I met was quiet and pleasant too, and not difficult. When two big guys, not unlike the Killers in Hemingway's story, walked past our table and, as luck would have it, one of them said something disparaging about Ernest, my companion rose dramatically to his feet and said to them, "I am Scott Fitzgerald." Before he could ask them to apologize, they muttered something and walked away. This was as close as he came to the edge of trouble that night, and I should like to report that of the four or five eminent writers of the Crazy Decade with whom I have spent the night hours drinking, Scott was the best behaved, the least menacing, and the quietest, and he held his liquor better than any of the others.

That was just one Scott, on only one night, to be sure, but it is the way I will always think of him. To some of his friends he was "extremely difficult," or "a bad child," but a man I talked to recently said, fondly, "he was a sweet guy." Each of us had his different Scott Fitzgerald. If Zelda had completely recovered in that lovely springtime, and if his novel had been well received by the critics, I think he would never have turned to the destructive drinking of straight gin and might be alive today, writing steadily, and possibly lecturing the rest of us on the advantages of moderation and the inner check. But he never had any luck.

When I mentioned *The Great Gatsby*, which I had read three times and expect to keep on reading, he snapped, "I don't want to talk about that book, I want to talk about my Testament of Faith." By this he meant *Tender Is the Night*, the writing of which had taken a heavy toll of his vitality. He told me that his hostess at a recent party in Virginia had brought him a copy of *The Great Gatsby* and asked him to inscribe it for her. "I will never write my name again in any book except my Testament of Faith," he told her coldly. It was one of those theatrical moments which Fitzgerald, the actor, could bring to such a high and embarrassing point. The situation fortunately had been saved when the lady squealed, "Oh, I surely must have *that* book of yours!" and rushed to her library to ransack its shelves for *Testament of Faith,* by F. Scott Fitzgerald.

He had in his pockets that night at least three dozen of the catalogues of Zelda's show, whose most arresting canvas, I found out later, was a sharp, warm, ironic study of her husband's handsome and sensitive profile, which she had called "Scott in Thorns." By midnight I must have had a dozen of these in my pockets because he kept absently handing them to me. At three o'clock in the morning, the hour he made famous, he suddenly said, "Do you know any good girl we could call on?" I got up and went to the telephone, although I was all for keeping the party stag. The first two good girls I called exclaimed, identically, "You and Scott Fitzgerald both at this hour? You must think I'm crazy." The third good girl I reached was an actress, who had not yet gone to bed, and she said, "Give me half an hour." Thirty minutes later—the drinking gentleman is meticulous in these matters late at night—we arrived at her apartment building and the night elevator man phoned up to say, "Mr. Fitzwater and Mr. Thurman to see you." We were indignant, but we took the gross insult in our dignified stride.

The next few hours were spent in tranquil conversation about a great many things. Most of the time I spent in another room, since it was he who had wanted to talk to a good girl. I understand that this was the year that Fitzgerald made several pathetically futile attempts to interest himself in other women, in an effort to survive the mental and emotional strain of Zelda's recurring psychotic states. In one of the stories that he wrote for the *Saturday Evening Post* later that year, the name of his heroine was the same as that of his hostess of the April morning. But it didn't mean much to him, because all that night Zelda was in his lap, and there were a million miles between him and the good girl who sat only a few feet away.

He was staying at the Algonquin, and he kept forgetting that I had a room there, too. When we drove up in front of the hotel in bright daylight, he got out and said to me, "You don't really

belong to my generation and you don't have a daughter." These
were two of his great obsessions, and he must not have been
listening earlier when I told him my age and talked about my
own daughter. "I am less than two years older than you," I told
him, "and I have a daughter." He got back in the cab and told
the driver to drive around the park. This trip lasted an hour, and
we talked about a writer who was much older than either one of
us and who didn't have a daughter, the late Ring Lardner, of
whom his young friend Scott later said, "He had a face like a
cathedral." When I got up late that afternoon, I found that I had
at least two dozen catalogues of Zelda's show in my pockets.
Later, when I talked to the good girl who had taken us in the
night before, she said, "I have about ten catalogues of his wife's
show. He kept handing them to me all the time." I keep going
back to that night and thinking what a difference a good sale and
a favorable critical reception of his novel might have meant to
his life. My God, one recent edition of *Tender Is the Night* has
sold 300,000 copies already—or is it half a million? He never had
any luck.

The sentimental notion, currently so popular, that Fitzgerald's
name began to fade in the 1930's and that he was completely lost
to literary view after his death, and had to be revived by Mizener
and, indirectly, by Budd Schulberg, simply does not stand up
under examination. In 1945 Viking brought out *The Portable
Fitzgerald* in a series devoted, in large part, to his living con-
temporaries, and not to resurrected ghosts, and in the same year
that fascinating and widely reviewed book about him called *The
Crack-Up*, edited by his friend Edmund Wilson, appeared; in
1948 the Columbia Broadcasting System's excellent "Studio
One" dramatized *The Last Tycoon* in an hour-long performance
that was lovingly done, excited much comment, and showed the
strength and fineness of this unfinished book; and in the summer
of 1949 the latest Hollywood remake of *The Great Gatsby*
opened in New York. Malcolm Cowley and Alfred Kazin and a
dozen other critics had been exploring and re-exploring Fitzgerald well before the so-called "revival," and there were countless other signs that he had not fallen into precocious neglect. For
one thing, his name has remained bright and constant in the

writings and conversations of American writers who can forget a man quickly enough when his time has come.

Much is now being made of the fact that *Tender Is the Night* sold only thirteen thousand copies. It so happened that Fitzgerald's books never were runaway best sellers, and Mizener notes that even *This Side of Paradise* had a remarkably moderate success for so famous a novel. It sold only about fifty thousand copies in three years. The infinitely better and far more readable *Gatsby* did not reach thirty thousand in its first twelve months, four years before the depression. A fair analysis of the comparative sales of *Tender Is the Night* would have to take into consideration the taste of the American reading public in 1934. I can't go into this in any great detail, but it is interesting to point out that two tremendous sellers of that year and the year before, *Goodbye, Mr. Chips* and *Anthony Adverse,* were well at the top of the list.

It is true that the critical reception of *Tender Is the Night* profoundly depressed its author, but many critics who reviewed it unfavorably have since revised their estimates upward, and Hemingway, on whose judgment Fitzgerald greatly depended, said in 1935 that the book seemed much better to him than it had when he first read it. As for all the talk about Fitzgerald's books having been out of print when he died in 1940, it should be remembered that this was a good six years after the publication of his last novel. Even the most popular books do not have a way of staying in print very long in a country of fickle and restless tastes that goes in for the Book of the Month, the Man of the Year, and the Song of the Week.

The good and simple truth is that Fitzgerald never disappeared into a lonely literary limbo. I am sorry if this fact disturbs the dreams of the careless romantics who like to believe that a quiet oblivion somehow sweetly suits the short, unhappy life of the "Symbol of the Twenties."

The stature of the writing Fitzgerald, the best of all the Fitzgeralds, has undergone many distortions, from emotional magnification to the sort of cold mental dissection that misses or minimizes his warm understanding, his indestructible honesty, the fine perception that always, in the end, saw through the illusions that plagued him, the charm of his "jeweled prose," and the literary grace and artistic soundness that were born in him. He thought of his talent as something that could be lost, like his watch, or mislaid, like his hat, or slowly depleted, like his bank account, but in his last year there it still was, perhaps surer and more mature than it had ever been. This is a happy thing to remember.

Culture After Breakfast

By Dean Acheson

In the years when I had some connection with the United States Information Service and the Voice of America I heard a good deal about American culture—from those who contributed to it, from those who absorbed it, from those who dispensed it, and from the Congress, which took a very dark view of it in any form. Only recently I have a new view from a young colleague who has just toured South Asia, the Soviet Union, and the eastern European satellites. Whatever, he reported, might be said about American foreign policy—and much was said—American jazz reigned unchallenged from Bombay through Tashkent, from Moscow to Warsaw and Belgrade. "How," he asked a Pole, "can you listen to this stuff?" "Ah!" said the Pole. "You ought to hear what we have had to hear for ten years!" Well, I thought, what gurgles like water in a weary land is worth a taste.

But the example of the Poles alone would not have been enough to make me switch on the radio in the morning. An occasional concert in the evening, yes; but after breakfast, never. What finally turned the trick was boredom. For years the summer-morning drive from our Maryland farm to Washington was a joy of fresh, clean day before the sullen heat had spoiled it. But now only the first few miles are that—the red-winged blackbirds and meadow larks along the honeysuckled fences, the wood doves here and there on a telephone wire, the mockingbirds with their aristocratic drawling flight, and their wings left open for an instant after alighting, like an eighteenth-century Corinthian about to raise his quizzing glass, cattle still eager for the damp grass, and my friend the nurseryman cultivating between his rows of box rootings. This soon ends as our rolling and twisting country road drains into the eight-lane divided highway and one development merges into another, each announcing itself as such-and-such Gardens, Hills, Knolls, Valley, or Arcadia. That is when I push the first radio-station button and begin to learn again what has grown dim since last year.

A female voice greets me singing, with depressing vivacity, "The most beautiful thing in Silver Spring is a Loving Chevrolet." Surrounded by this sprawling young metropolis—the second city of Maryland—flowing over farms, woods, and streams like lava from an urban Vesuvius, one acknowledges that she may well be right. And then the mind drifts off to wonder whether a Chevrolet really could be loving. I once had an open blue Chrysler with wings on the radiator cap that definitely was. But the music cuts off reverie.

There is something unique and categoric about all orchestral selections played from, say, eight-thirty to ten o'clock in the morning. The aim of the performers is, apparently, to make every wind instrument sound like every other wind instrument, and to make all of them sound like Donald Duck. The result is as disintegrating to the nervous system as a ray gun. Sheer reflex makes one press the next button, and the next. But it's no use. *Plus ça change, plus c'est la même chose.*

What a sheltered life one leads who reads books and listens to records chosen by himself! No preparation, this, for coping with the world around us. The radio listener is better conditioned. He takes what he is told he likes and likes it.

Then comes a respite—or rather it used to be a respite: the news. But this summer the news has been a depressant. Of course the facts have always been there, but my own experience has sheltered me from the kind of apprehension of them that has come from listening to the news this summer with our cook as I drive her into town on Thursdays. She is a woman of sense and sensibility, an old friend, from whom I have had many a shrewd, amused, and amusing observation on life as she sees it in and out of our house. Now a sense of shame comes over me, and a constraint comes between us as, together, we listen to reports of statesmen declaiming that to propose giving her simple rights of citizenship (she lives in Virginia) is a cunning scheme to rule the South with Federal bayonets; or race riots in Chicago over a picnic; of a minister beaten in Tennessee while protecting colored children on their way to school; of two colored youths kidnaped and beaten for trying to buy ice cream at a wayside stand serving white people only.

To turn the radio off would be worse than leaving it on. So we sit through it in silence. It is a relief—even when I am alone—to have the exposition of this side of our culture end.

For end it does, back comes the music, and with it what is becoming an absorbing interest, the song of matutinal appeal for the American disc jockey. What does it portend? Something significant I am sure, but just what I do not yet venture to say. Here are some tentative findings.

First of all, there is no doubt at all that between nine and ten A.M. the American radio is concerned almost exclusively with love. All the other great subjects of song from the earliest ballad and Icelandic saga down don't add up to two per cent of the time. War songs, marching songs, patriotic songs, drinking songs, songs of old times, songs of laughter and of lament, lullabies, mother-and-home songs—they can't hold a candle to love. It seems a little like ending breakfast with a stiff bourbon. But then, I once knew a Swedish entomologist who fortified himself for his morning with his net on beer, pickled raw herring, and goat's cheese. It's all in what one is used to.

But love songs, as sung over the morning radio, are quite a bit more varied in mood than one might imagine. In general they are keyed down, a sound concession to the hour so difficult for those whose zest for life gathers momentum slowly. Of this genre is the philosophical love song. The writer of one of these songs clearly was entrapped by the dilemma posed by Bishop Berkeley regarding the nature of reality. Can, for instance, a violet blush unseen when color is the effect produced on the retina of the eye by an object? This writer crashes right into the whole tangled mess. The issue about which he becomes lyrical is whether he loves his inamorata because she is beautiful or whether she seems to him to be beautiful because he loves her. Well, there you are. In my view, it's anyone's guess, though it might be a help to have a look at the girl before guessing. But my real puzzlement is over what difference it makes to him practically. Then, too, he ought to look at it from the girl's point of view.

Another type is the materialistic song, the one which believes that love can be bought. In one of these the troubadour promises to buy his lady a rainbow, and then in a burst of reckless extravagance throws in the moon, too. I am dead against this sort of idea being put in girls' heads. Some woman probably wrote it. It can lead to no end of trouble and might undermine the home.

"A Teenager's Romance" looks at the matter from a new and somewhat arresting point of view. To them, so he sings, love is only another facet of an old problem—their elders. This time the old spoilsports, who appear under the incognito of "they," have apparently insisted that the young Romeo and Juliet are not to be relied upon, as it is euphemistically put, to tell black from white. At first glance, "they" would seem to have something of a point, as the old man is probably trying to get him at least through high school unencumbered. Then one wonders how good, on the record, "they" are at telling black from white themselves. Most arguments between adults end by each telling the other that he is unable to do just that.

In the world of song "they" is a sinister concept. They can't take away the sunset, they can't take away the moon. "They" is what makes a man sorry for himself and usually is himself.

The songs in which love poses an unusual, and often unique, problem have a special interest for me. One never knows how they are coming out. I have two in mind, one sung by a man, one by a woman. The man's song is called "It's Not for Me to Say." The title suggests a wide field, but what he picks out as not for him to say seems very odd indeed—it is that his girl loves him. This seems so reasonable a proposition that one wonders what bothers him. He goes on to explain. All he has to go on, he says, is hope, as he holds her in his arms and presses his lips to hers, that perhaps day by day this may blossom into love. But if this is not to be and if fate sends them on their separate ways never to meet again, it has all been worthwhile. This man takes whatever the future may bring without flinching.

The girl has a different problem. She warns us not to be misled by the cold gleam in her eye because down below the flames in her heart fairly roar—so much so, in fact, that she suggests alerting the fire department before the next meeting. A very fair girl, a little aghast at her own potential, greatly to be commended for giving a man a break by posting the notice "Road open. Proceed at your own risk."

This brings us to the last and proportionately much the largest category—the songs of unrequited love. The early-morning troubadours can't resist these. They begin with the revived and much-sung favorite entitled "I'm Going to Sit Right Down and Write Myself a Letter." Conduct otherwise incomprehensible is explained by a lady so indifferent that the postman doesn't even ring once. This pathetic case is followed by "Love Letters in the Sand," whose depressing message needs no elaboration, though of course "aches" and "breaks" furnish needed rhymes throughout. My son tells me of the acme of defeat in love that used to come over the radio to the men in the Pacific during the war, perhaps played by Tokyo Rose, containing the morale-building thought that the singer was born to lose and now was losing her. In "Dark Moon," unrequited love goes into an astronomical phase. Why, the moon is asked, is its splendor gone; and the anthropomorphic suggestion is advanced that perhaps it shares the sorrow of a lost love. The moon is too much of a lady to reply that she is at her darkest just before the new moon.

A final note of hope among the ruins is "Love in the Afternoon." Are its title and thought perhaps a little reminiscent of Hemingway? At any rate, it brings to those who see the shadows lengthening the hope that between them and the chill of the evening there may still be Something.

As I turn into the garage and switch off the radio, I ponder the observation of Andrew Fletcher of Saltoun that if a man could write the songs of a nation, he need not care who should make the laws. Is it possible that between legislators and minstrels the score at the top of the ninth is nothing to nothing, with two out and no hits?

February 21, 1957

Cars, Cars, Cars; Roads, Roads, Roads:

A South African Looks at California

By Dan Jacobson

At nightfall, after thirty hours in the plane, we found ourselves level with the country we had been flying over during the day. We came out of the terminal building, and before us more parked motor cars than I had ever seen in a single place stretched in an expanse toward some kind of bridge in the distance. Cars were passing over the bridge and to the right and the left of the terrain of parked cars, and from the night sky broken by the chasing headlights there came a continuous rustle, a fall of sound—a whisper out of the throat of the night. The cars moved all about us; they moved above us, until where we stood seemed to be the center of a circle of country that gleamed and whirred, and wheeled entirely around us.

Then we were taken to a car, and we too were moving around the plain of parked cars, and the road we were on suddenly fell away in an arc and then went up again, and around us other roads were rising and falling in arcs. Which road we were on I no longer knew. A broad, black width of tar, tilted down and curving to the right, rushed toward our headlights, and by their light we saw that none of the other roads were lying on the earth, but all were moving up from it or stepping down to it on great concrete stilts. And they were all wide, wide, and ran as fast as the headlights of our car, which rushed down to another road, wider than any we had yet seen, and flat before us, at an angle to our arc.

Suddenly we were no longer tilted, but on a level with the big road. Then, though neither we nor any other cars slowed down to let us onto it, we were moving on this new road, and cars came past with a curiously close and confidential rustle at their rear wheels, for in comparison with them, it seemed, we weren't traveling so very fast after all.

The cars were swollen and shining; their colors were different above and below; they bulged in front and they bulged at the back. Never had I seen, never could I have imagined so many of them moving so fast all at one time. It is the movement, I suppose, that paralyzes the mind: One could imagine cars, just cars, stretched out indefinitely, but set them moving, set them moving at sixty or seventy miles an hour, set them moving three or four abreast, set them moving in two directions, and the imagination simply retreats and despairs; the mind is numbed.

In two directions, I have said, but there were more than two directions. As we had joined the road by hurling ourselves at an angle into it, so other cars were doing along other roads that came into ours from the right; and so too roads suddenly sheered off to the right, some running level but others climbing onto structures that swung each road around in mid-air so that it crossed overhead, though the cars on it had a moment before been racing pell-mell in front of our own. Now they passed across in mid-air, their headlights still flinging light on the tar and the concrete. On the other side of the road, as in a mirror where everything was reversed, cars that had been coming with their lights toward us now crossed from left to right above our heads. The sensation was that not the cars but the roads themselves were moving, like giant escalators, ferrying hundreds of cars at a time, fast, fast, fast.

We have been some two months in California now; but the biggest single impression is still of that road.

I have been up and down it now a few times, and have seen the shabbiness that the thousand neon signs hid from us the first time we drove down it. Then it was as if every motel or drive-in we passed was a place of light, bloated and palatial under the signs that stared and glared and gave each one of them a different name in letters three feet high. By daylight some of these places were not much better than shabby wooden lean-tos, or shabby brick-fronted buildings, or else cheap, jerry-built places vaguely Spanish in intention, with their plaster and arches and red-tiled roofs. None looks like its neighbor; they share no style, no size, they have no relation to one another but that imposed on them by the single thing they do share: a frontage on the road, a view of the traffic, a gaze across to the other side of the road where there are other motels, drive-ins, used-car lots, gas stations, other giant billboards, and other names—The Crown, Crazy Jack's, Ole Olsen's, Top-T Service, and a supermarket spaciously spelling out its name by a single letter in each of its stucco arches.

Even the shabbiest of them by daylight is resplendent with its colored lights by night. They sprawl wide, wide, drunkenly down the road, because each has to have sufficient parking space for the cars that it hopes will swing off the road, attracted for some reason to this drive-in rather than the fifty others in the last few miles, this supermarket rather than the last. Perhaps because in front of this one someone has advertised in huge black plastic letters on a white illuminated background "Celery 10 cents a stick." How can anyone go to so much trouble to sell even twenty or two hundred sticks of celery, one wonders, but one can wonder about nothing very long on this road, for in front of one a car is mounted on a platform twenty feet high, and slowly the whole platform turns around, bearing the car on its palm.

Below it and stretching away from it are other cars, acres of cars glittering in the open used-car lots; and then there is a service station, a motel, with all its little gabled, little Swiss chalets in a row, a second-hand furniture mart, a liquor store, more used-car lots. How to tell which of all the cars in ranks on the sand belongs to one lot and not to another I don't know, for there are no spaces between them; but there are names on poles, names on billboards, names as high as the little offices that bear them, and each name is different.

Beyond the lots rises the grandeur of a new shopping center. This looks something like the Palais de Chaillot in Paris. It is white; it gleams; it flings its arms open as if about to embrace not a terraced garden but a plain of parked cars as great as that first one we saw in front of the airport. These shopping centers are things we have never seen before—places that under a single sprawling roof house enough shops to supply the wants of a town. This one looks like the Palais de Chaillot; the next one is quaint, rural, timbered, with flagged walks, low buildings with overhanging eaves, at every corner a loudspeaker playing soft music.

And so the road goes away, all the signs and buildings, and the other roads that leap over it—giant-sized, like the cars that rush along it at all hours. To the one side it goes for all I know to Los Angeles, hundreds of miles to the south; on the other side the road comes to San Francisco, where the six and eight lanes of traffic are flung into swathes of tar and concrete that fill the sky in loops and curves dwarfing even the city beneath them as one approaches it. There the roofs of the cars, curved like the wing cases of beetles, flash above the concrete parapets in a hundred different colors; there are no shops there, no billboards; there are no people, and nowhere for people to walk but a kind of narrow catwalk along the side of the parapet where a man can clamber to the emergency telephones if his car breaks down. There, where there is no place for a man outside his moving car, the road reaches its purest, most abstracted state—it can be used for nothing but to carry cars from one end of its giant structures to the other. Its colors are black and gray; from afar it is desolate and beautiful, but unlike a natural desert it has no peace.

I am writing this some thirty miles away from those structures, outside San Francisco in a town attached to the road. In this case, the town seems to be the no man's land, not the road. Except for a house to live in, that road along its length is able to provide you with any material thing you might ever need. There are banks, travel agencies, money-lenders; real-estate agents who will sell you a house and furniture stores that will sell you the furniture to fill it with; there are bookstores and shops selling the latest selection of records; there are elegant little establishments that offer you tropical fish in bowls; there are at least three or four hospitals for dogs. But the curious, the frightening thing is that no one lives on the road; all these shops and facilities belong only to the road, and to no city. Nowhere along its length does the road contract, confine itself, center itself for a community around it. There are no parks, no statues, no plaques commemorating notable events; there are no vistas, no views, no streets that radiate from this point or that; no steps leading to public buildings. The road runs with all its businesses from San Francisco to here and beyond, and it is as if some kind of vital tendon has been severed, so that it can grasp nothing to itself, can enclose nothing in itself, can make no order of itself, but can only lie sprawling, incoherent, centerless, viewless, shapeless, faceless—offering all the products a community can need and yet making the establishment of a community impossible.

It is by that road and from that road that this town lives. Every morning half of its male inhabitants seem to get into their cars and go thundering to San Francisco along it, and every evening they come thundering back again; the women drive along it to do their shopping; the very air of the town is filled day and night with the whisper of the traffic along the road, and there has never been anything else. The road doesn't seem to have superseded something older and perhaps pleasanter, something that would in any case have forced the road to deviate, to have some respect for what had been there before it came. Or if the highway did supersede something else, it has done it so completely that now the highway seems coterminous with the towns set back from it and the townsfolk who do their shopping along it. They weren't here before the road, waiting for it; they came with the road as it ran from San Francisco, and built their indistinguishable, dependent, flat little towns. The highway being what it is, these towns seem nothing but appendages to it—equal parts of a brand-new nameless sprawl.

We hadn't been here for more than two days before it became obvious that we simply couldn't manage without a car. It wasn't a luxury here but a necessity; we had lived for three years in England without a car, but California was clearly different. When everyone has a car, everything is built on the supposition that everyone has a car. For the pedestrian the distances are defeating, and the public transport is bad. Because everyone has a car, the busses run rarely, and because the busses run rarely, everyone buys a car. The man without a car is caught in the middle of this circle, from which point he is able to watch what busses there are going at infrequent and indeterminate intervals along routes that only the bus drivers seem to know about. These busses never have more than three or four passengers, and the driver's air of boredom and disbelief in his own occupation can be seen from a distance of many yards.

Clearly we had to have a car. Everyone said so too. "You can't manage without a car here," they said. "You can pick one up cheaply, you know." They made it sound so easy I was ashamed to admit that I didn't know how one actually went about buying a car. People always underestimate the helplessness of the bewildered newcomer, who finds it difficult enough to walk to his temporary lodgings from three blocks away, let alone do anything as hazardous as driving the distance. And I wanted a cheap car, a really cheap car. I had thought of something in the neighborhood of a hundred dollars, but when I said this they frowned; they said that you had to be careful if you went down that low (there was all the more reason to be careful if you went any higher, I couldn't help thinking); they said—and here my heart sank into my boots—that at that price it was purely a matter of luck. Luck, I have a feeling—that sort of luck, the luck purely of the draw—has never been mine. I felt this acutely when my requests for the name of a reasonably honest used-car dealer were met with such humorous remarks as "Now you're asking for something!"

What I was secretly asking for was someone who "knew about cars" to lead me to one particular car among the several thousand cars on display in the open nearby. There was no way I could distinguish one lot from another, and they all looked like circuses to me.

Suspended over the rows of cars in every lot there were rows of multi-colored plastic whirligigs that spin around when the wind blows. There were strings of streamers as if royalty were soon to pass by. There were neon signs, banners, chalked-up signs, and painted signs promising the prospective buyer easy credit or a radio in every car. There were also the cars themselves. They were all the circus anyone could want. They were swollen, puffed-up monsters of cars, shining in all colors; inside they were like rooms, with their lounge seats and their radios and their heaters and their color schemes; their steering wheels looked as though they had been made out of ivory and whalebone and jade and pewter and other semi-precious substances; their dashboards looked like the things that jazz bands play in front of on the films. And they all looked factory-new to me. It had been nearly four years since I was in a country where American cars were in free supply, so the styles of the last four years were all equally new to me; and there were so many of them—so many styles, so many colors, so many cars, thousands upon thousands of them parked bumper to bumper in great rows, platoons, phalanxes, armies of gleaming and curved metal and glass. "Clean!" the signs shouted. Clean? These cars positively shone, they glittered; why tell me that they were clean?

This was no way to buy a car, but things moved as they always did, and the fifth morning after our arrival in California I went with a friend who knew no more about cars than I did to inspect a two-hundred-dollar car that it had been arranged I was to see. Mr. Dickson, we had been told, was expecting us, and we drove down the highway to him.

We found him in a wooden shack behind a phalanx of cars, under the usual bits of bunting and rows of whirligigs. Mr. Dickson was dressed in a lightweight suit that shone like some kind of metal; he had a tall, thin frame, the anxious, lined face of a victim of dyspepsia, and the tanned skin of an outdoor man. He was eager to please. He shook hands, said "It sure is hot," and guffawed suddenly, a surprisingly deep sound that matched neither his frame, his restless eyes, nor the smile through which the sound was uttered. He took us across the sand between the cars to the purple one we had come to see. "She doesn't *look* so good," he admitted, "but that poke on the door doesn't mean a thing. Look, it opens, it closes." He guffawed again. "If it wasn't for that poke in the ribs there we'd be asking three hundred for her. But that doesn't mean she can't run. Get in, try her, look around, take your time, make up your mind." His patter was exhausted; he attempted to revive himself with the deepest and most sepulchral guffaw we had yet heard from him.

He failed, and withdrew with a kind of listless tact to one side, leaving us to look around.

Tact was called for, for neither of us had much idea of what we should look for. I opened the hood and we both stared inside, and then I closed the hood. We opened and closed all the doors. We switched on the lights and switched them off again. We started the car and drove it around the lot; we revved the engine; we brought it back to where Mr. Dickson stood listlessly on the sand, his lean figure casting a lean shadow in front of him, and I saw at least how he got his tan.

We were back later that afternoon—my feeling about that highway was such that I was almost surprised we had managed to find the place again, that it was still there, that Mr. Dickson was still there, that Mr. Dickson recognized us, and that we recognized him. When I had signed the bill of sale, Mr. Dickson took it from me and looked carefully at the signature. "You won't regret it," he said. "You've bought a good car, Don."

Friends in England had written asking, "What's it *like* in California?" Until a used-car salesman in a lot somewhere along that highway has called you by what he imagines is your first name, you have no idea *what* California is like.

What the newcomer catches glimpses of here is a country of unimaginable size, to all appearances related only nominally to what past it has, peopled by millions of immigrants or the near descendants of immigrants, held together and apart by sprawling highways of frightening dimensions. Sooner or later he asks, "How does it keep together? Why doesn't it fall apart?" If the asking of such a question is one of the privileges of a newcomer, so too perhaps is having a guess at some small part of the answer.

I think anyone who comes to both England and America as a visitor cannot but be immediately struck by how much less he seems to have learned of contemporary America from the classic American novelists than he has learned about contemporary England from the English authors. Half the fun of living in England, one sometimes feels, is just that delighted confirmation of the expectations one has derived from literature. Dickens and George Eliot and even Jane Austen still seem to have far more

to do with the England of today than, say, Hawthorne with anything in this particular part of America. Indeed, Hawthorne, or
Melville, or James has so little to do with anything one can immediately see that the expectation that any one of them might
do so begins to look naïve in the extreme.

California, after all, is almost as far from New England as
England itself is; and Melville wrote mostly about the sea or the
Marquesas, anyway—these are the things one begins to tell oneself in tones of reproof. But while it is true that California is a
long way from New England, they are both, surely, American;
and if they are both American, why shouldn't one expect Hawthorne to tell one something about California? There is after all
a continuity of a particular kind that even the mountainous facts
of geography and history have not broken—and the suspicion that
one has learned nothing about modern California by reading the
classic American authors is unfounded. There is a persistence,
though unlike the English persistence it has little physical
about it, and is not to be found directly in matters of appearance, ways of speech, or overt social relationships. This continuity or persistence, it seems to me, may most simply be described
as the self-consciousness of Americans about being Americans.

It is obviously not a simple matter, no matter how simply a
two months' residence encourages one to describe it. And an
outsider is probably more aware of this self-consciousness than
he should be, and tempted to read more into it than he should,
for people always explain themselves to an outsider much more
than they do among themselves. Yet I am continually being surprised by how very much the Americans do it—and not only to
outsiders but to each other. The English, one might say exag-
geratedly, have the air of always being faintly surprised and
amused that there are any people in the world who are not English; the Americans, on the other hand, seem always a little surprised that they are Americans. Or if not surprised, at least they
believe that there is something so special in being Americans as
to demand exhortations to each other on the subject. In fact,
there seems to be a positive campaign about America that actively and continually engages the institutions of government,
the schools, assorted public bodies, and all the media of com-

munication; this is the simplest and most popular expression of what operates as busily on many other levels of sophistication.

The self-consciousness that in the books of James and Hawthorne and Cooper takes the form of a debate between a postulated "America" and a postulated "Europe" is hardly the same thing as that which at election time sends out the Boy Scouts with placards shaped like the Liberty Bell urging people to vote because it is the American thing to do, or that which prompts the marshaling of six-year-olds to salute the American flag at school every morning; but there is a connection between them, and it is not a tenuous one.

To put it no higher, this American self-consciousness has important work to do. The Americans are talking themselves into a relationship with one another and with what is around them; they are continually giving themselves a common name; they are continually, determinedly becoming Americans. They take neither themselves nor their country for granted, and it is precisely in this tension that they seem to know their identity as Americans.

Intimately related to this—and indeed a part of it—is another feature of American life which is easily noted and which has been remarked on often before: friendliness. To one who drives down the highway for the first time, it seems that here in California there are no neighborhoods, no communities, no possibility of the development of a sense of mere distinctive localness— let alone the associated virtues of neighborliness, parochial interest, and local pride. Yet never have I been in a country where so high a value was put on sheer friendliness. In exactly the same measure that conditions seem to make it impossible, the Americans *are* good neighbors, *are* community-minded, *do* busy themselves with good works locally, *do* hail by their first names their neighbors of a few weeks' standing, *are* friendly to one another and to strangers.

It almost seems that America is a vast, deliberate exercise of the will. There is something frightening in the thought, for we have the belief that the will never acts but against its own counterimage, and that the more forcefully it is exerted the less secure is the equilibrium it has imposed.

One begins to suspect that if these people weren't so deliberately exerting themselves to be "good" and friendly Americans, there'd be nothing to stop California from declaring war on Oregon, people ramming their cars into one another all over the highways, the radio announcers screaming obscenities over the air, and the whole thing going up in a smash of asphalt, concrete, shining metal, toppling TV aerials, and broken packages of frozen foods.

Yet the fact that the fantasy presents itself in this form shows exactly how much of a fantasy it is. Not that American society is without its own tensions, which could become critical, like those of any other society; but rather that the use of the word "will" in this connection—despite its attractions—is misleading. Perhaps one should confine oneself to saying that the American need to be explicit about social aims and relationships seems at this time, here in California, an attempt to deal with the central problem of community in a mass society. There have been worse attempts to solve that problem.

Hollywood: The Toll of the
Frenzied Forties

By Robert Ardrey

The best play ever written about Hollywood, *Once in a Lifetime,* came from a couple of Broadway provincials, George Kaufman and Moss Hart, who had never at the time been closer to Sunset Boulevard than East Liverpool, Ohio. And the first thoroughly convincing, comprehensive, in-and-out all-weather analysis of Hollywood's future that I ever encountered came to me almost ten years ago one Fourth of July in San Antonio, Texas, from a college boy who had never been nearer Broadway or Hollywood than the north bank of the Brazos.

Frank Duane is a bright young playwright around New York now; at that time he truly had youth on his side, and moreover was accustomed to the climate. He outlined with care the long future of American films, in terms of the impact of television. I listened enchanted. When I returned to the Coast a few days later I told Frank's tale around to various astonished friends in the industry. We all agreed that my young friend had something, and promptly went back to whatever it was we had been doing.

Duane's thesis was quite simple. As he saw it, television would draw the mass audience away from motion pictures. Perhaps five out of six American theaters would close. Major studios, dependent on mass production to pay the overhead, would vanish.

With the collapse of the theaters and the studios would come the end of present centralized systems of distribution and financing. All this was fairly obvious. What was enchanting in Frank's analysis, what made one forget the Texas heat and the chiggers, was his conclusion that the flight of the mass audience to television would sweep with it most of the inhibiting forces that emasculate American films.

Censorship would lessen; for censors are, in the end, concerned only with their guardianship of the great public. Exhibitors—who, Joe Mankiewicz once said, should return to their proper calling of scraping up chewing gum from theater carpets—would be reduced to a force of manageable proportions. The "money"—that vast New York thing which exercises such iron control on the major studios—would lose interest in an activity of smaller proportions and smaller stakes; the financial influence on films would come more to resemble that in the theater, where we customarily send the backer out for sandwiches. Increasingly comparable to the theater would be the role of the producer, an independent making two or three films a year, whose activity would be guided by what stories he had to tell rather than by what commitments he had to fulfill. There would still be some two thousand theaters—a lot of theaters—scattered across the land, and still in existence an enormous audience by anybody's standards. But the burden of bigness would have been removed from the daydreams of Hollywood's creative people, and an industry might at last turn into an art.

It was a magnificent vision—young, spacious, perhaps a little rosy—but basically sound. Ten years later I can pick no quarrel with it, and if Hollywood today were suffering from troubles no more serious than collapsing studios, guillotined executives, berserk stockholders, and panic in the streets, then I'd say that all was proceeding in the most splendid and orderly fashion. But unfortunately there are other troubles, and a college boy in Texas, in the hot shade of a mesquite tree ten years ago, may perhaps be forgiven if he did not foresee them.

The motion-picture industry has gone through two great periods of shakedown. In the early 1930's, moral conformity struck down the wild, wicked, legendary Hollywood of the 1920's. The industry's self-regulating facility, the Code, saw to it that in the future no screen sinner would escape unpunished. Studio supervision invaded the private lives of the hired help and saw to it that more lively sin, if it could not be entirely suppressed, would at least receive the minimum of publicity. Everything was done to meet the demands of an aroused public. The adult public responded by staying away from the theaters in growing numbers.

The second great crisis in the history of Hollywood's iniquity occurred in the late 1940's. This time it was the political waywardness of certain members of the Hollywood community that brought out the threats of various religious and veterans' groups. The industry responded as it had before, by siding with the pickets against its own members. The blacklist appeared. The morals clause in contracts was interpreted to include political depravity as an offense for which a contract might be broken. When, after several years of purges, the American Legion was still dissatisfied with the community's political purity, the industry graciously stepped aside and allowed its accused members to attempt to settle their individual accounts with the Legion's judges, with the understanding that to fail was to be fired.

I am not one of those who pretend to know what the public wants. It seems doubtful to me that what the American adult wanted in the 1930's was indeed more statutory rape, more manslaughter, and more paternity suits—and in the 1940's more Communists. I am sure that it is an unfortunate coincidence, and no more, that the final catastrophic decline of the Hollywood box office corresponded so exactly to the period of the blacklist. But what must be apparent is that moral and political conformity, both executed frankly in the interests of the box office, have had a variety of effects on Hollywood, not among them the saving of the box office.

Whether or not anybody in the early 1930's anticipated the effects of moral conformity on the creative spirit I don't know, because I wasn't there then. I am sure that in the atmosphere of that period it was as difficult to plead the case of wickedness as later, in the climate of political dissent. But there were certainly those in 1947, at the time of Representative J. Parnell Thomas (R., New Jersey), who saw with some clarity the rubber-stamp marks on the wall. That year's political wars gave Hollywood its most interesting season since Fatty Arbuckle was in his prime.

Although I was an established screenwriter, in 1947 I was a newcomer to the Hollywood community. This put me in the position of being a clean, attractive target without any holes in it. Also, I was that rarest of birds in the Hollywod aviary, a liberal who had never given a nickel to a Communist cause. While my new neighbors, suffering perhaps from swimming-pool guilt during the depression years, had been contributing generously to a wide variety of needy lettuce pickers and Spanish Loyalists and other premature anti-fascists, I had been confining my contributions to a string of hamburger stands in the Middle West. Abject poverty (some say innate stinginess) has presented me with a political record beyond House Un-American Activities Committee reproach.

This was the season when friendly witness after friendly witness appeared in Washington before Congressman Thomas's committee. Reputations rolled about like undergrade oranges. For the studio executive, frenzy became the normal office atmosphere.

No studio was harder hit than Warner Brothers. One lunchtime there, after a morning devoted exclusively to listening to the radio, Jack Warner is reputed to have rushed screaming into the Green Room. Someone in Washington had worked over virtually his entire contract list. He ran wildly about, jabbing his thumbs at his lunching help. "I can do without you!" he yelled. "And you! And you! I can do without you!" He came to Jerry Wald, who at that time was producing a good half of all the Warner Brothers films. "I can almost do without you!" he screamed.

It was a lively time. Opinions were still being exchanged freely on all sides, frankly and at the top of the voice. Cocktail parties were deafening, dinner parties a caution. The floor in any meeting of the Screen Writers Guild was a mass of combatants cheerfully assassinating each other's characters and impugning each other's political ancestry.

One fought on many fronts. I was a member of a non-Communist group, the Committee for the First Amendment, that raised almost fifty thousand dollars in a matter of days and flew off to Washington to protest the Congressional attack on the entire Hollywood community, and got into enough trouble to last some for the rest of their careers. I was a member of another group within the Screen Writers Guild fighting at the same time to break the power of the Communist faction within the Guild. We won and took complete control. Immediately we were confronted by the industry's announcement of the blacklist, and so we fought that too.

Until the coming of the blacklist a more or less united community had been defending itself. I know of only one studio head who favored the blacklist before its actual adoption. The new policy was dictated in New York, at the famous Waldorf meeting, by the studios' New York ownership. Accepted, it turned the industry against its own members.

Within our group of twenty-odd writers who had taken control of the Guild, there was little division of opinion. We were all anti-Communist, all liberals, all fairly invulnerable to attack, and all convinced that the principle of the blacklist held an ultimate threat against all nonconformist opinion. In our year's tenure of office we finished off, on the one hand, any threat to the Guild from its Communist bloc, and on the other we launched a suit against the studios through Thurman Arnold's law office in Washington. It sought to restrain any group of corporations from setting up a private court for the judgment of citizens, and from enforcing the decisions of that court through the police power of monopoly.

It was an excellent suit, but its support was scarcely unanimous. The Communist bloc, preferring the blacklist to litigation they didn't control, fought against the Arnold suit to the last. Meetings dragged on into meetings. When we raised money by private subscription to carry the suit some day as far as the Supreme Court if necessary, they boycotted the campaign. In the course of the single year I attended more than a hundred night meetings. Few broke up before one in the morning. On one rare night I found myself, a little stunned, standing in Hollywood Boulevard at ten-thirty. It seemed like noon. Near me stood a fellow board member looking dubious.

"What about a drink?" he said.

"A drink?" I was appalled. "Stop and have a drink when I've got a chance to go home at ten-thirty? Don't you want to go home?"

"I don't think I'd better," he said. He shook his head. "No. If I come home at ten-thirty, my wife's going to think I wasn't at a Guild meeting at all."

That was 1947, several years before the Senator from Wisconsin came to more than local attention. We had anticipated rather well the drift of things. But what we had not anticipated was what would happen to ourselves. When the Arnold suit at last reached the Federal court in New York, more than five years later, the 1947 board—plaintiffs in the suit—met with the current board. There was deep concern regarding the wisdom of pursuing the suit.

By now much had changed. What had been a scandal in Babylon was now a nation's. Instruments of assassination sharpened on movie necks had become household hardware. In every studio in Hollywood, the "security officer" had been added to the imposing list of higher executives. One was not supposed to laugh. Neither, when one received a list of "charges" from a studio, was one supposed to point out that the blacklist had come to have but the most remote connection with Communism. I received such a list, from a studio. It contained ten counts. One referred to a play that I had had produced in the 1930's by the Group Theater. One brought up my membership in the Committee for the First Amendment. Four charged me with having been a director of the Screen Writers Guild, and four more with having been a charter member of Americans for Democratic Action.

This was—and is—the stuff of which blacklisting, as practiced in the entertainment industry, was and is made. And so in 1952 we all met with Thurman Arnold to consider what should be done about a suit brought by time-tested non-Communist plaintiffs, a suit that had taken five long years to come to court and yet had arrived at the precise hour when it could do the most good.

Only three or four of the original plaintiffs spoke in favor of

pursuing the suit. There was some discussion of the poor effect
that litigation would have on the Guild's public relations. The
current board voted unanimously to drop it in exchange for a
statement from the Motion Picture Producers Association that
there never had been a blacklist.

I knew all the personal vulnerabilities that went into the vote.
It took little imagination to see the new wave of investigations,
headlines, and crushed careers that such a suit might bring on. I
realized that it was asking a lot of twenty-two professional screen
writers to take such an action in a time when only one Democrat
in the Senate had allowed the record to state his opposition to a
McCarthy appropriation. Worse, I knew that my own role as a
passionate advocate of the Arnold suit was something far less
than heroic, for I was a part-time screen writer with other fields
to turn to, and there was the accident of my political invul-
nerability. Even so, I have never attended another Guild
meeting.

Peck's Bad Boy has come a long way. The wild, wicked Hollywood of the 1920's, arrogant, uninhibited, creative, as vital as a
jungle plant, shocked and galvanized the earth's multitudes. It
will never be forgotten. But the untamed Hollywood of the
1920's became the domesticated Hollywood of the 1930's, going
to church, living in seclusion, taking the children to school, and
giving money to causes that would cause it further grief. Out of
further cataclysms of reform has come the star of today, the star
in the gray flannel suit. He is a corporation. His lawyers, his
business manager, his agents, his public-relations man combine to
choose his roles. He is arranged like a window at Lord & Taylor
or a bunch of flowers. If he has passions, he pours them into
Texas oil wells, or the ranch in Mexico; if he has instincts, he
suppresses them, for they have brought him nothing but trouble.
He is apolitical, like a sunset; mildly antiseptic, like boric acid;
and nonmoral, like a dishpan.

It has taken a deal of trouble, and a throbbing myriad of executive headaches, to produce this figure from the unlikely ancestry of Valentino and Chaplin. One must admire not only the
ceaseless application which the motion-picture industry has devoted to the problem of its own self-destruction; one must also

appreciate the speed with which the job had been done. Lysenko himself would be amazed at a genetics experiment that by the mere force of environment could produce such staleness in little over a generation. Finally, one must give all tribute to these giants of public relations who against all odds are achieving the bankruptcy of an industry in a period as unlikely as this.

Perhaps by confining this discussion to the effects of moral and political pressures, I have made the industry's achievement seem more heroic than in fact it has been. Actually, the public-relations brains of the industry have been confronted by a far richer variety of pressures to give in to. I am reminded of Joe Breen, in an office at R.K.O. back in 1940, listening to an airplane passing through the then smogless California sky, and how he said, rather wistfully: "Every time I hear a plane, I wonder if it's bringing a delegation from Memphis, Tennessee, to protest unnecessary references to silk as a symbol of success in Hollywood films."

Organized labor, as well as organized industry, organized religion, and organized minorities, have each contributed their bit to the public-relations man's opportunities. Watch yourself with the characterization of a waitress; there's a waitresses' union that's sensitive. While it's all right to make a religious figure athletic—in fact it's to be encouraged—any other human attributes will just make trouble. Keep the heavy a white Anglo-Saxon Protestant American: Negroes, Mexicans, coal-miners, Jews, Poles, Catholics, veterans, and virtually all others are out.

In one of my more recent films, "The Power and the Prize," I allowed the villain of the piece, played by Burl Ives, to say of the English in a genial mood: "They're a race of swindlers. They invented swindling. They perfected swindling. Then the super-swindlers, they even made swindling socially acceptable." In my simplicity, I assumed that the British in these times would be grateful for any crumb of praise. But the Hollywood trade press was shocked, and uniformly commented on the tastelessness of the line. Not even an American villain, out to swindle the English, should be allowed to say something which might conceivably hurt the British market.

How far the public-relations mind can go, in its unceasing

quest for pressures to give in to, can be demonstrated by a Hollywood taboo of which few are conscious. The rich dramatic material of the American Revolution remains all but untapped. Who has ridden with Paul Revere, or stood with the embattled farmers at a New England bridge? Who has lived through that winter at Valley Forge, or witnessed the writing of the Declaration of Independence? Who has heard the Liberty Bell toll out, or met General Washington at the nadir of his despair, or had a glimpse of Franklin, Jefferson, or the hot Patrick Henry? Scenes remain unmade, stories untold, for fear—for the single fear—of offending British sensibilities.

Hollywood has pioneered many of our most cherished institutions, and for these blessings we should be grateful: the California ranch house, the outdoor barbecue, House committees investigating un-Americanism, the use of sports cars, the hanging open of the mouth when a woman has her picture taken. Hollywood pioneered conformity when Madison Avenue was still a street of small shops. Now it pioneers bankrupcty while Dow Jones industrials press 500. Perhaps what motion pictures have pioneered most skillfully has been the creative role of the public-relations man in any walk of life, and the immense benefits to be gained, eventually, by those who listen to his sage counsels.

What will happen to American films? I don't know. There are those who believe that when eight out of nine motion-picture theaters in the United States have failed, and when the vast distributing organizations have gone bankrupt for lack of outlets, and when the last great traditional Hollywood studio has become a rental (or parking) lot, and when the last of the present generation of corporate stars has demonstrated through successive disasters that his presence in a film is worth something less than fifty per cent of the profits, then perhaps the few remaining independent film makers, harried by creditors, cornered, driven to the most desperate of measures, will turn to the making of better pictures. I find this view a little cynical.

All, in truth, that I do know is what has already happened. And what has happened, oddly enough, was best summed up for me by a lady visiting Chicago more than twenty years ago, when what has happened had scarcely begun to happen. This was deep in the unlovely period of my apprentice writing. I had had the grievous misfortune, some years earlier, of committing my apprenticeship into the hands of Thornton Wilder, who was a hard master and who treated my most inspired efforts as if they were obscene outrages to be hidden promptly from public view. Onto this dreary scene came Gertrude Stein and Alice B. Toklas, fresh from the West Coast in the midst of an American tour. I was commandeered, on several occasions, to make a fourth, with the strict provision that I should keep my mouth shut except to eat.

On one of these occasions to which Miss Toklas and I added decoration, Miss Stein talked about films. Her visit to America had coincided, not without cheerful forethought, with the very peak of the Stein craze. Wherever she had gone, she had been lionized mightily, and nowhere so mightily as in Hollywood.

At one stupendous party, at somebody's house, there had been nothing but the great as far as the eye could see. Sitting cross-legged on the floor at her feet, they had reveled for hours in the Stein wisdom. And then there had come a little pause in the questions, and a little silence, and Miss Stein had given one of her happy little laughs.

"Oh, I know what you want to ask me!" she said. "You want to know how I get my publicity."

At this there came an enormous laugh, because it was indeed a question that had been on not a few minds. The laugh was followed by a very real silence, for this was serious business, and there were those who wanted to know.

"Well, then, I'll tell you," said Miss Stein, in her most pleasant grandmotherly fashion. She lacked only a rocking chair. "You see, I write to please myself. I write to please no one in the world but myself, and so I please myself completely. And in doing that, I please a few others completely. I please them so completely that each one goes out the door and becomes my messenger. What you try to do is to please everybody. And this is a very great mistake. Because, you see, nobody can please everybody. And when you try to please everybody, you end up by pleasing nobody, not completely. And so you don't have any messengers. And you have to hire your publicity, and that isn't the same."

The Perils and Rewards of
Going into Trade

By Gore Vidal

I must confess right off that I am not at heart a playwright. I am a novelist turned temporary adventurer; and I chose to write television, movies, plays for much the same reason as Captain Morgan selected the Spanish Main for his peculiar—and not dissimilar—sphere of operations. The reasons for my conversion to piracy are to me poignant, and to students of our society perhaps significant.

If I may recall in nostalgic terms the near past, I did, as a novelist, enjoy a bright notoriety after the Second World War. Those were the happy years when a new era in our letters was everywhere proclaimed; we would have, it was thought, a literature to celebrate the new American empire; our writers would reflect our glory and complement the beautiful hardness of our currency. But something went wrong. The new era did not materialize and the work of my generation was finally dismissed—for the present at least—as a false dawn. And it *is* a fact that the novel as a popular art form retrogressed gravely in our reign. Not clever enough to interest the better critics, nor simple enough to divert the public, we lost the critics to pure criticism and the public to impure television. By the 1950's I and my once golden peers were plunged into that dim cellar of literature characterized as "serious," where, like the priests of a shattered establishment, we were left to tend our prose privately—so many exiles, growing mushrooms in the dark.

The passage of time has only confirmed the new order. Less and less often is that widening division between the commercially viable and the seriously meaningful bridged by the rare creator who is both. Most of the publishing events of recent years have been the crudely recollected experiences of non-writers. Apparently obliterated is the antique conception of the man of letters creating a life's work to be enjoyed by the common reader in continuity. True, that nineteenth-century phenomenon never quite took root in this country, and lovely though New England's Indian summer was, winter, when it came, was killing; nowadays our better literary men seek refuge in the universities, leaving what is left of the public novel to transient primitives and to sturdy hacks. Nor, let me say, are the serious writers themselves responsible for their unpopularity, as our more chauvinistic editorial writers would have it. The good work of the age is being done, as always. Rather it is the public that has changed. Television, movies, the ease of travel—so many diversions have claimed the attention of the old reading public that it is doubtful if the novel will ever again have the enormous prestige, the universal audience it had at that golden moment when an idler on a Mississippi wharf shouted to the pilot of a passing steamer: "Is Little Nell dead?" And, alas, Mistah Kurtz, he dead, too—solemnly embalmed by the Academy.

Today, the large audience holds communion in a new, more compelling establishment. I doubt if many Americans could identify a single character in a work of modern fiction, but there are few who could not describe in exact detail the night on television when Charles Van Doren failed to identify the king of the Belgians. And it is vain to deplore a cultural change. After two pre-eminent centuries, the novel no longer is useful to the public —yet only novelists need mourn, for it is a fact of civilization that each society creates the games it wants to play.

And though the main audience has turned back to the play (in all its various forms, both "live" and filmed), it is, nevertheless, a stoic consolation for those of us whose first allegiance is the novel to know that there will always be some serious interest in one's work, that the keys to the kingdom of prose will continue to be passed on from hand to hand. And though I rather suspect that in a century's time the novel will be as rare and private an art form as poetry today or that delicate and laborious process by which dedicated men fire glass with color, it will always be worth the doing.

There are, of course, compensations in any defeat. There is the sense of a hard duty done, and in the case of the artist who has become unfashionable or—worse still—whose art form has collapsed beneath him, there is an obvious grandeur in holding fast to the high altar as ominous fissures in the earth open and the columns fall. In one sense, I await oblivion with a martyr's complacency; it pleases me to write novels and I shall continue to the end, with or without readers. But making enough money to live presents a problem, and since I am not clever enough to go into business (much the wisest course for anyone who wants to be a serious writer, if only because one's literary faculties are not exploited by the day's work), I was forced to learn a trade. I chose playwriting. It did not tap the same sources of energy as novel writing. It was highly remunerative, and if one bothered to take it seriously, it could provide a marvelous megaphone through which to trumpet those fancies and irritable crotchets one would like the many to heed.

Over the years I attempted three stage plays. When I was nineteen I wrote a quasi-poetical work about, heaven alone knows why, a man who became a werewolf in Manhattan. I destroyed all copies of this early effort only to learn recently that a collector had somehow got hold of a copy, a ghastly prospect for some as yet unborn English major.

The next play I wrote was on an equally obscure subject, written in a Pindaric frenzy in the spring of 1948 at Shepheard's Hotel in Cairo. Later that summer, I gave it to Tennessee Williams to read. He pronounced it the worst play he'd read in some time, and I abandoned playwriting for good, I thought, after first pointing out to him that a literary form which depended on the combined excellence of others for its execution could hardly be worth the attention of a serious writer—adding with deliberate cruelty that I did not envy him being stage-struck and his life taken up with such ridiculous people as actors and directors. He agreed that I should not expose myself just yet to this sort of tedium.

Six years later, driven by necessity, I took the plunge into television, the very heart of darkness, and to my surprise found that I liked it, that it could be taken seriously, and that in spite of the many idiot restrictions imposed by those nervous men who pay for plays—the sponsors—it was possible to do a certain amount of satisfactory work. The thought, too, of a mass audience was awesome. New novels are not wanted. They are written because one wants to write them and that is that. But television needed plays by the hundreds. I don't think there has been anything comparable since the Elizabethan theater, when new plays were turned out with rich abandon to keep resident companies busy (no further comparison, of course, is possible).

Yet despite its raw youth there is a tradition already firmly established in television that comedies seldom work and that satire *never* does. Like most traditions, this one is founded on a small truth. For one thing, the comedy timing of stage-trained actors is inevitably affected by the absence of human response during a performance, and, for another, several people sitting at home glumly staring at a television set are not apt to find anything very amusing unless it is heavily underscored by laughter from a studio audience. And plays on television are performed without audiences.

Satire presents a further difficulty for the mass audience. If satire is to be effective, the audience must be aware of the thing satirized; if they are not, the joke falls flat. Unfortunately for our native satirists, the American mass audience possesses very little general information on any subject. Each individual knows his own immediate world, but as various research polls continually inform us, he holds little knowledge in common with others. Even political jokes, were they allowed on television, would not have much relevance. Recently one national poll discovered that almost half of those queried could not identify the Secretary of State. The size of the population of course has much to do with this collective ignorance. When Aristophanes made a satiric point, he could be confident that his audience would appreciate his slyest nuance because in a small community each citizen was bound to share with his fellows a certain amount of general information—literary, religious, and political. National units today are too large and, in America at least, education too bland to hope for much change. As a result, satire, unless done very broadly, like that of Mr. Al Capp, our national Hogarth (or the playing version of my *Visit to a Small Planet*), puzzles and irritates rather than amuses.

I have often thought that the domination of naturalism in our letters is directly attributable to the breakdown of the old homogeneous American society of the nineteenth century by, variously, the influx of immigration, the discovery of exciting new machinery, the ease of travel. Yet before this burst of population and invention, an educated man, writing allusively, could assume that his readers would respond knowledgeably to a fairly large number of references both literary and social. Since 1900 this has been less and less possible, and it is no coincidence that naturalism should be to this day the preferred manner in the novel, if only because the naturalistic writer, by definition, takes nothing for granted. He assumes that the reader knows no more than he chooses to tell. He constructs a literal world of concrete detail. His narrative is easily followed. He records the surface of life with a photographer's care, leaving the interpretation, the truth of his record to the reader's imagination: The result is that our time's most successful *popular* writing, aesthetically, is journalism—another dagger at the novel's heart.

The idea for *Visit to a Small Planet*—from outer space arrives a charming hobbyist named Kreton whose blithe intent it is to start a war: "I mean it's the one thing you people down here do *really* well!"—was rejected by three television sponsors before the Philco-Goodyear Playhouse bought it. I was told that the advertisers found the premise alarming, which was certainly disingenuous of them. Had I not spun my fragile satire about the one glittering constant in human affairs, the single pastime that never palls: war? In fact, one might say that *Visit* is the happiest of pro-war plays.

But only Philco saw the austere beauty of my conceit, and on the night of May 8, 1955, it was telecast. With some anxiety we waited for the roof to fall in; to our very real surprise it did not, and most people were pleased with my gentle heresy. I suspect it was Cyril Ritchard's fine performance which did most of the pleasing, but that was to be expected.

I was then informed that George Axelrod would like me to do a stage version that he himself would produce. And so it came to pass. Expansion was not difficult. As a novelist, I am accustomed to using a hundred thousand words to net my meaning. My problem theatrically has always been one of compression; left to myself, I go on and on. After the script was ready there were the usual trials, delays, problems of temperament; each participant confident the others had gone into secret league to contrive his professional ruin (and on occasion cabals did flourish —the theater is a child's world).

On January 16, 1957, the play opened in New Haven. From that moment until the New York opening on February 7, I was more dentist than writer, extracting the sharper (but not always carious) teeth. The heart of the play's argument was a scene in the second act between Kreton and the secretary-general of the United Nations. At each performance the audience, charmed by the fooling that had gone before, grew deathly cold as the debate began: This was not what they had anticipated (a fault, I own, of the dramaturgy—were I a better playwright the scene would have developed inevitably), and their confidence in the play was never entirely regained. A few days before we left Boston, I replaced the scene with a lighter one, involving the principals and giving the curtain to our subtlest player, the cat. The substitute was engaging; the play moved amiably; no one was shocked (some observers in New Haven had declared the entire conception unwholesomely menacing. If only they had seen the first draft of the play in which I blew up the whole world at the end, the perfect curtain.)

And so by deliberately dulling the edge of the satire, the farce flourished, giving rise to the misapprehension that the evening was delightful largely because of the comedic improvisations of two gifted *farceurs*. Our clowns were certainly gifted, but if I may be predictable and come to the defense of my squat but healthy child, they did *not* create, they played. The comedic invention was mine.

A number of reviewers described the play as a vaudeville, a very apt description, and one in which I concur, recalling a letter from Bernard Shaw to Granville-Barker: "I have given you a series of first-rate music hall entertainment thinly disguised as plays, but really offering the public a unique string of turns by comics and serio-comics of every popular type." That, of course, is only half the truth, but it is the charming half. In the case of *Visit,* the comedic approach to the theme tended to dictate the form. Having no real commitment to the theater, no profound convictions about the well-made or the ill-made play, I tend to write as an audience, an easily bored audience. I wrote the sort of piece I should like to go to a theater to see, one in which people say and do things that make me laugh. And though vague monsters lurk beneath the surface, their presence is sensed rather than dramatically revealed. My view of reality is not sanguine, and the play for all its blitheness turns resolutely toward a cold night. But happily for the play's success, the incisors were extracted out of town and the venture was a hit. But there in that word "hit" lies the problem.

I was obliged to protect an eighty-thousand-dollar investment, and I confess freely that I obscured meanings, softened blows, humbly turned wrath aside, emerging with a successful play which represents me very little—perhaps a good thing. It is not that what was fashioned is bad or corrupt. I rather fancy the farce we ended up with, and I think it has a good deal of wear in it. But the play that might have been, though hardly earth-shaking, was far more interesting and true. But although I feel hurt at the sort of reputation that hovers about my part of this venture, I cannot honestly make much of a case for myself. I played the game stolidly according to rules I abhor.

In extenuation I should like to say what many others have said before me: The theater and its writers are seriously, perhaps fatally, hampered by economic pressure. Because it costs too much to put on a play, one works in a state of hysteria. Everything is geared to success. Yet art is mostly failure. And it is only from a succession of daring, flawed works that the occasional masterwork comes. But in our theater to fail is death, and in an atmosphere so feverish it is difficult to work with much objectivity. Only the honest hacks have a good time of it. Cannily, they run up a banner: It's just us again, kids, trying to make a buck. And they are let off with genial contempt. It is the crankier, more difficult writers who must work at a disadvantage, and efforts to divert them into familiar safe channels are usually disastrous.

But things are as they are. No time has been easy for any of the arts. And, to take the longest view, one must recall that society does not exist for the express purpose of creating literature— a hard fact for many of us to realize. When certain forms lose their usefulness, they are discarded. It may be that the novel was a temporary diversion—less than three centuries old in English— and that the play, thanks to social changes and new machinery, has regained its ascendancy.

As for myself, I am divided at heart. I should never have been drawn to playwriting had it been possible to live by prose. Yet what I began in a fit of opportunism I have persisted in with some pleasure—at least in the actual work. Nor am I displeased with this unexpected change in course, for have I not, like one of those civilizations Professor Toynbee so enjoys inventing, risen to a desperate challenge, and survived? At least for now.

April 28, 1953

A Note on Santayana*

BY GOUVERNEUR PAULDING

It was always a farewell to everything, not just to arms. The first farewell was to Avila, where he might have become a canon of the cathedral, a canon who doubted his faith, or a lawyer occupied with endless litigation about the fields beyond Avila's walls, a lawyer skeptical of the law. His second farewell was to Harvard, escaping, he thought, from obvious danger: The perennial supply of youth provided by the better private schools would have forced him to observe the effects of age upon his own person rather than upon that of others.

But there was no escape. Oxford proved as perilous, because of the dons. Each year at Harvard young men came in, but four years later they went out into the world, where at least they progressed into senility out of Santayana's sight; the dons at Oxford were students who, never having gone out into the world, irritatingly grew old *in situ,* as the archaeologists would say, gluttonous or dull or religious. Santayana fled Oxford.

As long as he was saying good-by to places, no harm was done, for he kept places in his mind, with all their essential qualities, and here in this last volume of his memoirs the places are safe from all possible destruction. Avila is safe in his prose, as Toledo is safe in the Greco painting, and Rome, Boston, Oxford are

* On publication of *My Host the World,* Vol. III of *Persons and Places,* by George Santayana.

safe—in the sense that Nineveh and Tyre are safe, in a cold and perfect abstraction.

It is Santayana's farewell to persons in this book that is disturbing, because he could not make it a gracious farewell or even a farewell at all. He betrayed all his friends: He fled them because they could not remain forever young; yet they stayed with him, insistent reminders, horrid reflections perturbing this Dorian Gray to the end. One need not mention names: Here is a friend of his, an old man now, sitting in an English garden busying himself with embroidering a large design in gold thread; he has lost his figure, his money, his malice, and his wit. Here again is an English gentleman, married often and unwisely, and Santayana, after all the years, is still gossiping about him in the pantry. "People do not grow better when they grow older. . . . No: we are no longer charmed by their virtues or interested in their vices."

It is a wonderful thing to achieve serenity, terrifying to achieve it in emptiness of heart.

April 1, 1952

The Mormon Invasion of
New York City

BY ROBERT BINGHAM

Shortly before noon on one of those unseasonably mild days which occur in New York during February, I kept an appointment with six Mormon missionaries at the corner of William Street and Maiden Lane, just north of the financial district. The Mormons were going to hold a street meeting for the lunch-hour crowds.

Elder Stanley C. Kimball of Montebello, California, who had asked me to the meeting and who supervises the work of seventeen other Mormon missionaries in the metropolitan area, turned out to be tall, thin, and anything but elderly. He told me later that he was twenty years old. Explaining that Mormon missionaries always work in pairs, Elder Kimball introduced me to his companion, Elder Gary Nalder of Shelley, Idaho, who looked even younger. In marked contrast to Elder Kimball's narrow features, Elder Nalder's face was wide, not with fat but with bone. He shook hands with tremendous and disconcerting vigor, but by so doing prepared me for the heartiness of the other four elders who were to take part in the meeting. None of them could have been much over twenty and all of them hailed from the Far West.

473

While the others were in a huddle around their briefcases—arming themselves with tracts, getting out some kind of banner, and stacking their hats one inside the other to be left with the baggage once the meeting got under way—I had a little talk with Elder Kimball and with Elder Nalder, who stood with us somewhat impatiently, interrupting his chief from time to time. Elder Kimball told me that when he was called by his home bishop to go away on a mission he had been a freshman at the University of Utah, beginning a predentistry course. "We spend two years at this work," he said quietly, "and most of us get to feel that they're the two best years of our lives." He grinned, almost as if he were apologizing for his own earnestness. Elder Kimball stood several inches over six feet in height, and he had a way of inclining his head forward slightly so that he seemed to be looking up rather than down at shorter people. Elder Nalder volunteered the information that he had been studying pharmacy at Idaho State College, but that he had since decided to be a physician.

When I asked if all Mormon missionaries were of college age, Elder Kimball seemed to weigh his answer. Before he spoke, Elder Nalder broke in to say, "They are now, but you watch and see; in a few months we'll start to get the old ones—fifty and sixty years old, some of them married, even." He looked quickly at Elder Kimball for approval. "It's the draft boards," he said with a knowing nod. Elder Kimball explained that the 4-D classification which defers ordained ministers under the Selective Service system is given to Mormon missionaries for only two years, after which they are subject to the draft like anyone else. In Utah, where more than half the residents are Mormons, the draft boards have been hard put to it to meet their quotas, and the church has agreed not to use any young men for missionary work who are about to be called up for military service. "Those draft boards are really on the lookout for us when we get back," Elder Nalder declared.

"A year ago," Elder Kimball said with a touch of sadness, "we had 232 missionaries in the Eastern States Mission, of which our district here in New York is a part. Now we have 148. In a few months it will be even less." He shook his head. "You see, we have no paid priesthood. The bishop who presides over each ward—what you call a parish—is not paid for the work he does, and he doesn't, for example, preach the sermon every Sunday. Every man is eligible to hold some rank of the priesthood. Why, as soon as he turns twelve a boy can become a deacon." Once again Elder Kimball's grin seemed almost apologetic. "We Mormons like to get everybody into the act."

"Even the missionaries don't get paid," Elder Nalder put in, watching me closely for a sign of surprise, which I was quick to give him. "We pay our own way, traveling expenses, rent, and all the rest. It either has to come out of savings or from money our families can give us." This was a subject that interested both of the missionaries—not, as I suspected at first because they felt that the requirement was unjust, but rather because they were proud of it. Elder Kimball said that when called he had had no savings of his own whatsoever, and his father, an accountant and a former bishop of his ward, had been out of work for two years. "And as if that wasn't enough," he said, "my sister Janet was called to be a missionary down in Texas." Elder Kimball smiled. "At first I couldn't see how it was going to work out. But since then my dad has found a job and—well—everything's going all right." I was convinced that only his natural shyness prevented him from identifying more precisely what he believed to be the source of his good fortune.

The huddle around the briefcase broke up, and Elder Kimball excused himself. Striding purposefully out to the curb, he took up his position next to a subordinate who was holding a small American flag and a banner headed APOSTACY. Traffic on the sidewalk was heavy, mostly with people who appeared to be stenographers and clerks on their way to lunch. When Elder Kimball began to speak, a few looked up, but most hurried on toward their destinations. The rich aroma of freshly ground coffee blew up Maiden Lane from the East River.

Elder Kimball was as a man transformed. He shed his shy manner entirely, and his voice became clarion, every word distinct above the roar of traffic. He braced his feet wide apart and leaned forward aggressively.

"Friends of Manhattan," he bellowed, "we are some few

ministers of God, representing the Church of Jesus Christ of Latter-day Saints. We come to your street corner in this way so that we may share with you some of the mysteries of a great religion which has given strength to us and to our people, and which we know to be true." The other missionaries stood about singly on the sidewalk, as if they were passers-by pausing to hear what Elder Kimball had to say. Still none of the stenographers and clerks stopped. "We are not here as radicals or fanatics. We are but six of the five thousand missionaries and more who are sent throughout the world by our church. We're not here for our benefit. We're here for your benefit!"

A man with a pushcart had stopped at the curb a few feet from Elder Kimball, and a crowd of girls gathered around to examine some sweaters he had for sale. "These kind of sweaters ain't the inflammable kind, are they?" one girl demanded suspiciously. "I been reading a lot in the paper about sweaters they just go poof."

Pointing to the banner which his colleague was holding, Elder Kimball spoke of "the falling away of true belief," and this somehow attracted the attention of the girl who didn't want to buy an inflammable sweater. She left the pushcart and stood in the gutter, staring up at Elder Kimball with a mixture of suspicion and incredulity. "Going clear back to the beginning," Elder Kimball shouted, turning from side to side as if he were addressing a large audience, "the gospel was given to the prophet Adam. But the people would not live according to the word of God, and so it was taken from them." This process had been repeated, according to Elder Kimball, down through history. He described how the multitudes had fallen into corruption after the gospel had been given successively to the prophets Noah, Abraham, Moses, and Jesus Christ. One of the missionaries approached the suspicious girl in the gutter and offered her a tract. She gave him a sharp, nervous frown, waved him away, and started up William Street, staring back over her shoulder. Elder Kimball announced that the next speaker would tell how the gospel had been given to a prophet in our own times, and he beckoned to a red-headed missionary to come in and replace him.

For Mormons the spiritual is never far from the practical, and the next speaker chose to say nothing about the reception of the gospel by a modern prophet. Instead, he described the fine record made by the basketball team of Brigham Young University, which won the National Invitation Tournament last year. "They did it all by clean living and obeying the commandments of God," he asserted. What he left unsaid but clearly implied was that Mormon athletes, unlike some of their Eastern rivals, had not taken bribes from professional gamblers. As the new speaker proceeded anecdotally through some of the worldly successes of his church, I asked Elder Kimball to continue the theological commentary that he had begun at the curb. I said that I knew next to nothing about the doctrines of his religion. "If you're like most people," Elder Nalder inserted, "about all you know is that Mormons used to have a lot of wives," and all three of us laughed.

Elder Kimball kept on smiling, but it was not difficult to detect his fundamental seriousness. He wanted first to straighten out the matter of plural marriages. "At no time were more than three per cent of our families polygamous," he said firmly. "It was a serious matter, to be entered into only after a great deal of prayer. And since 1890 any man found to have more than one wife has been excommunicated." In answering personal questions, Elder Kimball had been more than a little self-conscious, but now he spoke rapidly and confidently in phrases that had been worn comfortably smooth in his mind by constant repetition since childhood.

"Essentially, what we believe," he began, "is that the same kind of divine revelation that God sent down to the prophets in ancient times He can and does send down in latter days. This has been proved to us in the life of the prophet Joseph Smith. In the early part of the last century, when Joseph Smith was only a boy of fourteen years, he happened to think about where it said in the fifth verse of the first chapter of James, 'If any of you lack wisdom, let him ask of God, that giveth to all men liberally, and upbraideth not; and it shall be given him.'" Elder Kimball repeated the quotation from James, this time more slowly and with greater emphasis. Elder Nalder was listening as if he had never heard the story and found it fascinating.

"And so Joseph Smith prayed," Elder Kimball recited, settling firmly into his subject, "and sure enough the angel Moroni appeared to him and entrusted to him the golden plates on which the Book of Mormon was written. The prophet found them buried on the Hill Cumorah, just south of Palmyra, New York. Now the Book of Mormon was written in what they call Reformed Egyptian, but Joseph Smith was able to translate it into English because the angel also entrusted to him the Urim and Thummim."

"The what?" I asked, with more of an edge than I had intended.

Elder Kimball nodded as if he had expected my question. "The Urim and Thummim," he repeated. "You'll find references to them in the Old Testament. They're magic stones for translating and things like that.

"Now in this Book of Mormon, which is 522 pages long, we get testimony as to how one of the lost tribes of Israel came to the Western Hemisphere six hundred years before Christ was born. This recent book *Kon-Tiki* proves how they got here. The same current that carried Thor Heyerdahl *away* from South America carried them *to* South America. It goes around in a circle, you know.

"Anyway, after Christ was crucified in Jerusalem, He appeared for three days among these people in South America and converted them. You get a proof of this in St. John, where Christ says, 'And other sheep I have, which are not of this fold: them also I must bring, and they shall hear my voice, and there shall be one fold, and one shepherd.' Now the people lived in peace for a time, but then wickedness sprang up among them. The Lamanites, who were dark-skinned people, killed off all the Nephites, who were white-skinned people. Mormon, a leader of the Nephites, gave the record of all this to his son Moroni, who buried it on the Hill Cumorah, where Joseph Smith received it fourteen centuries later."

Elder Nalder had been waiting for a chance to break in. "The Lamanites are the same as the Indians that white people found when they came over here later on. As a proof of that, do you remember when Cortez invaded South America? The Indians hardly put up any fight at all because they thought he was the Great White Father." Elder Nalder paused for effect. "They thought he was the Second Coming of Christ. That's what they thought."

"Actually we find in other writings revealed to the prophet Joseph Smith that Christ will appear in Missouri," Elder Kimball said with his usual quiet certainty. "And before that happens the Lamanites—that is, the Indians—will be converted, and they will rise up and wipe the place clean."

There was a shading of anger in Elder Kimball's voice when he spoke of wiping the State of Missouri clean for which I could not at the time account. It has since occurred to me that his anger might perhaps be traced back to the treatment Joseph Smith and his early followers received at the hands of an anti-Mormon governor of Missouri, Lillburn W. Boggs, who ordered that "The Mormons must be treated as enemies, and must be exterminated or driven from the state . . ." In 1844, a few years after the expulsion from Missouri, Smith, in fulfillment of his own prophecy, was murdered by a mob across the river in Illinois. It was then that Brigham Young, "the Lion of the Land," led the Mormons across the plains to the Salt Lake Desert, where in persuasive accord with another of Smith's prophecies, the Mormons have become "a mighty people in the midst of the Rocky Mountains." There are now more than one million Mormons, and the desert has become an oasis, but the persecution, the exodus, and the rigors of the march are still vivid tribal memories for many Mormons.

I asked Elder Kimball if the writings also told when the Second Coming could be expected. " 'No man knows the day or the hour,' " he quoted. He seemed to make a calculation in his head. "But it won't be long now."

Elder Kimball excused himself again and went to spell a missionary who had been speaking for some time. Elder Nalder hurried off to catch a boy in a leather windbreaker who had stopped to look at the banner; he seemed to be about Elder Nalder's age. The red-headed missionary was talking with a substantial-looking businessman in a dark-blue overcoat. The missionaries call people who display curiosity about Mormonism "investigators," and it seemed that the investigator in the dark-blue overcoat had been given some tracts the week before and had promised to read them. He spoke seriously and very courteously to the young missionary. "Now, mind you," he said, "I don't claim that this story about the golden tablets and the Lamanites and all that isn't true. I simply say that I myself cannot believe it. Now I may be wrong—" He held up his hand for caution, and the red-headed missionary hurried into the hiatus with a rapid flow of quiet but insistent argument.

Elder Nalder's investigator, who had dark, shining hair and a thin mustache and who may very well have been a Puerto Rican, seemed to be pained by what Elder Nalder was saying to him, yet unable to break away. Grasping the young man's elbow firmly and holding a tract open before him, Elder Nalder led him out of the main traffic of pedestrians.

The investigator in the blue overcoat was still unconvinced, but finally he agreed to take a copy of the Book of Mormon along with him. "All right," he said. "Mind you, I'm not promising a thing, but I'll look this over and then I'll let you know how it strikes me." The red-headed missionary said that that was fair enough and shook hands mightily.

I did some reading in the Book of Mormon myself a few days later. The rhetoric has an authentically Biblical ring, but I found that it did not hold my attention very well. Mark Twain, who did not care much for any of the native-born religious movements of the nineteenth century, once referred to the Book of Mormon as "chloroform in print." Joseph Smith, at the time of his death, was working on an extensive revision of the Bible, based on further revelations that had come to him.

After Elder Kimball finished his next stint of preaching, I asked him if he was by any chance related to Heber C. Kimball, who had stood next to Brigham Young in the early hierarchy of the church and who had gone to England as leader of the church's first foreign mission. "Why, yes," said Elder Kimball with some pride, "he was my great-great-grandfather." When I asked if he could tell me which one of the older Kimball's numerous wives had been his great-great-grandmother, he wrinkled his brow and looked down at his feet, but he could not bring the name to mind. All he could remember was that she was one of the eleven or more women who had been married to Heber C. Kimball "for time" and to Joseph Smith "for eternity." Elder Kimball explained this arrangement. "You see, the seed that Heber C. Kimball raised up in her was sealed for eternity to the genealogy of Joseph Smith." I asked if that didn't make him the great-great-grandson of Joseph Smith, and he modestly agreed that in a way it did.

The boy in the leather windbreaker had finally gotten away from Elder Nalder. As he made his way across the street, look-ing down at the tracts which had been given to him, his sallow face was still uncertain, still troubled. Elder Nalder gave a signal that he was ready and willing to take on the preaching assignment.

"Brothers and sisters," he began with penetrating resonance, "for over a thousand years the people have been confused, not knowing what to do, which way to turn. No one has shown them the way. It's as simple as that." A truck and trailer roared past behind him, and his voice became even louder. He seemed to be angry. "My brothers and sisters, the Bible is good, but the Bible is not enough. We need revelation to show us the way. How many of you," he asked scornfully, "can say that the organ to which you belong is divinely inspired? Well, we're making that claim to you today, brothers and sisters, and we're calling you to repentance." A shabby old man shuffled painfully by, carrying a sandwich board that advertised FOUNTAIN PENS REPAIRED. "If you don't repent," Elder Nalder shouted anx-iously, "you're going to be caught up and burned!" The old man with the sandwich board winced perceptibly and did all he could to hasten his arthritic pace.

Four or five investigators had stopped to hear Elder Nalder, and one of the missionaries asked Elder Kimball if it would be all right for him to take some pictures. The supervising elder gave his permission, and the amateur photographer got an ex-pensive Kodak out of his briefcase. When I admired the camera, he told me that he had bought it from another missionary re-cently back from Africa. "At the time I bought it, I thought I was going to be sent abroad too," he said. "But here I am in little old New York." Elder Kimball told me that about half of the Mormon missionaries are sent abroad these days. He himself had hoped to go to England, like his great-great-grandfather.

When the next speaker took over, Elder Nalder approached a short, fat man who was leaning against a fireplug and offered him a tract. The fat man, who was wearing a bright plaid overcoat and a gray Homburg, laughed heartily. "You got me all wrong, son," he said, quaking with mirth. "I'm just here to meet a man for lunch." Elder Nalder shrugged his shoulders and rejoined Elder Kimball and me near the building.

"You know, a man has so many people screeching at him in a big city like New York," he said, "that he can't pay attention when something like this comes along." Both of the missionaries agreed that their work had met with more success in the outlying districts, away from the city itself. (Elder Kimball's great-great-grandfather had encountered the same situation in London back in the 1830's. "We found the whole city given to covetousness," Heber C. Kimball wrote, ". . . and all doors closed against us. We did not hesitate to stand in the midst of the streets and, Jonah-like, cry repentance unto the inhabitants . . .")

"We actually don't do very much work right here in the city except for these street meetings," Elder Kimball remarked. Except for what he calls "spot-tracting," he regularly deploys his missionaries mostly in northern New Jersey and metropolitan Long Island. I asked him if he ever sent his people up north of the city, into Westchester for example, and he nodded thoughtfully. "That's good territory. But"—he shook his read regretfully—"I simply haven't got the manpower."

The missionaries try to steer the investigators into one of the local churches, and Elder Kimball estimated that there were about fifty conversions in his area last year—a creditable record, he feels, but not an outstanding one. "Down South they're getting converts right and left," Elder Nalder said. "But then I guess the people are just more religious down there."

I asked if any of the missionaries, leaving religious and usually rural homes for the first time in their lives to set up on their own for two years in a place like New York, ever found themselves tempted, ever felt their faith slipping away. Elder Nalder accepted the question as a challenge and launched into a zealous denial, but Elder Kimball interrupted him. "It sometimes happens," he said quietly, "but most of us find that our religion is strengthened by the experience of talking to other people about religion. At first you don't know what to say. But then it comes. And you find yourself talking right out, and glad of it."

Elder Kimball noticed that the missionary who was doing the preaching just then, a new man who had arrived from the West only a few months ago, was starting to run down, and he hurried over to relieve him. The lunch hour had ended and the sidewalk was no longer crowded.

"We want to thank you good people of Manhattan for cooperating in our street service," Elder Kimball shouted, "and for permitting us to share with you our testimony of these mysteries which we know to be true." He went on about the mysteries for a few minutes while the other missionaries were packing up their unused tracts and sorting out their hats, but there were no more investigators to hear him. In fact, no one was listening to Elder Kimball except the other missionaries and me.

The Managers

By W. H. Auden

In the bad old days it was not so bad:
    The top of the ladder
Was an amusing place to sit; success
    Meant quite a lot—leisure
And huge meals, more palaces filled with more
    Objects, girls and horses
Than one would ever get round to, and to be
    Carried uphill while seeing
Others walk. To rule was a pleasure when
    One wrote a death-sentence
On the back of the Ace of Spades and played on
    With a new deck. Honours
Are not so physical or jolly now,
    For the sort of Powers
We are used to are not like that. Could one of them
    Be said to resemble
The Tragic Hero, the Platonic Saint,
    Or would any painter
Portray one rising triumphant from a lake
    On a dolphin, naked,
Protected by an umbrella of cherubs? Can
    They so much as manage

To behave like genuine Caesars when alone
   Or drinking with cronies,
To let their hair down and be frank about
   The world? It is doubtful.
The last word on how we may live or die
   Rests today with quiet
Men, working too hard in rooms that are too big,
   Reducing to figures
What is the matter, what is to be done.
   A neat little luncheon
Of sandwiches is brought to each on a tray,
   Nourishment they are able
To take with one hand without looking up
   From papers a couple
Of secretaries are needed to file,
   From problems no smiling
Can dismiss; the typewriters never stop
   But whirr like grasshoppers
In the silent siesta heat as, frivolous
   Across their discussions,
Out of woods unaltered by our wars and vows
   Drift the scents of flowers
And the songs of birds who will never vote
   Or bother to notice
Those distinguishing marks a lover sees
   By instinct, and policemen
Can be trained to observe; far into the night
   Their windows burn brightly,
And behind, their backs bent over some report
   On every quarter
For ever like a god or a disease
   There on the earth, the reason
In all its aspects why they are tired, the weak,
   The inattentive, seeking
Someone to blame; then if, to recuperate,
   They go a-playing, their greatness
Encounters the bow of the chef or the glance
   Of the ballet-dancer

Who cannot be ruined by any master's fall.
    To rule must be a calling,
It seems, like surgery or sculpture, the fun
    Neither love nor money
But taking a necessary risk, the test
    Of one's skill, the question,
If difficult, their own reward. But then
    Perhaps one should mention
Also what must be a comfort as they guess
    In times like the present
When guesses can prove so fatally wrong,
    The fact of belonging
To the very select indeed, to those
    For whom, just supposing
They do, there will be places on the last
    Plane out of disaster.
No; no one is really sorry for their
    Heavy gait and careworn
Look, nor would they thank you if you said you were.

A Comment on the Poem

If Mussolini was a manager, if Hitler was a manager, if Stalin was a manager, then, for us and presumably for Auden, the difficulty is perfectly plain. But if Roosevelt was a manager, if Mr. Truman and Mr. Attlee are managers, the difficulty is obscure indeed.

When the managers are recognizably tyrants, when there is a clear evil, when there is tyranny by a man, or by a man and a party, or by a group of men and a doctrine, then everything is simple; you know you are slaves; and every instinctive desire for freedom opposes the man, the men, the doctrine, the party, that enslave.

But if the managers are elected by the people, responsible to the people, dismissable by the people; if they are well-meaning, there is another difficulty, in some ways a harder one. Because then we are faced with more than the problem of which men hold the power, or whether they deserve it, or how they came by it. We are faced with the problem of how much can be accomplished by power, no matter how carefully delegated and exercised.

We have recently elected Mr. Truman and wherever we live there is a Justice of the Peace who is not there just because he wants to be there; or there is the Mayor who is not there just because he thinks it is a good idea; there is the Governor of the State and the State Legislature; in Washington there are the Representatives and the Senators—and none of these is where he is, managing any thing at all, except by the mandate we have given him. All the committees and commissions, all the 2,050,200 employees in the Federal Executive Departments and Agencies (as of January 1, 1949), all the employees of all the states, counties, municipalities, townships, and villages, are our employees and they manage our affairs with our consent. All the judges, all the police, are delegated by us to administer a justice that they do not invent or improvise but that we have invented over the centuries.

These are our managers. They manage not us, but our affairs.

Everything should be all right. And, as a system, everything is all right—or, at least, there is no better system anywhere, none that we envy. We have made a government, and a system, the way we wanted it to be, and there is no other system of government (on the Moon, or Mars, in Russia, or Saturn) that we would prefer if we could have it. We have our managers and they are not alienated from us. They do not push us off the sidewalks. And they cannot forget us because we can see to it that they lose their jobs.

The American system is a fine system. It does not even present the drawback of being something that is there forever and that can only be looked at. It can be, and has been, and will be, amended and improved; it is flexible within its own unchangeable principles of freedom as thought is flexible within its own unchangeable limits of logic. The American system can never be archaic; it can never look like something that people have forgotten to bring up to date with the changing technologies of freedom.

We look back at our last manager-in-chief—that man who was

so weighted down and enchained (literally), and who was so
weighted down and enchained (spiritually) by the fact that he
had to take decisions of life and death and these decisions were
imposed upon him from outside, by events other wills provoked.
We look back at him, and he was a politician, he laughed, he
smoked too much; he was a great man or he was not, he got
angry and then he was vindictive, and he had fifty ideas a minute.
It simply is not possible for us to think of him as a master, or as
a manager managing our affairs in cold detachment from us.

Or we look at the man who managed the invasion of Europe,
and here he is writing to the Columbia alumni, telling them that
it has not been so easy to find out how to manage a university
but that he means well and that perhaps the university will need
a little more money sooner or later.

Or we look at Mr. Truman, and he does not frighten us because we know how it happened that he is where he is and it
is not because the Argentines and the Greeks put him there.

All this is very consoling, very reassuring, and all the more
so because it is not taken for granted: the managing done by
our managers is not taken for granted, nor are our freedoms.
There are all the committees worrying about our freedoms;
there are the press, the radio people worrying about their freedoms and, what is even better, there are citizens defending their
freedoms against the press and the radio; there are the states
defending their freedoms against the Federal State in Washington, and, what is even better, there is the man who writes to the
paper defending his village monies from the county.

Then everything is all right? Not quite. We have the best
system in the world, to be sure, but often we get to thinking
that we are no more than spectators at a play—with the right to
watch the actors (the managers) come and go, the right to ap-
plaud and hiss, and even to put on other actors. But not the
right to put on another script. For the play seems to be written
once and for all—and not by us.

What appalls us is that it is not written by the managers either.

It is the war, the two wars, of course, that have created this
anxiety. And it is not that they came to us against our will; it is
that they came to us from some zone that was altogether outside

the possibility of being affected by our will. The wars came neither by or against our will. Our appointed managers were at their posts; the wars enveloped them like fog drifting in from sea.

We are a democracy; our managers are closer to us than they would be under any other system. We control them as far as it is possible to control delegated power in the tremendous complexity and size of modern civilization. (We cannot come on Sunday into the cow pastures of a Swiss canton—with the bright flags, the refreshment booths—and have a show of hands.)

The agonizing question is what do our managers control? Without them, there is anarchy. With them, there is sometimes the feeling, not that they are remote from us, but that the matter they handle—the matter of life and death—is remote from them.

September 18, 1958

The Most Cheerful Graveyard
in the World

By Paul Jacobs

Along with amassing a comfortable fortune by convincing Los Angelenos that the only fitting way to begin a "happy Eternal Life" is by being laid to rest, in one way or another, at Forest Lawn Memorial Park, the cemetery he founded in 1917, Dr. Hubert Eaton, or "Digger" as he is known in the trade, has also succeeded in almost completely revising the dying industry.

The Digger, whose official title of "Doctor" is purely honorary, accomplished this revision by the simple but profound device of converting the hitherto prosaic act of dying into a gloriously exciting, well-advertised event, somehow intimately and patriotically connected with the American way of life.

Today, thanks to Eaton, dying in Los Angeles is something to be eagerly anticipated, because it is only after death that one can gain permanent tenure at Forest Lawn. Eaton, in one of his earlier roles—that of "the Builder"—described Forest Lawn as "a place where lovers new and old shall love to stroll and watch the sunset's glow, planning for the future or reminiscing of the past; a place where artists study and sketch; where school teachers bring happy children to see the things they read of in books; where little churches invite, triumphant in the knowledge that from their pulpits only words of Love can be spoken; where memorialization of loved ones in sculptured marble and pictorial glass shall be encouraged but controlled by acknowledged artists; a place where the sorrowing will be soothed and strengthened be- cause it will be God's garden. A place that shall be protected by an immense Endowment Care Fund, the principal of which can never be expended—only the income therefrom used to care for and perpetuate this Garden of Memory.

"This is the Builder's Dream; this is the Builder's Creed."

The Builder's Creed is chiseled into a huge, upright stone slab on Forest Lawn's Cathedral Drive, just outside the Great Mauso- leum and hard by the Shrine of Love. Viewed, usually in reverent awe, by more than a million visitors each year, Forest Lawn is, along with Disneyland, a favorite tourist attraction in Southern California, far outdrawing the concrete footprints in front of Grauman's Chinese Theatre.

A smaller inscription underneath the Creed points out that on New Year's Day, 1917, Eaton stood on a hilltop overlooking the small country cemetery which had just been placed in his charge. An unemployed mining engineer, Eaton had gone into the cemetery business after a vein of gold in his mine had suddenly vanished.

"A vision came to the man of what this tiny 'God's Acre' might become; and standing there, he made a promise to The Infinite. When he reached home, he put this promise into words and called it 'The Builder's Creed.' Today, Forest Lawn's almost three hundred acres are eloquent witness that The Builder kept faith with his soul."

Indeed, yes. The "almost three hundred acres" also bear elo- quent witness to the fact that Eaton, still digging holes in the ground, worked a vein of gold infinitely more reliable than the one that vanished from his mine—the "Science and Art," as he describes it, "of Persuasion." So strongly does Eaton believe the "profession of salesmanship is the greatest of all professions" that he has established The Foundation for the Science and Art of Persuasion at his alma mater, William Jewell College, Liberty, Missouri.

Forest Lawn reflects Eaton's skill in the "Science." The "coun- try cemetery" with only a "scant dozen acres of developed ground" has grown into Forest Lawn Memorial Park, with a permanent "population" of more than 170,000, increasing at the rate of approximately 6,500 a year.

In fact, business has been so good that there are now two additional Forest Lawn "Memorial Parks" in Los Angeles: Forest Lawn-Hollywood Hills, the focus of a bitter political struggle in the city, and adjacent to it Mount Sinai, designed to attract the growing Jewish population of Los Angeles.

Forest Lawn offers the largest religious painting in the United States, displayed in a building, the Hall of the Crucifixion, specially designed for it. There, for a voluntary contribution of twenty-five cents, the visitor sits comfortably in a large theater, in one of a "broad sweep of seats, richly upholstered in burgundy, rising tier above tier, matching the splendor of the architecture," and watches the three-thousand-pound curtain open on Jesus at Calvary, forty-five feet high and 195 feet long. A lecture about the painting, supplemented with a moving arrow, is delivered by a tape recording in the special kind of rich, organ-tone voice used throughout Forest Lawn.

There are also hundreds of statues, both originals and reproductions, scattered throughout the three hundred acres. Typical of these is an eighteen-figure group depicting Forest Lawn's solution to the "Mystery of Life." Interpretations of the eighteen figures are supplied: "(17) the atheist, the fool, who grinningly cares not at all; while (18) the stoic sits in silent awe and contemplation of that which he believes he knows but cannot explain with any satisfaction."

At the Court of David there is a huge reproduction of Michelangelo's "David"—with a large fig leaf added by Forest Lawn. An exact copy of the sculptor's "Moses" is displayed at the entrance to the Cathedral Corridor in Memorial Terrace, "the only one," according to Forest Lawn, "cast from clay masks placed directly on the original statue in the Church of Saint Peter in Chains at Rome, Italy."

So that the masks could be made, the Church of Saint Peter had to be closed for a day, something that had not happened before. "I gave a lot of dinners and I bought a lot of wine and I sent a lot of cables and St. Peter's was closed," Eaton modestly explains.

Color photos and post cards of the "Moses" statue can be purchased, along with thousands of other items, at Forest Lawn's souvenir shop. There, browsing visitors can choose from showcases displaying money clips, cocktail napkins, book matches, jigsaw puzzles, and charm bracelets—all decorated with Forest Lawn motifs. Prices range from a modest twenty-nine cents for a key chain to $125 for a glass vase etched with a Forest Lawn scene.

There are brown plastic nutshells containing little photos of Forest Lawn, ladies' compacts, cigarette lighters, cufflinks, salt and pepper shakers, picture frames, demitasse spoons, bookmarks, cups and saucers, pen and pencil sets, glass bells, wooden plaques, ashtrays, place mats and doilies, perfume and powder sets, jack-knives, and a great variety of other goodies, all with an appropriate Forest Lawn theme. Books like *The Loved One,* Evelyn Waugh's satire of Forest Lawn, are not on sale in the souvenir shop. (Eaton occasionally expresses resentment over the treatment given the cemetery by novelists—especially by one writer to whom he extended free run of the park only to be parodied later. But Eaton also understands that such novels have brought worldwide publicity to Forest Lawn and have not adversely affected his sales, which come not from England but from Los Angeles.)

Among the most popular items at the souvenir shop are those showing reproductions of Forest Lawn's three churches, the Church of the Recessional, the Little Church of the Flowers, and the Wee Kirk o' the Heather.

"Providing a dignified setting for final tribute," the three churches "serve also for the joyous and memorable ceremonies of christening and the exchange of marriage vows." Since the churches have opened, more than 43,000 persons have had "memorable" marriages in them. But Forest Lawn makes no money directly from marrying people, and the profits from the souvenir shop are used for the upkeep of the Hall of the Crucifixion. Forest Lawn's real business is burying people.

"The hardest thing in the world to sell," states one of the organization's top officials, "are 'spaces.'" ("Space" is the euphemism used at Forest Lawn for "grave plot.") The reason for the difficulty is that Forest Lawn's sales organization, which comprises about 175 people, concentrates on sales made "Before Need," another phrase in Forest Lawn's own peculiar language of the flowers. Selling cemetery plots "Before Need" rather than "At Time of Need" or "Post Need," although difficult, is very profitable, since under California law a cemetery pays taxes only on its unsold plots. Once a "space" has been sold, it is removed from the tax rolls. Thus it is to the obvious advantage of Forest Lawn to sell off its land as quickly as possible, without waiting for "Need."

There are approximately fifteen hundred individual "spaces" to the acre in Forest Lawn. Prices average $300 per space. There are also rather more elegant neighborhoods at Forest Lawn which are less crowded and therefore more expensive. In the Gardens of Memory, entered only with a special key, there are "memorial sanctuaries designed for families who desire the privacy and protection of crypt interment, but who at the same time long for the open skies and the natural beauty of a verdant garden bathed in sunlight. Under the lawns in the Gardens of Memory have been created a number of monolithically constructed crypts of steel-reinforced concrete."

In the area of ground burial, Forest Lawn has contributed a pleasant innovation. No tombstones are permitted, only markers, set flush with the ground so that there is in fact the pleasant appearance of a park with sweeping green lawns.

But one does not have to be interred to take up permanent residence at Forest Lawn. A number of other arrangements can be made, including being inurned after cremation in a columbarium for as little as $145 or entombed in a mausoleum crypt—which can cost as much as $800,000, as in the case of the Irving Thalberg mausoleum. One can also be placed in a large wall out in the open air. Families may be interred, inurned, or entombed as a unit to maintain "togetherness." Should one feel the need for fresh air while spending the "happy Eternal Life" in a crypt, it is possible, at added cost naturally, to have a ventilating system installed. In the mausoleum, tape-recorded music is played as well.

Inurnment is not restricted to a single form of urn. The law in California, which has a strong undertakers' lobby, provides that after cremation ashes must be buried or placed in a columbarium. A wide variety of urn designs can be seen, ranging from books and loving cups to miniature coffins.

The price for the casket or urn sets the approximate amount paid for the funeral itself, but here the range is far greater than for the "space." The least expensive casket, with the metal screw heads showing, is $115; the most expensive goes for $17,500.

Forest Lawn's rich, creamy advertising presentations combine the hard and the soft sell. On radio and television, the same institutional approach is as manifest as at the cemetery itself. Programs of church services and organ music are announced in deep, sonorous tones, and practically no mention is made of the company's product. The institutional approach is also used on billboards picturing stained-glass windows or the "Moses" statue. However, many of Forest Lawn's billboards are given over to the hard, competitive sell, featuring what is Hubert Eaton's original contribution to the American way of death: the concept of combining in one place mortuary functions, such as embalming, with funeral services and burial, thus obviating the necessity for outside undertakers, florists, funeral chapels, and long processions to the cemetery. Forest Lawn successfully undertook the elimination of the undertaking middleman.

Today, Forest Lawn's hard-sell slogans of "Everything In One Beautiful Place" and "Just One Phone Call" are widely copied, as are the ads which usually feature back or side views, sometimes in color, of two dry-eyed, well-groomed people talking to a distinguished-looking, gray-mustached bank-president or diplomat-type man, identified by a discreet sign on his desk as a "Funeral Counselor." Sometimes only the "Counselor" is shown, answering the "Just One Phone Call" with the dedicated air of a statesman. It is clear from the ads that at Forest Lawn, where the concept of death has been abolished, the standards of accepted behavior demand no vulgar signs of outward grief.

But even though its competitors copy Forest Lawn today, Eaton faced a bitter battle when he first attempted to bring a mortuary into the cemetery. Forest Lawn's permit to operate a mortuary was given only after a determined struggle waged against him by some of the undertakers who foresaw disaster for themselves in the new trend of combined services. It was during this period that Forest Lawn began to build up its own political operations, which today make it the most powerful spokesman for the industry in the state.

There have been a number of occasions when, in its self-interest, Forest Lawn has had to do battle, sometimes in ways that might have been frowned on by the dignified gentlemen in their ads. From the 1930's to the early 1950's, Forest Lawn was in a running argument with the county assessor's office over the tax assessments made on its property, with Forest Lawn always claiming that the assessments were too high and almost always getting them reduced, even as much as fifty per cent, by the county board of supervisors. Some supervisors did consistently oppose Forest Lawn's plea for tax reduction and supported the assessor, but when the votes were taken a majority always supported Forest Lawn.

In 1938, in one of its early appearances before the board of supervisors, Forest Lawn requested a tax reduction, claiming that the vacant property in the land it then owned would remain unsold until 1973. At the time, the county assessor pointed out that Forest Lawn had "acquired additional property when they said it was going to take thirty-five years to sell out what they now have, yet they go to work and buy seventy-five acres adjoining at a big price."

Ten years later, in 1948, the issue of how long it would take to fill Forest Lawn's vacant "spaces" became one of the central points in a bitter political hassle within the Los Angeles City Council, and the cemetery completely reversed its argument of ten years earlier. At issue was Forest Lawn's request for a zoning change to permit the use, as a cemetery, of 480 acres of land adjoining Griffith Park, a public park and playground in the Hollywood area.

Forest Lawn's first request to develop this new cemetery was submitted to and rejected by the city planning commission in 1946. When the request was again rejected in 1948, Forest Lawn appealed, claiming, in contrast to its 1938 plea of unsold land, that "by the year 1965 all of the available grave spaces in existing cemeteries will have been exhausted."

The odds against Forest Lawn's gaining approval for its plan to open a new cemetery seemed formidable. The planning commission opposed it, the park department opposed it, the board of health commissioners opposed it, the water and power commission opposed it, the board of public works opposed it, the Hollywood chamber of commerce opposed it, and a variety of community groups opposed it. But the "Builder's Dream" triumphed, and on March 9, 1948, the city council voted 11-3 to permit the opening of the cemetery.

Never an organization to leave stones unturned, within a few hours Forest Lawn had hastily dug six holes in the ground and buried six bodies in them; a move which, under state law, immediately qualified the area as a commercial graveyard that could not then be disturbed or moved except under very specific circumstances.

"We got the bodies we buried through the county hospital or from their next of kin in advance," states Ugene Blalock, vice-president and general counsel of Forest Lawn, "and we made no charge for our services. If the vote in the council had gone against us, we would have given them a free burial elsewhere."

In fact, however, the council vote has rarely gone against Forest Lawn, even when the city fathers were voting on whether to give Beverly Hills the street where Eaton lives, thus providing the Digger with a more distinguished address. Although he hasn't moved, Eaton now lives in Beverly Hills.

No one is quite sure about the exact basis for Eaton's influence; or if they are, they're not willing to talk about it for the record. Blalock states that Forest Lawn as an institution has not made, as far as he knows, any campaign contribution in eighteen years, although he adds, "Individuals may make political contributions." But politics aside, it is Hubert Eaton, master salesman, who is chiefly responsible for Forest Lawn's success.

It is from Eaton's mind that has come the creation of the Council of Regents of Memorial Court of Honor, twenty-two "outstanding business and professional men" who advise "on all matters concerning the growth of the Memorial Park as a cultural center of religion and fine arts."

Its members, who include the president of Occidental College and the chancellor of the University of Southern California, wear a handsome, flowing red robe, trimmed with velvet, and an elegant round red hat, also trimmed daintily with velvet, while around their necks hangs a kind of Maltese Cross decoration, perhaps the Order of Forest Lawn.

Such touches as these distinguish the imaginative Eaton from his colleagues. Eaton's devotion to salesmanship, as evidenced by his creating special heart-shaped children's sections at Forest Lawn, named Babyland and Lullabyland, began early in life, according to "The Forest Lawn Story," his biography sold at the souvenir shop.

The son of a college professor, Eaton, states the biography, "sat in his little cubbyhole behind his father's bookshelves ostensibly studying but actually eavesdropping on his father's conversations with callers. Invariably they came for advice on one thing or another but more often than not, it was advice on matters affecting money. From these conversations he learned the word salesmanship and what it meant."

It was Eaton, too, who initiated many Forest Lawn public-service activities—the inspirational speaker made available to service clubs, the thirteen half-hour Bible films, and the giving of the Forest Lawn Awards for Persuasive Writing as a "practical service to students and Christian liberal arts colleges."

Long interested in "small, independent, liberal arts colleges" as being "America's last bulwark against the march of Socialism . . ." Eaton believes that "most" college professors are "semi-socialists at heart" who teach young people that salesmanship "smacks of chicanery, demagoguery, of influencing people against their wills. . . ."

But Eaton isn't always so serious. Even when he was at college himself, he always had a "good sense of humor." His biography relates that one of his favorite tricks was to persuade a visitor to allow a funnel to be inserted into the top of his trousers and then to make him balance a penny on his chin and try to drop it into the funnel. While the visitor was in this position, young

Hubert "or one of his cronies would pour a cup of cold water into the funnel."

Eaton's "good sense of humor changed little in succeeding years," states his biographer, and it certainly hadn't changed much the night when Eaton gave one of his usual huge, lavish parties for a group of friends and guests. It was called "An Enchanted Evening in the South Pacific," of which "Trader" Hubert Eaton was the master of ceremonies. Elaborate Hawaiian acts were presented, and guests received a large, beautifully printed eight-page souvenir program in color, in which Eaton had himself depicted as "Your Happy Planter," jumping from page to page on a golden-shovel pogo stick.

On the cultural level, the printed program carried a large reproduction of the "David" statue, with a fig leaf, a Hawaiian lei, and a girl curled around its neck, all illustrating a poem, "The Secret of Hubie's David," which described just how it was decided to add a fig leaf to Forest Lawn's copy of Michelangelo's "David" in order not to shock "the ladies of L.A."

But surely the greatest of all the improvements that Eaton has made on the past is Forest Lawn itself. Here, what might have been just an ordinary "country cemetery" has been parlayed into a solemn institution, profitable and widely imitated, looking like Edgar Guest's idea of Heaven brought to earth, while representing a social level to which all people can aspire after death. And in the future, says Hubert Eaton, "When the place is all filled up, my idea, from a financial standpoint, has always been to make Forest Lawn into a museum and charge admission."

February 23, 1956

Meditations in an Empty Room

By Marya Mannes

In a corner of the curve of the U.N. General Assembly Building
is a small place called the Meditation Room—built in 1952, according to a small plaque, and furnished by public contribution.
It is windowless and rectangular, but rounded at one end, cur-
tained from floor to ceiling in off-white, carpeted in off-white,
and lit by beams from spotlights in the ceiling. About twenty
armchairs of American pine with barrel-stave backs, five to a row,
face the curved end of the room, in the center of which is a
polished reddish tree trunk about four feet high and three feet
across; and on top of that is a cluster of philodendron in a re-
ceptacle. A separate shaft of light is directed on this, as if it
were significant.

The room was empty. I tried to think what it reminded me of.
The basement lounge of a small movie theater? The showroom
of a wholesale fur designer? But they are not so claustrophobic.

The information desk told me that the room was conceived
and executed by the Laymen's Movement for a Christian World,
as a place of communion or worship, where men might pray or
ponder in peace, preparing themselves for that verbal battle of
attrition, that exploration of hope, which is the U.N. And since
it was for the use of scores of nations and many religions, the
mandate was clear to avoid any symbol that might offend any
believer. Even the United Nations flag, once there, had had to

be removed. So now there were the trunk, the plant, and the chairs.

It seemed to me standing there that this nothingness was so oppressive and disturbing that it became a sort of madness, and the room a sort of padded cell. It seemed to me that the core of our greatest contemporary trouble lay here, that all this whiteness and shapelessness and weakness was the leukemia of noncommitment, sapping our strength. We had found, finally, that only nothing could please all, and we were trying to make the greatest of all generalities out of that most singular truth, the spirit of man. The terrifying thing about this room was that it made no statement whatever. In its opacity and constriction, it could not even act as a reflector of thought.

Outside, in the city, I began to see this noncommitment everywhere. I looked at the new buildings, the glassy aluminum boxes rising everywhere in place of the old. They made no statement. They offended no one. They had no stamp upon them. They were faceless. This was the kind of taste that is no taste, not even bad taste.

I thought of hour upon hour and month upon month of radio and television, produced to please all by offending none. The people who commanded audiences of thirty to fifty million, men like Perry Como and Ed Sullivan, did so because at no time did they commit themselves to anything but their sponsors' products. Once in a blue moon a play would make a statement, only to retract or temper it in a show of neutrality. It takes an ultimate act of adjustment—the twin of conformity—to make sixty million people look at the same thing at the same time. And they do, nearly every day.

That is why any statement, any commitment of self, is a stab of joy, on television or anywhere else—a rush of plasma into the draining bloodstream of our condition. And that is why gratitude should go in particular to NBC's "Elder Wise Men" series, those quiet conversations with men and women whose entire lives have been statements of their singularity. You have only to look at their faces—Arnold Toynbee, Bertrand Russell, Edward Steichen, Pablo Casals, Robert Frost, Jawaharlal Nehru, Wanda Landowska—to see how their features have been cast in the forge of the spirit's privacy, how immeasurably removed they are—in time, alas, as well as in form—from all of us. And when the great cellist Casals—a little stubborn round-shouldered man in a sweater—says in difficult English that he will never stand for the kind of political immorality that tolerates Franco; when Nehru speaks without rancor of his eight years in prison, a most tangible commitment; when Robert Oppenheimer (on last year's memorable interview with Murrow on CBS) gently tries to define truth, his face illuminated by the search; when Russell dares to be quizzical about accepted values and attitudes—then we know what we are missing every day of our lives in the pallid company of the uncommitted.

In a highly provocative new book entitled *Must You Conform?*, psychiatrist Robert Lindner presents one cure for this spiritual leukemia: "I suggest that the answer . . . lies in the mobilization and implementation of the instinct of rebellion. We must, in short, become acquainted with our protestant nature and learn how to use it in our daily lives, how to express it ourselves, how to infuse it throughout all levels of our culture, and how to nourish it in our young."

If we don't, presumably the spirit of man will be both represented and worshiped in rooms like this one in the U.N.—a quiet place of detachment where we can look at the philodendron in their light from nowhere and meditate on nothing.